EMPOWERMENT AND THE LAW

Strategies of Third World Women

Edited by Margaret Schuler

EMPOWERMENT AND THE LAW

Strategies of Third World Women

Edited by Margaret Schuler

OEF INTERNATIONAL

1815 H Street, N.W. ■ Eleventh Floor ■ Washington, D.C. ■ 20005 ■ USA

Associate Editor: Robin Forrest

Production and Design: Richard Moss Publishing+Design
Cover Illustration: United Nations
Cover Design: Carol Porter
Printed by: McNaughton & Gunn, Inc.

Library of Congress Cataloging in Publication Data
86-62721

IBSN 0-912917-11-3

To Rosalie Goodman, whose generous bequest to OEF International made possible the early initiatives of a global women, law, and development program and the publication of this book. Rosalie's life was devoted to the economic and legal advancement of women and to the human rights of women and men everywhere.

CONTENTS

Part I
An Approach to Women, Law, and Development

Part II
Confronting Patriarchal, Class, and Ethnic Biases in the Law: The Issues

Part III
Using or Challenging the Law: The Strategies

Part IV
The Nairobi Meeting of the Third World Forum
on Women, Law, and Development

FOREWORD

OEF International takes pride in presenting this collection of case studies documenting women's efforts throughout the Third World to overcome the legal constraints that hinder their participation in the benefits of development.

We believe the Women, Law, and Development (WLD) Program has broken historic paths as Third World women fight to achieve and protect their rights. We believe an irreversible process has been set in motion and we are proud to have played a role. Recognizing the link between law and development, and the growing number of women's groups working independently throughout the Third World to enhance women's rights, OEF decided in 1983 to commit itself to a long-term program which would support their efforts, facilitate new ones, and serve as a vehicle for their collaboration.

The first phase of the WLD Program culminated in the five-day Third World Forum on Women, Law, and Development, which took place in Nairobi in July 1985 as part of the non-governnmental activities connected with the United Nations Decade for Women. With over 60 panelists and workshop presenters and 500 attendees daily, the WLD Forum provided the opportunity for groups working in this field to document their strategies for improving the legal status of women in their countries and to share learnings. The participants generated a new momentum for collective action among Third World women on a regional and global level.

Both the Third World Forum and this collection of case studies represent a significant contribution to the emerging field of women, law, and development. We would like to call attention to the following areas of achievement.

Conceptual Framework. The WLD process is contributing to the development of a common framework for analyzing and addressing the many issues related to the law which concern Third World women today.

Emphasis on Strategies. The program is helping to link theory with action by encouraging women to design new

xi

strategies based on a careful analysis of legal obstacles facing women, to document those strategies, and to evaluate their effectiveness so others can learn from actual experiences.

Human Rights for Women. The program has also focused world attention on violations of women's human rights and the special problems they face which have not been addressed by traditional human rights programs.

Comprehensive Focus. The WLD framework for analyzing strategies draws from and is applicable to a wide range of issues affecting Third World women's participation in development: from rights in the workplace to inheritance laws, from credit issues to the effect of ethnicity on women's status, from the conflict between constitutional and personal laws to domestic violence and the right to divorce.

The Women, Law, and Development Program complements OEF International's other programs in Asia, Africa, and Latin America, which focus on economic development. The unique contribution of the WLD Program is that it reinforces economic empowerment efforts by touching the political, social, cultural, and religious dimensions of women's lives as well.

OEF is inspired by the growing enthusiasm and commitment among Third World women who have made the WLD Program a powerful and effective tool for confronting the obstacles posed by the content, culture, and structure of the law. OEF supports this new global network of WLD practitioners as a vital force addressing issues concerning the rights of Third World women. OEF also supports their continued work toward the demystification of law, and, ultimately, toward women's ownership of the law.

We want to congratulate the women from around the world whose dedication, commitment, and hard work have made these achievements possible. A special note of appreciation also goes to the Director of the WLD Program, Dr. Margaret Schuler, for her vision and leadership. We know this is only the beginning of our collaboration to break down legal barriers and to open up opportunities for women everywhere.

WILLIE CAMPBELL
President
ELISE SMITH
Executive Director

OEF International

xii

Acknowledgments

First and foremost, I thank all the contributing authors, whose papers represent more than the pages in this volume would indicate. Their struggle and commitment to the cause of women's rights throughout the Third World has been a constant source of encouragement, inspiration, and learning to me. In particular, I want to thank the Women, Law and Development Planning Committee whose members are Luisa Campos, Radhika Coomaraswamy, Sonia Dávila, Terri Kantai and Ranjana Kumari for their hard work, thoughtful contributions, and commitment to making the WLD Forum in Nairobi a productive platform for interchange and learning.

The actual production of this book required the help of many people. I would like to begin by acknowledging the contribution of Robin Forrest, whose dedication and assistance in every phase of the production of the volume as well as in the day to day management of the project has been invaluable. The thorough, quality work of Carolyn Gates made a significant contribution to the editorial integrity of this book. Guillermo Delgado's editing and translation of many of the Spanish papers was a major contribution as well. Richard Moss's talent and enthusiasm were critical to the book's design. Carol Porter did the artwork for the cover; Deborah Ziska provided advice on design, Norma Adams, Nena Terrell, Anna Corrales, Robert Richardson, and Jennifer Crawford all helped in the translation of many of the papers; and Elaine Reuben and Linda Dominic contributed editing and proofreading assistance, respectively, in the book's final stages. I also want to thank Diane Dodson and Valerie Miller for their valuable advice and suggestions and Elise Smith, OEF Executive Director, who provided the institutional backing needed for production.

A very special thanks goes to the Ford Foundation, the United Methodist and Presbyterian Churches, the Skaggs Foundation, and to the many other institutional and individual contributors who provided the financial support needed to make this book and the WLD Program itself possible.

Finally, I want to express my sincere appreciation to Nancy Rubin whose belief in the Women, Law, and Development Program and commitment to seeing it become a reality has been an inspiration to me since the program's beginning and especially to Willie Campbell, President of OEF International, for her vision and encouragements over the past three years.

Margaret Schuler
Washington, D.C.
October, 1986

INTRODUCTION

This book is about Third World women and the law. It is about how society creates and reinforces female oppression, and about women's efforts to confront that oppression. This book is about the empowerment of women who suffer the double burden of being poor and being female. It is about women deepening their understanding of the legal, cultural, political, and economic underpinnings of their subordination and gaining the skills needed to **utilize** the system (where possible) or **challenge** and even **subvert** it (where necessary) to assert rights, redress injustices, and access economic and political resources. It is about partial successes and tentative understandings. It is about ongoing processes of articulating ever more adequate analyses and implementing ever more effective and congruent action strategies.

The fifty-five case studies contained in this volume document the problems confronting women in thirty-two countries of Asia, Africa, and Latin America. The papers also document the strategies and programs women are using as they struggle to take their place as participants, contributors, and beneficiaries of development.

Looking at *Women, Law, and Development*

Development is essentially a process of allocating and utilizing resources for the social and economic benefit of society. Unfortunately, the net result of many development processes in the Third World today is the political and economic advancement of certain groups and the marginalization, exclusion, or subordination of others. Women comprise one major social sector systematically excluded from full economic and political participation in the production and benefits of development. They are often the last to benefit from formal development efforts due to their inferior economic, social, and political position which results in a continuous lag in opportunities for them in education and training, employment, health, and public life.

1

Since 1970, much *women in development* activity has attempted to remedy this situation by increasing the potential of women to produce and dispose of income at the individual or micro level. The goal of such activity has been to incorporate women into development—essentially increasing their stake in the existing system—by altering policies which limited women's access to economic benefits and providing greater opportunities for generating new sources of income. But such activity has not addressed major systemic or structural issues, particularly those of power and the limitations of the modernization development model.

Critiques of this approach note the insufficiency of its underlying analysis and the failure of its programs. They identify two key and mutually reinforcing variables as critical to understanding both the problem and thus the solution of women's subordinate role in development: the structure of production and hierarchical sexual stratification.[1] They point to the inadequacy of modernization as a viable development model and to the tenacity of patriarchal social structures in maintaining women in a subordinate position, irrespective of the model of development used. Additionally, the issues of racism and ethnic identification have been isolated as contributory factors in maintaining the subordination of women and in the failure of development to respond to the social and economic needs of the entire population. Thus, class, patriarchy, and race or ethnicity have become critical analytical categories in understanding and remedying the problem of women in development.

The Role of Law

In the last few years, awareness has been growing among Third World women activists about the role the law plays in supporting the classist, racist, and patriarchal structures of society and thus in upholding and legitimizing women's social and economic subordination and marginalization in the development process. They have seen how the law functions as an instrument of control by promoting or inhibiting access to certain resources while supporting attitudes and behaviors that maintain oppressive social structures and relations.

Essentially the law regulates access to **economic** and **social** resources, such as land, jobs, credit, and other goods and services, and to **political** power, that is, control over the allocation or administration of those resources. This regulation is accomplished through one or a combination of the following mechanisms:

❑ the formulation of laws and policies that are skewed toward the benefit of some and the burden of others;

❑ the arbitrary or selective application of laws or policies;

❑ attitudes and behaviors that reinforce and condone the existence of inequitable laws and inconsistent application of the law. (These may take the form of a **conscious acceptance** of detrimental laws and practices or a **lack of understanding** and awareness about the intent and procedures of the law. The result is the same.)

The outcome in most Third World countries is a pattern of legally sanctioned, and, in some instances, constitutionally guaranteed, subordination of women. Subordination is manifest in several key areas, particularly labor law, penal law, and civil law which governs legal capacity, rights and obligations in marriage, guardianship, inheritance, income, land rights, and participation in public affairs. In some instances women's inferior status is formally **legislated**; in others, it is produced and maintained through **prejudicial social practices** as well as through ignorance of the law by its intended beneficiaries, who consequently are unable to exercise the minimal rights the law does provide.

Moreover, the very concept of rights is conditioned. The *public sphere vs. private sphere* ideology as expressed in law is a key measure of society's perception of **women's** rights. The private sphere (domestic life, home, and family) is considered the traditional domain of women. The public sphere (work and politics) is accepted as the domain of men. This public/private dichotomy is deeply ingrained in the law. Regardless of the operative legal system or cultural context, laws touching the public arena (*e.g.*, labor law) have been modernized, that is,

3

brought into line with more enlightened thinking, while family and personal laws in the private sphere have been left untouched by the state, despite the fact that they reinforce women's oppression. Thus, the law plays a critical role in maintaining sexual stratification and in shaping the inferior social and economic position of women in society, functioning as both legitimizer and as regulator.[2]

In sum, women most often bear the brunt of economic and political disadvantage in the development process, and the law plays a critical role in this inequity. The problem of the inferior legal status of women centers around three key issues:

❑ The laws themselves are often unjust or discriminatory, limiting the rights of women;

❑ The application of the law—even when adequate—is often arbitrary or prejudicial toward women; and

❑ Women tend to be unaware of their own legal status, of the rights they do possess, of the effect laws have on them, or even that they are the objects of injustice.

The Development of Legal Strategies

Growing awareness about the relationships among *women, law,* and *development* brought about the further realization among Third World women that the law is also an instrument that can serve women. It can be both an obstacle to, and an instrument of, social transformation. While its repressive functions are often more easily identified by the disadvantaged in society, the potential also exists for a liberative function at the service of the disadvantaged—in this case, women. The concepts of *people's law, alternative law,* and *legal resources* represent articulations of alternative approaches for using the law as an exercise of political power. Each of these approaches contains the assumption that the poor and disadvantaged can be empowered to act on their own behalf and to use law as a political tool.[3]

As the UN Decade for Women (1976-1985) stimulated interest in women's participation in development, the idea of using the law as a political resource fused with the develop-

4

ment of feminist thought in the Third World. Coincidentally, a willingness by funding institutions to support public interest law and human rights programs provided the means to experiment with the use of law as a strategy for improving the status of women.

In various countries of Asia, Latin America, and Africa, women's organizations began implementing legal programs to educate women about their rights, to redress grievances, and to change discriminatory legislation and policies. Many of these programs were well-articulated and coherent and exhibited considerable creativity and variation; but often they were forced to develop in a vacuum, isolated from the lessons learned from others' experiences. In this early phase, viable programmatic models were, thus, limited.

Available documented experiences tended to a) deny the legitimacy of a specific focus on women, b) be sponsored by academic institutions or government agencies, c) be grouped under the rubric of legal aid, or d) focus exclusively on legal services or entirely on lobbying efforts aimed at the policy-making level. Unlike other social programs for which remedies had been formulated, tested, evaluated, and refined over the years, programmatic efforts to improve the legal status of women were still charting a new course. The reservoir of theoretical and practical wisdom was limited to isolated pockets of experimentation. While studies documenting the status of women *vis-á-vis* the law in its written form did exist, there were few studies of program processes and strategies which offered insight on what could be expected to be effective in women's efforts toward social transformation.

The Women, Law, and Development Forum

The growing experimentation with legal strategies and the wide divergence in interpretations and approaches to the problem created the need for a global dialogue on these issues, which materialized in the Third World Forum on Women, Law, and Development. At the 1985 gathering of non-governmental women's organizations in Nairobi, Kenya, the WLD Forum brought together women working on issues related to women, law, and development from numerous Third World countries. Later, the WLD Forum began to take on a life of its own as an ongoing forum organized at both regional and inter-regional levels.

The specific objectives of the WLD Forum in Nairobi were:

❑ To broaden, systematize, and document understandings about:

- ◆ the relationship between the law and the socioeconomic development process as it affects women,

- ◆ the legal and cultural mechanisms which maintain women's marginal status, and

- ◆ successful strategies to improve women's legal status.

❑ To develop a network among Third World women working to promote and improve the legal status of women.

❑ To contribute to the articulation of effective action strategies utilizing both the law and other innovative methodologies.

❑ To encourage women's organizations to develop and implement their own action-oriented programs and strategies.

❑ To focus world attention on this issue and heighten general awareness about the significance of the law in conditioning women's participation in development.

Given these objectives, a major task for the WLD Forum became one of clarifying the relationship between the law and the social, cultural, and economic structures of society, and thus explaining the ways the legal system functions to promote or hinder women's participation in development. As a means to this end, the Forum Project proposed to examine the concerns and experiences of Third World women who had developed and implemented action strategies to raise the legal status of women. It provided a mechanism and a framework for documenting and critically analyzing those strategies and promoted an interdisciplinary dialogue among Third World women lawyers and social scientists, academics and activists.

Prior to the Forum itself, seventy-five potential individual and organizational participants were identified from this emerging "field" of women, law, and development. Using the framework provided to systematize their analyses and draw on their own expertise, all were invited to prepare program case studies analyzing their particular strategies or to document the most critically relevant issues facing women in their countries. Drawing on these resources, a representative planning group of Third World women designed the forum and selected the presenters. Sixty of the core group of potential participants presented papers at the Nairobi Forum. Hundreds of other women participated in the discussions.

Essentially, the Forum offered a platform for dialogue around shared experiences of discrimination and exploitation, and divergent strategies to eliminate such injustices. By bringing together practioners and grassroots activists as well as researchers and academics to discuss and learn from each other, the Forum also contributed to the integration of theory and practice. Often the theoretical insights gained from research remain the domain of researchers and academics and do not make their way to the service of the concrete program or grassroots worker. The Forum sought to provide a vehicle for practitioners to participate in research by articulating learnings from their own experiences, and by engaging both practitioners and academics in a dialogue focused on developing from their experiences new theoretical insights that would be useful to the work in the field.

Moreover, the dialogue was interdisciplinary. Both law and the social sciences have something important and unique to contribute: each has its own methodology and set of categories for looking at reality. No one discipline could adequately provide a framework suited to the demands of the field of women, law, and development.

The goal of the continuing dialogue remains that of developing more adequate frameworks as tools—not cookbook solutions—that empower women to understand their own oppression and the social forces that shape and maintain it,

7

and to create strategies capable of confronting and overcoming them.

The papers contained in this collection represent the starting point of that ongoing dialogue, not the synthesis. They therefore present neither definitive solutions nor fully elaborated frameworks. In many ways, they mirror the unevenness of the field in its capacity to analyze critically and create innovative solutions. Therefore, the reader will note varying degrees of depth in the articulation of problems and solutions.

There is also variation here in political perspective and in methodology. Some papers are more academic in tone, referenced in detail, and theoretical; others are practical and descriptive. Some focus on substantive issues with only brief mention of strategies, others concentrate exclusively on programmatic approaches to the problem, and still others give equal weight to issues and strategies.

It is important to note, however, that the papers and the variation found in them also mirror the dynamism of the field. This collection of fifty-five papers represents *the state of the art* in women, law, and development. The papers document the extent and creativity of the pioneer efforts of Third World women to confront the structures of inequity in their societies and to identify new and effective means of transforming them. The value of these papers is that they document how Third World women are challenging the limitations of culture, as it is expressed in the law, and questioning the credibility of the official reproducers of culture. This collection calls attention to the fact that women throughout the Third World are beginning to mobilize force to this task.

The WLD Forum in Nairobi was structured around the themes which surfaced from the papers and case studies, themes that are both issue-specific and strategic: they identified the principal legal constraints facing women, and described collective action strategies in response to these problems. This book is similarly structured. It is divided into three parts. Part One is entitled *An Approach to Women, Law, and Development: Conceptualizing and Exploring Issues and Strategies*. Part Two, *Confronting Patriarchal, Class, and Ethnic Biases in the Law: The Issues* looks at the effect of those factors on certain substantive areas of law concerning women as well as particular issues identified by the contributors. Part

Three, *Using or Challenging the Law: The Strategies* looks at collective action and other kinds of programmatic responses. The report and recommendations of the conference and keynote addresses follow in a separate section.

There are three substantive themes in *The Issues* section. The first, **The State, Law, and Development,** focuses on the character of law in a given state and the state's response to the needs and demands of women. It makes reference to constitutional issues and development policies. Specific areas of interest here are land tenure systems, labor laws and practices, and family law. The second theme, **Custom, Religion, Law, and Ethnicity,** discusses attempts to bring to light and resolve the the contradictions that exist among state law, custom, customary law, religion, and women's rights. Finally, the theme of **Violence and Exploitation** explores efforts to identify and confront the ways in which society legitimizes violence against women, particularly rape, prostitution, domestic violence, exploitation in the workplace, and human rights violations. *The Strategies* section is itself divided into three parts: education and organization, law reform, and advocacy.

Given the integrated nature of the problem, that is, the fact that strategies cannot be easily isolated from issues, nor issues from some suggestion of an appropriate response, the papers in this collection have been distributed across themes and strategies somewhat artificially, according to the element they appear best to exemplify. The overview of each section notes the exemplary element of each paper.

Empowering Women

I hope this book will provide the basis for further theoretical insight and practical application in the area of women, law, and development for women throughout the Third World who are struggling creatively, and many times against great odds, to overcome the many injustices they suffer. I hope the insights offered may spark new experimentation and greater depth, both in analysis of the issues and in the approaches taken to meet the challenges they present. They are offered, as well, to women and other readers in the First World who are interested in and working on similar issues, so that they too can learn from the experiences of the Third World.

PART I

AN APPROACH TO WOMEN, LAW, AND DEVELOPMENT

1/Approach

Conceptualizing and Exploring Issues and Strategies

Margaret Schuler

The issues and strategies included in this collection present striking variation and striking commonality. Delimiting variables are found in the specific context of each issue or program discussed; at the same time, the problems faced by women in one cultural or political milieu are easily recognized as similar to those being confronted by women in another, even though similar problems are not always confronted with similar strategies.

It becomes extremely important, therefore, to identify functional categories or concepts for comparative purposes so that useful learnings will emerge at the cross-cultural level as well as at the level of the individual program. What is needed is a set of concepts that will help order the data, allow patterns of similarity and difference to surface, and articulate a new and deeper comprehension of the structure and utility of the efforts described.

The need for useful categories was brought home to me dramatically as I traveled around the world making contacts and observing many of the programs and strategies described in this book. I realized to what degree our analysis is circumscribed by the terms we use. Often, seeing the work of a group in action reveals a very different picture from the description given of it by the very people who are involved in the action. Many times excellent and innovative contributions are not recognized even by the innovators.

I was also struck by rhetorical cliches whose required usage makes them devoid of meaningful content. It is popular to speak of "mobilization" and "empowerment," for example, but what do they really mean and how do you do them? "Educating women about their rights" is another popular phrase. But what kind of education?

For program designers and implementers to respond critically to the question, "what are you doing and why are you doing it that way?" so as to reveal the power or the limitations of the strategy at hand, a high level of awareness or analysis is required. The better we are able to name the phenomena in which we are immersed, and to share those names, the more useful our experiences become both to ourselves and to others.

This chapter proposes a series of simple definitions and categories to help name these experiences. It presents a conceptual framework which identifies the major legal issues facing women in the Third World and offers some elements toward a thematic analysis of them. Secondly, the framework explores strategies by defining them in a generic sense, classifying them by activity and focus, identifying the content of typical strategies, listing conditioning factors critical to their development, and suggesting criteria for judging their value.

This framework is not intended to limit discussion but to be a tool for exploring and assessing strategy effectiveness and value in its own context, and for identifying common patterns and broader applications.

The Issues

All the programs or strategies included here are directed in practice toward some specific issue of relevance or urgency to women. They do not have as an objective changing the status of women in general, but rather target one or several specific issues of concern. Following is a list of the most common substantive legal issues for which these strategies are developed.

Constitutional Issues
Equality
Human Rights
Civil Rights
Political Rights

14

Economic Issues
Credit
Ownership & Control of Property
Inheritance

Labor Issues
Wages
Working Conditions
Maternity Benefits
Social Entitlements
Opportunities for Employment
Protective Legislation

Family Relations
Marriage
Divorce
Child Custody & Guardianship
Reproduction

Health
Health Entitlements
Birth Control
Abortion

Violence and Exploitation
Rape
Other Forms of Violence Against Women
Prostitution
Pornography

Merely listing the issues, however, does not convey the nuances which point to commonality or variation in the legal problem areas facing women in the Third World, or the strategies taken to confront them. One way of approaching issues is to organize them by themes, or points of reference, as we chose to do for both the WLD Forum in Nairobi and this book.[1]

The themes we identified are: 1) the State, Law, and Development, 2) Custom, Religion, Ethnicity, and Law, and 3) Violence and Exploitation. Any of the substantive legal areas discussed might be considered from each of these perspectives, though some fall more obviously into one than another. Indeed, it is hoped that these three major themes or points of reference will be useful for exploring various issues and in this way facilitate a richer analysis.

State, Law, and Development

The first point of reference, the **State, Law, and Development**, looks at the relativity of law from the perspective of the state and the national and international economic system. Recognizing that the character of law is linked to the character of the state, the need for reference to a political and economic analysis becomes critical in considering laws affecting women in the development process. From this perspective, the struggles for equality are necessarily linked to the varying political and economic realities of Third World countries where these struggles unfold.

Appreciating contextual differences helps us to understand the relative success, failure, and variations of strategies women design to achieve *de jure* and *de facto* equality. The nature of the task in countries currently engaged in nationalist struggles, for example, is different from that in countries with relative political and economic stability. Whether the strategy is to press for the ratification of the Convention on the Elimination of All Forms of Discrimination Against Women; to push for a new family code, an equal rights clause in the constitution, or the interpretation of current constitutional provisions favoring women; or to change entrenched attitudes toward women by the courts or police, the nature of the struggle is linked to the larger political and economic issues that give character to both the state and the law.

This contextual emphasis becomes particularly vital when considering development programs and women's participation in them. Only a political understanding of development can locate the patriarchal, class, and ethnic biases of such programs and help delineate how legislation and policy serve to exclude women from economic development through capitalist or sexist or racist land tenure and credit systems, technical training, and other programs. Recognizing the problem areas and limitations of women's participation and empowerment within a given context can guide the design of legal strategies that get to the heart of the problem.

The character of the economic system has special relevance to the situation of women in the area of labor law. In most of the Third World, "women's occupations" afford few rights and little protection: their jobs are usually not in an organized sector and thus expose them to great exploitation. Developing strategies for organizing the women engaged in occupations like domestic labor, vending, and other jobs in the informal sector calls for special attention to the structure of the economy in order to secure the minimal protections afforded men and women in other "non-female" occupations.

In family law, an area most often weighted against women, the degree to which the system will permit legislative changes or applications of the law favorable to women is also conditioned by the character of law and the state. Likewise, the possibilities for the development of effective strategies focused on family law are linked to economic and political factors.

Custom, Religion, Ethnicity, and Law

The second theme, or point of reference, for considering major issues facing women is **Custom, Religion, Ethnicity and Law** a theme particularly critical in Asia and Africa where ethnic revivalism and religious fundamentalism, contributing as they do to the public/private dichotomy, have played a major role in circumscribing the status of women. It is not irrelevant, however, to Latin America, where custom and religion have also affected the majority of women in many areas of their lives.

Both revivalism and fundamentalism exist within religious and ethnic communities for a variety of reasons. In conflicts between ethnicity and womanhood, a woman will often opt for her ethnic group over her own rights so as not to lose or challenge her identity as member of the group. The two phenomena of fundamentalism and revivalism have been

17

recognized as generally detrimental to women only relatively recently and pose a challenge to develop approaches that creatively confront the contradictions they present.

The two most relevant aspects of the theme of custom and ethnicity are customary law and religion. In many countries of Asia and Africa, customary law (dating from the pre-colonial era) governs relations within the family (especially inheritance, marriage, divorce, maintenance, and child custody) while state law governs all other matters. Although customary law is not always detrimental to women, in many contexts it affects women adversely, especially when supported by patrilineal customs of marriage, divorce, and inheritance which, by definition, always favor men. The challenge is to create strategies which promote those aspects of custom not detrimental to women while replacing those which are.

Religion poses a similar concern to women, especially where fundamentalist interpretations have reinforced practices that maintain women's subordinate position in society. There are differences of opinion as to whether a religious approach or a secular one is more appropriate for combating these religious interpretations that discriminate against women, and this difference presents a challenge to women in the future. Fundamentalist tendencies have emerged in most of the religions of the world, and there are numerous recent instances of reversals of gains for women due to the strength of fundamentalist movements.

Violence and Exploitation

The final point of reference for considering legal issues facing women is **Violence and Exploitation**. The growing recognition among Third World women of the link between violence and the factors of class, race, and patriarchy makes this a theme of considerable importance. Given the political and economic dimensions of these three critical variables, it is often Third World women who are most vulnerable to sexual and labor exploitation and violations of human rights.

The law generally condones domestic violence by "protecting" the patriarchal family from intervention by outside forces. Victims of violence, including genital mutilation, battering, rape and murder of women (all attempts to control female sexuality) are often further victimized by legal systems that treat the perpetrator with leniency. This is clearly the case in prostitution, to which women are increasingly resorting for economic reasons. The exploitation of sexuality in the form of prostitution has a clear relationship to development in many Third World countries. In fact, in certain countries, "sex tourism" has developed into a veritable industry vigorously promoted by the state. While society usually condemns prostitution as undesirable, it is generally the prostitute and not the client who is prosecuted. In all of these areas, penal codes in most countries are out of step with the reality of violence directed toward women. Therefore, many strategies are focusing on changing penal codes as well as offering the victims interim relief through various programs.

Another area of exploitation related particularly to women and development is labor law. The proliferation of Free Trade Zones in the Third World is predicated on the abundance of cheap and docile female workers. The most exploited of industrial workers, women in Free Trade Zones are unorganized and without legal protection. Migrant domestic servants and unskilled workers who leave their own countries in search of jobs elsewhere also suffer gross exploitation. If in their own countries they have little protection, the situation in most "host" countries is intolerable, with little or no regulation.

Political and human rights violations are another form of violence. "National security" states in the Third World are notorious for their repression of opponents and disregard for human rights. Women are not excluded from political repression. The extent of torture and imprisonment of women for political reasons has only recently been documented, and it can be shown that violations of individual human rights are linked to larger issues of social, economic, and cultural rights.

In enumerating these issues and linking them to the larger political and economic realities of the Third World, we are reminded that the legal constraints women face are survival issues—often life and death concerns. Women's struggles for equality and justice are not peripheral to development but, in many ways, measure the quality of development unfolding in their societies. They are part of the larger search for general social justice.

The Strategies

Our attention now turns to strategies developed to confront these issues. We discuss here primarily what we mean by "strategies," various kinds of strategic activities and methods, how strategies are put together, and the way they work to produce change. In the exploration of strategies that follows, some of the content is definitional and descriptive, some is evaluative.

Definition of *Strategy*

Confusion often results when people use different words to describe the same phenomenon. Conversely, confusion occurs when they use the same word to describe several phenomena. Consider, for example:

> Programs
> Organizational responses
> Strategies
> Collective action
> Action strategies
> Experiences

All of these words have something in common and all have been used to describe similar phenomena. Yet each has its own particular nuance and none is adequate to convey the richness of the list taken as a whole.

For example, in certain circles, *program* has bureaucratic connotations and is rejected for its association with oppressive institutions. *Strategy*, on the other hand, can have militaristic or manipulative overtones. The term *experiences* is concrete and conveys a more humanistic sense of group activity, but can also convey a certain passive or reactive quality.

The dictionary defines strategy as:

> the science and art of employing the political, economic, and psychological forces of a group to afford the maximum support for adopted policies; a careful plan or method; the art of devising or employing plans toward a goal.[2]

The critical words here are *group, plan,* and *goal.*

Making the definition more explicit for our purposes, a strategy

❑ has clearly articulated goals and objectives,

❑ has a series of planned activities—not spontaneous or serendipitous—designed to fulfill these goals,

❑ is carried out over a period of time in a systematic fashion—not occasionally or sporadically, and

❑ is carried out by a group in a collaboratory and organized fashion.

These characteristics are also implied in the terms *program, organizational response,* and *collective action.*[3] The terms have different nuances, of course, but for the purposes of our present task, we will use *strategy* as the functional term for all planned group activity geared toward a specific goal.

According to this definition, then, a strategy may be a series of activities carried out over a relatively short period of time for a very specific purpose, or it may be a long-term complex of activities and tasks geared toward achieving a series of goals and objectives.

What makes a strategy a **WLD** strategy, is, of course, its women, law, and development content. We use *women* here to refer to those strategies that have as a major goal raising the status of women or empowering women. We use the term *law* as synonymous with legal system, including not only written formulations (in constitutions, legislation, policies, regulations, *etc.*) but the practical application of the law and the attitudes and behaviors of the population toward it. We use the term *development* to mean the process of generating, allocating, and utilizing resources for the benefit of society. We have defined the term *strategy* to mean all planned group activity geared toward the achievement of some goal. Thus we define a **WLD Strategy** as

a series of organized actions that either challenge or use the legal system to empower women economically, politically, and socially.

Challenging the legal system can be accomplished in a number of ways, from consciousness-raising to litigation to civil disobedience. Using the legal system also has multiple

21

possibilities, from public education about legal rights to proposing new laws to legal assistance. Somewhere in between, but touching both complementary poles, are the strategies that articulate alternatives to current norms and practices. There is, in fact, an enormous range of activities and approaches that will fit our definition.

A Framework for Examining Strategies

Having defined a WLD strategy, we will now categorize various kinds of strategies and their components. Following is an analytical framework for doing this. (It appears graphically on page 23.) This framework presents a constructed simplification of the features, components, and processes of WLD strategies. As an analytical and diagnostic tool, it is a summary statement, grounded in the observation of numerous programs and strategies throughout the world, about what appear to be essential program foci.

The framework we present follows Friedman's approach to understanding the structure and interactions of the legal system by breaking it down into three components: the substantive (the content of the law), the structural (the courts, enforcement and administrative agencies of the state), and the cultural (shared attitudes and behaviors toward the law).[4]

Components of a Legal System

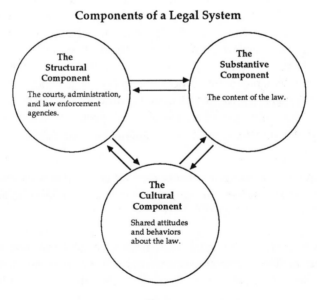

The
Structural
Component

The courts, administration,
and law enforcement
agencies.

The
Substantive
Component

The content of the law.

The
Cultural
Component

Shared attitudes
and behaviors
about the law.

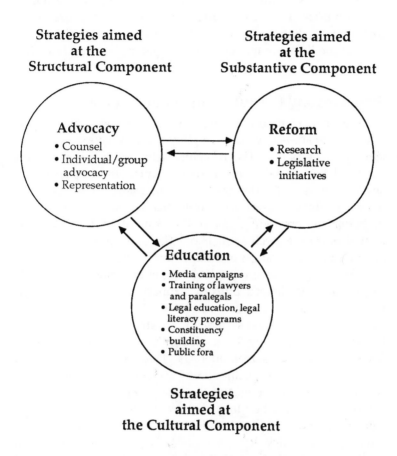

Strategies aimed
at the
Structural Component

Strategies aimed
at the
Substantive Component

Advocacy
• Counsel
• Individual/group
  advocacy
• Representation

Reform
• Research
• Legislative
  initiatives

Education
• Media campaigns
• Training of lawyers
  and paralegals
• Legal education, legal
  literacy programs
• Constituency
  building
• Public fora

Strategies
aimed at
the Cultural Component

Relationship between Components
of the
Legal System and Program Strategies

As the diagram above illustrates, activities aimed at law reform
target the substantive components of the legal system; those
aimed at educating people about the law target the cultural
component; and those aimed at advocacy within the courts and
administrative agencies focus on the structural component of
the system. Just as the system components are integrally linked
to one another, so program component imply a relationship and
an interaction. The arrows describe this interaction.

The structure of legal strategies can also be analyzed in terms of the structure of the legal system since the activities that comprise a strategy correspond to one or more of its components. Following is a description of strategies that address the three components of the legal system and how they interact to produce change.

Strategies and the Substantive Component

A strategy focusing on the substance of the law is made up of activities geared toward changing discriminatory or unjust legislation or policy. The principal activities it might include are legal and social research to determine the impact of the law on women, and the drafting of alternative legislation and policies. When these efforts fulfill their objectives, they result in better understanding about the content of the laws and related policies as well as their practice and impact on women, and they produce changes in the laws themselves.

However, research and lobbying efforts alone are unlikely to produce the desired outcomes unless they are consciously linked to other strategic activities that target the other components of the legal system, *i.e.*, its structure and culture. To be truly effective, any legal change benefiting must women respond to women's real interests. This can be assured only through the active participation of a conscious constituency of women in the formulation of the law, its implementation, and enforcement. Thus, building a conscious constituency through education and organization is a necessary complement to research and policy level activities. Nor is it sufficient that equitable laws exist and that people are aware of them. For such laws to be effective, there must be some means to assure access to the system at the structural level for those the law is meant to serve.

Strategies and the Structural Component

A strategy focusing on the structural component of the legal system will have as its objective making the law functional for those who have least access to resources within the legal system and thus are the most vulnerable to injustices. Strategies of this type include activities such as formal legal representation, counsel, and advocacy in various forms. (Most legal services programs fall under this category of strategy.) But again, without direct interaction between lawyer or "advocate" and client or "participant," these activities will not achieve their objectives. The women clients themselves need to become participants, aware of the law and how it affects them, and to see their own problems as "legal" problems in order to gain the confidence they need to press their demands. Thus, the success of advocacy services is, to a large degree, contingent upon activities which focus on education or awareness-raising (cultural level activities) to complement program activities aimed at increasing access to the resources of the legal system at the structural level.

In addition, should a program focusing on the structural dimension remain uncritical with regard to the substance of the law, strategic effectiveness will be weakened. In fact, such a program might actually contribute to the maintenance of the *status quo*. There is an additional requirement, therefore, to include strategic activities geared toward the "substantive" as well.

Strategies and the Cultural Component

Educational strategies, which focus on the cultural component of the legal system, can take a variety of forms: *e.g.*, structured, community-level legal education programs, media campaigns, public fora, reform of law school curricula. Their main purpose is to change attitudes and behaviors by raising awareness about the legal status of women and how the law functions to women's detriment. Educational efforts are directed primarily toward women, particularly those whose access to such information is limited by their social status. They are also, however, directed toward men and those who serve as advocates, policy-makers and legislators. Indeed, as previously mentioned, awareness is a critical factor in making advocacy and reform strategies

25

effective. Awareness alone, however, is insufficient and creates frustration unless accompanied by access to the courts and influence over legislative and policy-making levels.

Since application or enforcement of the law depends on the attitudes and biases of judges, lawyers, administrators, and citizens in general, activities geared toward equitable application of adequate laws generally target all three components of the legal system, with particular emphasis on the cultural. The task becomes one of creating the force to place political pressure on the system at its structural and substantive points.

In sum, this framework suggests that the law can be used as an effective—though not sufficient—means to promote structural as well as attitudinal and behavioral change. It suggests, moreover, that the interaction of the structural, substantive, and cultural components of the legal system has implications for the development of effective strategies. Thus, any program aimed at improving the status of women *vis-à-vis* the law, if it is to achieve this goal, must include activities that will address all three components of the legal system.

Strategy Orientation

Strategies are responses to a problem. They tend to emphasize one approach or another depending on how the problem and the best way of solving it are perceived. Building on the framework outlined above, we see that WLD strategies respond to problems which generally are perceived in one of the three following ways.

Firstly, it may be seen as **a problem of substance,** the content of the law. There may be elements lacking in the law; there may be flagrant inequality and injustice, or there may be ambiguities that make the law inadequate at least and repressive at worst. With this perception of the problem, the emphasis of the strategy is on changing the content of laws and policies, eliminating them, or adding new laws.

Alternately, it may be seen as **a problem of the institutions** which uphold and apply the law, the structure of the legal system. Often, legal institutions and structures are seen as inaccessible or unable to respond to the interests of the people they are meant to serve, especially the poor. Strategies derived from this perspective generally emphasize transformation or creation of more responsive and accountable structures for the administration of justice.

Finally, it may be viewed as **a problem of attitudes and behaviors**, the culture of the law. From this perspective, the problem stems from the manner in which those who administer the law, as well as the population in general, have been conditioned to regard the law. Cultural issues may range from acceptance of discriminatory and unjust practices to basic ignorance about the possibilities and limitations of the law. Where the problem is perceived in this way, strategies tend to emphasize the empowerment of women through increased awareness of their rights and through their active engagement

How Analysis of the Problem Predicates Strategy Choice

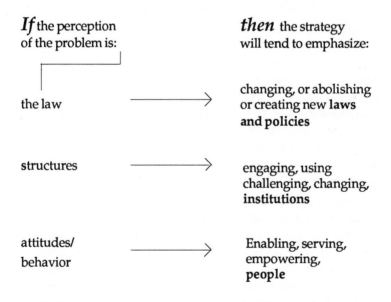

If the perception
of the problem is:

then the strategy
will tend to emphasize:

the law ⟶ changing, or abolishing or creating new **laws and policies**

structures ⟶ engaging, using challenging, changing, **institutions**

attitudes/
behavior ⟶ Enabling, serving, empowering, **people**

The graphic above relates stategy to the perception of the problem. For example, if the problem is perceived as one of attitudes and behavior, then the strategy of choice is likely to be enabling, serving, and empowering the people. Thus, the graphic posits three perceptions and notes the corresponding strategy.

in the development of resources to defend those rights.

While strategies generally address several aspects of a problem, there is usually one aspect that is perceived as the most problematic. Therefore, strategies and the activities that make them up tend to target one of the major components of the legal system: content, structure, or culture.

The Strategy Matrix

The Strategy Matrix (see page 30) summarizes the major categories of strategies according to focus, goals, objectives, activities, and terms used to describe the activities. The structure of the matrix suggests that in addition to the three components of the legal system (structure, culture, and content), an additional analytical category (application) is useful for identifying the kinds of activities contained in strategies that focus on assuring the just application of the law. As mentioned earlier, application strategies target all three components of the legal system.

This matrix, like any analytical model, is an oversimplification. The major limitation is that it fails to convey the interaction of the components and activities. (We have already noted the importance of addressing simultaneously the several dimensions of the legal system and have included a graphic presentation of this concept. (See page 23.) The strategy matrix can, nevertheless, be useful in ordering and categorizing the information and descriptive material presented in this book and can serve as a starting point for a critical analysis of the activities contained in legal strategies.

The matrix also addresses the imprecision of terms that are often used to describe various kinds of activities. "Legal services," for example, is most generally considered synonymous with "legal aid," but in some circles it has been used to include every activity represented in the matrix. "Advocacy" is another term that can cover a multitude of activities. The matrix attempts to clarify terms and concepts by defining and categorizing activities **functionally**. Once activities can be located according to their function, we can more easily assess their validity and value. Thus, the matrix is intended primarily as a tool for categorizing relationships among components of strategies.

Empowering Strategies

In the last analysis, WLD strategies refer to various approaches to the exercise of political power by women-- approaches which use or challenge the law. When we speak of empowerment, we refer to the capacity to mobilize resources to produce beneficial social change. The concept of empowering strategies, therefore, contains important methodological implications for the development and assessment of legal strategies for women.

Whether the strategy initially targets inadequate legislation or policy or focuses on legal services or legal literacy, we can identify three critical dimensions that are part of a process leading to the acquisition and exercise of power. The process begins with the development of consciousness about issues, leads to organization, and, finally, results in mobilization. Using these categories, any strategy can be assessed by the degree of empowerment it effects.

At the first level are those activities geared toward raising individual consciousness. They are primarily focused on developing an understanding of the problem (in this case, women's subordination as manifested in a variety of issues) at the level of personal awareness. Activities geared toward individual consciousness-raising are not limited to legal literacy or legal education strategies alone, but are also included in legal reform and services strategies as well. Developing explanations about proposed legislative changes, working with a woman involved in litigation to help her understand her case, conducting research, and implementing media campaigns about a given issue are all examples of integrating consciousness-raising into various kinds of strategies. The critical element is the presence of activities that increase awareness or consciousness about the nature or cause of the issue identified as detrimental to women.

At the second level is organizational consciousness. Understanding of the problem moves from the individual toward the group and an identification with other women as objects of injustice or discrimination. This collective element is manifest in activities which increase the capacity of women to work together for the achievement of common goals based on a common understanding of the problem.

29

Focus	Culture	Structure
Terms	Consciousness-Raising, Legal Education, Legal Literacy	Legal Advocacy, Legal Aid, Legal Assistance, Legal Services.
Goals	Empowerment of women through increased awareness of their rights and the development of resources to defend these rights.	An accessible legal system, functional and accountable to those it is meant to serve
Objectives	**Sensitizing women to** ❑ their inherent rights ❑ their actual status ❑ the intent and provisions of the laws and policies affecting them ❑ the limitations of the law ❑ the structural sources of powerlessness **Demystifying the legal system**	**Opening up access to the legal system in order to** ❑ secure the enjoyment of rights ❑ redress injustices
Activities	❑ Seminars, conferences, and workshops by and for experts ❑ Community education programs on the laws ❑ Mass media campaigns (radio, press) ❑ Publication of scholarly works ❑ Dissemination of information through popular literature and art forms: comic books, posters, dance, brochures, theatre, poetry, *etc.*	❑ Legal services available to women (especially low-income women) ❑ Use of litigation, focusing on test cases with the greatest potential impact ❑ Class action suits ❑ Developing alternative approaches to resolving disputes ❑ Training and use of para-legals, social workers, and psychologists in advocacy skills

Content	*Application*
Legal Advocacy, Legal Reform	Advocacy
Existence of adequate and just legislation and policies	Effective use and application of laws and policies meant to benefit women
Eliminating discriminatory law and policies **Replacing or adding new, more just laws and policies**	**Assuring enforcement of laws and policies**
□ Legal and sociological research on current and proposed laws □ Design of new laws and policies □ Lobbying at policy-making levels □ Building effective organizations at the grassroots □ Public pressure on policy-makers and legislators □ Collective action and mobilization □ Civil disobedience	□ Monitoring enforcement at administrative levels □ Monitoring enforcement policies in the courts □ Systematically documenting discrimination in public and private sectors □ Developing arguments and building cases □ Building networks and organizing public and private protest mechanisms

Four Major Categories of WLD Strategies

Activities at this level can also cut across the major categories of strategies, ranging from legal literacy to reform to advocacy. They include organization and the development of political, organizing or legal skills at the collective level. These kinds of activities, however, assume the presence of consciousness of the issue or problem at the individual level. Sometimes organization and consciousness-raising are done simultaneously, but they represent two different dimensions of empowerment and imply a sequence.

The third level is mobilization. The collective skills and resources of the group are translated into action to produce the desired changes. At the point of mobilization, the exercise of political power reaches its highest expression. Mobilization necessarily builds on consciousness at the individual and collective levels and the capacity to organize at the group level. It is toward this goal, mobilization, that all the resources and energies of a given strategy are ultimately geared.

Methodologically, this implies that any strategy aimed at raising the status of women by using or confronting the law should include not only formal legal remedies and methods, but political ones as well. For example, effecting desired changes in legislation requires an organized, conscious constituency, able to articulate grievances and exert influence. The tasks of building this constituency and exerting pressure are political ones and, therefore, require political methods. Drafting new legislation and building persuasive arguments to justify it are technical tasks and require legal skills and methods. Most strategies imply a combination of legal and political methods.

Looking at strategies from this perspective, we can identify criteria for assessing their validity and value. Not all efforts aimed at "legal education," for example, are of equal value, nor are all efforts to change legislation or ensure enforcement equally valid. What gives them value as strategies is not their stated goal but their capacity to amass power and, ultimately, to effect beneficial change, that is, social transformation.

Further, to achieve the goal of empowerment, the educational component of any strategy is critical—with the caveat that only certain educational orientations are likely to produce empowerment. A necessary condition of an effective strategy is the use of methodologies that help women acquire the functional knowledge and skills they need to assure the law protects their interests.

The concepts of Paulo Freire, the Brazilian educator, perhaps best express this approach.[5] Applied to women, the basic premise of Freire is that the ignorance and powerlessness of the poor and by implication, women, are rooted in social structures that determine the unequal exercise of power in society. The remedy is social transformation, for which education is a prerequisite—an education that enables people to reflect on themselves and their roles in both the old and new societies and to develop the capacity to participate rationally, critically, and democratically in public life. This capacity is developed through a process of achieving critical understanding of one's socio-political context and of acquiring the skills to transform unjust power structures and relationships. Since human beings are essentially creative beings, significant change will come from their own

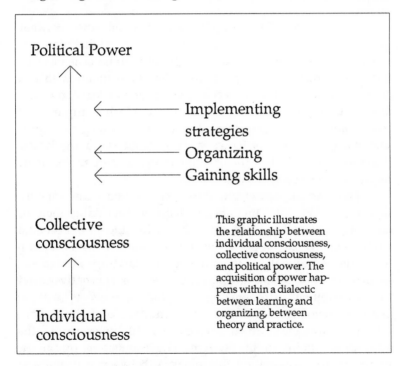

Political Power

← Implementing strategies
← Organizing
← Gaining skills

Collective consciousness

Individual consciousness

This graphic illustrates the relationship between individual consciousness, collective consciousness, and political power. The acquisition of power happens within a dialectic between learning and organizing, between theory and practice.

Building Empowerment

33

transforming action. The role of the educator in this process is to engage in a "dialogical praxis" with the participants, recognizing that they are equally knowledgeable, if not more so, about their own situation. Implicit in this method is a critique of traditional educational approaches, particularly extension training, which assume that the educator possesses the knowledge needed by the "learners" and that this knowledge can be imparted to them.

The "alternative law" and "legal resources" approaches to using the law as a political tool also acknowledge the need for education and see the legal advisor as "facilitator." In the words of Baxi, the role of the legal advisor is to "help people to play creatively within the space the system concedes them."[6] This requires the use of participatory, problem-posing approaches to leadership that are neither manipulative nor impatient, but respectful of and confident in the capacity of women to understand the sources of their oppression, to act on their own behalf, and to move effectively within the legal sphere.

This methodology implies an effective link between grassroots and policy-making levels. Often, a dichotomy is posited between these two as though only the latter is of value and the former, while "interesting," has little to do with real change. To the contrary, no change in policy or legislation will lead to social transformation without the input and mobilization of the grassroots. Empowering strategies assume that the grassroots has the capacity to understand the issues, develop the skills to articulate alternatives, and mobilize its resources to press for effective change.

Empowering strategies, thus, use methods that catalyze this force. Whether they begin with legislative change or advocacy, or another focus, they always include an educational component which progressively moves women from learning about rights and injustice toward an understanding of the causes of their inferior status, to the articulation of alternatives, and the development of organizing and political skills. With these skills women are equipped to formulate and implement effective strategies which create political pressure at the appropriate point in the system. The acquisition of power, therefore, happens within this dialectic between learning and organizing, between theory and practice.

Variables Influencing Strategy Design and Structure

One last issue remains in developing our framework for understanding and assessing strategies. We have already indicated a series of elements considered critical to the effectiveness of a strategy. However, there are probably few strategies that include all of the ideal components. We suggest that there are certain factors that influence which elements are included in a strategy and the degree to which they can be implemented. These factors, described below, influence the design and structure of a strategy as well as its efficacy, success, validity, and value.

Socioeconomic and Political Context

The social, political, and economic character of the society in which the strategy is developed is significant in defining both the opportunities for, and the limitations of, action. What can be done within a liberal democracy, for example, is not the same as in a military dictatorship or in a post-revolutionary society or a theocratic state. To be more specific, a government orientation which is neither democratic nor participatory (in the sense of providing mechanisms for its citizens to have any meaningful input into policy formation) would influence whether policy or legislative activities might be effectively included in the strategy.

Similarly, where grassroots organizations are either not allowed to develop or are repressed when they do, the risks involved in working to change the *status quo* are obvious. (On the other hand, the very repressive character of a society can sometimes inspire a militant challenge.) Clearly, the openness of the society has an important influence on the possibility of implementing certain activities aimed at promoting political consciousness and mobilization at the grassroots level.

Ideological Orientation of Strategy Organizers

Another important variable is the ideological orientation of strategy organizers with regard to the issues of women, law, development, class, race, and patriarchy. For example, a feminist perspective, *i.e.,* one which emphasizes the role of patriarchy in creating and maintaining the subordination of women, would incline the strategy to a different direction than one that does not consider this factor important. Either perspective will influence both the kind of activities and the kind of women to include in the strategy. Moreover, even within a feminist perspective, there are differences about the best way to approach the struggle.

With regard to development, there is also a wide range of perspectives. An approach that sees economic development within the current system as the cornerstone of women's empowerment would focus primarily on those legal constraints that hinder or facilitate women's incorporation into the free market economy. An approach, on the other hand, that sees women's empowerment in political rather than strictly economic terms, would focus on women acquiring power to alter inequitable structures. Each of these perspectives implies a different strategic response.

With regard to the law, there is also variation. Some strategies or programs clearly articulate the use of the law as a means of exercising power; others see it as a means for increasing awareness at an individual level, leading to the exercise of rights, and still others as a means to access economic resources at the micro level. Some provide law as a service to the needy; others promote it as a political resource.

Another variation on this theme of ideological orientation would be the weight the strategy organizers give the issues of class and race, in addition to patriarchy. A clear and progressive perspective on the need to transform social relations in the economic sphere does not always imply that a need for change in gender relations is acknowledged. On the other hand, feminist perspectives can also be void of understanding about class and ethnic factors. However defined, these views have a strong effect on the strategy's design and methodology.

Organizational Sponsorship and Leadership

The organizational setting of the strategy is also an important factor. Specifically, leadership, skill, and commitment to the strategy by the sponsoring organization play a major role in shaping its design, structure, methodology, and content.

Variations here are almost unlimited. For example, sometimes strategies are carried out by one group alone and other times they are a collaborative effort of several organizations. Often it is a women's organization, as such, that develops the strategy, but sometimes women attached to a university or some other institution create and implement the strategy. Even under the rubric of "women's organizations" there is variety. Some are large, voluntary, and national in scope, while others are local or limited to members of a single profession. Some are issue-focused (health, labor, *etc.*) and others have a more generalized concern about women's situation. Some organizations developing legal strategies around women's issues are not women's organizations at all, but are development or research institutes with a concern for women.

All of these institutional frameworks can be equally effective, provided they develop and implement strategies which promote a comprehensive understanding of the problem and implement empowering strategies leading to the exercise of political power by women. Nevertheless, we can point out a few of the factors that will have a bearing on the way a program or strategy is conceptualized, organized, and implemented. A development group will have a different approach, for example, than will a political group or an academic group, or an *ad hoc* group organized to confront a specific issue. The composition and experience of the group in designing strategies, organizing, and implementing them is another factor. A group composed exclusively of lawyers will have a different perspective from one composed of lawyers, social scientists, educators, and psychologists.

Of course, leadership and management styles figure as factors and will be reflected in the structure and style of the strategy. An organization with a hierarchical structure will tend to reproduce this characteristic in the design of the strategy. Similarly, a group which operates within participatory structures will tend to produce a strategy with participatory methodologies.

Funding

A final, perhaps obvious, variable in the development and design of strategies or programs is the availability of funding, which of course, determines the extent to which activities can be carried out. The interest of funders in supporting certain kinds of strategies determines to a large degree the existence and even design of programs. If there had been no interest in human rights, public interest law, and legal services over the last decade, many of the program described in this book would not exist. Nevertheless, resource availability is not the only critical variable in the establishment and design of programs. Many, after all, are self-financed or began modestly before they received outside support. Still assuming commitment, skill, and vision on the part of the leadership, resources play a major role in the possibilities for action in the execution of legal strategies.

❦❦❦❦

PART II

CONFRONTING PATRIARCHAL, CLASS, AND ETHNIC BIASES IN THE LAW: THE ISSUES

The State, Law, and Development

The papers in this section cover a range of legal constraints facing women in the Third World and offer a glimpse of the role played by the state and the law in defining them as obstacles. Some of the problems are constitutionally based and some relate to the way the law is administered and interpreted, but none is isolated from the social, cultural, political, and economic realities of the state in question. While they do not cover the totality of issues confronting Third World women, the papers point to the types of problems women face. Given the political context of law and policy formation and implementation, these papers also suggest, without elaborating the specifics, that organizing, pressure and mobilization by women are essential to achieving effective change.

Reflecting on the nature of law and the state, *Paredes* makes the general observation that discrimination is part of the law's legitimation function through which it supports the interests and conduct of the powerful.

In the next paper, *Pimentel* explores the importance of juridical equality between men and women being expressed as a constitutional precept, but she notes the difficulty of subordinating other laws and customs to this principle. *Bhuiyan* further explores this challenge and describes the interplay between the legal contradictions which exist in Bangladeshi law and other social factors that impede the removal of discriminatory laws and the adequate implementation of those progressive laws which actually exist. Given the inadequate nature of the laws themselves, the cumbersome legal system, the prejudices of law enforcement and implementation agencies, and the historically passive attitudes of women, she demonstrates how the inferior status of women is perpetuated.

Reiterating this assertion, *Goonesekere* notes that one particular source of conflict in Sri Lanka exists at the level of the constitution. It recognizes equality and the right of equal protection of the law, but it simultaneously protects the unrestricted observation of religious and cultural traditions. She calls for efforts toward a consensus of values which can be used to formulate a uniform family code. *Jethmalani* recounts recent decisions by Indian courts in labor discrimination, dowry death, divorce, and maintenance cases to demonstrate that the parallel regimes of constitutional and personal laws have conspired to create a situation of stagnation and oppression for women. She also demonstrates the link between women and development as mediated through the law. In particular, Indian labor laws have adversely affected women either by not being enforced or by mandating an inferior status. Moreover, marriage, succession, and inheritance laws, largely formulated through customary religious or ethnic practices, reinforce women's economic powerlessness.

Velásquez points out that legal reforms benefiting women in Colombia were often the result of economic necessity. Many of these reforms, while delivering women from certain patriarchal bonds, have also served to incorporate women into the capitalist economic system as less privileged wage earners. And although Colombian women are in a favored situation regarding legal rights and guarantees, the absence of effective enforcement mechanisms has rendered progressive legislation hollow.

Badri explores the ways Sudan's land registration and tenure laws, which limit women's right of control over land, adversely affect development. These laws respond to the exigencies of expanding agricultural enterprises entailing large capital expenditure, cash crops, and wage labor, thereby reducing the participation of women in agriculture. Food production is consequently reduced. *Chopra* looks at property rights of women in India from the perspective of the effect of rights to property on status within the family. Tracing women's rights to various categories of property (agricultural and ancestral, principally) according to the operative legislation governing the various ethnic/religious groups (Hindu, Muslim, Christian, Parsi, tribal, *etc.*), Chopra demonstrates that virtually all Indian women are limited in their right to own property.

❧❧❧❧

Venezuela: Women, Law, and the State
Rosa Paredes

Women and Family Law

In numerous countries, family law discriminates against women. This discrimination impedes the full participation of women in society. It is also an obstacle to establishing healthy family relationships and equality within marriage. In the past ten years of the UN Decade for Women, several Latin American countries have placed the theme of family law within the realm of women's political and social issues. Some countries like Venezuela have legislated judicial reforms that give women an equal status within the institution of the family. Other countries are still in the process of obtaining legal equality for women through family law.

At present, in all of our countries, a dilemma regarding the types of reforms that should be sought exists. On the one hand, we can continue to work for partial legislative reform, which is feasible; or on the other, we can work for more comprehensive reform, which would satisfy a greater number of working women, but which would also be far more difficult to achieve. One way that we have faced this dilemma is to link women's reproductive roles (as mothers) with their productive roles (as workers). In this way, we can begin to improve women's family, working, and social conditions.

The State and Legal Rights

The state is based on a juridical-legal structure which permits the different segments of society to express and pursue their interests and rights. This structure is the most fundamental of the state's mechanisms to support, control, or repress actions as well as ideas and people within the society. The model of conduct, which the state imposes on its citizens, is implemented through legislation.

The law does not respond uniformly to all interests. Instead, it tends to reinforce the interests of the more powerful, and thus, it becomes a mechanism for furthering the dominance of that social class. It also determines the relative welfare of the different social groups. Hence, the law legitimizes the interests and conduct of the powerful, and it works against those of the weak. It is clear that the law has discriminated against one of the weaker groups in society, women.

Women's Organization's Struggle for Legal Rights
The popular women's groups in Venezuela have attempted to further women's legal rights by working with private and governmental organizations to pressure the legislature to introduce various legal reforms.

They have also organized mass meetings to discuss and to mobilize popular support for the legislation and implementation of these reforms. To create popular support for these reforms, they have also written and distributed pamphlets to explain their necessity and implications. Furthermore, they have undertaken informational campaigns and projects to encourage the acceptance of legislative reform.

Rosa Paredes is Vice-President for Latin America of the International Council for Adult Education.

Brazil: Constitutional Reform and Women
Silvia Pimentel

Introduction
A critical examination of the Brazilian socio-juridical reality shows that we continue to live under *cultural colonialism*. As a result of the political and economic colonialism that has dominated Brazil, a great number of Brazilian laws are transplanted from European or American legislation.

The cultural, political, and economic dependence of Brazil has had a significant influence on the development of its law and, specifically, on the rights of women. The historical examination of our constitutions reveals progressive evolution of the rights of women in the work force. However, specific studies and surveys indicate that the integration of women in the job market is still, as Heleyeth Saffioti says, "a peripheral integration."

45

For Saffioti, a sociologist and professor from São Paulo, the problem of the marginalization of female labor and, therefore, of the women themselves is historically and culturally related to capitalism. Although there has not been a massive exploitation of female labor in Brazil to accelerate the accumulation of capital, the employment of women has always permitted the appropriation of larger profits due to their lower wage scale.

Saffioti claims that capitalism nourishes the myths and prejudices that support the role of women as homemakers. The great majority of men, viewing women as competitors in the labor market, cannot perceive that both the female and male conditions are determined by the historical totality in which both are embedded. Saffioti cites Bernard Muldwork when she adds: "To free woman from her alienation is, at the same time, to free man from his fetishes."

The class structure in capitalist society limits the human potentialities so that myths are necessary to justify either *de jure* or *de facto* discrimination. However, capitalism alone is not responsible for inequality and discrimination against women. Female subordination to men occupies a long history that predates the introduction of capitalism to the West in the 18th century.

Historical transformation—especially in technology—in changing attitudes and values and in increasing the participation of women in society is creating conditions for the progressive affirmation of women's labor rights. Brazilian law has unevenly incorporated these advances, although it has often reflected international pressures more than demands of our social reality.

Evolution of Women's Rights under Constitutional Law

In 1934, for the first time, the Brazilian Constitution recognized the equality of all persons before the law. It expressed the legal status of women by prohibiting inequality based on sex. The 1937 constitution suppressed the expressed reference to the juridical equality of both sexes, returning to the generic formula of the principle of equality in the Brazilian constitutions of the previous century. In 1967, when the first Brazilian Constitution was promulgated after the affirmation of the Universal Declaration of Rights, it again expressly recognized the equality of all before the law.

The juridical equality of men and women is now an expressed constitutional precept. All other laws and customary norms are to be subordinated to this principle. Nevertheless, an objective examination of our legal and social systems shows that the law, attitudes, and custom have not always respected this constitutional imperative. Flagrant examples of the unequal treatment of men and women by civil law can be cited. The husband is the head of the household. He—not the couple—has the right to choose the family residence, to administer the property of the couple, and to seek divorce.

Nevertheless, reforms are being made to improve the legal status of women. Among the principal modifications of the new civil code approved by the lower house of the legislature is the establishment of equal legal rights of men and women. With these changes, husbands and wives will have equal marital rights and equal voices in choosing their domicile. Both spouses will have the right of leaving the domicile for professional and private reasons, and they will share equally in making major decisions about their marriage, home, and family. Regarding inheritance under the new code, a woman will share equally with her children in the inheritance of her husband's property.

Final approval by congress of the new civil codes has been postponed. The advances brought by the new code must be defended by lobbying congress to permit the code to proceed independently of the approval of the new constitution. In this way, other provisions (*e.g.*, the issue of concubinage) can be added. A second and more important means, which does not exclude the former, is the explicit affirmation in the new constitution of the equality of rights postulated the new code.

The constitution affirms that the family "has the right of being protected by society and the state and to the fulfillment of all conditions which allow the personal realization of all members." It defines the protection of the family as:

the promotion of its social and economic independence; the promotion of family assistance (such as daycare centers) to mothers;

the dissemination of family planning methods; the establishment of fiscal, social and legal policies that benefit the family; and the establishment of a political system that promotes family life.

One important advance for women can be taken from the Portuguese Constitution. It states:

fathers and mothers have the right of being assisted by society and the state in the realization of their irreplaceable action regarding their children, namely, as to their education, their professional realization and their participation in the civic life of the country.

Conclusion

This comparative and historical analysis of women's constitutional rights demonstrates that the affirmation of the rights of women in the new Brazilian Constitution will be a fundamental step towards a true democracy. A new constitution will be of little or no use if it reflects once more the ideals of a dominant minority. The aspirations of the majority must be fulfilled. Women, who are actively participating in the betterment of society, have a significant responsibility. They must help create a new juridical and social order to respond to the needs and expectations of the people. Let us begin!

Silvia Pimentel is a professor of law at the Catholic Pontifical University in São Paulo, and Director of the Juridic, Economic, and Social Sciences Center.

Bangladesh:
Personal Law and Violence Against Women
Rabia Bhuiyan

Evolution of Personal Law

Bangladesh is a densely populated country, containing a Muslim majority. Personal law, which governs marriage and divorce, is based primarily on the religion of the community to which a person belongs. As a result of legislative modification, personal law has evolved significantly. Apart from the constitution, legislation makes the greatest impact on the legal

48

status of women in Bangladesh. Even though the constitution bestows equal rights upon women, some discriminatory provisions are found in legislation concerning marriage and divorce, *inter alia*. In the areas of marriage and divorce (*talaq*), significant changes have occured as a result of the Muslim Family Laws Ordinance, 1961 (as amended), and the Muslim Family Laws Ordinance, 1982 (amendment). Still, a Muslim wife does not have the unilateral right of divorce like her husband. If circumstances do not permit a woman to file for divorce under the previously mentioned ordinances, she must sue under the Dissolution of Muslim Marriage Act, 1939. Under the 1939 act, a divorce can consume an inordinate amount of time because of the complicated legal system. (*Runa Laila v. Khawaja Javed Kaiser*). Another major change is the addition of restrictions on polygamy. Husbands who wish to take additional wives are required to notify the chairman of the Arbitration Council under the Muslim Family Laws Ordinance, 1961. While violaters are subject to punishment, few men obey the law. Wives who lodge complaints rarely receive justice because of legal and socioeconomic barriers. The issue of jurisdiction poses a serious problem to a wife attempting to obtain legal remedies (*Shahnaz Parveen Khadem v. Abdul Alim Bhuiyan*). To improve this situation, the Institute of Democratic Rights has submitted a draft proposal of reforms which is under consideration.

The socioeconomic obstacles that women face, compounded by illiteracy and ignorance, limit the scope of the law to protect them from violence and deprivation. Various forms of violence related to the wife's dowry are common occurrences in Bangladesh. The most publicized is the case of Sufia whose throat was slashed by her brother-in-law with the help of his family relations because of non-payment of a promised dowry (*State v. Abdul Jabber and others*).

The Dowry Prohibition Act, 1980, was enacted in response to the proliferation of dowry-related violence, including murder. Dowry is defined as any property or valuable security given, either directly or indirectly, by one party of a marriage to the other party at, before, or after marriage, as consideration for the marriage (although it excludes certain forms in Muslim marriages). The violation of the law is an offense punishable by imprisonment and/or fine. It is, however, very difficult to prosecute a case successfully under the Dowry Prohibition Act, due to the weakness of the law and often to a lack of evidence (*Dr. Mazharul Hoque v. Jahura Khatun*).

Private organizations continue to pressure for the reform of laws dealing with violence and discrimination directed against women. The recent Child Marriage Restraint Act Ordinance, 1984, has amended the Child Marriage Restraint Act, 1929 by raising the marriageable age of females from 16 to 18 years of age, and for males from 18 to 21 years of age. The Cruelty to Women (Deterrent Punishment) Ordinance, 1983, has outlawed the kidnapping or abducting of a woman of any age for the purpose, *inter alia,* of prostitution or other unlawful or immoral acts. It also mandates the death penalty or life imprisonment for causing the death of a rape victim. In addition, the 1983 act provides for capital punishment of a husband and his family for murdering or attempting to murder a woman to obtain the dowry.

Additional changes are still needed in this area of the law. Recently, the government has taken a decision to introduce stringent legislation to outlaw the act of throwing acid on another person; almost 100% of the acid burn cases involve women. In spite of the continuing efforts of the government to raise the legal and actual status of women and to achieve the objectives of the UN Decade for Women, few women are able to exercise their rights in Bangladesh.

Obstacles to Implementing Legal Reforms

Firstly, the laws are defective and vague, thus making the task of implementation extremely difficult. Secondly, corrupt law enforcement agencies and complicated and cumbersome legal procedures place legal remedies out of the reach of poor and uneducated women. Thirdly, a big gap still remains between, on the one hand, the provisions of the constitution and general legislation and, on the other, Muslim and Hindu personal law. Fourthly, the pervasiveness of social attitudes, including the traditionally defined sex roles, and socioeconomic conditions such as poverty, illiteracy, unemployment, economic dependence of women continue to impede the implementation of equal opportunity and legal rights for women. In spite of all of the government's efforts, legislation alone cannot bring about change. Clearly, it is a difficult battle to remove age-old traditional attitudes, customs, and prejudices. Hence, much of the struggle to enforce the legislation depends on women themselves.

Moreover, women are doubly victimized. While the existing personal laws continue to discriminate against women, women must also fight for the enforcement of the progressive areas of the legislation. Apart from the unequal legal status of women is their actual position in society: it is a position of inferior status. This struggle has only begun.

Strategy

Beyond the need for reforms in the legal system, a most urgent consideration is the provision of adequate legal assistance, the establishment of legal literacy programs, and the dissemination of legal information. At present, several organizations are providing legal assistance to poor and helpless women. For example, the Institute of Democratic Rights provides free legal services. In particular, it helps women who wish to initiate class-action suits or those with cases that have wide-ranging legal implications. Finally, women's organizations must strive to bring about attitude changes in both men and women. They must pressure government and convince the society at large that changes to increase women's self-reliance, rights, and opportunities are essential.

Rabia Bhuiyan is President of the Bangladesh Women Lawyers Association and Director of the Institute of Democratic Rights.

Sri Lanka: Legal Status of Women
Savitri Gooneskere

Introduction

At the time the United Nations' Decade for Women was inaugurated, the concept of gender equality in Sri Lankan law was not a current or controversial issue. Gender equality was accepted in the colonial period by the statutory law that regulated most areas of public life. This legal position was maintained in the first decades after the independence of Sri Lanka. It is this ideology of the assumption of gender equality by the law, rather than a positive policy forbidding discrimination, that is revealed in the first indigenous Sri Lankan Constitution of 1972. This constitution did not specifically refer to gender equality in its list of fundamental rights or in its principles of state policy. It defined the fundamental right of equality before the law and equal protection in general terms. The constitution established a distinct prohibition of discrimination on the basis of sex only in regard to public sector employment. An exception to this article, which enabled the state to reserve certain posts or classes of posts for one sex or the other, did not provoke controversy.

The government, which promulgated this constitution, also introduced significant socialist reforms in regard to property ownership and modified the formal laws pertaining to the administration of justice. A marginal concern to articulate liberal legal values in regard to women is apparent in the latter reforms. However, women's property rights were sometimes prejudiced under the new legislation because of the failure to monitor its impact on women. These inconsistencies were inevitable since the issue of women's rights was not a specific concern of official state policy.

The United Nations' Decade for Women had no impact on the legal system of Sri Lanka in the first few years after 1975. The Sri Lankan Constitution of 1978, which replaced the 1972 constitution, however, indicated the government's awareness that the concept of gender equality should be specifically included in the constitution. Hence, the drafters of the constitution appear to have been influenced by the international concern for equal legal rights and protection of women. Although those who drafted the constitution had liberal intentions, the constitution in fact categorized women with children and disabled persons by suggesting that beneficial laws shall not be deemed to discriminate against other citizens! Other fundamental rights were, nevertheless, described as available to all persons or citizens; thus, women enjoy the same legal protection as men. Some claim that the Indian Constitution does not perceive a woman as an individual citizen with independent rights of her own. None can argue that this position applies to the Sri Lankan Constitution.

Despite the positive stance in regard to women's rights in the 1978 constitution, there has been an attitude of passivity throughout the decade in regard to using or challenging the legal system to advance the position of women. Legal educators, legislators, law reformers, women's organizations, and legal administrators have not focused their concerns on women's issues. The legal position of women has been discussed in an isolated research publication, an occasional seminar, or lecture which invariably attracts the same participants. The concept of developing strategies to remove legal constraints on women has not been adopted by existing women's programs. The Decade for Women has had a positive impact on some areas of Sri Lankan women's lives, but few women have viewed the legal system as relevant in initiating creative change, except in a marginal sense.

The general apathy about the legal system in Sri Lanka is in sharp contrast with its reality, which imposes significant constraints on some aspects of women's lives. These constraints inhibit the full participation of women in both the public and private spheres of society. This paper will examine the practical significance of sex discrimination in the legal system, the apathy in this regard, and the prospects of developing creative strategies for change.

Areas of Discrimination

In the areas of fundamental civil and political rights, education, and professional training, Sri Lankan women have enjoyed equality with men for many decades. The rights to vote and to stand for Parliament were granted by the British colonial regime to all citizens at the same time. The Sex Disqualification Removal Ordinance of Sri Lanka was introduced in 1933 to remove obstacles that generally excluded women from entering the legal profession. The Education Act (1939) empowered the minister to make regulations imposing an obligation on both parents to educate all children between the ages of 5 and 14 (up to that time, the age limit was lower for females in some communities). Men and women receive the same rights to welfare facilities, equal wages and retirement benefits in public sector employment; women receive some additional benefits, such as maternity leave. The law protects men and women equally in labor matters.

In general, women are not legally excluded from public life, nor is the public sphere viewed as the exclusive preserve of the male. Those women who are victims of discrimination in the work force are protected by legislation that aims to prevent the exploitation of women workers. This protective legislation, however, is now under review because there is immense pressure to absorb women into the industrial work force in today's market economy.

Although the formal legal system takes a basically egalitarian view of women's rights, weaknesses can be discerned in the content of the law. Besides problems of enforcement of the laws, apathy and indifference hamper women's progress. Compulsory education of all children has not yet been mandated. This neglect perpetuates the sex discrimination of the previous regulations. Administrative and executive actions that violate civil rights guarantees can be challenged in the courts. Yet, due to the absence of an effective system of legal aid and the costs of litigation in the superior courts, it is difficult to assess whether the constitutional guarantees on fundamental rights afford real protection. Moreover, only proposed legislation, not past laws, can be challenged in the courts under the constitution.

Some legal provisions which discriminate against women workers (*e.g.*, wage differentiations between men and women in the area of unskilled and manual work) cannot be challenged under the constitution. Furthermore, one system of customary law restricts the economic rights of women through legal provisions that require the husband's consent to make immovable property transactions. Due to the lack of a consistent legal approach, isolated provisions are enacted which do not conform with the egalitarian approach to women's rights of most areas of public law. For instance, amendments to the Land Settlement Legislation in 1981 do not repeal anachronistic statutory provisions on the devolution of property, which are out of harmony with the generally egalitarian pattern of inheritance laws. Because legislative reform has not been adopted, contradictory laws—often with unintended consequences—are implemented. Thus, recent legislation allows women to work at night, but it exposes them to exploitation because existing protective industrial laws and regulations are violated with impunity. Women and men have made impressive gains in obtaining labor protection through industrial courts. Yet, delays and costs of labor litigation often negate the meaningfulness of these gains for women workers.

The same contradiction between the formal laws and the reality of their application can be observed in criminal law. Women and men are generally treated equally under formal Sri Lankan criminal law. Under the Penal Code of Sri Lanka which was inspired by the inegalitarian Indian Penal Code, there are no marital laws permitting the treatment of women as the property of men. Adultery is not a crime, but is a matrimonial offense against either spouse, whereby a divorce and civil damages may be obtained. Prostitution is a criminal offense only if the woman is "a common prostitute wandering in a public place and behaving in a riotous or indecent manner," while the client who solicits in any public place is guilty of a more serious offense. Pimping is also a criminal offense. Yet, the police invariably use these laws to prosecute women rather than their clients.

Rape laws are designed to protect women from violence. Moreover, the penal code limits permissive attitudes of certain customary laws about child brides. Yet, the strict abortion laws, the defense of consent, and the treatment of women as accomplices in rape cases all deny women the protection the law seeks to accord to them. Successful prosecutions of abortion without the woman's consent are difficult to obtain. Time-consuming procedures, legal complexity, and delays guarantee that the whole legal process in a rape case is weighted against a female victim. These problems have never been seriously considered by legal experts or reformers. Nor has there been a reassessment of the validity of existing laws, even within the framework of the accepted criminal justice system.

Discrimination against women in the legal system has the most significant impact in the area of family law. Laws of some minority ethnic groups, usually based on indigenous custom or religion, seriously prejudice women's rights in the family. However, the majority of Sri Lankan women enjoy equal rights in regard to marriage and divorce, matrimonial property, and inheritance. These gains are weakened only by delays in the judicial process.

The tendency of the judiciary to apply the norms of Roman-Dutch law to the legal system has resulted in some legal principles unfavorable to women. Such unfavorable principles are observed in regard to parental rights, and the property and contractual rights of women, which are governed by a system of customary law known as Tesawalamai. Women who are governed by that system of law have been denied the right to contract or alienate property without the consent of their husbands. The lack of such rights has had a negative impact on the ability of these women to obtain bank credit or to make other financial transactions.

The Culture of the Law

A major cause of the inadequacies in the legal system *vis-à-vis* women's rights and the continued apathy in this regard is the lack of legal literacy of women. Women have not shown a great concern with personal issues. Cultural constraints affect women in some communities; women are often reluctant to take public positions on issues which may conflict with conservative social and religious values. In addition, certain areas of legal discrimination may only touch their lives marginally. The concept of testamentary disposition in Sri Lankan law, which is used by all communities, helps to ameliorate the discriminatory inheritance laws of some minority ethnic groups. Moreover, the availability of wider family support and the practice of settling custody issues privately signify that only a few women who must resort to litigation have to cope with the weaknesses of the law regarding parental rights over small children. As opposed to personal issues, women have proven to be more outspoken about their legal rights in employment, particularly in the sphere of public sector white-collar jobs.

Law reformers, legislators, and administrators have shown the same apathy in regard to women's issues. This situation partially results from a general assumption that the law does not discriminate against women in public life. Customary laws are also considered an area of concern to the particular ethnic and religious minority. Although a separate unit has been established in the Ministry of Labor to handle women's affairs, recent legal reforms in regard to equal pay for equal work on agricultural plantations were introduced due to pressure from other quarters. Furthermore, labor officials concede that they are helpless in enforcing labor laws in many industries.

The task of introducing necessary legal reforms has been conferred by the Ministry of Women's Affairs upon the Ministries of Labor and Justice. Their attention has been focussed on areas of the law that urgently require review and reform. While these were exposed at a national symposium in 1982, little has been done. The government and nongovernmental organizations, instead, have concentrated their assistance to women in the areas of social welfare, nutrition, and family planning. Not surprisingly, the law is viewed by most people as remote and irrelevant.

Conclusion

The Sri Lankan experience demonstrates that the legal system has not been viewed as a tool for achieving positive gains for women's rights. In this matter, strategies should focus on the mobilization of people to use the legal system for the betterment of women. Efforts must be made to introduce a uniform family relations code to replace the current diverse systems of family law. Legal education must be reformed and legal literacy programs must be developed. Such strategies are crucial to reform in the content and application of the law. However, past experience has shown that *ad hoc* reform efforts are reduced to academic research projects. Furthermore, without the necessary infrastructure to implement new legislation, reforms remain ineffective. Therefore, rather than pushing for hastily conceived legislation, women's and other interested organizations must employ strategies that will motivate planned and pragmatic programs for legal change.

The Sri Lankan Constitution itself has not resolved the contradiction between, on the one hand, recognizing a fundamental right of equality and equal protection before the law and, on the other, an unqualified freedom to observe and follow religious and cultural traditions. As in other multi-ethnic and sectarian societies, discrimination against women in Sri Lanka can be perpetuated in the name of religion and culture. Unlike many other countries with similar problems, however, Sri Lanka has a long legal tradition of uniformity in the law, which has displaced religious and cultural diversity in some significant areas. Nevertheless, efforts must be made to enlist the support of influential groups in all communities to agree upon a consensus of values which can be used to formulate a uniform family law code.

Another important strategy is to increase awareness of women's issues in all institutions of legal learning in the country which will help transmit egalitarian values throughout the legal system. One example of implementing this strategy is the introduction by the Open University of Sri Lanka of a focus on women's rights in its undergraduate law degree program. Programs of legal literacy at the popular level can sensitize both men and women to the inadequacies of the law and can make them conscious of their rights. They may help to remove the existing apathy and to politicize the efforts to change the legal system. Such programs can also encourage women in obtaining the protection that the law confers upon them.

The legal and cultural ethos in Sri Lanka has generally shown considerable liberalism towards women. While economic conditions and the essentially patriarchal social structure have had a negative impact on women, these structures have not excluded women from sharing some of the economic and social gains in Sri Lanka. Feminist tenets, such as the denunciation of the patriarchal family and male domination and the devaluation of motherhood, will not appeal to the majority of Sri Lankan women. These women find real meaning in the cultural values of maternity, family devotion, and loyalty.

Hence, taking doctrinaire positions which are totally out of harmony with the social and cultural milieu of Sri Lankan women is counterproductive. It could impede legal gains for women in other areas. A puristic feminist crusade can have, at best, a small impact on Sri Lankan women and men who have supported women's progress in the past. Thus, to avoid a male backlash, legal strategies to improve the lot of women should enlist male support. As Simone de Beauvoir once noted: "The battle of the sexes is not implicit in the anatomy of men and women...and the cleavage of society along the line of sex is impossible."

Savitri Goonesekere is a professor of law and dean of the law school at the Open University in Colombo, Sri Lanka.

India: Law and Women
Rani Jethmalani

Constitutional vs. Personal Law

The constituency of women has been frequently betrayed by the law, the courts, and recently by a government allegedly wedded to taking us to the 21st century. Feminism began with the recognition that patriarchal power structures have to be altered fundamentally for women's lives to change. Governments throughout the world have demonstrated that they are quite prepared to use women for their own political purposes.

The marginalization of women in the current struggle between forces of tradition and modernity is increasing notwithstanding the constitution's egalitarian and secular ideology which finds expression in:

Article 1. The State shall not deny to any person equality before the law and equal protection of the laws within the territory of India.

Article 15(1). The State shall not discriminate against any citizen on grounds only of religion, race, caste, sex, place of birth or any of them.

Article 3. The State shall in particular direct its policy towards securing (a) that the citizens, men and women equally, have the right to an adequate means of livelihood; (b) that there is equal pay for equal work for both men and women; (c) that the health and strength of workers, men and women and the tender age of children, are not abused and that citizens are not forced by economic necessity to enter avocations unsuited to their age and strength.

Article 51-A(e). It shall be the duty of every citizen of India to renounce practices derogatory to the dignity of women.

This progressive and dynamic philosophy in the Constitution has been considerably diluted by a parallel regime of personal law which affects inheritance, custody, and succession rights. The latter has been stagnant, unchanging, and oppressive to women.

The state's non-intervention to redress inequalities in the law is sought to be justified on the ground that such a liberal approach is consistent with the constitution's secular ideology. Since article 25 guarantees the fundamental right to practice, profess, and propagate religion, it is argued that personal laws, even if detrimental to women, must prevail, even if in the process they violate article 14. The saga of Shah Bano and the enactment of the Muslim Women (Protection of Rights on Divorce) Act, 1986, reflect the lack of political commitment to women's issues.

Section 125, the maintenance provision in the secular Criminal Procedure Code, which could be availed of by all wives (including divorced Muslim women), was clearly a valid piece of legislation since it related to public order and morals and was designed to prevent vagrancy and immorality of women in economic penury. The newly enacted Muslim act, apart from being discriminatory, is devious, tedious, and unworkable. It reduces women to financial parasites eternally dependent on a hierarchy of reluctant relatives.

While an agenda for human rights for women has received low priority from the government, the Supreme Court, in contrast, has responded with remarkable sensitivity. In the air hostesses case, *Air India vs. Nargesh Meerza* (AIR 1981 SC 1829), the service conditions framed by Air India for air hostesses and male stewards were held to be clearly discriminatory. The services of an air hostess could continue up to 35 years but were terminated if she contracted marriage within four years of her recruitment or on her first pregnancy. The Supreme Court, while upholding the condition for terminating the service on marriage within the four years, invalidated the condition which terminated the service on the first pregnancy. The court regarded that condition as unreasonable and arbitrary and held that it compelled the air hostess not to have children and this was against the ordinary course of human nature.

The epistolary (letter) jurisdiction of the court, by which the Supreme Court entertains writs even on the basis of letters, has increased access to the courts; by liberalizing the principles of *locus standi*, the court has enabled women's organizations and coalitions to approach the highest court for redressal of social injustice to women. In *Neelam Verma and others vs. Union of India*, seven dowry victims and two women's organizations addressed the Supreme Court, alleging that their rights under articles 21 and 14 of the Constitution of India had been violated. They submitted that the police authorities had not complied with their statutory obligations under the Criminal Procedure Code by refusing to register complaints regarding dowry harassment. It was contended that the right to life includes the right to live with human dignity.

Similarly, in *Satya Rani Chadha vs. Subhash Chander and others*, a private complaint was filed by the complainant's mother since she believed that her daughter had been burned to death for dowry when she was six months pregnant. The complainant stated in her petition to the Supreme Court that she had filed a complaint under section 200 of the Criminal Procedure Code in the magistrate's court since the police had registered no case under section 302 in spite of a lapse of 18 months, and that after the filing of the complaint, an unduly long date had been given by the magistrate for the recording of evidence. The Supreme Court immediately issued Notice to the State to show cause.

In the *Indian Federation of Women Lawyers vs. Laxman Kumar & ors.* (1985 (2) Scale pg. 701), the complainant—the brother of the deceased Sudha Goel who had been burned for dowry by her husband Laxman and his mother Shakuntala Devi—along with 14 women's organizations filed a Special Leave Petition to challenge the acquittal of the two by the High Court (and also Laxman's brother, Subhash) after the Sessions Judge, S.M. Aggarwal, had sentenced all three to death. The Supreme Court reversed the acquittal of Laxman and his mother and acquitted Subhash. The State (Delhi Administration) had also filed a separate appeal against the High Court judgement. The highest court's well meaning sentiments expressed in the judgement reflect a benign paternalism and conform to the stereotype of women who are either deified or demonized.

The Sudha Goel case not only highlighted an obnoxious social evil which demeans women and reduces them to the status of a secondary sub-caste, it focused on the compelling need for women's organizations to tenaciously pursue through joint efforts issues which cry for reform. Women's problems must ultimately be the concern of women in redefining the social order. Women cannot be shy of the fact that feminism is politics—because it intends to change and transform power structures which have made women invisible, oppressed, and subservient.

The High Court did not approve of the strategies adopted by women's organizations to express their disapproval in acquitting the murderers of Sudha Goel. It issued a contempt notice to the Mahila Daxata Samiti (see case study by Kumari) and other organizations for having carried what it considered offensive placards outside the High Court denouncing the judgement. In *S. K. Datta vs. Mahila Daxata Samiti* (unreported) Justice Rajinder Sachar and Justice Leila Seth, while not doubting the genuineness and humanitarian motives of the respondents, proceeded to draw the line on the limits of protest within the permissible parameters of the law. The court held that the respondents' conduct amounted to contempt but it decided to take no action against them in view of the respondents' justified indignation over dowry atrocities.

In *Shahnaz Sheikh vs. Union of India*, the Muslim personal law has been challenged as being oppressive and discriminatory to women. Section 10 of the Indian Divorce Act which makes divorce almost impossible for women among Christians has also been challenged by the Joint Women's Program. In *Bharata Lakshmi vs. Union of India*, sections 6(1)(a) and 19(1)(b) of the Hindu Minority and Guardianship Act, 1956, which provide that the natural guardian of a Hindu minor shall be the father, and after that the mother, have also been challenged as violating article 14. All the petitions are pending final hearing in the Supreme Court.

While the State's non-intervention to advance women's rights has been motivated by the ballot box, its occasional *avant gardism* has been somewhat baffling. The Irretrievable Breakdown of Marriage Laws Amendment Bill was introduced to provide a new ground for divorce on the basis of the modern theory of no fault on the incompatibility between spouses leading to breakdown in marriage in the Hindu Marriage Act and the Special Marriage Act. The bill was opposed by the Mahila Daxata Samiti since it was ill-conceived and premature, as it failed to ensure community of property, *i.e.*, division of all property belonging to both spouses at the time of divorce. Further, in the absence of statistical data, it was difficult to conclude that the bill was pro-women. For most women, marriage is still the ultimate security. This view was not shared by many women's organizations who supported the bill on the ground that it was a basic human right to be free of an oppressive situation. The bill was dropped in the absence of consensus.

Much the same sentiments was expressed by Justice Choudhary in *Saritha vs. Venkatasubbaiah* (AIR 1983 A.P. 356 pg.) where he held that a decree for restitution of conjugal rights constituted the grossest form of violation of an individual's right to privacy, which is a part of article 21. The Supreme Court in *Saroj Rani vs. Chadha* (AIR 1984 1653), however, held that section 9 of the Hindu Marriage Act, which provided the remedy of restitution, was not coercive and hence not violative of article 21.

Recently, the right of a matrimonial home, *i.e.*, the right to claim a share or live in the matrimonial home on divorce, was upheld by the High Court of Andhra Pradesh, where it held that a company that had rented premises to the husband of the petitioner wife could not evict the wife and children upon estrangement of the marriage and the failure of the husband to provide shelter to his wife and children, particularly where the renting company (BHEL) was an instrumentality of the State.

In an equally significant decision, *Swaraj Garg vs. K.H. Garg* (AIR 1978 Delhi 296), both husband and wife were gainfully employed but at two different places. The husband sued for restitution of conjugal rights on the ground that his wife had withdrawn from his society without reasonable excuse. In rejecting the husband's plea, Justice Deshpande held "that there is no warrant in Hindu Law to regard the Hindu wife as having no say in choosing the place of the matrimonial home. Article 14 guarantees equality before the law to the husband and wife."

Equal Burden, Unequal Wages

Women do not control resources, so how can women be contributors and beneficiaries of development? Women have been excluded from even access to resources, so how is autonomy possible? Women have been deprived of land, jobs, credit, and other goods and services—how can women then have control over their lives? How can women's access to resources be promoted when those who administer and make the law condone the existence of inequitable laws or enact backward laws like the Muslim Women Protection of Rights on Divorce Act, 1986, that deprive women of even the crumbs for survival and dignity?

As author Robin Morgan states in her remarkable anthology *Sisterhood is Global*, "women are the world's proletariat and have no source in even defining what 'work' means." [1] Women do two-thirds of the world's work, receive five per cent of the world's income, and own less than one per cent of the world's assets—yet women's work has received little attention. Housework is not counted as work nor is it paid, and it is dismissed as trivial, mindless, and marginal. The Gross National Product (GNP), supposed to be the total value of goods and services produced, includes only goods and services exchanged for money. Women's unwaged work has been left out. In addition, house-based work, *i.e.*, execution of work done within one's own domestic premises, does not figure as work in official statistics. This includes a whole variety of work taken for granted, including, according to government statistics, 2.25 million workers making *bidis*, several women employed in the garment and packaging industries, and others who do embroidery.

Where women are employed in factories, industries, offices, and other establishments, the situation is different since they are less exposed to exploitation, but this is only in theory. Protective welfare legislation for the woman worker, such as the Equal Remuneration Act, 1976, and the Maternity Benefit Act, 1961, governs the conditions of work in industries and contains special provisions for women. The Factories Act, 1948 and the Factories and Mines Act, 1952 also contain special provisions for women. In the Maternity Benefits Act, it is obliga-tory where more than thirty women are employed to make arrange-ments to provide creches for women. This, however, has adversely affected women's employment since most employers are men who consider an investment in women unnecessary and cumbersome. Similarly, in 1964 when the Supreme Court struck down the *marriage clause* which permitted retrenchment of women on marriage, employment statistics showed a steady decline in women's employment.

Despite article 39 of the constitution that directs the state to formulate its policy in such a way as to secure equal pay for work for both men and women, there is discrimination in the matter of payment of wages and stereotyping of work assigned to women. This work is generally back-breaking, poorly paid, and less challenging than the work reserved for men. The Equal Remuneration Act, passed unobstructively during the emergency to commemorate the International Women's Year in 1976, to provide "for payment of equal remuneration to men and women workers and for the prevention of discrimination on the ground of sex against women in the matter of any employment," has been rarely used to advance women's status as a worker during the decade after its enactment. However, in the *People's Union for Democratic Rights and ors. vs. Union of India* (1982 (2) SCC p. 494), the Supreme Court directed the Union of India and the Delhi Administration and the Delhi Development Authority to take necessary steps for enforcing the Minimum Wages Act and the Equal Remuneration Act, by contractors engaged in the construction work of the stadiums to be built for the Asiad Games. The petition was brought by addressing a letter to the court, and in response to this public interest litigation, the court nominated officers for the purpose of inspecting sites of the construction work where women were employed.

In the *Self-Employed Women's Association vs. The Municipal Corporation of Ahmedabad*, it was through the intervention of the Supreme Court again that the Municipal Commissioner was directed to work out equitable arrangements to permit women vegetable vendors to handle their wares in areas within the limits of Ahmedabad, since refusal of permission would be in violation of article 19(1)(g) of the constitution—the fundamental right to carry on any occupation, trade, or profession.

While the courts have shown an awareness that development and high technology are meaningless where tangible benefits do not percolate to the beneficiaries of welfare laws, the Ministry of Personnel, Public Grievances, and Pension displayed refreshing bureaucratic candor in issuing clarifications, demanded by women's organizations, that unmarried female government servants would be entitled to maternity leave, which had till then only been allowed to married female employees of the government. Since the word *female* in the Central Secretariat Service Leave Rules, 1972 did not specifically refer to the marital status of the female and the word *married* is not prefixed to the word *female* it was held that leave was admissible.

There has not been much exploration of the potential possibilities of using the Equal Remuneration Act to end the triple discrimination that women suffer as workers. The situation in India contrasts to the US where innovative use has been made of the belatedly enacted Civil Rights Act, 1964—surprisingly the first comprehensive package of anti-discrimination legislation. The frustrating struggle and trauma over passage of the Equal Rights Amendment Act, 1973, which ended in futility when it failed to receive the requisite ratification of the states in the US, is a significant illustration of the overwhelming impediment in cultural environments supposedly more progressive than our own. Clearly, women's inferior status is formally legislated—as was witnessed in the passage of the Muslim Women's Protection of Rights on Divorce Act, 1986, or as in the US in the failure to pass the necessary legislation. What is common in countries so totally divergent are the cultural attitudes, which with tenacity reinforce that status and endorse women's powerlessness.

Succession and inheritance laws are a striking example of the inequitable control and distribution of resources. The laws of inheritance are not uniform and are once again based on considerations of religion. Under the Hindu Succession Act, 1956, the interest in joint family property or co-parcenary property is acquired on birth only by the son. No female can become a co-parcener or owner of co-parcenary property, except in Andhra Pradesh which has recently amended the Hindu Succession Act to declare daughters as co-parceners who are entitled to claim partition with a view to eradicate the pernicious dowry system. Some females like the widow, wife, mother and the grandmother are entitled to obtain a share in the co-parcenary property if a partition takes place, but the right to demand and effect the partition is available only to men.

In the self-acquired property of a male intestate, if the property consists of a dwelling house which was, at the time of the death of the intestate, occupied by the male heirs of his family, female heirs are denied their rights to ask for a partition and demarcate their share. They are given only a right of residence in the dwelling house. In case of daughters, this right is available only to unmarried daughters. Married daughters do not even have right of residence in the house of their father unless they are widows or judicially separated from their husbands.

Among Muslims who are governed by the Muslim Personal Law Shariat Application Act of 1937 and among Parsis governed by the Indian Succession Act, 1925, females get a share which is equal to half the share of their male counterparts, e.g., a daughter's share is half the share of a son and a sister's share is half the share of a brother. Within Muslim communities governed by the Ithna-Ashari Law, a childless widow is not entitled to inherit immovable properties of her husband, while the widower in the same situation does not suffer from such a disability.

Until the Supreme Court's decision in *Mary Rao vs. State of Kerala* (1986 (1) Scale p. 250), a daughter's right among Travancore Christians to family property ended when she was given *Stridhan* on marriage, the amount being fixed at Rs. 5,000 or one-fourth of the value of the son's share. The widow had only a life interest in her husband's property. This ended with her life or on her remarriage.

Succession laws expose how women have been invalidated by denial of ownership rights to them and, unless women control resources, they will continue to have little or no control over their lives. Tribal laws in Bihar, protected under the Chhotta Nagpur Tenancy Act, prevented inheritance of land by females, while the HO tribal unmarried women living in their parents' home had only the right of user till the time of their marriage. Such women do not have a right to bequeath land to anyone of their choice. Similarly, the wife had usufructory rights to her husband's land during her lifetime. If her husband died, she could claim maintenance rights from the male relatives of her husband since only they inherit the land and not her.

These customary tribal laws have been challenged in the Supreme Court in *Madhu Kishore vs. State of Bihar* on the ground that such laws affect women in various ways. Among the HO's, at least 80% of all agricultural operations, except ploughing, are performed by women. Performing such work without owning the land devalues women's labor and women themselves. Such devaluation has made women peripheral in the economic and political life of the tribe. Further, HO women are excluded from the Tribal Panchayats and all other political decision-making institutions. Their powerlessness is directly related to the denial of land rights.

In *Pratibha Rani vs. Suraj Kumar and another* (1985, 2 S.C.C. 370), the Supreme Court dealt with a critical and recurring problem: whether *Stridhanam* given to a woman by her parents at the time of marriage can be the subject matter of criminal complaint by the wife against the husband. *Stridhanam* is a concept of the Hindu Law of Succession which means and includes any money or ornaments, or in lieu of money or ornaments, any property, movable or immovable, given or promised to be given to a female, or on her behalf to her husband or to his parents or guardians, by her father or mother, or after the death of either or both of them, by anyone who claims under such father or mother, in satisfaction of her claim against the estate of the father or the mother. Pratibha Rani had demanded upon estrangement with her husband the return of her jewelry, clothes, and silver articles. On his refusal to do so, she filed a complaint for criminal breach of trust, an offense under sections 405 and 406 of the Indian Penal Code. The Supreme Court rightly held that handing over the articles in question to the husband and other relatives at the time of marriage constituted entrustment. The Court's intervention on behalf of Hindu women will not only go a long way to redress a serious injustice which has deprived them of control over their assets, but will hopefully be applicable to the determination of questions of spouses belonging to other religious communities.

Notable changes in criminal law have made a positive contribution to minimizing the exploitation of women, but these have not brought about a noticeable change in social attitudes and perceptions of women. Credit for changes in the rape law following the Mathura rape case where a young tribal woman was raped while in police custody must be attributed to the relentless campaign of four activist professors of law of the Delhi University. The salient features of the amended rape law make it clear that consent is vitiated under several circumstances and an essential ingredient to the offense of rape is the absence of true and genuine consent given by a woman who is mature enough to sive such consent.

Custodial rape invites a ten-year imprisonment, though the maximum punishment in other situations is seven years. A new section amending the rules of evidence puts the burden of proof on the accused in aggravated rape cases like gang rape and custodial rape, *i.e.*, rape while in custody of those in positions of trust. The court, in such situations, shall presume that the woman did not consent.

Without the freedom to control one's own body, no other right would have any meaning for women. In America, the rights to reproductive freedom have been justified on the theory of the constitutional right to privacy. It was as late as 1971 when the American Supreme Court decision handed down the historic *Roe vs. Wade* decision upholding the right of a pregnant woman to have an abortion. It was only in the 1960's in *Griswold vs. Connecticut* where the same court held that it was unconstitutional to outlaw the sale of contraceptives to married persons.

The Indian law on abortion, the Medical Termination of Pregnancy Act, came into force on April 1, 1972. The proposal to do so was made by the Central Family Planning Board in 1964. It modified the provisions of the Indian Penal Code, 1860, by legalizing abortions previously considered illegal under the code under specified and limited conditions. Section 4 of the act insists that abortion must take place in either hospitals established by the government or in an approved place. This is a most restrictive and unwholesome provision. However, under section 4(b) of the act, approval by the government can also be extended to other places.

Unfortunately, the liberal provision of the act has been grossly abused, as is evident in the shocking resort to amniocentesis—the chromosome test done on the amniotic fluid in the womb of a pregnant woman to predict whether an unborn fetus is male or female—followed by abortion if it happens to be a female. Such selective sex determination tests, carried out in the All India Institute of Medical Sciences in the 70's, were discontinued when the purpose for which the tests were being used was discovered. Women have been freed from the bondage of compulsory pregnancies, yet they continue to be threatened by new insecurities. Nor have the old insecurities vanished, as statistics on female infanticide unfold this gruesome reality.

Unfortunately, political leaderships have not been helpful in molding social attitudes in the Third World. Aging dictator Ferdinand Marcos of the Philippines remarked that his female opponent in the 1986 presidential elections was not a proper rival because a woman's place is in the bedroom. Comments Richard Falk, professor of International Relations at Princeton University,"such regressive patriarchy does not even give the woman the freedom of the home but confines her figuratively at least to the bedroom."

The evaluation that the fight for women's rights in India is a Western concept, can only be termed as facile. Regardless of such observations, women will pursue the quest for human rights, even if it is resisted as an idea that is borrowed or as an idea that has come before its time.

Rani Jethmalani practices law in the Dehli High Court and the Supreme Court of India.

Colombia: Legal Gains for Women
Magdala Velásquez Toro

Introduction

Colombia is generally perceived as one of the few democratic countries in Latin America. It has been governed by civilian authorities, a president, a congress and active judiciary. For 35 years, however, the country has been under a political system of exceptions, resulting in suspension and restriction of citizens' freedoms and of individual guarantees granted by the National Constitution. The ever-increasing interference of the military in civilian life, the great socioeconomic inequalities, and a political system that is dominated by the traditional liberal and conservative parties (and excludes other ideological parties) have brought about popular discontent, and urban and rural violence. Historically, various forms of repression have existed including the standards of exception and lack of structural solutions or partial changes to the unjust distribution of wealth.

Nevertheless, the present government is moving forward by engaging in public policy debates and pushing for democratic reforms in the National Congress. The enactment of measures to democratize the economic life of the country encounters great difficulties due to the private interests of a minority of people who illegally monopolize large areas of land and dominate big industry (e.g., the multinationals). The traditional political parties, which control the congress, serve the interests of the powerful landowners and industry; hence, they oppose popular reforms, such as land and labor reforms.

Colombia, like most Third World countries, and specifically Latin American countries, is currently undergoing severe economic changes whereby the conditions of life for the majority of people have deteriorated further. With a foreign debt of $11 billion and pressure by the World Bank to satisfy the austerity plan of the International Monetary Fund, the Colombian government finds itself in a dilemma: the IMF recommendations would be futile, even if there existed the political will to carry them out.

The Law and Colombian Women

Latin American nations, as independent states with colonial ties, were influenced by the French and American Revolutions' ideologies of equality, freedom, and brotherhood for all men. In theory, these democracies were to be governed and organized not only by and for the landowners and the bourgeoisie, but by and for all men.

The rights of women were never considered, even at an abstract legal level. While women had no rights, they held many responsibilities. The constitution excluded women from intervening in state matters after 1821. This situation influenced the treatment of women by other Colombian institutions. The Constitutional Reform of 1936 granted women the right to hold administrative posts, accompanied by its authority and jurisdiction. The Constitutional Reform of 1945 established the legal right of citizenship, but the franchise and the right to stand for public office was bestowed exclusively upon men. Only in 1954 was that right granted to women, but it could not be exercised because the country was under military dictatorship. Subsequently, in 1957, a period characterized by economic chaos, violent social contradictions and upheaval, and a civil war that killed 300,000, women were given the right to vote—symbolizing the hope for peace and civility in the district assemblies.

Under the Napoleonic law, a woman was viewed essentially as a wife and mother, and thus, remained under the absolute authority of a male, who also managed her property. The civil or patrimonial rights of the married woman were recognized by Law 28 in 1932. However, legal equality of the sexes was only declared in 1974. A presidential decree abolished a husband's authority over his wife, and both parents were given authority over their children. A husband could file a complaint against his wife if she was caught in adultery, which would result in her imprisonment for up to four years. Until 1980, a husband could legally kill his wife or restrict her freedom for committing adultery.

Women were not granted the right to an education. What little instruction they received concentrated on the duties of a wife and mother, such as domestic work and educating children. Some women were permitted to study acceptable subjects for a degree. However, until 1933, women could not obtain a technical or university education because they were not allowed to matriculate for the B.A. degree. In 1968, the inequality of male and female education was officially abolished.

The process of legal emancipation of Colombian women has been distinguished by two major factors: it has been dominated by men, and hence, women have not been its principal advocates. While feminist and suffragist movements pressed for the extension of basic human rights for women, progressive governments have been the moving force of change through their recognition of women's individual and social rights and responsibilities. However, economic necessity catalyzed this historical process of reform. During the 1930's, when the country was recovering from the Great Depression and expanding its industrial base, women were recognized as a legal entity. To incorporate women into the capitalist system as wage earners (previously, any income would have been controlled by the husband), it was necessary to free women from patriarchal family relations. Similarly, women began to enter technical and higher centers of learning as the demand for educated and skilled labor increased.

Women's Economic Situation

Although employment opportunities, remuneration, and benefits for men and women are equal by law, the following data characterize the actual situation of women.[1]

❑ 300,920 women comprise 25% of the total labor force in the manufacturing sector. They are concentrated in apparel and footwear and, to a lesser extent, in plastics, chemicals, and textiles.

❑ In restaurants, hotels and businesses, they comprise 23.34% of the labor force. In relation to the total active economic population (APE) there are approximately 286,000 women.

❑ According to the Colombian delegate to the Interamerican Commission on Women, women occupy only 0.1% of the leadership positions and 0.2% of the technical positions in the country.

❑ In Colombia, the law provides for equal work and pay for men and women (Article 143 of the Substantive Labor Code). In reality, in both the public and private sectors, women are paid lower salaries than men who do the same tasks. Statistics of average monthly wages, according to occupation and sex, show that in 1978 women on the average earned 53.6% of what men in the same occupation earned. In 1980, the figure grew to 65%.[2]

Despite the dire economic situation, women have not comprehended the necessity to organize themselves to defend their interests. Furthermore, employers tacitly allied with the state quash any movement towards organizing unions in their companies. (Such suppression of the workers' rights is legally prohibited.) Nor do the unions actively negotiate with the large firms about the rights of women workers.

In Colombia, labor legislation protects the working mother through: licensing for salaries; providing sanctions against employers who dismiss or suspend pregnant women; holding companies responsible for establishing child daycare centers in factories, *etc.* In reality, however, pregnancy has become a cause for female dismissal and unemployment. The capitalist class is not prepared to assume the economic cost of reproduction. Hence, employers have established a series of illegal practices to circumvent maternity rights and benefits: they require laboratory proof that a woman is pregnant, and they often terminate work contracts solely because a woman gets married or appears to be pregnant.

As a result of the non-enforcement of maternity legislation, women must accept serious economic consequences of their pregnancies. They must endure unemployment, social sanctions, impoverishment of their families, and sometimes death. Deaths often occur due to illegal abortions. In Colombia, some 250,000 abortions are performed annually. Thirty-five percent of these are performed because of economic reasons. As abortions are illegal, they are performed in secret, unsterile conditions; they often result in deaths caused by infection.[3]

In Colombia, there are approximately 2,480,000 housewives living in urban areas. This segment of society has no legal protection, nor does it receive state medical assistance (for home accidents), disability insurance, or old age pensions. This group of women is in great need of state protection. Although these women greatly contribute to the enrichment of the lives of their family and of society, they are not rewarded or protected because they are not wage-earners.

The Social Reality of Colombian Women

The real issue for women living in a bourgeois democracy is the extent of actual exploitation and domination. While there are formal declarations of legal principles and norms granting women rights and prerogatives, millions of women must confront a less sanguine daily reality. The problem of women is not exclusively a class issue; it crosses all socioeconomic boundaries. It is present throughout the culture, and therefore has particular manifestations in the economy, politics, society, and sexual relations. However, the manifestations of oppression and discrimination of women have different effects on the various strata and social classes.

The social situation of women contributes to the political, economic, and social problems of the country. However, it is not possible to believe that a social revolution will eliminate all forms of discrimination against women. A social revolution may

A social revolution may improve the lives of the majority of the population, including women. But, if the power and attitudinal relationship between men and women does not change, the patriarchal and *machismo* ideology will continue to exist and to be reproduced in society.

From the point of view of legislation, Colombia might be viewed by a foreigner as a women's paradise. Women are granted almost all basic legal rights and aspirations. In 1981, the U.N. Convention of the Elimination on All Forms of Discrimination Against Women was approved by the legislature. The essential problem centers on the absence of effective enforcement mechanisms. Because the progressive legislation has not been accompanied by an educational campaign aimed at the masses of women and men, in general, the laws are no longer observed or enforced.

Magdala Velásquez Toro is a legal historian.

Sudan:
Women, Land Ownership, and Development
Balghis Badri

Introduction
This paper draws attention to the limited nature of land ownership by women in the Sudan—a problem which was further aggravated after the system of traditional communal ownership was replaced by a legally-mandated land registration and tenancy distribution. It will relate the lack of women's ownership of land to slowed socio-economic development and to restricted food production.

We start by asking several questions about female-owned property in Sudan.

Does land ownership motivate women to increase agricultural production?

Does land registration affect women's land ownership in rural areas?

How does the concept of women's property, and its application to the private domain only, affect the size of land owned by women?

What is the impact of the introduction of technology on women's land ownership?

What are the other socio-cultural and political factors that influence women's land ownership?

How have these various factors affected national development?

What should be done to improve this situation?

Secondly, this study assumes certain premises. The most important is that male planners have preconceived notions about women, property and work which have had a negative impact on the advancement of women and on general social development. Male planners have postulated that:

■ Women do not actively seek private land ownership.

■ Women are not sufficiently motivated to increase agricultural production even if they own land.

■ Women participate in land relations and agricultural production through their husbands.

■ Women participate principally in food production for the private domain, and hence, contribute little to the expansion of national economic development.

We refute the assumptions held by male planners. In fact, we will show that when women are denied land ownership, their participation in agricultural production is very low (particularly, in private agriculture). Case studies done in the Sudan disclose that there is a direct relation between female ownership of land and motivation of women to expand production. In general, it appears that as social acceptance of women's work grows, their participation increases.

Statistical data on land ownership in Sudan is scarce. However, we can offer a few facts to place the female role in perspective. According to the 1973-1974 census, women own no more than 12% of agricultural land in the tenancies surveyed. Specifically, women owned 11.7% in the Gazira scheme; 3% of the White Nile Pump Schemes of Kasti; 9% of that of Al-

Diem; 10% of the land in Kutum (Darfur); and 3% of land in the Rahad Scheme.[1] It is estimated that female participation in agricultural production amounts to 87% in the traditional sector of the non-market economy, dropping to 10% in the modern sector.[2]

While the material used to support the propositions of this paper is limited, it does indicate trends. To highlight the trends and to argue the premises put forward, it will draw from many recent case studies undertaken in different parts of the Sudan.

Regional Case Studies

Kutum[3]

Active participation by women in the production of both millet and horticultural crops is common in Wadi Kutum. The researchers note: "In fact, the historic right of women to work in fields was never a subject of dispute or challenge by men...."[4]

The case of Wadi Kutum indicates that 80% of the total labor force is women. Women's production does not significantly vary from that of men, and in some cases it is better. According to the study, the respondents' answers reveal that 46.4% of farms are owned by women. However, after the government introduced a system of farm registrations, only 10% of the small plots were being registered in women's names. The government wanted to give credit and extension service to the farmers as well as to encourage the formation of cooperatives. Women, according to the authors' explanation, view credit and cooperatives as part of the public domain. Because the public domain is associated with men, women lose their rights to land ownership. Thus, 90% of land is formally registered in male names even though it is women who do the cultivation.

Another study by Dr. I. Fuad maintains that extension services in the same region are carried out by male advisers while the majority of farmers are women.[5] Women, who are barred by custom from free association with foreign men, did not receive the extension services. Rather, it is men who receive this assistance; and in most cases, they do not share it with women.

It is clear that both the system of land registration and distribution of agricultural services have hurt women. Specifically, they have reduced female ownership of land. Because of the male-dominated society, ownership and economic responsibility are falsely associated with men. However, female economic participation (FEP) has not decreased because of the acceptance of women's role as farmers and the need for their labor due to the mass male migration. Yet, it seems that if land registration regulations had been coupled with other social factors that devalue women's work, then a lower FEP would have taken place. This is the situation that occurred in the northern region.

The Northern Region

The northern region has the lowest female economic participation—about 1.4%. Cultivation in the region is divided into five categories according to land ownership.[6] *Public pump schemes*, which are worked by males, compose 25.2% of the land area under cultivation. *Private pump schemes*, which are generally large-scale schemes owned by the rich (25% being owned by one company), make up 62% of the cultivated land. In the third category, 9% of the land is *mitrat*. Basin cultivation, comprises another 3.6% and *sugias* accounts for .02%.

Women's agricultural participation and land ownership is concentrated in the last two categories of land, which consists of small family-owned plots. Because pump cultivation requires start-up capital and because credit facilities are closed to women, women's participation is limited in the largest type of land exploitation. In fact, since the 1930's when pump schemes were introduced, a noticeable retreat in female participation in agriculture has taken place. As a capitalist mode of production was introduced into Sudanese agriculture, reflected by the introduction of irrigation, peasant workers were transformed into day-wage laborers. Day laborers traditionally migrate from area to area to obtain work. Hence, not only did men own the pump schemes, women were also discouraged from participating in agriculture by cultural prohibitions against working outside the family.

This region also suffers from male migration, which has increased in the 1970's as men sought work in the Arab gulf region. Male-owned land has not been cultivated because women have relied on their husband's remittances for their needs. The end result has been a deterioration in land and a shortage of food production, a situation which the government attempts to remedy through large-scale agricultural schemes. Logically, this will lead to a decrease of female ownership and production in a favorable economic climate; and in a depressed economic situation, it may result in increasing numbers of women becoming wage-workers, perhaps in the big private agricultural schemes.

Due to the economic recession in the Gulf countries, Sudanese workers will increasingly be forced to return to Sudan. With the changes that have occurred in Sudanese agriculture, they will find in most cases no land to cultivate. Therefore, they will also be forced to work as wage-laborers in the large-scale farming enterprises. These factors will no doubt change the nature of Sudan's agriculture. More importantly, if women were encouraged to cultivate the land by their direct ownership of land, then men would be able to return to their wives' land to farm with them. Ultimately, such a situation would increase the female economic role as property owners and as farmers. This would benefit a region where only about 2% of women are economically active. Moreover, it is possible that male migrant workers would invest money in their wives' property. This situation would have a favorable impact on agriculture, women, and on marriage stability.

This case suggests that male-ownership of land does not motivate women to cultivate it. It is particularly true in a situation where divorce is easy and the threat of polygamy exists. Cultural, legal, and political factors have all played great roles in reducing women's economic participation and ownership in agriculture.

Nomadic Tribal Society

The case of nomadic tribal society points out the fallacy of planners who assume that women's economic activity occurs mainly in the private sector and has had an adverse effect on development. In nomadic society, women are responsible for milking the herd and for processing and marketing the milk.[7] Currently, Sudan spends S£11 million annually to import milk powder and milk products because the government has neglected to invest in the dairy sector—a sector which is monopolized by women and nomads.[8] Given the low status of both these groups, production of milk products has been completely ignored. Instead, the Sudanese government chose to support large-scale dairy enterprises as typified by the establishment of the Babanusa Milk Factory which failed in 1965. If policy-makers had concentrated their efforts on building modern dairy farms (based on the introduction of appropriate technology) which women would manage and operate, milk production could have been increased. Moreover, the Sudanese government could have expanded milk production with little capital by continuing the nomadic style of linking dairy farming with the male-operated fattening farms. However, the government chose to import milk and to permit large Arab companies to establish capital-intensive dairy enterprises. These companies, which operate in Khartoum province, mainly employ wage-labor, displacing women from their traditional role in milk production.

Irrigation Schemes of Gazira, Rahad, White Nile, and Khartoum Provinces

The majority of the modern large-scale irrigation schemes are owned by men. In this sector, 49% of the men are economically active as compared to 10% of the females. In the traditional sector, 85% of the women participate.

The regulations that apply to the state agricultural schemes (which compose an important share of the large irrigated farms) exclude the majority of women. According to the regulations, the head of the household will be given a tenancy provided that he will cultivate it, holds a Sudanese National Certificate and has a family that will help him. The concepts of head of household and family help eliminate women's tenancy. Moreover, obtaining a certificate is a difficult process. Both legislative and customary factors hurt women whose mobility is restricted, particularly among the tribes of the middle region where these schemes are concentrated. Furthermore, the new complex system of irrigation and crop rotation used in these schemes is not suitable for the majority of women who are mothers of young children. Therefore, only a woman who proves she is different is able to gain land tenancy.

According to Gassim Al-Seed, the low agricultural participation of women who do not own land is due to the element of hard work and the lengthy distance from the house to the farm. Furthermore, husbands prefer lower profit and production rates from hiring workers rather than allowing their wives to work in front of other men in an activity that they do not highly value.[9] Al-Seed adds that from the women's point of view, this work is not profitable because husbands do not pay them or landlords (non-husbands) pay them little.[10] In both cases it is not worth their effort. In the few cases where women work their own tenancies, however, they have produced more than men. According to the 1983 data, the prize for the best tenancy was won by a woman.

In contrast to Al-Seed's assertions, Badri and Bashir note that in the Gazira scheme, male tenants prefer women wage-laborers to men and about 63% of all pickers are female.[11] They also mention that the average productivity of female tenants in the Gazira is quite high.[12] The economic incentive for women to work in the Gazira is great since day-laborers receive S£2 per day.[13] According to the 1973-1974 survey, 30% of tenants' wives work on their husbands' land, and 57.5% work on farms other than those of their husbands.[14] Despite the high wages, we still find that many resident women prefer to farm their own small plots of land.

In the White Nile Schemes, the case is a bit different. We find that 50% of the wives of tenants work on their husbands' land as compared to the 30% in the Gazira Scheme.[15] The main reason is that in the White Nile, the tenancies are smaller and closer to villages; and the people are poorer in Gazira. Hence, all family members must work since one hired worker can cut the profit by half.[16]

The above cases indicate that women will only work on their husbands' farms when there is a great need for them to do so, when it is not more profitable for them to work as wage-laborers, and when they have no other land to cultivate. Nevertheless, land legislation has adversely affected female ownership of property in both the modern and traditional sectors of agriculture.

From these cases it is evident that women's economic participation in agriculture is important even though they own small amounts. Women make economic calculations of the remuneration of their work in determining the extent of their agricultural activities. As women increase their ownership of land, their participation and economic role in agriculture will expand significantly.

To improve the situation of women in agriculture, specific actions must be taken. First, women's consciousness of their rights and of the importance of their ownership of land must be increased. Credit and agricultural services should be extended to women who are already in agricultural production. The female graduates of agricultural and family science colleges should train women as local agricultural advisers and produce appropriate educational materials to assist women farmers at the grass-roots level. Furthermore, all technical, financial, and agricultural services should be dispensed through an expanded network of women's organizations.

Women's organizations should also pressure the government to reform land tenancy laws. Policy makers must be made aware of the adverse effect of current land registration laws and tenancy regulations on development. Moreover, this system of registration should not be introduced to areas under traditional forms of ownership. But the government and women's organizations should encourage the participation of women in agriculture by assisting in the establishment of small farms operated by women.

The expansion of big agricultural enterprises that entail large capital expenditure, cash crops, and wage-labor should be eliminated. Large-scale capitalist agriculture has excluded women so it can obtain quick profits. Apart from the negative impact on women's participation in agriculture, these large-scale schemes have reduced food production.

We must fight for a suitable model of agriculture. Such a model will ultimately increase women's participation in agriculture and their economic and political power. It will also feed us. One suggested model is a return to the traditional system of agriculture whereby appropriate village technologies are introduced.

Strategy

Women's organizations clearly have a key role to play in developing an appropriate model of agriculture. They must work collectively to help women directly and to pressure policy makers to assist women by fairer land legislation, better development training, and more equitable distribution of services. In addition, more field work must be undertaken to understand women's problems. Grassroots involvement can be encouraged by organizing a workshop to establish a program to attain these objectives. Hence, women must organize to increase their economic, social, and legal power. These measures, then, will permit women to advance in agriculture and all other spheres of Sudanese society.

Balghis Badri is a lecturer at Khartoum University, Department of Sociology and a member of the Scientific Association for Women's Studies (SAWS) in Omdurman, Sudan.

India: Women and Property Rights
Chandermani Chopra

Introduction

The spectrum of legislation about property rights clearly demonstrates that women fare much worse than men. Indeed, there are certain areas in which there is a complete and total denial of women's rights. However, discrimination does not occur only between men and women, but also between women and women because of personal laws. In spite of the principles of the constitution stating that there shall be a uniform civil code, this objective has not yet been achieved. This paper will examine the areas of egregious discrimination against women regarding property rights and the relationship between women's right to property and her status within the family.

Agricultural Land

Agricultural land in India forms the bulk of property. Most states in India adhere to traditional views of property rights which discriminate against women. Some claim that the Hindu Succession Act, which was enacted to improve radically the rights of women, does not apply to agricultural land. This assertion is not correct. Section 4, subsection 2 of the act declares that nothing in the act is deemed to affect any law which provides for the prevention of fragmentation of agricultural holdings, for the establishment of ceilings on holdings, or for the modification of tenancy rights in respect to such holdings. Several states in India have successfully excluded widows and daughters from inheriting agricultural land (*e.g.*, U.P. Zamindari Abolition and Land Reform Act, 1950; Delhi Land Reform Act; and other land ceiling laws, adopted in states like Punjab or Madhaya Pradesh). These laws are not justified. The denial of the rights of widows to inherit this property is inconsistent with other laws. However, under the pretext of the necessity to avoid land fragmentation, and in spite of women's protests about this issue, nothing has been done so far. Clearly, the Hindu Succession Act to equalize laws for women has miserably failed.

Ancestral Property

It is only under the Hindu Succession Act that a distinction is made between succession to ancestral property and succession to self-acquired property. The right of women to inherit ancestral property is inferior to that of men. The law that governs ancestral property is the Hindu Succession Act, section 6. However, before examining this section, it is necessary to define co-parcenary. A co-parcenary is a body other than a joint family, consisting of only those persons who, because of birth, have taken an interest in the property of the present holder for the present and who can inherit the property at the time of the holder's death. The co-parcenary begins with common male ancestors and it includes a holder of joint property and only the male descendants who are not removed from him by more than three degrees. Thus, a son, grandson or a great-grandson is a co-parcener; the great, great-grandson is not a co-parcener because he is removed by more than three degrees from the holder. (Co-parcenary is limited because in the Hindu religion, only descendants of three degrees can provide spiritual administration to an ancestor.) All females are excluded from

85

the co-parcenary. Co-parcenary property is defined as ancestral property. By virtue of section 6 of the Hindu Succession Act, co-parcenary has been preserved, but at the same time, some rights have been given to females. Co-parcenary is maintained by the application of the principles of succession to co-parcenary property by survivorship and not by inheritance. Therefore, only co-parcenars who are members of the co-parcenary can inherit the property.

The situation has been mitigated by establishing a provision under section 6 of the act. Thus, in the case that the co-parcenar dies leaving behind a female relative in class 1 of the schedule or a male relative specified in the class who claims rights through such female relatives, the interest of the deceased in the Mitakshra, co-parcenary property devolves by testamentary or intestate succession and not by survivorship. Briefly, it means that in the case of a daughter, or a grandson being the son of a daughter, a notional partition will occur, and the share of the deceased devolves upon his heirs who are designated as class 1 of the schedule. In this process, the sons get larger shares of the ancestral property than the daughters.

One Indian state, Andhra Pradesh, has recently introduced an amendment to section 6 of the Hindu Succession Act, in order to improve the rights of women to inherit ancestral property. This is a very laudable step and should be followed by other states as well.

Right to Partition

Section 23 of the Hindu Succession Act makes a special provision about the rights of heirs to a dwelling house. Section 23 reads as follows:

Where a Hindu intestate has left surviving him or her both male and female heirs specified in class 1 of the schedule and his or her property includes a dwelling house wholly occupied by members of his or her family, then, notwithstanding anything contained in this act, the right of any such female heir to claim partition of the dwelling house shall not arise until the male heirs choose to divide their respective shares therein, but the female heir shall be entitled to a right of residence therein.

Provided that where such female heir is a daughter, she shall be entitled to a right of residence in the dwelling house only if she is unmarried or has been deserted by or has separated from her husband or is a widow.

It is clear that through Section 23 an attempt has been made to maintain privacy of the family against an outsider, *i.e.* a son-in-law. When there is intestate succession, it restricts the right of the daughter to a residence. Through this provision in the law, there is discrimination between married daughters and unmarried daughters, apart from other forms of discrimination. It is debatable whether the denial of the right of partition in the interest of the preservation of the family is justified or not.

Succession under the Indian Succession Act

The Indian Succession Act was enacted in 1925 to consolidate the large number of different laws which were in existence at that time. However, the laws of succession of Muslims and Hindus were excluded from the act. Under this act there are two schemes which have been adopted: one dealing with the succession rights of individuals such as Indian Christians, Jews, and those married under the Special Marriage Act of 1955; and the other dealing with the succession rights of Parsis.

In the first instance, when a person dies intestate, leaving a widow and a lineal descendant, the widow is entitled to a fixed share of one-third of the property, and the children, irrespective of their sex, would share the remainder equally.

Christians in Kerala

There is also a diversity of laws that apply to Indian Christians. The Travancore High Court held that the Indian Succession Act did not apply to the Christians of the state. Thus, Christians in Kerala are governed by laws that are different from the ones governing Christians in other jurisdictions. This discrimination against persons within the same community has been highlighted in the report of the Status of Women Committee submitted in 1973.

In Travancore, the old notions of Hindu law of inheritance, which discriminate against women, still persist. A widow or mother inheriting immovable property takes only the life interest terminable on death or remarriage, and a daughter's right is limited to Istri Dhan.

Christians in Goa and Pondichery

The Christians of Goa are governed by the Portugese Civil Code. The result is a legal system which is totally different from the ones prevailing in the rest of the country.

The code makes no distinction between brothers and sisters, and it relegates the widow to a very low position. With the existence of sons and daughters, the mother does not inherit anything. In the order of legal heirs of a person, a man's sons and daughters inherit property in equal shares. If there are no children, his parents inherit, followed by the brother and his descendants. The widow inherits only if there is no heir in these classes. The widow becomes the owner of "agricultural commodities and fruits," meant and necessary for the consumption of the conjugal couple. She will, however, lose even this right if she is divorced or separated from the husband. Unlike Christians in the other states of India, a person cannot will or give away his entire property, thereby excluding his legal heirs.

Parsi Intestate Succession

Regulations of intestate succession of males have the characteristics of Islamic law, namely, a male heir receives twice the share of a female heir. If a male Parsi dies, leaving behind one or both parents, a widow, and children, the property is to be divided so that the father will receive a share equal to half the share of a son, and the mother shall receive a share equal to half the share of a daughter. Thus, the inheritance rights of a mother are inferior and different from those which prevail under the Hindu Succession Act.

The Indian Succession Act and Hindu law (i.e., both Mitakshara and Dayabagh) place no restrictions on the power of testation. It is one of the major factors in perpetuating the evil of dowry. Even when the bill on the Hindu Succession Act was being debated at Lok Sabha, it was pointed out that the rights of female heirs would be violated by the unrestricted power of testation. The objection, however, was brushed aside. The report of the Status of Women Committee notes that:

an analysis of the inmates of rescue homes in this country will prove how many of those women are those who have been thrown out of the joint family. . . The committee's own experience in many places, but

88

particularly in Banares, more than proves the point that there are many women who had been reduced to destitution and beggary because their families have deprived them of all support. It is, therefore, necessary that the right of testation should be limited under all laws relating to succession as not to deprive the legal heirs completely.

Matrimonial Property

The various personal laws in the country are uniform in recognizing the obligation of a husband to maintain his dependent wife, but the right of the wife to claim part ownership of the property acquired and enjoyed jointly by the husband and wife during the marriage is not recognized. In the socioeconomic situation prevailing in India, the contribution of the female to the family's economy is not recognized. A large number of women participate in the family's economic activity, but they are considered unpaid family workers. Even when they do not work to increase the family's income, the economic value of their household activities permits the husband extra time to pursue his profession or vocation. Nevertheless, it is not recognized as a direct or indirect economic contribution.

Most married women have no independent source of income. Furthermore, many women give up their jobs after marriage. Others do not accept employment for many years after marriage in order to devote their full time to family obligations. They are, therefore, economically dependent on their husbands. In most of these cases, property (both movable and immovable) acquired during marriage is purchased from the husband's earnings. If a matrimonial home is acquired, it will be registered in the husband's name. Household goods are legally owned by the husband because the wife has not contributed economically under the law. Hence, the principle of determining ownership on the basis of financial contribution is unjust and works inequitably against women. The demand for the recognition of the wife's contribution in terms of household and family responsibilities is growing in many other countries. A legal recognition of the economic value of a housewife's contribution must be made for the purpose of determining property ownership, instead of the continuation of the archaic test of actual financial contribution. It is, therefore, recommended that, in the case of divorce or separation, the wife should be entitled to at least one-third of the assets acquired at the time of and during the marriage.

Other Recommendations
The succession laws must be amended to remove discrimination. Furthermore, research on the right of rural women to inherit agricultural land must be examined. Then, proposals can be initiated to expand their rights and improve their situations.

These suggestions, however, are not new. As far back as 1971, the Indian government appointed a Status of Women Committee to examine comprehensively these issues. The committee studied myriad aspects of the socioeconomic status of women and property rights. Their recommendations were submitted on June 29, 1973 in the form of a report. Unfortunately, until the present time, no follow-up of these proposals has taken place.

Chandermani Chopra is an advocate of the High Court Chambers in India.

Custom,
Religion, Ethnicity,
and Law

As an introduction to this section and of particular relevance to the case studies presented here, *Coomaraswamy* (Sri Lanka) offers a theoretical framework for analyzing the relationship between ethnic identity and women's status. The first part of her paper elaborates the inadequacy of other paradigms for studying the social reality of the Third World, particularly with reference to women and ethnicity. As exclusive frameworks for analysis, none of these paradigms (nationalism, modernization, class analysis, ideological analysis, and radical feminism) provide sufficient insight, since all fail to integrate ethnicity, class, and gender as essential to their analytical schema. The second part of Coomaraswamy's essay identifies several factors of critical importance to an analysis capable of transcending the particulars of culture and ethnicity. These factors include sexual subordination, unequal family relations, economic dependence, absence of participation in public life, physical violence, and rights to sexuality.

Coomaraswamy concludes that women "must preserve their ethnic identity while fighting for social reform and social change within their own ethnic group."

The other papers in this section provide examples of the role of religious and customary laws in determining the rights of women. *Patel* begins by documenting how the interpretation and enforcement of Islamic laws in Pakistan are detrimental to women. Her observations are particularly relevant in a Muslim country such as Pakistan because the Shariat Court system holds sway over the majority of the population in those aspects of life governed by Islamic law. Patel's organiazation defines the issue as one of "combating the misinterpretation of Islam," in the courts and legislature.

Molokomme's careful look at the interaction of state law, custom, and customary law begins with a definition of customary law, a term she notes is often misused. The paper goes on to analyze the position of women under customary law in Botswana with regard to marriage, divorce, inheritance, property rights, guardianship, and other family-related issues. Using an historical perspective, Molokomme argues that today customary law can be shown to be detrimental to women: contemporary customary law corresponds to conditions which prevailed in an earlier time but are no longer relevant; also, customary law has been unable to accommodate rapid changes in Botswana. Molokomme concludes with a few suggestions for strategies, noting the need for positive state intervention, non-governmental assistance, and increased women's awareness.

Mamashela, from neighboring Lesotho, compares the rights of women in marriage under customary and civil laws and concludes that the status of women is virtually the same under both sets of laws—since a woman remains a minor during marriage. Mamashela explores how those laws affect women economically—particularly when their husbands migrate in search of work outside the country, a situation common in Lesotho. In such circumstances, the woman becomes the *de facto* administrator of the joint estate and head of household. Nonetheless, her legal status as a wife precludes her entering into any contracts without her husband's permission. This abandonment by the husband in search of work is particularly burdensome.

El Dareer focuses her paper on the obstacles Sudanese women face in their changing roles and position in society. Many of these obstacles are deeply rooted in religion, culture, and social heritage. Beginning with the traditional attitudes of both men and women, the obstacles women face include unequal application of the law and traditional practices favorable to men and sanctioned by law. She notes examples such as the failure of divorced men to provide child support, the stringent laws against adultery applicable only to women, and male-only initiation of divorce proceedings. These cultural and traditional practices discourage women from seeking their rights. El-Dareer calls for strategies which encourage both men and women to participate jointly in efforts toward change.

(Papers in other sections of this book also deal with issues of custom, religion, and ethnicity. See, for example, *Kumari* on the institution of dowry in India, *Tai Young Lee* on Confucianism in Korea, *Moghaizel* on crimes of honor in the Middle East, among others.)

Sri Lanka:
Ethnicity and Patriarchy in the Third World
Radhika Coomaraswamy

Introduction

A conceptual framework of ethnic identity and the status of women cannot endeavor to be comprehensive. No framework can be general enough to encompass all societies and still be sensitive to minute details of social life as they are actually experienced by women in any particular social context. The purpose of this framework is, therefore, not to present a tapestry of the social experiences of women in diverse cultures but to help identify certain analytical factors which will allow for a cross-cultural comparison.

At the same time, this paper does not purport to be value-free. It is primarily concerned with confronting the negative features of patriarchy, *i.e.,* "the social organization of the family, the community, and the state, in such a way that male power is reinforced and perpetuated."[1] Secondly, though it accepts as self-evident the diversity of cultural forms and social experiences, the paper is primarily concerned with factors which perpetuate and transform sexual hierarchies in the modern period, even though the "founding persons" of the past may have had a different social purpose. Thirdly, the paper is written in the context of human traditions—of diverse ethnic origins—which have been committed to the elimination of inequality and exploitation of women, not only as ends in themselves, but also, as Nawal El Saadawi so convincingly argues in her book, "it is no longer possible to escape the fact that the underprivileged status of women, their relative backwardness, leads to an essential backwardness in society as a whole. For this very reason it is necessary to see the emancipation of women as an integral part of the struggle against all forms of oppression."[2]

A conceptual study with regard to the status of women in diverse ethnic settings must come to terms with the independent but interlocking variables which characterize: a) the nation-state in which the women live; b) the ethnic group with which the women identify; c) the specific class to which the women belong and d) the status of women in each context. In addition, these variables would have to be analyzed through diverse historical periods—the ideology and practice of which continue to regulate social life, giving rise to present day contradictions and realities.

The Ethnic Factor

Studies on women in Third World societies have concentrated on the general status of women in a particular nation-state. Within these states, social scientists have analyzed the position of women either in terms of class or ethnic group. The two sub-divisions have usually been self-excluding categories except in cases of what Rudolpho Stavenhagen calls *ethnic-class*, an ethnic group as a whole shares the same characteristics of a social class (*e.g.*, Blacks in the US or South Africa, the Mayan Indians in Latin America, Tamil estate workers in Sri Lanka). However, though the social reality of women in the Third World is greatly conditioned by both her ethnic identity and her economic status, ethnicity in traditional societies has gathered a dynamic social momentum which has not been fully appreciated by Western feminists interested in the social advancement of women. Since the 1940's ethnic identity or race has become a primary factor in the politics and social life of Third World societies. Without coming to terms with the ethnic factor, it would be impossible to understand why Iranian women took to the *chador*, why nuclear families have not emerged in India even in the large cities, why Tamil women in Sri Lanka have yet to become politically articulate, why Andean women have reacted strongly against land reform, why American black women have remained hostile to and resisted the call to feminism. The purpose of these studies is, therefore, not to exclude other criteria such as economic development, national political ideology, or social class, but to focus on an area of analysis which has yet to be researched empirically and studied systematically in a cross-cultural context. Keeping this purpose in mind, this paper will first attempt to summarize past paradigms which have been used to study social reality in Third World societies and analyze them with specific reference to ethnic identity and the status of women.

It will also attempt to isolate certain factors which are said to characterize the social practices of patriarchy and then analyze them in the context of diverse ethnic contexts.

Past Paradigms for the Analysis
of the Status of Women

Nationalism:
The Two-Edged Sword

Until the advent of radical feminism, ethnic identity and the status of women have always been analyzed from the perspective of general social theory aimed at understanding the processes of change and development in Third World societies. In this context, nationalism and nationalist movements have played an important part in defining the terms under which women would have to live in post-colonial Third World societies. Kumari Jayawardene, in her book, *Feminism and Nationalism in the Third World*, puts forward certain conclusions after analyzing nationalist forces in six Asian and African societies.

Women's participation in the struggles against colonialism and imperialism and the campaign for improved social conditions for women were important components in Third World nationalist movements.

The impact of nationalism on the status of women was greatly determined by the class composition of nationalist leaders.

Women's active participation in nationalist movements created a greater feminist awareness and led to social reform and to the organization of women's groups. Unfortunately, after independence, many of these movements lost their momentum and women reverted back to their basically subordinate roles in society.3

Post-independence nationalism with its emphasis on ethnic pride and national glory has had unforeseen consequences throughout the Third World, as nationalism is often linked to the predominant ethnic identity within a given nation-state. The symbolism of this national-ethnic identity has been an important factor in strategies for social mobilization. The status of women in these societies has also become a fundamental concern for those projecting the symbolism of a particular ethnic group. If nationalism contained a modern social reform component, nationalist leaders, once they achieved power, attempted to discard the more cruel practices against women so as to purify the image of their ethnic group and to make the reforms part of a general package of social mobilization and transformation.[4] However if nationalism did not contain a social reform component, then the status of women was seen as a fundamental aspect of the ethnic identity or a testament to the uniqueness of a particular community.[5] Any attempt to challenge the status of women was, therefore, seen as a threat against the whole community. This social reform component is, therefore, the factor which distinguishes a nationalism which has a negative effect on the status of women and those movements which have generally improved women's position in society.

As a general rule, since the concept of self-determination and the political basis of nationalism have their roots in liberal and socialist theories of the modern era, nationalist movements, with only a few exceptions, did contain the necessary social reform components.[6] However, the ethnic identities of minorities presently living within a nation-state do not necessarily accept the component of social reform. The particular state of insecurity which ethnic minorities face in Third World societies often makes them defensive, insular, and resistant to changes emanating from the center. As in the Punjab in India, defending the inferior state of women within their identity can become an issue of minority rights.[7]

Nationalism and the assertion of ethnic identity may, therefore, be a two-edged sword, greatly dependent on the vision of the leadership and the consciousness of women within the group. History has shown that mass nationalist movements need the resources and energies of women; hence, an ideological appeal to equality and the creation of women's groups has been an important aspect of the nationalist period. However, a threatened ethnic or nationalist identity, with a fundamentalist leadership and a dependent female population, may actually initiate changes which will result in reversals with regard to the status of women in society.

Modernization: The Differential Impact

The vast majority of Third World women, regardless of ethnic identity, live under conditions of abject poverty. It has often been argued that modernization of the economic modes of production and political life will automatically alleviate the condition of women. Modernization theories center around economic planning that aims at capital accumulation and national development. However, data and experience in Third World societies show that modernization does not necessarily improve the situation of women. In fact, in certain contexts, modernization may lessen women's social status and economic independence. Research clearly shows that modernization differs in its impact on women in various societies.

The impact of modernization on the agrarian sector is analyzed by Madhu Kishwar's study of agrarian relations in the Punjab, India. Kishwar concludes that the Green Revolution and agrarian reform have actually resulted in the systematic subjugation and seclusion of women.[8] The Green Revolution displaced subsistence agriculture, in which women had an important economic role to play. With the introduction of tubewell irrigation and mechanization, female participation was reduced, and the new peasant elite valued seclusion of women as an indicator of success and prosperity.

Modernization in the urban, commercial, and industrial sectors has led to wage-labor and capitalist enterprise. Throughout the modern period, regardless of ethnic group, the demand for women's labor has grown, especially in the area of textiles (China, Japan, India, Turkey, Iran) and in the plantation sector.[9] In addition, the urban centers permit capitalist initiative regardless of sex or ethnic origin. As a result, the differential impact of modernization on the status of women in these sectors was not inherent in the policies themselves, but often a result of the social ideology as fostered by a particular ethnic group. This is clearly brought out if one again examines the empirical data in diverse case studies.

Susan Bourque and Kay Barbara Warren's study of patriarchy in the Peruvian Andes clearly shows that contrary to the agricultural sector, in the commercial center of southern Peru, modernization has had a positive impact. Many of the enterprises are run by women, and they make economic decisions and participate fully in the economic life of the town. However, there is still no sexual parity, since men control the larger enterprises and have access to the inter-regional markets.[10]

In Egypt, women's participation in the commercial and industrial sectors is minimal (less than 20%), primarily because women need the consent of their husband to work and because social ideology frowns upon women working outside the home.[11] Modernization policies in the urban, commercial, and industrial sector do have a differential impact on women (*i.e.*, access to skills and technology is still less for women than men), but the degree of differential impact is greatly dependent on ethnicity and social ideology. The difference in attitude between the Andean women interviewed by Bourque *et al* and the Egyptian women discussed by Nawal El Saadawi indicates that the ethnic dimension is in fact a determining factor as to whether women participate fully in the organized commercial sector.

Modernization with regard to legal status and political rights has generally been welcomed as progressive. However, in certain ethnic contexts, modern laws do have unanticipated social consequences. For example, the introduction of monogomous marriages in Africa deprived a whole class of women—concubines—of their traditional rights under customary law. In addition, the stress on the individual and the nuclear family has brought about a new type of economic dependence which was not present earlier.[12]

Modernization paradigms and development theories in general are greatly dependent on a centralized state mechanism to implement their policies. This reliance on a powerful state, especially one which has the ethnic characteristics of one group in society, often results in different policies toward different ethnic groups. Women in minority ethnic groups can often claim double discrimination or double oppression: firstly, as members of the ethnic group, and secondly, as women within an ethnic group.

Many feminists have argued that the decline in the status of women cannot be traced to changes in the mode of production, but to the emergence of centralized states which have regularized the practices of patriarchy through legal and administrative procedures. Nawal El Saadawi in her book on Arab women shows clearly how tribal organization prior to the rise of the great Islamic states accorded women a higher status.[13] Saadawi argues that the rise of great empires coupled with the importance of private property resulted in the oppressive forms of social organization which today characterize the lives of Arab women.[14]

Class Analysis: Women Divided

Marxist theorists have often argued that ethnicity and sex are dependent variables, ultimately conditioned by the nature of a society's class structure. An analysis of ethnic identity and the status of women would first focus on the social formation of a particular ethnic group and then the position of women within each stratum.[15] This type of analysis is, of course, essential, especially in developing societies, where class differences are especially acute. Madhu Kishwar and Maria Mies, in their analysis of India, are agreed that the Indian national movement gave a special position to middle-class, politically articulate women. Their presence in the Indian national movement allowed for the easy enactment of post-colonial legislation on the right to vote, property rights, access to education, access to employment, *etc.* However, these laws are often meaningless in a context where only 25% of women are literate and less than 5% own property. "What prevents lower class women from sharing in equality is not only male chauvinism alone but patterns of socioeconomic inequality."[16] The Indian context is an extreme example of the advances of one segment of the female population, while the majority face increasing political and economic marginalization.[17]

Class analysis, however, does not explain the status of women in all social contexts. In India itself, in the Punjab, rich peasant women are more likely to suffer dowry deaths and physical seclusion than women at the lowest end of the social spectrum. In Egypt, Sudan, and in most of Northern Africa, women of all classes are subject to the systematic mutilation of their genital organs so that they will not feel sexual pleasure. Hence, the factors of sex and ethnicity are often independent variables, complemented by class analysis. In certain contexts, (*e.g.*, the Adivasis in India, Tamil estate workers in Sri Lanka, Mayan Indians in Latin America) class, ethnicity, and sex appear to be interdependent. In other ethnic contexts such as Saudi Arabia, and the Punjab, Ashanti women in Ghana, being a female has an independent, often subordinate, dynamic of its own. To dismiss these different contexts is to ignore the important role of social ideology, and the independent nature of certain structures of patriarchy.

Ideology: Manipulation of the Social Mind

Ideological analysis is basically concerned with the realities of who controls the values, symbols, and culturally-created myths of a particular society. In whose interest are these myths perpetuated; and in securing these interests, which group is denied its full potential in terms of human expression and expectation? From Levi- Strauss in anthropology through Lacan in psychoanalysis and Foucault in history, the structuralist-ideological school is perhaps the most dynamic in current social theory. The vulgar manipulation of symbolic systems and thought processes to perpetuate power-relations is evident in developing societies. Ironically, with regard to ethnic identity and the status of women, this school of analysis has perhaps the most universal application. In practically all societies, myths and symbols are manipulated to perpetuate a system of patriarchy. Women are exalted as Earth Mothers or denigrated as vulnerable children; they are ignored as apolitical homebodies or feared as powerful behind-the-scene negotiators. Their domestic labor is minimized as not being *work* and men who are influenced by women are laughed at as being *Sarco-Largo*—wearing a straitjacket.[18]

Stereotypes with regard to the female disposition are often accentuated by equally simplistic ethnic stereotypes—the Geisha Japanese, the spiritual Indian woman, the powerful Black woman, the docile Arab woman, the passionate Latin lover, the sexually-licentious American. These are all stereotypes which not only refuse to accept the other woman as a multidimensional full personality, but also have a material force in society. These images, however, are not *ad hoc* but have been systematically developed over time and used by different groups for different purposes. These systems of thought or ideologies continue despite the fact that social reality remains in contradiction.

Ideologies are not only static and inherited; they are also dynamic and ever-changing. As Madhu Kishwar illustrates in the Punjab, new ideologies are created in light of new social conditions. Given the fact that there is a perpetual tension

101

between ideology and reality, the fact that the status of women in society has been the subject matter for mystification by men in all ethnic groups, the ideological approach is perhaps that which is most applicable to women's reality in any ethnic context. Though it cannot stand alone and needs to be augmented by economic and historical analysis, it does provide an important starting point for extracting common belief-systems across cultures which continue to prevent women from participating fully in social and economic life.[19]

Radical Feminism

With the increase in empirical data and research in women's studies and the growing awareness of women about the special, independent nature of the social indicator of gender, there have been recent attempts to construct a social theory of radical feminism. Firestone in *Dialectics of Sex* argues that the domination of women by men is *the* fundamental social division upon which all others rest.[20] This analysis has two implications: firstly, that the material basis for this division is that women's labor is devalued and appropriated; and secondly, that ideological systems are built around the male-female dichotomy and help perpetuate men's power over women.

There is a danger in placing the issue of women as the focal point of social theory. Though sex is an independent variable, especially in developing societies, it is difficult to accept the proposition that it always displaces poverty, class, and ethnicity as the most determining variable. Its centrality depends on social context, the economic forces of production, and political and ideological forces. In analyzing the issues of female labor, women's identification with an ethnic community, or class position in society, radical feminism cannot stand alone.[21]

Patterns of Inequality and Exploitation

Conditions under which women live, work, and die vary according to their socioeconomic origins and ethnic backgrounds. There is still much research which is necessary to analyze systematically the patterns of inequality and exploitation which cut across cultural and ethnic lines. A general survey of some of the anthropological and social science material available on women and the Third World points to the following factors which appear to cut across culture and ethnic identity.

Sexual Subordination

In general, women appear to be sexually subordinate to males. They are either considered inferior, or they are dependent on male hierarchies. Their labor is often the least valued in society. This state of affairs contrasts with sexual parity, a context in which women are considered independent and autonomous individuals in control of their personality and their labor.[22] This state of subordination is not static, but is a product of changing social processes and structural relations. Especially in the context of changing societies, the notion of sexual subordination must be understood over a particular time period.

Less Control Over Her Body

In many societies women lack control over their bodies. The classical cases of female circumcision are the primary examples of this.[23] Furthermore, in most societies abortion is illegal. In the Catholic countries of Latin America, abortion is an unforgivable sin. In Northern Africa, abortion is illegal in most of the countries, although economic considerations have led Tunisia and Somalia to legalize abortion. In the countries of Asia, despite overpopulation, abortion remains illegal. The arguments for abortion in developing societies are both moral and practical. According to Dr. Nawal El Saadawi, in Egypt, one out of every four embryos is illegally aborted.[24] Legalization would, therefore, only bring these abortions under medical supervisory care.

Akin to the fact that women do not have control over their bodies is the prevalent ideology of seclusion which exists in many communities in Asia and Africa, especially for women whose labor is seen as unnecessary. Seclusion has definite social consequences for women. It prevents freedom of association, independent sources of income, and independent access to information. They become completely dependent on males. In certain parts of Asia, such as northern India, child brides are taken away from their parental home to their in-laws where the ideology of seclusion prevents them from visiting their own parents. Emotional, sexual, economic, and political dependence then becomes the accepted way of life, idealized in the figure of Sita, the selfless wife of Lord Rama.[25]

The Separate Sphere: Unequal Relations

In general, family life is composed of unequal relations between males and females. The degree and intensity of this inequality vary greatly, especially according to ethnic group, but there is a patriarchal bias in most family structures.

The traditional argument supporting the sexual division of labor is that biology has determined *the sphere of the woman*. It is argued that adversarial concepts should not invade family life and that notions of harmony uphold the complementary character of women's work in maintaining the household while the man works in the public world of business and politics.

Yet, even in the female sphere, rarely do women make most decisions or control family relations. While women rarely make decisions within the family, unless they have strong, outstanding personalities which have challenged structural limitations, they often lobby or attempt to influence the making of decisions by the males in a non-adversarial manner. This form of socialization leads to a certain passivity and inaction in confronting injustice in public life. Moreover, even though women rarely make decisions for the whole household, older women are free to exercise control over the younger women in the family. The hostility between mother-in-law and daughter-in-law, defies the harmony theory. In India, for example, mothers-in-law have frequently been involved in dowry deaths, according to court records.

Nevertheless, there are a few exceptions to the powerlessness of women, even in the separate sphere. For example, some African women and American Black women have gained economic power and autonomy due to their particular socioeconomic circumstances. Despite these exceptions and even though all societies attach a positive value to woman's role as mother, for most women, the family is not the nostalgic separate sphere, the secure retreat from the harsh realities of the world.

Another component of the unequal relationship between men and women is marriage. Polygamy still persists as a common practice in Africa and some parts of Asia. In Zaire, thirty-one percent of all marriages are polygamous.[26] Even where there is no polygamy, the practice of concubinage is common in Africa, in Malaysia, Singapore, and East Asia. Confucian customary law recognizes concubinage as a special status entitled to certain rights. In many parts of the world, a woman enters marriage not as an equal partner, but as one of many. The sharing of affection and economic decision-making among these wives or concubines is at the discretion of the male. In fact, the Arab concept of Beit El Ta'a (House of Obedience) is used to describe the relationship between the male head of household and his many wives and dependents. Even if they leave him for physical cruelty, he has the right to bring them back by force.

Female labor is perhaps the most important and energetic component in the family home. This element appears common to all ethnic groups. In subsistence communities, women take an extremely active role. In southern Peru, they are responsible for cooking, harvesting, storage, and housekeeping. Yet, it is also interesting that when families do become richer and have access to modern technology, household work done by the woman is the last to be modernized. A cassette player will often precede an electric cooker. In rich Indian peasant homes, the women still cook over a smoky *chula* or a brick oven stove.[27]

The concept of a woman's power in her separate sphere appears therefore to be more a myth than a reality. Though there are exceptional cases, family structures as they obtain throughout the Third World, appear to foster unequal relations among the sexes.

Women in Economic Life

In all societies, active working women are respected even though the work is confined to the home and its immediate environment. Not all societies encourage women to work outside the home, to become economically independent and socially free to associate with other working men and women. In Islamic countries, women cannot work without their husband's permission. This social barrier allows them minimal participation in the workplace. However, in other developing countries

Sri Lanka for example, women compose about forty percent of the workforce. Women's participation in national economic life greatly varies and is dependent on culture and context. Regardless of the diversity of women's circumstances, all suffer from the dual burden of working inside and outside the home.

Women's participation in economic life must be analyzed in terms of access and equality. Do women have equal access to the technology and skills in a particular sector and do they receive equal treatment?[28] In the agricultural sector, in low-skill farming, women and men in Peru, Zimbabwe, and northern India appeared to share work equally. The concept of "separate but equal" was of greater relevance. However with greater modernization, men began to monopolize access to certain resources—irrigation, tools, animals, transport, *etc.* These resources have given men better access to technology. A cross-cultural comparison of marketing agricultural products shows that in Peru, men control transport in the more lucrative inter-community inter-regional markets. On the other hand, Ghanian middlewomen control the foodstuff trade in their society.

In the urban, industrial sector in some parts of the world, women dominate the low-skilled jobs. In Indonesia, the Philippines, and Malaysia, women are also increasingly displaying entrepreneurial abilities and are entering all professional fields.[29] Despite all the drawbacks, urbanization and industrialization have made women more independent economically. The gender factor is increasingly becoming less important in the ASEAN world. However, in India, the proportion of working women in the organized sector continues to decline. Though a professional elite does exist, the 25% literacy rate among women and the nature of bonded agrarian relations have contributed to the perpetuation of a female-dominated informal, highly exploited, and unskilled sector.

The degree of women's economic independence depends greatly on ethnic and class backgrounds. Both of these factors will determine whether a woman will benefit from participating in the economic life of her community.

Women's Participation in Public Life

Despite the fact that there have been a handful of female heads of state, the participation of women in public life has been minimal in most cultures. In Sri Lanka, only eighteen members of Parliament have been elected since independence, and none have actively worked for women's organizations. In Egypt, though women have the vote, only one-half of one percent actually go to the polls! Even at the local level, despite the importance of decisions to their lives, women do not actively participate in decision-making. In Peru, the local level cooperatives and community groups are dominated by men. In India, the Panchayat system continues to be nearly one-hundred percent male, even though the government has encouraged female participation.[30]

Even during the period of nationalist movements when women were active participants, their activities tended to center around social services and the needs of male members.[31] In socialist societies where women's equality is an essential aspect of revolutionary slogans, women are not active participants or decision-makers.

Research has shown us that most ethnic groups have perpetuated an ideology which inhibits women from actively participating in public life. This ideology is increasingly being challenged. However, the reticence of women to claim their positions in public life reflects patriarchal structures that have discouraged or prohibited women from organizing and exercising their political power.

Physical Violence

Physical violence directed against women is a brutal reality for women of many ethnic groups. The pre-Islamic practice of female circumcision has already been mentioned. Rape is another act of physical violence directed against women of all ethnic groups. However, women from under-privileged ethnic groups are especially vulnerable, as the studies on Indian untouchables and American ghetto women show. Wife-beating is also a common practice among most ethnic groups.

Physical violence against any individual is usually an arbitrary criminal act. However, in the case of women, certain practices have been systematized and institutionalized over time. For instance, Indian plantation landowners often feel it is their custodial right to sleep with landless women in their plantations; they would not view this act as rape.

107

Other legally-sanctioned practices (*e.g.*, circumcision and the right to chastisement) only perpetuate structures which legitimize violence against women. Though the type and degree of violence varies with each ethnic group, the inherent vulnerability of women to physical abuse is common to all.

Women's Right to Sexuality

It is often said that women are the moral guardians of a society. They are expected to protect the integrity and dignity of a family upon which all other institutions rest. As Nawal El Saadawi so rightly puts it, this morality rests on "a fine membrane called honor," the chastity of the female.

Even though the myths and symbols of a society may be sexual, women may be taught to repress their sexuality and to see it only as a vehicle for reproduction. As El Saadawi argues, female sexuality is seen as a threatening and destructive force which can tear the fabric of society. Strict laws on adultery and fornication in some societies are often accompanied by the systematic socialization of women to sublimate and repress their sexual desires.

This has not always been so. Polyandry was recognized in the pre-Islamic Arab World, and Zawag al-Muta'a (contracts for pleasure) also existed. In India, courtesans and devadasis were accorded high social respect as artisans and artists.[32]   In southern Peru, trial marriages for a period of one year were recognized and accepted. However, colonial rule and ideological developments in some societies have led to the prohibition of sexual expression outside marriage.

Many activists have argued against the bourgeois concept of marriage. Nevertheless, we must conclude that because the vast majority of women have not been socialized as men's equals, marriage laws are viewed often as protecting women. Hence, the institution of marriage becomes the only means by which a man is accountable for the children he fathers; and it provides women with a certain amount of security in terms of inheritance and maintenance rights, especially as they are rarely economically independent. Until women are socially and economically equal and independent, the destruction of the institution of marriage may, in fact, make them more vulnerable to exploitation and manipulation.

Conclusion

Women must preserve their ethnic identity while fighting for social reform and social change within their own ethnic group. They must develop among themselves a consciousness so that women's groups would not be frogs in a well but would have the capacity to unite with other women's groups from other communities to press for change and reform in the society as a whole. In fact, in an ethnically biased world, this may be the only option available for Third World women. In the past, women, especially in minority ethnic groups have failed to raise issues because they did not wish to seem disloyal and insensitive to racial discrimination directed against their men. However, a socially active consciousness from within and without will allow women to add the social reform component to their ethnic identity and enrich the social and political lives of their men. As Madhu Kishwar writes,

Our cultural traditions have tremendous potential within them to combat reactionary and anti-woman ideas; if we can identify their points of strength and use them creatively, the rejection of the harmful is easier than attempts to overthrow traditions totally or attack them arrogantly from the outside. We must realize that if we fail to acknowledge and help reinvigorate the deeply humane portions of our heritage, none of our other efforts are likely to succeed.[33]

Radhika Coomaraswamy is Associate Director of the International Center for Ethnic Studies in Colombo, Sri Lanka.

Pakistan: Muslim Women and the Law
Rashida Patel

Introduction

At the birth of Pakistan in 1947, hundreds of thousands of Muslim refugees flowed into the new country. A core of women volunteers, led by Begum Raa'na Liaquat Ali Khan, cared for the needs of these refugees. This group of women formally organized itself as the All Pakistan Women's Association (APWA). A significant amount of the APWA's work has been concerned with improving the legal and actual status of women in Pakistan. This work has involved a focus on women's education, employment, and health.

Education

The APWA initially tackled the problem of prejudice against the education of girls in Pakistan. Learning centers for girls were set up all over the country in every available space, even under trees and bridges. These educational centers grew to become schools and colleges. Upon the nationalization of educational institutions in 1973, they were taken over by the government. The APWA continues to work for the education and training of women by acting as a pressure group on the government for the allocation of equal and sufficient funds for women and by exposing discriminatory attitudes. A network of APWA training centers operates all over the country. The centers teach arts and crafts, tailoring and embroidery, food preservation, and secretarial courses as well as hygiene and nutrition. Many of the APWA branches have preschool daycare centers, and they have again organized primary school projects. A college for women and a hostel for working women have been established by the APWA Lahore Branch. The APWA has long worked to improve the education and literacy of women, and it has received the UNESCO adult literacy award for this work. The members continue to view this project as a most important task.

Employment

The number of women in the labor force has been reported as 2.1%. These figures, however, do not include the unpaid family labor of rural women. Moreover, the amount of female workers is enormously under-reported. In urban areas, a small number of women can be found in every branch of work. Women work as lawyers, judges, , bankers, doctors, nurses, paramedicals, professors, teachers, executives, administrators, architects, engineers, accountants, secretaries, clerks and industrial laborers.

Pakistan is not a signatory to the ILO convention of equal pay for equal work. The Pakistan government has legislated protection for women factory workers which prohibits overtime and night shift work for women. Women factory workers and women in the organized sector are also entitled to maternity benefits. APWA continues to actively support the expansion of rights and opportunities for Pakistani working women. At various levels, it takes up the complaints of discrimination by women workers. The APWA is working to inform rural women about appropriate technology (*e.g.*, bio-gas). At the same time, it is pressuring the government to increase training facilities for women, especially in the field of new technology. The APWA must expand its program on women's employment as the needs are vast.

Health

Women of the underprivileged classes in Pakistan suffer poor health due to numerous pregnancies, lack of healthcare facilities, and malnutrition. In its various centers, the APWA has established projects to supplement the diets of women and children by providing them with biscuits made with special nutritional substances. The APWA also runs a number of maternity and childcare programs and a mobile healthcare unit. Population planning and family welfare are among our top priorities, in view of the high rate of population growth, nearly 3%. While abortion is illegal—except to save a mother's life—no laws ban the use or dissemination of contraceptives. Nevertheless, obscurantist attitudes opposed to family planning are spread by many religious leaders. The APWA takes a positive attitude by promoting family welfare through education and its various activities and institutions.

111

Legal Status of Women

APWA's contact with the public has made it very aware of the discriminatory laws against women. Our first priority was to reform family laws. In the 1950's, we began our struggle, based on a two-pronged strategy: creating an awareness and a demand among the people for reforms, and acting as a pressure group on those in power. The Muslim Family Law Ordinance of 1961 stipulates procedures to reconcile a couple before a divorce becomes effective; restrictions on polygamy; the minimum age of marriage as 16 for women and 18 for men; and the compulsory registration of marriages. This law has been under constant attack by Muslim fundamentalists who claim it is not Islamic. The APWA opposes any move to repeal this law. Although it does not fully protect the rights and needs of the wife and family, it is a step in the right direction. In addition, the APWA continues its campaign for further reforms.

One impediment to the progress of Pakistani women is their lack of awareness concerning their rights. Apart from that problem, women are exposed to misinterpretations of Islam by their religious leaders. Muslim clerics often lead women to believe that they are inferior and have a limited role to play in society. Legal literacy among women is very low. The APWA has been attempting to rectify this situation by organizing discussions and seminars, and publishing information to educate women about the law and their rights. Recently, APWA published a translation in Urdu of my book *Women and Law in Pakistan*. It has been distributed freely to schools, colleges, libraries, welfare organizations, trade unions, and other institutions all over the country.

Another aspect of APWA's work is legal assistance. A legal aid center is operated by the APWA, Karachi Branch. In other places, legal assistance is given to women on an occasional basis. Every complaint received by APWA's headquarters is studied, and action is taken. Unfortunately, in recent years, certain segments of the fundamentalists, who do not accept the content and spirit of Islam in regard to the equality and development of women, have been preaching against the equal status of women and their participation as workers. The APWA has been constantly countering these attacks with the support of several thousands of forward-looking men and women.

Laws Challenged as un-Islamic

The Offense of Zina (Enforcement of Hadd) Ordinance 1979, which for the first time made adultery and fornication a crime in Pakistan, has been challenged as un-Islamic. A petition has been filed before the Federal Shariat Court that certain sections of the law contradict the injunctions of Islam and must be struck down. The petition contends that according to the *Holy Koran* and *Sunnah of the Holy Prophet*, *zina* (adultery and fornication) can only be punished if proved by the evidence of four adults, who have witnessed the actual penetration. The law makes *zina* punishable even if such evidence is not available, and hence, it is un-Islamic. The exclusion of a woman's testimony in the enforcement of this law is also being challenged before the Federal Shariat Court. The challengers contend that there is no justification under Islam to exclude the evidence of women since no such discrimination in the *Koran* or the *Sunnah* exists.

Two proposed laws, the Qisas (retaliation) and Diyat (compensation) Ordinance and the Qanoon-e-Shahadat (Law of Evidence) were strongly opposed by the APWA and other women's organizations because they contained sections discriminatory against women. So far, the proposed Qisas and Diyat Ordinance has not been made law due mainly to the consistent opposition by women. The Qanoon-e-Shahadat Ordinance was promulgated in 1984. The proposed discriminatory sections, however, have been considerably modified as a result of the protests by women.

Women Judges

The All Pakistan Women's Association and the Pakistan Women Lawyer's Association opposed a petition before the Federal Shariat Court challenging the right of women to be judges in an Islamic state. At the outset of this case, the court stated, "what is not prohibited by the Holy Koran and Sunnah is permitted, and the burden of proof about anything being prohibited is on the person who claims it to be so...." The Court held, "the imposition of conditions on an appointment of a woman Qazi [judge]." The court, referring to Universal

Declaration of Human Rights published by the Islamic Foundation in London observed:

...it gives a list of human rights recognized by Islam. The third right, which deals with equality before law, entitlement of equal opportunities, and protection of the law also provides, firstly, that all persons shall be entitled to equal wage for equal work and, secondly, that no person shall be denied the opportunity to work or be discriminated against in any manner or exposed to greater physical risk by reason of religious beliefs, color, race origin, sex or language. This view supports our position.[1]

In an enlightened judgement, the Federal Shariat Court held that the Holy Koran approves of equality between men and women. The court also observed that Islam places men and women on the same footing in marriage, in economic independence, property rights, and legal processes.

In retrospect, the time and effort spent on this case was well spent for the women of Pakistan. At present, the conjunction of law and development is receiving a lower priority by many. But if the decision had disallowed women judges, the advancement of women would have suffered a setback. While there is a great deal of criticism of paper laws, Third World countries still need them to help women achieve a modicum of rights and opportunities.

To improve women's position in Pakistan, it is essential that the true spirit and intent of Islam are accepted. As the world has changed since the founding of Islam, it must be reinterpreted and reapplied to fit present day conditions. The progress of humanity, the innovations of science and technology, and the demands and needs of present day life have to be considered. Members of the APWA and all forward-looking Muslim men and women in Pakistan and the rest of the world are working for the rediscovery of the intrinsic purity and justice of Islamic law. We seek to distinguish a pure Islam from historical traditions and customs that have been added to it. Customs and the misinterpretation of Islam have prevented some Muslims, particularly women, from obtaining its full benefits. Therefore, we are working towards eliminating the influence of local customs and traditions on Islam which impedes the emergence of the true values of Islam, namely, justice and equality for men and women.

Elections have been recently held in Pakistan. A majority of men and women in the assemblies take a positive modern approach to Islam and women. Most of the orthodox elements have been defeated; not more than five to ten percent of the legislators propound orthodox Islam. We are looking to the legislators, especially the women members, to stand up for women's rights and against the suppression of and discrimination against women.

The work described above is not a comprehensive account of the APWA's efforts. Much more is being done, even in the remote corners of Pakistan. Thousands of women volunteers work at the APWA's local, district and provincial branches, and at its national headquarters. The APWA also employs professionals. We salute Begum Raa'na Liaquat Ali Khan, whose consistent work and concern for the APWA and for the women of Pakistan has made it possible for the women volunteers and professionals to struggle for women's progress in Pakistan. Because of the APWA's many committed volunteers, our work will be moving forward continuously. At times, we become despondent about the conditions of life around us. At other times—such as at this conference—we are filled with enthusiasm and expectation that the women of the world, including the women of Pakistan, will progress onward to their rightful place in society.

Rashida Patel is Vice-President of the All Pakistan Women's Association and an advocate of the High Courts and Supreme Court of Pakistan.

Botswana: Women and Customary Law
Athaliah Molokomme

Introduction

This paper looks at the relations and contradictions of the law regarding the state, custom, and customary law and their impact on the status of women. This subject, which is rooted in cultural and political history, is particularly complex. An examination of customary law is made difficult by its very nature as it is not always uniform, often varying from tribe to tribe in a country as ethnically diverse as Botswana (and indeed, many African countries). Finally, the term *customary law* is itself not precise and is often used carelessly to refer to different things, specific to varying historical contexts.

The term *customary law* must be used carefully, but many writers, lawyers, sociologists, and politicians have not always been precise. The way it has been used and understood has tended to result in over-simplification, or worse, total misunderstanding. Western anthropologists have frequently sought European equivalents in African law. When they did not find them, some have concluded that these societies have no law. Rather, they operated in accordance with customs, habits, and usages which were generally accepted by members of their communities. As a result, the oral and traditional modes of behavior were grouped and labeled customary law, or as the British colonialists would have it, *native law and custom*. Customary law, therefore, simply referred to apparent legal forms which existed before colonial intervention (and later modified by colonial regulations). This approach has numerous weaknesses which will not be exhaustively treated here. Suffice it to say, however, that it is based on little understanding of the cultures of these societies; also it ignores the changing historical contexts within which various events were taking place. In sum, adherents of this approach have viewed customary law simply as indigenous African law handed down from generation to generation.

Recent studies of African law have been more sensitive to its complexity and tried to place it in historical perspective.[1]

Historical analysis of customary law is imperative to understand its origins and relationships with the social, political, and economic forces in African societies. W.M. Reisman's suggestion that customary law has had three shifting meanings is particularly useful. The first refers to norms, patterns of behavior, expectations, and other processes that obtained in pre-colonial Africa.[2] According to Reisman, this normative system was based on its own features: a traditional technology of production and distribution; a certain population level; fixed patterns of consumption and demand; and a variety of other contextual features of pre-colonial Africa. A second meaning refers to the legal forms which were permitted to continue, often in diluted versions, by the colonial powers. "This transformed customary law can be viewed as much of a colonial European artifact as an authentic African customary law."[3] The third sense in which the term is used encompasses the "ongoing generation of norms about appropriate behavior."[4] Reisman explains that these norms are derived more from social interaction than from formal, explicit legislative action and that often people are quite unaware but deeply conscious of these norms. He concludes by warning that we must distinguish among these three meanings to ensure clarity to our audiences.

The Evolution of Customary Law in Botswana

Professor Reisman's warning is particularly apt in the case of Botswana's customary law. The country known as Botswana is a configuration of areas inhabited by different tribes which existed prior to the colonial period. In general, these tribes were composed of people of the same stock, and they had a broadly similar social structure and normative system. What little is known about the organization of these pre-colonial chiefdoms is found in recorded oral histories. Anthropological writings, which were written during the colonial period after some changes had already occurred, also reveal information about these tribal structures. As with most pre-colonial African societies, no clear distinction was made between social and legal norms; the normative system was very closely related to the culture. The legal position of women was, therefore, dependent upon and synonymous with the role and status accorded to them in the society. By the time the territory was made a protectorate—known as Bechuanaland—in 1885, some aspects of Tswana life had already changed due to contact with European society. Nevertheless, the basic traditional pattern of social organization persisted. The society was organized into hierarchical units and groups, ranging from the family and household at the bottom to the family group, the kingroup, the ward, and the section, all of which composed the village. At the apex of each unit was a male head who was responsible for all its members and also to the head of the next higher unit, continuing up to the chief. Based as it was on kinship units, emphasis was placed on the groups rather than the individual. The position of women, as part of the group, was clearly defined.

The colonial period introduced new social norms and values, just as Christianity had previously done. Although some people were converted to Christianity and others were British-educated, the majority of people in the protectorate continued to live according to their traditional norms and values. The British colonial administration did not interfere in this system, except to relieve traditional leaders of their authority to deal with serious matters (*e.g.,* political offenses or serious felonies). However, the colonial administration introduced a new system of law, the Roman-Dutch law. Although originally applied to Europeans only, the new legal regime was eventually made available to Africans. Even so, the majority continued to abide by traditional norms. Thus, the colonial period did not substantively change the indigenous normative system, although the society was not static and unresponsive to the social, economic, and political changes that were taking place in the protectorate. Hence the traditional structures were not significantly altered, particularly the gender relations which prevailed within the society at large. The dual legal system simply provided options for Africans in their personal law, but most remained within the domain of their own system, which was labeled *native law and custom.*

At independence in 1966, this traditional normative system was retained as *customary law*. It continued to coexist with the Roman-Dutch law, now called common law, which includes the Acts of the Botswana Parliament and other law that is not customary law. As was the case during the colonial period, customary law remains unrecorded and must be determined in the courts of general jurisdiction. Contemporary courts use the writings of anthropologists who recorded the customary law during the colonial period, mainly the Handbook of Tswana Law and Custom, compiled by Professor Isaac Schapera.[5] This book, written in 1937 at the request of the British colonial administration, is based on research done from 1929 and is regarded as the most authoritative work on Tswana customary law. Later writings on the subject and statements by experts on customary law supplement this book. Therefore, when one speaks of customary law in Botswana today, it is understood in all three senses explained by Professor Reisman; it encompasses the traditional norms which continued to be permitted by the colonial period as well as the changes that took place until the present. However, a uniform system of customary law does not exist because of the varying pace of change among the different tribes and districts. Nevertheless, we will look at the position of women under customary law, taking into consideration varying time period and changes.

The Public Status of Women Under Tswana Customary Law

Traditionally, women played no leadership role in politics and government. Leadership was a male preserve even though there were two instances of regency (in the Ngwaketse and Tswana tribes) during the colonial period. The *kgotla*, the central political council which decided public issues and adjudicated disputes, was closed to women unless they were witnesses or litigants in a dispute. Each of the previously mentioned social units was headed by a male. Status was based on gender and age and strict regulations ensured the perpetuation of the system.

The public role of women did not change during the colonial period. As the colonial legal regime discriminated against Africans, the position of women worsened. Colonial educational and employment opportunities were given primarily to men, and even where women were employed in the same jobs as men, they received less pay and no maternity benefits. During the preparations for independence, no women technically women could vote and stand in the election prior to independence.

The period after independence saw little improvement in the public role of women as far as senior posts and leadership positions were concerned. Although either sex is legally qualified to be appointed to these positions, they are dominated by men. One notable exception is the chieftanship which is still determined by tradition. However, the state president has the right to appoint any fit and proper person to a tribal position. Custom and culture only partially explain the absence of female leaders because similar situations exist elsewhere.[6] As has been argued elsewhere, while tradition and culture have excluded women from certain things, other aspects of the culture have been conveniently discarded "to respond to social, economic, and social change."[7]

Women's Position in the Family

It is generally agreed that the structure of the family and its relations with other institutions largely determine the role and status of women. The organization of the family in most societies is established by a sexual division of labor. Traditional Tswana society allocated domestic tasks (*e.g.*, rearing children, cooking, and caring for the family) to women. Men were given public (*e.g.*, decision-making) and family support (*e.g.*, hunting) roles. Although there appears to have been an overlapping responsibility for the tilling of fields, in general, the division of labor between the sexes was strictly observed. This division of labor generally continues to the present day. It affects education and employment throughout the society. However, the status of women under traditional and contemporary customary law is often determined by marital status.

Single Women

An unmarried woman in traditional Tswana society remained under the guardianship of her father or other male family member irrespective of her age. Only the guardian could execute legally-binding transactions on her behalf. If she were raped, it was her guardian who could take legal action against the perpetrator. Moreover, a child born out of this situation would fall under her guardian's control and care. However, a woman past marriageable age acquired a significant amount of independence and was permitted some privacy and property.

Daughters were not permitted to inherit male property (*e.g.*, cattle, wagons, guns, etc.), nor did they qualify to become principal heirs, unless their father had absolutely no male relative. This practice was justified by the desire to retain wealth within the family. Because daughters would marry into another family, property would be dispersed if women were permitted to inherit the bulk of the family estate. The *tshwaiso*—a custom by which a father would earmark specific animals to be given to his children (including daughters) upon his death—somewhat mitigated the inheritance customs that discriminated against females.

Today, changes in inheritance laws are occurring at an uneven pace, and much is left to the discretion of the customary courts and family heads. Without any standards, the rights of single women in inheritance matters are at best uncertain. They are dependent upon the generosity of their fathers, and failing that, on formal courts.

Married Women

The perpetuation of marriage is made a high priority in customary law. A distinct feature of the marriage law is that it entrenches and legitimizes patriarchy by giving the husband the sole rights of decision-making and control over the wife, children, and property. Because of the emphasis in traditional African society on the kinship group, it is incorrect to view the social status of women in terms of their individual rights. Furthermore, a wife has traditionally commanded significant respect and power within the family domain. Having stated these caveats, we will proceed to analyze the legal aspects of current customary marriage that adversely affect the status of women.

The potentially polygamous nature of customary marriage has adverse implications for women. Although it has been argued that polygamy sometimes provides an economic resource for women, it is obvious that only reasonably wealthy men today can provide adequately for more than one wife and family. A polygamous husband who has few resources often inflicts economic hardship on his wives and families. In addition, a wife has little say in her husband's decision to take another wife, despite its impact on her family.

Secondly, the institution of *bogadi*, the bride price, has affected women's status within marriage. The most important function of *bogadi* is the transference of the reproductive power of the woman from her family to that of her husband. An important consequence of *bogadi* is its conferral to the husband of power and control over the wife, which he otherwise would not have. For example, as a rule, a man who has not paid *bogadi* cannot chastise his wife; this privilege is given to men who have paid *bogadi*. At the same time, a woman married with *bogadi* is held in much higher social esteem than the woman without it.

Thirdly, the customary law limits the rights of married women regarding their legal standing (*locus standi in judicio*). Upon marriage, the husband becomes the legal guardian of his wife. Hence, the husband is the ultimate decision-maker in all aspects of family life, and the wife must obey him. The only relief available to a wife against an abusive husband is to appeal to the two families. If that fails, she may sue him for divorce, but this action is usually not to her advantage. Any infidelity on the wife's part is not tolerated, whereas her husband may have a concubine without any social or legal sanction.

Similarly, the wife's property rights are dependent upon her husband. Although she may independently acquire property and engage in commerce, she must receive the consent of her husband. Her personal property is legally kept separate, but the husband administers this property. In the household, the husband controls the cattle, fields, huts, and other family property which is not owned by the wife personally. There is no equivalent of the Roman-Dutch matrimonial property regimes of *community of property* and *out of community of property*. Therefore, the wife's right to family property depends on the attitudes of her husband and his family. However, the family is no longer a safeguard to the neglected wife, particularly in view of the disintegration of the extended family and the trend towards individualism.

Fourthly, the legal status of married women can be adversely affected by divorce laws. Both the husband and wife in a customary marriage traditionally have possessed the right to sue for divorce, although attempts to reconcile the couple by the family were required before the couple could bring the matter to court. Recognized grounds for divorce have included excessive cruelty and financial abandonment of the family by the husband; other grounds are barrenness as well as sorcery, repeated adultery, and non-performance of domestic duties by the wife. Since a man's infidelity is generally tolerated by society and polygamy is a recognized institution, the husband occupies a far better position. He is able to take a concubine or another wife if he tires of a current wife. Moreover, a woman has more to lose in a divorce than a man due to myriad legal and social consequences.

Upon divorce, women traditionally have lost all claims to the children unless the husband has not paid the *bogadi*. Today the courts often decide the custody of the children on the factors of the guilty party in the divorce and the age and sex of the children. Furthermore, wives tend to lose more than half of the property when their marriages are dissolved. Normally, a woman will retain her personal property and household goods, while the husband keeps the home and cattle. Another consequence is the stigma attached to a divorced woman which makes remarriage unlikely.

The fourth and final aspect of customary marriage laws that adversely affect women is the dependent position of the widow. The death of a husband does not terminate a woman's relationship with her in-laws; frequently, she must remain at his family's home under the guardianship of his heir. Today, most young widows return to their own families, but they must leave both the children and the family property behind. In Tswana customary law, therefore, a widow can only inherit her late husband's estate if she remains with his family.

Conclusions and Recommended Strategies

This paper has outlined the legal status of women under Tswana customary law and has sought to place it within the various contexts in which it arose and continues to exist. We have argued that customary law, which obtained during the pre-colonial period, was related to conditions prevailing at that time, but which no longer exist today. Nor is customary law accommodating the rapid changes occurring in Botswana. Women, who in traditional society have been dependent upon the family and other institutions for material and emotional support, have been the major losers in society. The improvement of these circumstances requires state intervention, non-governmental assistance, and women's awareness and efforts. The law can also be used as an important tool to improve women's economic and social position. Many who argue that an increase in women's legal rights does not necessarily ameliorate their material situation ignore certain aspects of the legal system. Through legislation, the state can effectively allocate resources among men, women, and institutions; it can decide who gets what, how, and when. Once law is viewed in this manner, it is clear that the legal system makes an impact on an individual's material conditions. Some practical strategies to empower women to make the law relevant and beneficial to their lives are suggested below.

First and foremost, an essential strategy to improve women's status is the organization and participation of women from all strata of society, particularly the lower and middle classes. Any struggle against oppression can succeed only if there exists mass organization and active participation of those affected. Women's organizations have often failed to serve the interests of the masses because of their mono-polization by a few women from the elite. This tendency has resulted in the alienation of women from the grassroots. Therefore, to improve the situation of the majority of women, ordinary women must be involved in organizing, designing, and running programs for themselves. Educated and skilled women have the duty to teach other women so that all can participate in addressing various issues that face them.

A second strategy focuses on information and education about pressing issues. In our case, this strategy centers on teaching women about legal issues and principles that affect them. Thus, it would be a process of demystification of the law and its relationship to social, political, and economic structures in society. The use of posters, pamphlets, handbooks, radio programs and other media will show women how legal policy is formulated, as well as teach them how to influence the process. In the specific context of Botswana, the handbook *The Women's Guide to the Law*, written in English and Setswana for the Women's Affairs Unit, will be used. The Women's Affairs Unit has so far distributed this book among social welfare educators, social workers, women's organizations, and other relevant institutions so that they may disseminate the information to a wide audience of women. Radio programs, which wlll discuss women's legal problems and the law in general, are also underway.

A third strategy is assisting needy women with legal and support services. At present, no system of legal aid exists except for persons charged with murder; they are financially assisted by the state in the preparation of their defense. However, social welfare legislation, such as the Deserted Wives and Children's Protection Act and the Affiliation Proceedings Act, permits women to secure financial support from their husbands without incurring normal court charges. This legislation could be expanded by providing a system of paralegals to handle these matters at little or no expense to women. Women who have been raped, deserted, or abused should also be assisted by the proposed system. Modifying the legal system to respond better to women's needs also includes training of more legal workers and enforcing the magistrates' judgements in women's cases.

Finally, a campaign must be launched to make the general public, and men in particular, aware of the burdens of women, especially in the family. Perhaps an awareness and an appreciation of the vital role of women in society will improve the attitudes of the policy-makers, legislators, administrators, and the public about women's legal and social status. It is, no doubt, a challenging task, as attitudes are most difficult to transform. Nevertheless, it is a necessary prerequisite for the success of other strategies to improve the lot of women.

Athaliah Molokomme teaches law at the University of Botswana and is an attorney in the High Court of Botswana.

Lesotho: Women, Marriage, and the Law
Mothokoa P. Mamashela

Introduction

Lesotho, like all former British colonies, inherited the legacy of an imposed foreign legal system. Roman-Dutch law and customary law operate simultaneously in Lesotho. This study focuses on the inequities in both legal systems regarding women, particularly married women. It examines the legal status of women in relation to personal laws, *i.e.*, the effect of marriage on women's legal status in the areas of property rights, inheritance, and custody and child support.

From time immemorial, women have been relegated to an inferior position to men. This discrimination and unequal treatment of both sexes is discernible in both industrial and traditional societies. Unconvincing theories aimed at explaining and justifying this unequal treatment between the sexes have been expounded. They range from sheer frailty of the female sex to division of labor between the sexes.

The Lesotho Marriage Act No. 10 of 1974 provides for recognition of two types of marriages, namely, a civil Christian marriage and a customary law marriage. This paper addresses the personal and proprietal consequences of both types of marriages by focusing on the marital power exercised by a husband over his wife's person and property. It highlights specific areas where a married woman's position is adversely affected by marital power.

This paper will point out that with more than fifty percent of the young men away from home for a good part of the year, they are not physically present to exercise the martial power. On the contrary, it is the married woman who heads the household during her husband's abscence. It is therefore absurd that a *de facto* head of household, who not only manages the daily household chores, but also at times makes important decisions in connection with children, fields, and cattle should be accorded the status of a minor.

Marriages under Roman-Dutch Law

A civil Christian marriage is under community property unless the parties have entered into a prenuptial contract. Both spouses jointly own all property brought into and acquired after the marriage. In theory, they have equal shares in the property. But in reality, this ideal is never realized because of the unequal legal status of the woman. Hence, the wife rarely obtains an equal share of the estate.

Along with the community property regime exists the husband's authority over his wife's person and property by virtue of marriage. This is called the marital power. Upon marriage, a woman becomes a minor, and her husband becomes her legal guardian. The guardianship of the husband over the wife's property confers on him the exclusive right of managing all property belonging to the joint estate. He is also entitled to administer the wife's personal property even though a prenuptial agreement may have excluded community property rights. This situation can only be avoided if the contract excludes the marital power and reserves to the woman the right to manage her own affairs.

By virtue of the marital power, the husband is entitled to alienate, pledge, or mortgage the wife's movable or immovable property without her consent. Even though it may prejudice the interests of the wife, he may disburse property or payments—provided that it is not deliberately done to defraud the wife or her heirs. The wife may, however, take steps to protect herself by applying to the court either for separation of goods, *separatio bonorum*, or for a restraining order barring the husband from distributing her property.

As the husband is the sole administrator of the joint estate, an unsuspecting wife frequently is unaware of the threats to her half-share due to the husband's maladministration. Even if she suspects mismanagement, it is very difficult to prove deliberate fraud. Furthermore, a restraining order can only be obtained when a wife is instituting separation or divorce proceedings, and only if she has reasonable grounds to fear that her husband may dispose of her property or her share of the joint estate in the anticipation of a granted divorce or separation. (*Rambooa v Rambooa*, 1967-1970, LR90.)

These remedies are too late to help the wife secure her part of the estate. Moreover, a wife is equally liable for all debts contracted by her husband, even without her knowledge during the marriage or even after his death. As in the case of minors, the wife has no judicial status or *locus standi in judicio*. She cannot appear in court without the sanction and assistance of her husband; she can sue or be sued only through him. A married woman has no right to dispose of either her own property or property belonging to the joint estate. She cannot enter into any contract without the express or implied consent of her husband. If she does make a contract without such consent, the contract is null and void. However, if the couple benefits from the said contract, it is binding upon both of them. She can validly incur debts in matters connected with household necessities. If the husband willfully withholds his consent or if it is impossible to obtain the husband's consent, the court will sometimes permit the wife to enter into contracts or to deal with the common property without the husband's consent.

There are two exceptions to these regulations that restrict the wife from appearing in court or making a contract without the husband's consent. In the first case, the wife has reserved to herself the management and control of her separate property by a prenuptial contract. In the second, she is engaged in business with the express or implied consent of her husband. Under such circumstances, she may sue and be sued and enter into contracts with regard to all matters pertaining to her business.

Under this system, therefore, the legal status of a married woman is reduced to that of a minor. Moreover, the so-called partnership begins only at the dissolution of the marriage, either by death or divorce. Not only is the wife an inferior partner in the marriage partnership, she is also a very powerless one.

Marriage Governed by Customary Law

A married woman's situation is virtually the same under customary law as under Roman-Dutch law. In strict legal theory, a woman never attains majority under customary law. She is a minor under her father's guardianship until she gets married. Upon marriage, her husband assumes guardianship over her. If her husband dies before her, her father-in-law becomes her guardian. Where a marriage is terminated by divorce, she reverts back to her father's guardianship if he is still alive. If her natural father is dead, a family heir assumes responsibility for her.

The concept of an emancipated spinster exists under customary law. It refers to a woman who has remained at home without getting married until she has "gone past the age of marrying" under customary law. It is not easy to define that age with any precision. Suffice it to say, by custom, young girls get married at puberty. Thus, a thirty-year old woman likely would have "passed marriage age" according to customary law.

One main difference between Roman-Dutch and customary law is that under the latter system a husband is always expected to act in consultation with his wife in the administration of the joint estate. He is not allowed to alienate family property without obtaining the wife's opinion on the matter. She is entitled to challenge any major transaction involving the joint estate if it were undertaken without her knowledge. To challenge such transactions, she may call a family meeting to solve the matter amicably, or as a last resort, she may institute court proceedings.

Although women married under customary law have these rights, most are unaware of them. Those who do know their rights may encounter numerous obstacles in enforcing them. For example, the convening of a family meeting depends upon the wife's relationship with her in-laws and her own parents. Without a cordial relationship, her efforts will meet difficulties. However, if she proceeds to court, the wife may be refused a hearing because she is a minor under the law and, thereby, has no *locus standi in judicio*.

Women's Responses to the Migration of Male Workers: A Report on Field Research

A remarkable feature of Lesotho society is the very old and widespread phenomenon of temporary migration of the Basotho males to obtain work in South Africa. Statistics show that as many as 50-60% of the adult male population is affected. The most obvious implication of this migration is that female-headed households are on the increase. A married woman is a *de facto* administrator of the joint estate during the husband's absence. When a husband abandons his family for a lengthy period or for good, the wife is left to fend for her family. To make ends meet, she must seek employment. However, she is legally a minor and cannot enter into any valid binding agreements without her husband's consent.

To document how abandoned married women circumvent these well-defined laws, we are conducting a study. Our investigation, which is still underway, has resulted in fieldwork being undertaken in rural areas of the four out of ten districts in Lesotho. It also seeks to find out which strategies women have adopted to bypass the legal barriers and the results if the strategies fail. We are also attempting to determine if an informal system has evolved over time that allows a married woman to enter alone into legally binding agreements. If a system has developed, we will investigate its rules and how it interacts with the formal legal system. Finally, we will examine if the women's strategies could be utilized to reform the present laws.

The picture that emerges from the data collected so far is inconclusive. It appears that three main categories of practice occur. At one end of the scale exists a very liberal practice whereby a husband gives his wife an unlimited mandate to do whatever needs to be done during his absence. She will account for her decisions when he returns (if he comes home frequently) or by letter. It should be pointed out that even with this blanket mandate, there are some transactions which her local chief would not allow her to do on her own (*e.g.*, the granting of *bewys*, animal identity cards, or selling a cow.)

Another practice has developed whereby a couple discusses and decides together on major family matters that will need to be done. The wife is charged with the duty of execution during her husband's absence. At the other end of the scale is the wife who must write to her husband for instructions or permission to enter into any transaction.

The last practice is obviously the most cumbersome and time-consuming. It impedes the wife's ability to make independent, judicious, and timely decisions. The first two practices are more practical in that they allow the wife some maneuverability during her husband's absence. But, they do not in any way eliminate the wife's legal disadvantages. Because married women in Lesotho are *de facto* administrators of their estates, the law must recognize the recent and irreversible phenomenon of mass migration of the Basotho men to South Africa.

Analysis of Alternative Arrangements

While some argue for the adoption in Lesotho of the English system of total separation of the estates to enhance the status of married women, there are problems associated with such a system. In real life, the wife usually spends the first few years of her married life unemployed due to family responsibilities. Undoubtedly, her estate would suffer during these early years, while that of the husband would flourish. Another reality is the usual *de facto* merger of the two estates during marriage with the husband as the administrator. Moreover, the failure to recognize the non-working woman's contribution to the household creates a mere semblance of equality in most marriages. This point was vividly made by the late Mr. Justice Toom Van Den Heever in *Edelstein v. Edelstein:*

The basis of community is the Frankish notion of *collaboratio*; in other words, whatever spouses acquire during the marriage, they do so by reason of their combined but specialized efforts. The deceased could not successfully have conducted his bag and bottle business if his wife had not cooked the dinner and minded the children.

In a system of separation, the family savings are usually placed in the husband's name; where freedom of testation rules (as is the case in Lesotho), the wife may be left penniless upon divorce or the death of her husband.

Another alternative would be for Lesotho to adopt a deferred partial community property regime. During the marriage, each spouse owns and administers his or her own separate estate, thus allowing independence and freedom of action. But a deferred community property system is not simple; it consists of, "fairly complex calculations. Also, presumptions concerning the initial and final values of the two estates are necessary, and inflation gives rise to the problem of illusory accruals."

The need to protect the eventual claims on the estate leads to restrictions on each spouse's freedom of action during marriage; the results are not dissimilar to those produced by the traditional community system. Because of the anomalous situation whereby about 60% of married women are for long periods of time *de facto* heads of their households—a reality the law does not recognize—we recommend that the husband's marital power be abolished. Then, a married woman's legal status would be equal to that of her husband. The abolition of the marital power would permit the wife to help administer the estate. Thus, as an equal partner, she would be consulted about major financial decisions, and she would have the right to challenge her husband if he did not ask for her advice. Furthermore, she could enter into contracts without fearing that her actions would be declared void.

Women and the Right of Inheritance

Under common law, when a marriage is dissolved either by divorce or death of the husband, the wife is entitled to half the estate. The children, if any, share among themselves the remaining half of the joint estate. The advantage of the universal community regime is that the widow is assured of her half of the estate. The husband cannot divest her of it even by his will. But in practice, the wife's position is precarious. Since the husband is the sole administrator of the joint estate during his lifetime, he could easily dispose of a large portion of the estate without consulting his wife. As a result, her actual share of the joint estate would consist of less than her rightful entitlement.

The Administration of Estates Proclamation No. 19 of 1935 introduced an English-style system of executorship into Lesotho. Section 3(b) provides that the proclamation shall not apply to the estates of Africans which will continue to be administered according to customary law provided that:

such law and custom shall not apply to the estates of Africans who have been shown to the satisfaction of the Master (of the High Court) to have abandoned tribal custom and adopted a European mode of life and who, if married, have married under European law.

The Intestate Succession Proclamation No. 12 of 1953 was introduced to supplement common law by conferring rights of inheritance upon a surviving spouse when the deceased fails to leave a will. It provides that over and above his/her half-share of the joint estate, he/she is also entitled to some share of the children's estate. If the deceased leaves no children, parents, or siblings, the surviving spouse would be entitled to the entire estate. However, very few widows have been able to take advantage of this provision because it only operates in specific circumstances where the Administration of Estates Proclamation applies.

Under customary law, where a marriage is dissolved by death, the widow falls under her eldest son's guardianship; if there is no son, she becomes the ward of her deceased husband's brothers. Previously, the son or her brothers-in-law administered the estate and provided for the welfare of the widow. In the recent past, however, a widow is allowed to administer her late husband's estate (*Mokhethi v. Mokhethi* and *Mohapi v. Mohapi*).

Customary law protects the rights of an heir. According to section 14(1) of the Laws of Lerotholi, any person may dispose of his property by means of written instructions. Such instructions, however, are only valid if they do not deprive the heir of the greater part of the estate. This provision tends to safeguard the rights of the customary heir.

Our study shows that the attitude of married women has changed toward matters of inheritance. They feel that the present law is long overdue for reform. They believe that legally they should be entitled to part of the joint estate which they have helped sustain for their lifetimes. They also challenge the customary laws of inheritance which support the principle of primogeniture. Their position is based on the equality of their children in the rights of inheritance.

Conclusion

Because of the numerous similarities between Roman-Dutch law and customary law in the field of family law, we recommend that the concept of universal community property with all its present tenets (with the notable exception of marital power) be introduced. It would not only enhance the status of a widow, it would also ensure equitable distribution of property among all the deceased's children.

The universal community property system reflects the realities of the average household where incomes of both spouses are pooled with little thought being given to the ownership of the acquired assets. It provides both spouses an equal share in the household's wealth, which frequently consists of no more than the matrimonial home (in most cases, rented), a car, cattle, horses, and sheep. The disadvantages of a universal property community regime are the following: a poor spouse can become rich overnight by marrying someone rich; joint debt liability exposes any contribution by one spouse to the claims of the other spouse's creditors; and without the exclusion of the marital power, the status of the wife is reduced to that of a minor.

On the other hand, the advantages of the system outweigh the disadvantages. Specifically, it is not unfair that the assets of a household pay the debts it has incurred. And the objection to the marital power of the husband can be overcome by abolishing it: marital power is not essential to the universal community regime.

With regard to inheritance, the universal community property regime is advantageous to the widow because she is assured of at least her half of the joint estate. Where there are no children to inherit the other half, she would be entitled to the whole estate. We would, therefore, recommend that the right to sharing in the estate should be extended to a customary law wife, who is sometimes left destitute when divorced by her husband.

Mothokoa P. Mamashela is a member of the Faculty of Law at the National University of Lesotho.

Sudan: Custom and Customary Laws
Asma A. El Dareer

Introduction to Sudanese Society

Sudan is a vast country which covers an area of approximately one million square miles and has a population of about twenty-two million. It lies in the northeast corner of Africa and is bordered by eight countries. Ethnographically, Sudan can be divided into two main areas. A mixture of indigenous peoples and immigrant Arabs live in the north; this region is predominantly Muslim. The southern region contains many different African tribes; while both Muslims and Christians live in the south, the majority of the population follow their own tribal rituals. The common language of the vast majority is Arabic, although there are a large number of dialects.

The Role of Custom

When we speak of custom in the Sudanese culture, we mean the traditional problem-solving procedures or local responses which have existed for a long period of time. If these local responses were perceived to be successful, they have become acceptable, familiar, and habitual.

When customs, habitual practices, or social behavior patterns continue over a long period of time in a particular community, they become so established that they have the force of law. They become customary law. In Sudan, customary law dominates the private and public lives of women far more than it does those of men.

This may explain the exclusion of women from the decision-making process in both the political and social realms. In Sudanese society, people pay tremendous attention to social norms. Therefore, although women enjoy equal rights and freedoms according to the law, certain practices are observed which completely ignore women's legal rights.

Women, the Family, and Social Change

The family is fundamentally important to Sudanese society. The origin of the family is deeply rooted in the religion, culture, and heritage of that society. Within this concept of the family, the woman has the specific functions of procreation and socialization. In addition, she is the emotional anchor of her husband and children. Sudanese women are socialized to assume this role and accept these family responsibilities.

At present, Sudanese women live in a changing society. Certain aspects of this change affect women profoundly. Economic development, the expansion of technology, the rising cost of living, and changing social institutions influence women's lives. Increasingly, some women need to be relieved of time-consuming domestic activities in order to support their families financially, or to participate more fully in social and community life. Other aspects of this changing society can be felt in the areas of religion, law, education, tradition, and values. As a consequence, many varied forces are influencing change of the women's role in the family.

Emancipation of Women and the Challenges It Offers

Social change is said to be a force for the emancipation of women. In Sudan, women have achieved some of their legal and human rights through their own struggle and through new revolutionary legislation. Women have had to fight their exclusion from the political decision-making process and from the economic marketplace. Moreover, they have had to fight against overprotection by men which, in most cases, is not beneficial to women. Their achievements raise problems and require social adjustment to the new situation. A new value system must be strong enough to withstand challenges and obstacles that are promoted by traditional customary law.

These challenges are not universal. They differ from culture to culture. However, the variations are always in quantity rather than in quality. The challenges can be characterized in terms of the obstacles which threaten the progress and development of women.

Some of the Obstacles Faced

A major obstacle to women's progress is the attitude and belief of men who are not prepared to accept women into their world. These men fear that an acceptance of women would cause a serious breach in the male-female relationship. Some conservatives maintain that women should remain in the home because they believe that women are intellectually inferior. Others support the tradition of segregation based on religious grounds. They argue that women should not be allowed out of a sheltered existence because they are too fragile to cope with a mixed and complex society.

Another barrier consists of women—some of whom are educated—who fear the loss of security and protection if the traditional role of women is altered. Hence, they support the domination of customary law even though it suppresses their freedom. Problems are also caused by physical, climatic, and social factors which limit the equal application of the law to women. For example, the position of women in higher social classes in urban areas is totally different from that of poor or rural women. Therefore, the obstacles they face differ.

Legislation passed in the interest of women is successful in some areas, but ineffective in others. Family and personal law sometimes favors women, but it is frequently underutilized. Women are either unaware of the provisions, or they are unwilling to go to court. The attitude of men towards the *nafaga*, alimony and child support, illustrates this problem. Frequently, divorced men abandon all of their responsibilities towards their children. They disregard the law that clearly states that a former husband is solely responsible for all family expenses such as lodging, education, medical treatment, *etc.* While divorced men are legally required to allocate between one quarter and one half of their earnings for family support, many evade the law by not declaring their actual income. Other men argue in court that since the former wife is working, she can take full financial responsibility for the care of the children.

Marriage relationships, which tend to be governed by customary law and social practice, present another obstacle for women. Dissolving a marriage is the man's prerogative according to Islamic law. Although under Sudanese law a woman may also obtain a divorce, this right is restricted to specific circumstances and must be exercised through the court.

Frequently, women find themselves having to assume all responsibilities for raising and supporting their children. Islamic law clearly states that child rearing is the mother's responsibility, and supporting the family financially is the father's. Custom and tradition, however, discourage her from seeking her rights. Consequently, because men feel little or no obligation of support after divorce, they do not regard the matter seriously.

The law and custom towards adultery also favors the male. While the law views both parties culpable in adultery, society treats such behavior as acceptable and normal for men. For women, however, adultery is regarded as a most serious and shameful crime. In an adultery case, the public opinion supports a man who asks for a divorce under customary law on the grounds of his wife's unfaithfulness. State law, which now follows Islamic law, requires that four witnesses affirm that adultery has been committed before the punishment of stoning both partners to death can be enforced. Due to the difficulty of obtaining such evidence, the penalty under state law is the beating of both parties.

Critique of Strategies

No society can achieve full maturity without the interaction of both sexes. Under all circumstances, the female role in the family must be preserved. As a mother, she must instill the society's values in the children. Hence, women must consider humanity at large when working towards the goal of the improvement of their conditions. Women should not feel that they are fighting or challenging men.

However, society will continue to be apprehensive about women's progress. If women work and study, some people will question women's commitment to bearing and raising children. Others worry about the job security of males if women prove to be efficient and accept lower wages at the same time. To combat these fears and to promote the best interests of the society, our efforts must facilitate a new interaction between, and coexistence of, males and females in our developing society. In this way, a balance between customary and modern values can be struck which will benefit women.

In adopting strategies to confront barriers to women's achievement of equal legal and social status, we recognize many factors affecting this objective. The various strategies include protest and political action; passing new legislation and amending existing laws; and encouraging women's solidarity and unity.

The formation of the Women's Union has proved to be the most important political strategy in the fight for women's rights. Opposition to the formation of the union was considerable. Conservatives objected on religious and social grounds. However, the support and participation of women from all classes and backgrounds and the encouragement of the independent press and other groups have made the Women's Union a success. The politicization of the issue of women's rights is another strategy which proved successful. A number of politicians and groups have supported women's rights in the hope that women would vote for them in elections. Women have also protested against the opposition by writing and lobbying the politicians and by conducting demonstrations. Hence, women have made progress through their solidarity and unity and through the belief that they could overcome the opposition.

Conclusion

The conflict between women's actual status and their legal position is partially a result of the prevalence of customary law regarding women. The passing of legislation favorable to women has helped women to overcome some of the injustices they face. But, it is clear that the real position of women will not be improved until traditional mores and customs are reexamined.

Women, therefore, must individually and collectively work to remove the obstacles traditionally placed upon them. By so doing, the detrimental customary laws will gradually be replaced by more favorable statutory laws. Women will then be able to appeal to the law to protect their fight for equality.

Asma A. El Dareer is a noted writer on women in the Sudan, particularly on the problem of female circumcision.

4/Issues

Violence
and
Exploitation

Opening this section, *Tambiah* explores the multiple forms of violence and exploitation of women, beginning with a discussion of genital mutilation. She asserts that this particular aggression, as well as other manifestations of aggression, is geared ultimately toward controlling female sexuality. Battering of women, perhaps the most extensive and the least discussed type of violence toward females in the Third World, is also related to patriarchal domination of women. Rape, violence of a sexual nature, is another. It is important to note that in the Third World particularly, factors such as class, caste, and ethnic background accentuate the vulnerability of women to one or more of these forms of violence. Tambiah also explores pornography and its function of linking violence to sexuality, as well as gynæcide (the killing of women) in several contexts, particularly that of dowry deaths in India and Muslim practices of killing women who have been willing or unwilling participants in sexual acts outside of marriage.

In discussing exploitation, Tambiah notes that the distinction between violence and exploitation is vague and that violence is often accompanied by female labor exploitation. One of the most obvious instances of simultaneous exploitation of both labor and sexuality is prostitution. However, the Free Trade Zones provide an example of labor exploitation that is not necessarily but often accompanied by sexual abuse. Finally, Tambiah discusses women agricultural workers on the family farm as another case of exploitation. Women work longer hours, rarely control the family's cash income, and often receive the least nourishment despite their greater need—a consequence of a longer workday and frequent periods of pregnancy and lactation.

Throughout her analysis, Tambiah links violence and exploitation to patriarchy and the preservation of male supremacy in society. She also notes that while all Third World women share vulnerability to violence, poor women are more vulnerable to becoming victims of exploitation.

Perpiñan's paper discusses the phenomenon of sex tourism and links it with the factors of class division, neocolonialism, sexism, and racism. Poverty on the one hand and the lure of quick money on the other—supported by economic strength in the tourist industry—brings many women to the service sector where they often end up in sexual servitude. The sexist and racist attitudes of Caucasian and Japanese men support the development of a sex tour industry in the Philippines and other southeast Asian countries, particularly Thailand. Moreover, the paper points out that economic and geopolitical factors, particularly the presence of U.S. Army bases in the Philippine Islands, support the continued existence of the industry. The remainder of the paper deals with strategies to end sex tourism and assist in the rehabilitation of those exploited by the industry.

Letelier looks at violence toward women political prisoners in Chile. The paper documents the methods of torture used by the Chilean military dictatorship against women as well as the conspiracy and silence of the legal system in processing cases of this type. One of the most physically and psychologically damaging aspects of imprisonment for women political prisoners is, of course, torture, including the constant threat of rape, sleep deprivation, sensory overstimulation, simulated executions, witnessing torture, hypnosis, drugs, and electric shock. Another of the unique problems facing women prisoners who are also mothers is the domestic dislocation imprisonment brings about, whether the children accompany their mothers to prison or live with friends or relatives on the outside.

Moghaizel's paper presents a comparative study of legislation in Arab and Mediterranean countries dealing with crimes of honor. The paper establishes the conditions under which a full or partial excuse may be obtained in the commission of homicide or inflicting serious bodily injury in cases where a woman is surprised in the act of illicit sexual relations by an "aggrieved" party (a male relative: husband, brother, *etc.*). An excuse may be obtained even in cases where it is suspected that a sexual act is **about** to occur. While there is some variation from country to country, Moghaizel shows that this type of legislation discriminates against women since the victim is always female. It also stands in contradiction to the Universal Declaration of Human Rights. More serious still, legislation of this type establishes the right of individuals to pursue their own justice. While this paper is limited to the Middle East and the Mediterranean, it should be noted that the concepts are relevant to many parts of Latin America, as well as other regions.

Porte's paper deals with the violence and exploitation of women industrial workers in the Philippines and Southeast Asia. It explores the issues of wages, job security, working conditions, sexual abuse and harassment, maternity benefits, living conditions, and trade unions as they affect women workers. Employed mainly in the assembly lines of garment, textile, and electronics factories, women of Southeast Asia are a vast reserve of workers that is often easily manipulated and controlled. The result is that women in this sector receive low wages, work under substandard working conditions, have insufficient social benefits and no job security. Because of the availability of low-paid labor and the complicity of the governments involved, unions are weak and the women are left with little recourse.

❧❧❧❧

Sri Lanka:
Violence and Exploitation
Yasmin Tambiah

Violence

Men's violence towards women knows no boundaries, neither age, caste, class, nor ethnicity. In a patriarchal society, which demands that certain men control and manipulate others in order to consolidate their professed supremacy, violence is probably the most sanctioned means to maintain social control over women. It is through bonding with or subjugating their own and others' women that men determine their worth in each other's eyes. Women are extremely vulnerable, placed as they are on the rim of the coin whose two faces read *male = protector* and *male = predator*.

Violence against women has many facets. In the Third World, they range from genital mutilation and women battering to pornography, rape, and death.

Genital Mutilation

Genital mutilation of young girls occurs mainly in Islamic societies. Like most types of aggression against women, it is directed at controlling women's sexuality. The control and suppression of women's sexuality is directly, but not exclusively, linked with patriarchy's need to secure women's reproductive and productive capacities to maintain the patrilineal mechanisms of inheritance. This mutilation, which involves the excision of the clitoris and sometimes even the suturing of the vaginal aperture until marriage, is intended to deny a woman sexual pleasure and inculcate a sense of shame about her body. It is hoped in this way to ensure that she conforms to the patriarchal ideals of the virtuous woman and the faithful wife. The neuroses and physiological complications that often result from the procedure and the inhumanity of the process continue to be ignored in most societies despite criticism by concerned Third World women.[1]

145

Battering of Women

Women battering is condoned by patriarchal society and deemed acceptable among all social classes. Among the types of violence directed at woman, this is often the least discussed. Because it is executed within the institution of the family, the sacrosanct cornerstone of the patriarchal power structure, outside intervention is strongly discouraged. A woman whose behavior is viewed as erring—irrespective of what she might or might not have done—can be beaten by her husband, male lover, or male guardian with impunity. Because she is socialized into passivity and often acquires a socially induced guilt complex (whereby she believes that the battering is due to some fault of hers, rather than the inadequacies and fears within the batterer himself); and because the macro-social reality is weighted heavily against her (*i.e.*, dependent children, economic deprivation, dependence on the male, discrepancies in the law, *etc.*) the victim may deem herself hopelessly trapped. Violence within the family is an act of aggression by an individual; it is also the manifestation of the power dynamic in a micro-social context and the physical expression of the power struggle in the society at large.[2]

The battering of women is now increasingly addressed by Third World women's groups. It is sometimes addressed in the context of a struggle against multiple social oppressions. For example, in the struggle for land in Bodhgaya, India by landless agricultural laborers and in Maharashtra, India by landless tribal peoples, the issues of alcoholism and women battering were incorporated. In both cases, women organized against these social ills and were initially opposed by the men. In time, when men were forced to acknowledge the role of women in the struggle for land, they also had to acknowledge women's right to dignity.[3] Often, however, it is more likely that the women's struggle is subordinated to what men deem as more important concerns, and issues specific to women's oppression are not addressed.[4]

Rape

Violence directed at women is often sexual in nature. The male interchangeable roles of protector and predator are directly related to woman's sexuality and to the treatment of her as a chattel. The honor and status a man acquires among his peers is dependent on whether he can protect the sexuality of his female chattel from falling into the possession of other men. On the other hand, male kudos to his manliness accrue in direct proportion to the number of successful sexual forays he can make among the female chattel of other men. Women are caught once more on the tightrope of a male-created contradiction. Society places an unnatural value on women's virginity and sexual fidelity to men. In contrast, it lauds masculinity in terms of the sexual conquest of women (who are preferably another man's property). While women are subject to draconian penalties for forced or voluntary sexual infidelities, men as protectors-turned-predators often go free. Women's sexuality and bodies, therefore, are the means by which men respect or humiliate each other.

The universally pervasive fear and reality of sexual violence has been an effective means of undermining women's empowerment. The complex and intertwined web of imposed morality on women, the general limitation of the male protector's power and influence, and the predatory male sexuality are deterrents to women's employment outside the home and, hence, to their economic, social, and political autonomy. The opinion that an economically independent woman is also sexually promiscuous is fairly widespread; the link between the free expression of sexuality and autonomy is made by both the oppressor and the oppressed. This assumption is used by men for their own ends.[5] Women are subjected to various types of sexual harassment in their workplaces, ranging from sexual favors demanded by the management in return for promotions, wage bonuses, *etc.* to rape by male colleagues or strangers when returning home. The myth about the working woman is a self-fulfilling prophecy; it enables the oppressor by his act of aggression to justify his fabricated concern for female safety. Within the confines of the home, she will be secure. Moreover, she will be able to challenge neither his sexual freedom, nor her socioeconomic dependence on him.

The rape of women has been a major motive force in history, one seldom acknowledged by men chronicling the past. Systematized rape carried out *en masse* has been used to intimidate the enemy's women—and through them—the men. Pakistan's invasion of Bangladesh, the American presence in

147

Vietnam, and the Lebanese civil war provide vivid examples of this form of violence.[6] Men's self-ascribed role as protector of women's sexuality has also been used to force the migration of political opponents such as the example of Palestinian Arabs in the 1967 Arab-Israeli War.[7]

Sexual violence against women has also been used in the context of class and caste. In the feudalism that still prevails in certain Third World states, the social hierarchy (whether based on caste or class) decrees that the women, men, and children who work the land are the property of the landlord. Because women are the lowest on the social scale, the landlord professes and maintains sexual rights over the women.[8] This prerogative of rape ensures the powerlessness of peasant men to defend the sexuality of their women. The same intention is evident in the organized struggle of landless laborers against the unjust appropriation of land which is undermined through the gang rape of militant women protesters or women spectators by hired thugs of the landlords.[9] In such cases, the rape of women of lower classes and castes is a particularly effective weapon wielded by the powerful. Since patriarchy demands that men control others, the sexual control of women is the only mode of socially acceptable control available to poor men, and the sexual violence directed at their women leaves them entirely impotent.[10]

In the Third World, therefore, it is not just the daily threat of sexual violence with which most women must contend. A woman's caste, class, and ethnic background will also determine the degree of the threat. In certain countries, women who face constant threats due to their class or caste identity have taken the onus of protecting themselves.[11]

The issue of custodial rape (*i.e.*, rape of women in police custody) has become a major concern recently. Women prisoners are subjected to a great deal of humiliation and even torture, especially if they are from economically deprived sectors of a society or if they espouse political beliefs that run contrary to those of the regime in power. Sexual assaults of various types, particularly rape, have been reported.[12] Because the offenders are supposed to uphold the law, either no charges are brought against them or they are transferred elsewhere to ensure that they will not be prosecuted. There have also been instances where the offenders have been brought to court, but later freed due to revoked verdicts.[13] Such instances have highlighted the weakness of the law and the biases of those who dispense justice. Poverty can also reduce the opportunity of redress in court. In general, because of society's assumption that a woman has no autonomous existence but is a man's property, and because of the censure directed at rape victims, individual women still find it difficult to seek justice. In some countries, women's organizations have arisen specifically to address the issues of social and custodial rape (*e.g.*, the anti-rape movement in India).[14]

Pornography and Media Violence

In the Third World, pornography has become an issue with the rise of consumerism. Perceptions of the female body as a commodity and of women's sexual subjugation through violence are expressed visually through the media. While helping to consolidate attitudes toward women already prevalent in patriarchal societies, the sensationalized visual and audio-visual presentation of these attitudes probably intensifies the violence directed at women. Pornography projects sexuality as being inextricably linked with violence and as a commodity worth exploiting in itself. Its open humiliation of women and their portrayal as subjugated sex objects contrast starkly with the male-created ideal of the virtuous woman. Again, women are forced to comply with the contradictions created by their oppressors.

Gynæcide

In male supremacist societies, a woman's mind, body, and life have always been disposable. The value of women has been linked primarily with maintaining patriarchal structures. The term *gynæcide* is consciously used here to denote the killing of women because they have acted contrary to the roles defined for them by patriarchal society or because they were unable to comply with such expectations. The two most glaring examples of this phenomenon are the gynæcide in the Arab World and the dowry deaths in India.

The gynæcide in Arab countries is intimately linked with women's sexuality. A woman may legitimately express her sexuality only within the institution of marriage. A high value is placed on women's virginity and sexual fidelity to ensure

149

property, paternity, and the inheritance rights. A woman who (voluntarily or forcibly) has engaged in premarital or extramarital sexual acts may be killed with impunity by a male member of her family. She may be stoned to death according to certain Islamic laws.[15] In some countries where rape is defined as *unlawful sexual intercourse,* or where rape even falls under the category of adultery (*i.e.,* implying mutual consent between the parties involved), the legal system further victimizes the rape victim, while permitting the offender to go free.[16] A woman can be stoned to death if found guilty or be sentenced to a public flogging if she is more fortunate.[17] Such violence, therefore, is directed specifically at women. As is consistent with the dynamics of power, the constraints and penalties are rarely imposed on men. Victimization of women by the law is greater among the economically deprived sectors of society where lack of wealth and influence make it difficult for them to skirt the law.[18]

The much publicized dowry deaths of North India further attest to women's lack of autonomy and to their low value. Young married women are either driven to suicide or murdered by their husbands and in-laws.[19] Within the last three years, over 1000 deaths have been reported, and it is likely that the actual number is much greater.[20] These deaths have been caused by the dissatisfaction of families with the dowries of the sons' wives. Though legally banned in India, doweries are given by many, particularly among the middle class. The material demands made by the husband's families on wives and their families are attempts to improve the status of the husbands' family. (Custom also dictates that the men are responsible for their sisters' dowries, hence, the pressure on the women they marry). At one level, women share the status of the material commodities they bring into marriage; at another, they are the instrument through which property and goods may be secured, passed on to posterity, and used to improve the social status of men. Women whose families fail to comply with the demands will be subject to constant verbal and physical harassment by their husbands and in-laws. These acts often lead to suicide or murder. The publicity of the protests against the dowry deaths has had some impact on the public and the legislature.[21] However, many people still are not very concerned as they view the problem as a mere family affair. Law enforcement officials often ignore it or even list the murders as suicides.[22] Nor are actual suicides perceived as constructive murders in these contexts. As in the case of women battering, whatever happens within the walls of a home is ignored by societies that sanction the patriarchal family.

Exploitation

Although the discussion on exploitation is dealt with separately in the interest of clarity, in reality, it is difficult to draw clear distinctions. Violence often accompanies the exploitation of women's labor and person, as the example of pornography indicates. Of the many types of exploitation to which women are subjected, three will be discussed: prostitution, work in the Free Trade Zones, and labor on the family farm.

Prostitution

Prostitution is one of the most obvious instances of exploitation of both women's labor and sexuality. In fact, their labor is their sexuality. As in the pornography industry, women are perceived exclusively as exploitable sexual commodities. There are few women who have voluntarily chosen prostitution over other vocations. Most are sold to brothels by their families or by abductors. Some take to prostitution because of poverty. In the brothels, they are exploited by their patrons and owners, sometimes being little better off than indentured slaves. There is little protection against violence. In certain Southeast Asian countries, sex tours have been organized for foreign tourists, thereby increasing the scale of exploitation.[23] Agitation by women's groups, however, has been successful in terminating some of the more egregious offenses.

The choice of prostitution may also be an inevitability in a society that provides only two contradistinct roles for women: the virgin or the harlot. A young woman who has had a premarital sexual relationship might view herself and be viewed as a fallen woman; the resulting self-hatred and negative social role may make prostitution a choice.[24]

Free Trade Zones

In the exploitation of wage workers, women share the predicaments of their male counterparts. However, there is also sexual exploitation to which they are subjected. The

151

classic argument invoked in advanced capitalist societies to justify lower wages for women focuses on the man as the head of the household who is paid a family wage, and hence, women's earnings are merely supplementary. This argument is also applied to the Third World situation. It creates enormous problems for female-headed households which are both prevalent and increasing in many of our countries. Such households often subsist at poverty level. These women face discrimination and longer working days. Nor is there compensation—economic or emotional—for the reproductive tasks she performs at home. The exploitative tendencies of capital and patriarchy are closely linked in the lives of such women.

In the sphere of labor exploitation, the Free Trade Zones (FTZs) that have been established in various parts of the Third World have caused great concern to women activists. Their primary objections are to the *ghettoization* of women workers, the denial of opportunities to organize, and the enslavement of women workers by foreign capital.

The FTZs however, pose a very complex problem and must not be dismissed as simply an issue of labor exploitation. They do exploit workers, particularly women workers. Nevertheless, the FTZs open up various opportunities for the women who work in them. The women are brought from the unorganized sector into an organized sector of the labor force. An assessment of available data indicates that many of the women come from economically deprived backgrounds where few or no opportunities for wage employment are available.[26] In addition, it is highly likely that these women were exploited by members of their families and communities. Their comparatively isolated existence gave them little chance to become conscious of their oppression. Their participation in the labor force permits the development of political activism, class consciousness, and feminist consciousness. Even if trade unionism is prohibited within the Free Trade Zones, activists have demonstrated that it is possible to politicize the workers by meeting with them outside the zone. Women working in the FTZs are reported to experience a qualitative improvement in the treatment they receive back in their homes, due to their monetary contributions to the family and to their relative independence as women.

Thus, while criticizing Free Trade Zone labor policies,

supporting the struggles against them, and searching for better alternatives, it is also necessary to recognize the opportunities to politicize these women, both as workers and as women.[26]

The Family Farm
Because many of our countries have large rural populations, the exploitation of women agricultural workers is a significant issue. Production on small family farms consists of either subsistence or larger-scale farming. Where the latter occurs, a process of super-exploitation often results. The price at which the farmers sell the produce to the middlemen does not reflect the cost of production. The produce is often sold below cost. Remuneration from the sales rarely provides many improve-ments for the farmers' quality of life. While the family as a whole is deprived of the rightful value of its collective labor, women are generally subject to greater exploitation.

Firstly, women work longer hours than men when both productive and reproductive labor time is considered.[27] Sometimes, their workload is greater even in the productive area, particularly during peak seasons.

Secondly, despite the fact that a woman may carry out a disproportionately large share of the family's workload, she seldom controls much of the family cash income.[28] Available evidence also indicates that men often control the earnings from women's labor. Family consumption patterns indicate that men tend to spend their income largely on their own needs, while women spend it on the entire family. In Africa, for example, women are responsible for producing food for the family on their own separate plots; in addition, they must try to generate a surplus for household expenses. In contrast, men do not usually contribute to the latter. The income from the men's own land, where women also work, is generally spent on liquor, *etc.*

Thirdly, women very often eat last at a meal, while the men are given the choice bits. Consequently, women tend to be far more malnourished than the men even though they work longer hours and require greater nourishment during pregnancy and lactation.[29]

Finally, some rural households are headed by women, and the denial to them of easy access to land and capital exacerbates their difficult conditions. The various development aid projects, which assumed that the heads of households will be exclusively men, have marginalized women farmers through the mechanization of agriculture. Not only have women been deprived of traditional agricultural jobs (outside the family household), they have also been forced into unemployment because of the assumption that women cannot master mechanical skills.[30] With the increase of mechanization, female-headed households are left destitute. Moreover, poorer families that are dependent on female labor for their subsistence have experienced a drop in the quality of life.[31]

In other areas, a woman's loss is a man's gain. In the Indian region of the Punjab, the green revolution has enabled the wealthier peasants to rise in social rank through material wealth, which has resulted in the increased seclusion of their women. The latter has been accomplished by hiring laborers to work the fields where previously the entire family worked.

Concluding Remarks

Violence and exploitation are realities in the lives of many women in the Third World. Every woman—irrespective of her caste, class, and ethnic identity—is a potential victim of violence. However, some categories of women are more vulnerable to becoming victims of exploitation. Violence against women is closely associated with the preservation of male supremacy in society. The processes of exploitation benefit either patriarchy or capitalism, often both. A careful analysis of women's oppression reveals that the inferior status accorded to her by patriarchy is often exacerbated by other oppressive forces. Hence, women must create a multi-faceted struggle to achieve freedom, dignity, independence and autonomy.

Yasmin Tambiah is a researcher for the International Center for Ethnic Studies in Colombo, Sri Lanka.

The Philippines:
Prostitution and Sexual Exploitation
Soledad Perpiñan

Introduction

The United Nations Decade for Women corresponds with the years that saw the growth of organized sex tours and the reappearance of other formats of sexual exploitation in the Philippines. In the mid-1970s, development plans in Third World countries called for the promotion of the tourist industry due to the compelling need for foreign exchange to save shaky economies from collapsing. For debt-ridden countries that clung to the lifeline of the International Monetary Fund and the World Bank, dollar-earning tourism was an important component of the conditions to obtain loans.

Advertising and publicity in the West and Japan have blatantly used sex to entice potential tourists to several Asian countries. With the promotion of tourism, the related amusement industry has flourished. Hotels, restaurants, discos, bars, saunas, massage parlors, and brothels have mushroomed in the tourist areas. The industry generated a need for service employees, particularly in the expanding field of *sexploitation*.

Hundreds of thousands of people were recruited from the impoverished countryside and given quick employment in the sex industry. In countries like the Philippines and Thailand, the lure of sex and youth imposed sadistic violence upon females and the very young. By 1980, over a million men on *sex tours* were coming to the Philippines. In Manila, it was a common sight to see 200 or more Japanese males disembark from a plane, be whisked to a hotel, and taken to a brothel where they pick a bedmate for their three-day sex stint. These developments were brought to our attention during an international workshop on tourism, an alternative conference to the World Tourism Organization convention held in Manila in 1980. We will present a case study of actions taken to confront these problems over the next four and one-half years.

155

Overview

The problem of prostitution tourism is complex and multi-faceted. It is related to the economics, culture, and politics of Third World countries. Other issues associated with this growing phenomenon are class divisions, neocolonialism, sexism, and racism. To understand prostitution tourism, it is necessary to understand both the structural and functional factors involved.

The *economic conditions* of these countries encourage this growth industry. Poverty, which is largely due to stagnating agricultural development, a national financial crisis, and an international economic recession, pushes young women into prostitution. Furthermore, there exists the lure of fast and easy money. Associated with these factors is a strong force of economic expansion in related industries: the airlines, hotels, tourist agencies, bars, restaurants, drugs, government, and protection syndicates.

Many policies and development programs—such as tourism—have adversely affected the people and the culture. Women have been reduced to sex objects. The *cultural aspect of this phenomenon* can be traced to the insidious effects of a patriarchal ideology on the society. Religious patrimony, feudal values, and colonial attitudes also contribute to the acceptance and growth of prostitution tourism. The *influence of the geopolitical realities* of the Philippines, reflected by the existence of American military bases and rest and recreation centers, have institutionalized large-scale prostitution.

Women and men in the Philippines suffer from the consequences of *neocolonialism, underdevelopment, and poverty*. Because of limited opportunities in agriculture and industry, they find it difficult to obtain productive work. Where employment is available, neocolonial interests and the international division of labor greatly exploit workers. As a result of unemployment and exploitation, thousands get drawn into the service sector. They often end up in the sexploitation industry where they become little more than commodities for sale. Women in the Third World are doubly oppressed because of *sexist attitudes*. Employment opportunities for women are limited to *female work*. In addition Third World women must assume certain roles, perpetuating colonial images of docility and servitude. The male ego of the chauvinistic Caucasian, Japanese, or Arab demands this—perhaps to give him a sense of power in a highly competitive world.

Tourists from the rich countries oppress Asian women in ways that liberated women in their own countries will not permit. *Race is stronger than gender.* For instance, at a meeting in Metro Manila, upper and middle class Australian women, whose husbands work in the Philippines, sided with Australian men on the issue of Filipinas who are drawn into the misery of the marriage market. Another example is provided by American women who are apathetic about prostitution that is proliferated by U.S. military bases. They project an attitude of "as long as the sexually exploited are Asians, who cares."

Responses of Women in the Philippines

With the amalgamation of complex issues that contribute to the explosion of prostitution in the Third World, holistic and analytical strategies must be developed to understand and fight this problem. The general objective is to confront prostitution tourism effectively by tackling the root causes as well as the symptoms. Through this struggle, we aim to raise the status of women in the Philippines and the rest of the Third World. They must be treated as human beings with innate dignity, worthy of respect by all in a society on the road to justice, equality, and peace.

To accomplish these goals, the Third World Movement Against the Exploitation of Women (TW-MAE-W) has engaged in four principal activities. The first is building networks and solidarity. It mobilizes and links individuals and groups to undertake concerted action and to exert international pressure. The second activity is consciousness-raising and informational and educational work. This aspect of the strategy uses the media, workshops, seminars, conferences, women's studies programs, and informal talks. The third involves research and publication. Surveys are conducted, research is initiated and monitored, and papers are written for conferences, seminars, and meetings. This activity also includes disseminating manuals, pamphlets, bulletins and other information to the masses. The final activity focuses on organizing marginalized women and forming support groups to empower them.

Strategy Development

A chain of militants and a spiral of activities are behind TW-MAE-W. Before the Philippine group was mobilized, South Korean women protested against the Kisaeng sex tours involving Japanese men; Japanese women, who were in solidarity with their South Korean and Taiwanese sisters, also denounced these tours.

The first action in the Philippines was a letter of protest addressed to the Japanese ambassador. The author of this paper wrote the letter in response to the proddings of a Japanese delegation, mainly journalists. After soliciting signatures of hundreds of people representing all classes of society from the urban poor in Tondo to the rich of Makati, the letter was presented to the Japanese embassy on Human Rights Day, 1980. At a celebration of human rights, the letter was read, and it was subsequently supported by the assembly of students, workers, and church personnel of the ecumenical circle.

Not daunted by the futile dialogue with the first secretary of the Japanese embassy, the group decided to pursue the protest internationally. Fortunately, women workers from the ASEAN capitals were visiting Manila, and together we planned to stage a series of protests during the January 1981 visit of Prime Minister Suzuki to the region. The women workers flew back home and did their own mobilization of groups such as the Friends of Women in Thailand.

Meanwhile, a second letter was written, this time addressed to the Japanese prime minister. A public forum was held on January 8, 1981, the day of his arrival in Manila. From then on protests escalated, taking various forms, such as a street play and a picket of the Japanese embassy in Bangkok. This was the birth of the Third World Movement Against the Exploitation of Women.

One month later, another letter was written. It expanded the issue of sex tourism to include military prostitution, specifically the whoredoms created by the presence of the U.S. Naval Base at Subic Bay and the Clark Air Base in Angeles City. The letter was presented to Pope John Paul II during his visit to Manila and copies were sent to the heads of state of the United States, Japan, and the Philippines.

A working team of TW-MAE-W, based in Manila, continued to organize the intensifying activities surrounding the issue. Numerous aspects of sex tourism were brought to our attention: mail order brides, international beauty contests, nudist resorts, child prostitution, and pornography, among others. We clearly analyzed each situation to determine the most effective mode of action. As a result, all activities were part of a conceptual framework; none was *ad hoc* or sporadic.

The process of strategy development also involved another chain of events. At the mid-decade UN Conference for Women in Copenhagen in 1980, a handful of women took up the issue of prostitution. The matter was pursued, and two years later, Philippine and Asian meetings were held about this issue. Since TW-MAE-W had gained renown for its involvement in the area, its coordinator was invited to present the country paper and was later chosen to represent the Philippines at the meeting of the International Feminist Network held in Rotterdam, The Netherlands in 1983. There she worked with other participants, who represented twenty-four countries to pull together several strategies to combat forced prostitution and violence against women.

Back in the Philippines, the TW-MAE-W coordinator shared these strategies with the local organizations. A few months later, STOP (Stop Trafficking of Filipinas) was launched on November 25, 1983, designated at the Rotterdam Meeting as the International Day Against the Exploitation of Women. The TW-MAE-W coordinator formulated the STOP strategies whereby discussions moved from the local to national to regional to international levels, then returned to the national arena to be solidified at the micro level.

Focus

The STOP program has been implemented nation-wide during the past eighteen months. STOP is directed primarily against the pimps, protectors, agents, recruiters, managers, and brothel owners, all of whom are behind the trafficking in women and children both locally and internationally. The yellow, red, and green traffic signals of the campaign are as follows:

Warning Yellow
Educate girls and their parents in the rural areas about the pitfalls of migrating to the city and of working abroad.

Expose the recruiters to the people.

Warn the people about questionable penpals, marriage bureaus, and offers abroad.

Involve local groups and organizations and obtain their commitment to a specific campaign activity.

Stop Red

Stop the recruitment of girls at the place of origin (*e.g.*, the pier or bus terminal).

Stop the operations of pimps, brothel owners, and agents of the "sexploitation industry."

Stop rape and sexual assault by the military in remote areas and places of detention.

Stop foreigners from sexually exploiting our women.

Stop foreign and local businessmen from the financing of and profiteering from the sex industry.

Stop sexual harassment in factories and offices.

Stop the media from exploiting women's bodies.

Go Green

Set up alternative economic opportunities.

Establish a tuition loan or scholarship fund.

Promulgate and enforce stricter laws against those who profit from the sex industry. (Note: existing laws subtly aim to make prostitution safe and clean for the customers.)

Create local and international networks to expose this situation.

The focal point for the STOP plan of action is education. There is great need for consciousness-raising and for deepening the awareness of the problem. Only through these means can there be a holistic and radical approach to solve this problem. Information is basic to the prevention and the rehabilitation of those exploited by the industry. It is also essential to take legal action or to conduct research.

TW-MAE-W, which operates internationally, focuses on networking and solidarity work through the dissemination of its action bulletin and the traveling of speakers and workers, among other activities. A problem like prostitution tourism is international in nature, and therefore the solution must also be international in scope. Working with groups in other countries is crucial. In 1985, the issue of child prostitution has received much attention. The campaign against it has largely involved the lobbying and pressuring of government ministries by the STOP sub-committee.

Legal Issues

TW-MAE-W has utilized international law to increase its clout. A case in point was the organization of protests against the publication of *Tengoku Hyoryu* (Drifting in Paradise), subtitled *Guide for the Night Life of Nymphomaniac Filipinas*. It was published by Sanwa Publishing Co., Ltd. and printed by Toppan Printing Co., Ltd. in Japan. At a confrontation with the company in Tokyo, the TW-MAE-W coordinator gave Mr. Goto, the Sanwa president, a copy of the letter from the movement addressed to the heads of state of Japan and the Philippines. The letter cited the UN Convention for the Suppression of Traffic in Persons and the Exploitation of the Prostitution of Others, which was ratified by both countries in 1949. By virtue of international law, we firmly demanded that our governments should take strong immediate measures including the elimination of trafficking in persons; the closure of tour and travel agencies employing sex tourism publicity; the closure of all quarters where sex abuse is practiced; the prosecution of syndicates that make money from trafficking in persons and sex tourism; and the imposition of penalties upon the parties behind pornography.

At the foreign ministry reception for the participants of the United Nations Economic and Social Commission for Asia and the Pacific (UNESCAP) pre-Nairobi meeting, this letter was given to the Japanese foreign minister with the request that he present it to Prime Minister Nakasone. Following the interventions made by the TW-MAE-W coordinator at the UN ESCAP meeting held in Tokyo in March 1984, most delegations urged that strong legal measures be taken to punish the exploiters, pimps, and traders in sex. Some participants suggested the decriminalization of prostitution, the monitoring of the media and propaganda, the rehabilitation of the young women, and the adoption by government of strong measures against those involved in the prostitution trade.

In the Philippines, a legal committee of STOP was formed to study several documents : Presidential Decree 603, which authorizes the prosecution of any person caught in the act of abusing a child; City Ordinance 842, which imposes a curfew on minors; Parliamentary Bill No. 4311, which mandates the prosecution of anyone caught exploiting a child; and the adoption law. Currently in the Philippine Parliament, a revision of Parliamentary Bill No. 4311 has been introduced so as to provide stronger deterrents against child prostitution by imposing stiffer penalties and by amending articles 340 and 341 of the Revised Penal Code.

Organization and Participation

The Third World Movement Against the Exploitation of Women has affiliated individuals and groups in forty-five countries of the Third World, the industrialized North-West, and the Socialist Bloc. From the very start, participation has been international. The synchronized protests against sex tours from Japan involved people and groups in the ASEAN capitals. The subsequent protest against the proliferation of prostitution by US bases witnessed the mobilization of thousands of individuals and groups on almost all continents. Other activities have involved inter-country groups, such as the protests against the marriage market in Belgium, Germany, Switzerland, Australia, and New Zealand. Furthermore, Japanese are involved in the rescuing of enslaved women. TW-MAE-W is also concerned with other forms of exploitation, *e.g.*, the plight of migrant workers. We have ties with organizations working with migrants in the Arab Gulf States, Europe, Hong Kong, Singapore, the United States, and elsewhere. Even in places as far away as Finland, efforts by women's groups to combat sex tourism are assisted by the studies and materials made available by TW-MAE-W.

TW-MAE-W has gained valuable experience and organizational links by its participation in numerous international conferences. The TW-MAE-W coordinator has also been invited to participate in speaking tours around the world. In addition, international groups have facilitated our visits to Eastern and Western Europe, and South and Southeast Asia. All of the conferences have been occasions for an exchange of ideas and the coordination of plans. Due to the problem of logistics, it was only in December 1984, that a much awaited Third World

Women's Workshop materialized. At that 1984 meeting, TW-MAE-W stated its principles of unity and announced the formulation of regional plans.

On the local level, public interest has been aroused by the mass media. National organizations have been mobilized, and several units under the name of Parish Movement Against Exploitation of Women (P-MAE-W) have been established. Through STOP, progress has been made in reducing the trafficking of women and children and exposing sex tourism. Most provincial groups have centered their specific activities on an educational and informational campaign.

The United Nations has also utilized the work of TW-MAE-W. Reporting to the UN Economic and Social Council, Jean Fernand-Laurent cited the contribution of TW-MAE-W in his "A Synthesis of the Surveys and Studies on the Traffic in Persons and the Exploitation of the Prostitution of Others." The UN Economic and Social Council for Asia and the Pacific requested the TW-MAE-W coordinator to write a background paper and to present a country report on the prevention and rehabilitation of prostitutes at two different meetings of experts in June 1985. UNESCO also commissioned TW-MAE-W to prepare an annotated bibliography on prostitution in East and Southeast Asia. Currently, a major research project on child exploitation in the Philippines is being coordinated by this writer.

A historic event has recently developed: for the first time in Philippine history, prostitutes are organizing. After a half-day seminar on May 3, 1985, 100 prostitutes from seventeen sex amusement clubs in Poro Point, La Union (the location of the U.S. communications center at Wallace Air Base) agreed to form an association called the Junction Club. (Junction is the name of the strip where most of the joints are located, and J.C. connotes the initials of Jesus Christ.) A council of representatives was formed, and officers were elected. Simultaneously, the TW-MAE-W team organized a support group among the citizens of San Fernando, La Union. A dialogue between the two groups was scheduled so that the entertainers themselves could tell their story and express their needs. In this manner, the participation in the strategy becomes most meaningful.

163

Results

Tangible results were seen immediately after the series of protests occurring during Prime Minister Suzuki's visit to ASEAN countries. The number of male Japanese tourists in the Philippines sharply declined; and a 25% decrease has occurred in Thailand. The remarkable drop in packaged sex tours forced Japan Airlines to reduce its flights to Manila. Advertisements for Southeast Asian tours in Tokyo dailies changed from depicting exotic ladies to showing seashores and mountains.

Protest letters sent to various heads of state and national and international organizations have exposed the nature and extent of prostitution tourism. Moreover, our work has been met with enthusiasm by solidarity groups around the world. TW-MAE-W papers and studies have been widely used here and abroad. Around the world, many have been able to make use of the TW-MAE-W Databank on Women Resources.

The Philippine Parliament is deliberating about the proposed bill against procurers of child prostitutes. TW-MAE-W is also pushing for a law which prohibits the trafficking in women. Steps to empower women have been taken. Special efforts have been directed toward the prostitutes themselves. The purpose of the TW-MAE-W survey in 1981-1983 was to provide a vehicle for the prostitutes to express their perceptions, self-images, and attitudes toward change and for the views of society about prostitution. The responses of 614 prostitutes from five major centers of prostitution—Metro Manila, Angeles City, Olongapo City, Batangas City, and Cebu City—and 100 more from Poro Point, San Fernando City provided an empirical basis to establish programs and direct services (one directed towards prevention, the other towards rehabilitation). From this survey emerged a baseline for other studies. The Poro Point connection has resulted in the organization of the prostitutes, a milestone in the empowerment of our marginalized women.

The emancipation of all women, especially those in the Third World, is a strong undercurrent in the educational campaigns sponsored by TW-MAE-W. They aim to highlight the gender question and discriminatory attitudes about women. The TW-MAE-W hopes that a recognition by all women of a common bondage will prevent upper and middle class women from patronizing the activities surrounding prostitution. It is essential to eliminate these divisions among women.

Lessons Learned

It is very difficult to outwit the forces of evil. As a consequence of the successful protests against the sex tours, the businessmen behind sexploitation tourism circumvented the constraints placed on the industry. For instance, they changed venues. Instead of landing in Manila, Japanese male tourists fly directly to Cebu. When package tours became unpalatable, the Japanese imported Asian prostitutes. Australians and Europeans have taken the lead in this area. Meanwhile, the Americans have not been deterred in their enjoyment of *R and R prostitution*. What is self-evident is the link between prostitution, tourism, and all other forms of imperialism. Hence, we must fight on all fronts. Precisely because of our weakness in confronting a multifaceted enemy, we must stress the use of collective and creative efforts. The collective aspect ranges from working with groups to mobilizing the masses. It involves obtaining the cooperation of as many diverse organizations as possible. The creative aspect covers a combination of factors. We must find the Achilles heel of the enemy, analyze the appropriate and effective counter-measures, and execute them at the proper time with extensive media coverage. Thus, the power of solidarity, creativity, and conviction in the service of a just cause can overcome imperialism in its many guises.

A final outcome has been the development of a Third World feminist perspective in confronting prostitution tourism. To empower all women—whether they are the victims, the activists, or the supporters—is a dynamic challenge. Doing so within the context of the Third World in an age of neo-imperialism has produced a Third World feminism that dares tackle the problems of class, sex and race in a holistic and radical matter. Only then, can women in partnership with men of conscience, gain true equality, genuine development, and lasting peace.

Sister Mary Soledad Perpiñan, a Good Sheperd Nun, is the Coordinator of the Third World Movement Against the Exploitation of Women.

Chile:
Response of Political Women
to the Dictatorship
Fabiola Letelier

Introduction

During the 1970-1973 democratic government of Dr. Salvador
Allende, there was little or no violent repression in Chile.
After the *coup d'etat* against the Allende government, the
society was radically changed by the introduction of the concept of *internal enemy*, which could be applied to anyone
regardless of sex, age, or socioeconomic background. Since 1973,
the Chilean people have been violently repressed; their situation is similar to people in other Latin American countries ruled
by military regimes.

The military dictatorship has reimposed a traditional
role on women, an attitude supported by the dominant conservative, military ideology. Women who dared to wear trousers
on the streets have been attacked, and their clothes were
publicly torn. Female public officials were forced to wear
feminine clothes to work. The records compiled by our organization specifically deal with repression against women, their
children, relatives, and friends during the past twelve years of
military dictatorship. Our present report will focus on a group
of women in the San Miguel prison in Santiago.

Repression of Women
under the Chilean Dictatorship

The military dictatorship was unable to execute its economic
and political program until it liquidated the popular vanguard
and leftist parties, whose rise in the early 1980's was notable.
To implement their objectives, the military dictatorship
declared war on an internal enemy: international Marxism.
Repressive actions followed. At one moment, these actions
struck at the masses; at another, they attacked the individual;
still, at other times, they were indiscriminate. The large-scale
repressive acts of 1973 brought about the military control of the
whole country in less than 48 hours. They cost the Chilean
people 8,000-30,000 deaths and more than 50,000 prisoners of

war. It is estimated that in Santiago and its environs, there were ten women executed and some 800 women imprisoned with men and subjected to brutality.

During these years, the imprisoned women were interrogated and searched in such a way that they would appear to belong to, or be connected or sympathize with, a leftist party. Many of them were held hostage while their leaders, sons, or husbands were being hunted. With the appearance of the National Intelligence Administration (DINA) and its secret torture chambers in 1974, forty-nine women of whom we know were taken to these chambers in the period between 1974 and 1977. They are still missing. In June 1974, the first concentration camp for women, *Tres Alamos*, was opened. It continued to operate until November 1976, and it held between 100 and 200 women.

Beginning in 1977, the dictatorship attempted to revitalize and stablize the economy, following the destruction of the parties and leftist movements and the dissolution of all guilds, unions, and social organizations. Coinciding with these events was a reign of terror inflicted upon the majority of the people. The women political prisoners of the dictatorship have been systematically tortured to extract information or confessions. There have been few cases of women prisoners who were not tortured. Some of the forms of torture have included: deprivation of sight; sexual humiliation and violence (rape, insertion of objects and animals into the vagina); beatings; burnings; hangings; forced body postures; dry or wet asphyxiation; electric shock; solitary confinement; sensory deprivation; drug use; and psychological manipulation. Other common forms of brutality are blackmail, pressure, fake executions, *etc*. Furthermore, according to the nature of the dictatorships offensive, it has utilized diverse techniques of overcrowding, biological weakening, and psycho-physiological destabilization.

The concentration camps were abolished and the activities of the (CNI) National Information Headquarters, which replaced the DINA, began in 1977; since that time, physical torture has been administered with inhuman savagery. The regime aims to use methods of psychological torture which annihilate the prisoners without leaving any physical traces.

167

With similar objectives, and to safeguard its international image, the repressive apparatus of the dictator-ship resorts to concealed assassinations. Deaths by faked con-frontations, which have replaced the disappearances, are represented nationally and internationally as governmental opposition to extremists. This method became an habitual practice during this period and has continued in various forms.

From 1976, the women of the Associations of Victims of Repression began to confront the regime about state violence. The popular movement was revitalized beginning on May 1, 1978. Women participated in the movement through the unemployment office, popular restaurants, and community kitchens. As a result, women were unofficially imprisoned for short periods of time to intimidate them. Another form of political repression emerged: the appearance of the Avenging Martyr Command (COVEMA), a pro-military government squad (separate from the official security services) which kidnapped, tortured, and killed people. It was composed of members of the CNI and the Bureau of Investigation, both governmental organizations.

The testimonies of women who were first taken to detention centers confirmed that military and police officials had received training and indoctrination from the American military services. In addition, the methods and structure of the repressive apparatus have demonstrated the collaboration between the Chilean Armed Forces and other Latin American military dictatorships. Since 1980, the number of women political prisoners has risen as the dictatorship has reacted to the progressive women's organizations, students, associations of relatives and victims of repression, and unions. During the period between 1980 and 1983, the average number of women arrested annually was about 250. However, the government and its counter-insurgency apparatus varied their means of repres-sion during this period. (It was the time when the 1980 constitution was enacted, an economic crisis hit, and the people were mobilized.) On the one hand, with the announcement of the decree laws protecting the new constitution, repression was made illegal. On the other hand, the CNI, *Carabineros* (National Police Force), and Bureau of Investigation continued their violent activities, totally ignoring the law. Executions and faked confrontations increased, and their modes of torture became more perfected.

As the mobilization of the opposition grew, groups of unidentified civilians reappeared. They stopped the street demonstrations and carried out operations with the police and military to intimidate, imprison, and kill the masses. In 1981, the National Coordinator of Political Prisoners (NCPP) was created. The political prisoners also organized to respond to the dictatorship from inside the prisons. Social organizations supported women prisoners helping to break the regime's enforced silence about their situation. At the same time, the NCCP improved the communication and coordination among all political prisoners.

In May 1983, the women participated in demonstrations that rapidly spread throughout the entire country. They innovated many forms of protest: boycotting commercial enterprises and their children's schools; beating on empty pots and pans; marching in and barricading the streets; and organizing the means of self-defense, first aid, and health services.

Political Prisoners
at the San Miguel Prison During 1984

This report was written with the assistance of twenty women political prisoners at the San Miguel prison in Santiago through their testimony and interviews conducted by committee counsel. This information has been directly obtained from their relatives and the Association of Relatives of Political Prisoners. From the data collected, we have seen that the Chilean legal process is extraordinarily slow, as demonstrated by its actions of conspiracy and silent compliance. Of the twenty cases processed, the prisoners averaged 19.4 months of imprisonment (sentences ranging from five to fifty-two months); six people have been released on bail; and only one case was terminated. That prisoner was sentenced to 102 days of imprisonment and up to four years of exile after having completed four years in prison.

To characterize the political prisoners, we have studied the educational data of the twenty women. The results have shown that they were not average Chilean in terms of social origin and socioeconomic factors. The average age of one-half of them was twelve years at the time of the 1973 military coup. In this group of twenty women prisoners, fifteen had a technical university education; of those, eight are from working class backgrounds, six from the lower middle class, and only one of middle class origin. The dictatorship suppresses discussion about their higher educational achivements , as it claims that the women are "delinquents,""socially marginal," and "psychopathic terrorists."

Mothers in Prison

The imprisonment of mothers—and, for more than half of these cases, fathers—creates a state of family dispersion and domestic dislocations. The following data is gathered from the twenty-six children of the twenty women prisoners.

Five children were born and raised in prison while three children are living with a relative in Chile, but not necessarily the father. Six children are living in exile with or without immediate relatives. Two children have become political prisoners (in this case, two young men of 19 and 20 years of age, whose fathers are political prisoners). Seven children are living alone because both parents are imprisoned. Two adult children are free and live relatively normal lives. One child was imprisoned since 1974, and his whereabout are now unknown.

For all these mothers, having children has made their political work more difficult. In general, the women are burdened with the responsibilities of the children, although they are supported by their comrades. This reality reinforced the determination of the women. In no case has it paralyzed them. These women have educated their children about the ideas for which they are fighting; today, many of these children have joined the struggle. Some women, on the other hand, have left their children to protect them from the risks of their situation. In other cases, the comrades temporarily leave their children only when they return to active struggle (which can only be done in secret). Two women, whose children were born in prison, decided to separate from them so that they would develop in a more normal environment. Obviously, the experience of separation is very painful, but the political mothers consider it a necessary and correct decision.

With respect to the economic background of the families

of the prisoners, we have classified them in three broad categories. Five families had good circumstances; four families had moderate means (*i.e.*, encountering some problems with minimal subsistence); eleven families had serious subsistence problems.

The Arrests

The police and military agents, who operate with impunity, use a great amount of force to arrest offenders. Threats, imprisonment, and physical abuse begin immediately upon arrest. Of the twenty surveyed prisoners, only one was not victimized by the authorities because she required immediate emergency medical treatment. She had been detained in a police bus and was wounded by *carabineros* who shot with small bullets from a short distance.

The duration of abductions varied, ranging from less than a day to more than sixteen days. Only one case was kidnapped less than a day, while seven cases were abducted for one to five days. Six cases were abducted for six to ten days. Two cases were abducted for eleven to fifteen days and four cases for sixteen days. The four abduction cases with the longest duration were carried out by the CNI. One of the prisoners, wounded by shots from security agents, was held eight days in the Santiago Military Hospital. To obtain information from her, she was systematically induced to believe (with the collaboration of medical personnel) that she was in a private clinic.

On Torture

We define torture as stipulated by article number 1 of the *Declaration on the Protection of All People against Torture and Other Cruel, Inhuman, and Degrading Treatment or Punishment*. In all cases, the acts of torture ("serious physical or mental punishment or abuse"), were conducted to obtain information and/or a confession; to punish an act committed or suspected of having been committed; or to intimidate that person or third parties. In every case, the rights of prisoners have been intentionally and systematically violated through the use of public organizations or at the instigation of public officials (security and police agents). The testimonies abound in details verifying the institutional character of the use of

171

torture. Interrogation and torture techniques are custom designed according to the needs of the organization.

The Impact of Torture

In general, victims of torture speak with great difficulty about their experiences. Others deny the circumstances or evade questions. This group of women prisoners, however, clearly faced their experiences of torture. They analyzed and viewed it within their overall political commitment. Torture is very humiliating. The women's clothes were taken away to pressure and blackmail them and they lived in constant fear of being raped. They were degraded. Futhermore, serious psychological traumas have resulted. The sophisticated methods of psychological torture are frequently applied to political prisoners. The modes of psychological torture include sleep or sensory deprivation or overstimulation; the simulation of executions; the witnessing of torture; behavioral modification; hypnosis; and the use of drugs. Physical torture was also employed: twelve of the twenty prisoners were subjected to electric shocks.

We should note here that nine of the cases detected the presence of women guards, the majority of whom were agents of the CNI. This indicates that women have been integrated into the repressive organization created by the dictatorship.

Even more difficult than obtaining information about torture is acquiring a description of the reactions of those tortured. However, it is possible to characterize the reactions and attitudes of prisoners undergoing interrogation and torture. Most frequently, they experience diffused anguish; a fear of imminent death; rage against their captors; a determination to withhold information; increased alarm; a feeling of impotence; and resignation to death. Less frequently they react with discouragement; hallucinations; de-personalization and detachment from reality; loss of muscle control; mutism; emotional dissociation; and the fear of disappearing.

It is common to find that prisoners claim they did not experience physical pain. Panic and fear are far more usual reactions. Moreover, in this group of women, numerous responses of rage against executions by the regime and of tenacity to resist cooperating with the authorities are significant. Their reliance on their consciences enables them to endure the horrible experience; it also fosters the process of recovery from torture. The twenty women suffer from various symptoms attributed to torture and/or to imprisonment. Most frequently they continue to feel uneasiness; anguish; diminution or lack of concentration; nightmares and insomnia; migraine headaches; depression, and paranoia. In addition, to the psychological effects, there are persistent physical and psychosomatic problems.

Organization of Women Prisoners

Abuse, brutality, and oppression have not prevented the women from developing organized prison activities. In her testimony, one prisoner reports the following about prison life.

The group is organized in its internal and external tasks; in addition, we belong to the National Organization of Political Prisoners. Group activities include handicrafts, cultural and recreational activities, and political analysis. Individually, prisoners read, study, and exercise. All prison activities are organized by ourselves. No activities are initiated by the gendarmerie or prison officials. Political activities are prohibited; and visitors are not allowed to bring in documents and tape recordings or to play music....Relations among the prisoners are good. We try to live in the greatest possible harmony, solving problems and antagonism through discussion...We try to avoid privileges or preferences in order to maintain the logical priority of friendship.

Fabiola Letelier is a lawyer working with the Committee for the Defense of the People's Rights (CODEPU).

The Arab and Mediterranean World: Legislation Towards Crimes of Honor
Laure Moghaizel

Introduction

We will examine a number of legislative measures dealing with *crimes of honor* in the Arab World (in Egypt, Iraq, Jordan, Kuwait, Lebanon, Libya, Syria, and Tunisia) and five Mediterranean countries, namely, Spain, Italy, France, Portugal, and Turkey. The principle of this legislation grants a full or partial excuse for one who commits homicide or causes injury if certain conditions are met.

A full or partial excuse may be obtained for an intentional homicide, one in which the perpetrator intended to kill the victim and not merely injure him or her. Among the most serious of crimes, intentional homicide, violates the first natural right protected by the law and guaranteed by the Declaration of the Rights of Man, It is punishable everywhere, often by a life sentence at hard labor or even by capital punishment.

While the penal code condemns the perpetrator of intentional homicide to punishment as serious as execution, the provisions concerning the *crimes of honor* may permit a full or partial excuse, thereby reducing the penalty or exempting the murderer from punishment altogether.

Legal Excuse: Crimes of Honor

The excuse is strictly regulated by statute with respect to its origin and influence upon the eventual punishment. A full excuse exempts the culprit from any punishment. It absolves and pardons the perpetrator. A judge may not punish the guilty party. A partial excuse does not prohibit punishment, but rather it lessens the sentence established by law. The party who is granted a partial excuse may later benefit from circumstances particular to his case which will further reduce his sentence. A legal excuse is imposed on the judge, while circumstantial mitigation of the penalty is left to his discretion.

A partial excuse reduces the sentence to a greater degree than does any considered circumstantial evidence. Factual

174

justification eliminates the infraction entirely; excuses do not. This is because factual justification, determined by law, removes the legal aspect and, consequently, eliminates the infraction.

In contrast to the cause of non-imputability, an excuse does not eliminate responsibility. In order to individualize the penalty (due to minority status, mental disorders, handicaps), causes of non-imputability are established by law. While recognizing that an infraction has occurred, these causes of non-imputability eliminate the responsibility of the act On the other hand, an excuse is granted on the understanding that the subjective and objective conditions of penal responsibility are satisfied, but they reduce or eliminate the penalty. Hence, the law recognizes that a homicide has been intentionally committed and that the perpetrator is responsible, but its mechanisms provide for the elimination or reduction of the penalty.

We should point out that, with the exception of the Jordanian, Lebanese, and Syrian penal codes, the Arab legislative measures under study do not grant full excuses, only partial excuses. The nature of these measures consists of a legal presumption. The law establishes a presumption of the total abolition of liberty of the person who surprises another caught in the act of adulterous *flagrante delicto* or illegitimate sexual relations. Subsequently, that person is absolved of the penalty of his actions.

Likewise, this law establishes a presumption of reduced liberty of the person who surprises his victim(s), found in *questionable attitudes*; his punishment is subject to mitigation. The presumptions are inferences which the law (or the judge) draws from what is known to what is unknown. The legal presumption is that which is linked by the law to certain acts or facts. It dispenses of all proof against the person to whom the law applies. In addition, no evidence can be admitted contrary to the legal presumption. In the framework of the texts we are now considering, the legislation establishes this legal presumption based on the recognition of certain facts relative to the case.

If a brother proves that he has surprised his sister *flagrante delicto* and committed his act at that very moment, he is not responsibile to prove that he acted in a moment of unreflected anger or that his feeling of infuriation abolished or

175

diminished his liberty. Once these facts are established, the law itself deduces that the perpetrator of the crime must be excused. Moreover, the public defender is not permitted to admit evidence that the accused did not act on a sudden impulse (*i.e.*, he knew about the misbehavior of his sister). Avoiding a legal investigation is precisely the legislative objective in granting the excuse, based solely on the circumstances surrounding the incident.

Legal Conditions of the Excuse

The circumstances and conditions necessary for the application of the excuses are as follows: the perpetrator surprised his victim (as the excuse cannot be applied if he was aware of the victim's relations with the third party); the victim was caught *flagrante delicto* for the case of a full excuse; the perpetrator committed his act during the initial period of his anger. Only momentary anger sparked by witnessing the offense is excused.

The *questionable attitude* of the victim is left to the discretion of the judge and can be interpreted in a broad or narrow sense. This concept, which is determined by the judge, is unique to Lebanese and Syrian law. Other Arab jurisdictions in question do not provide for the questionable attitude; they are more precise, requiring the act *flagrante delicto*. The notion of the questionable attitude has been greatly abused. For example, a brother sees his sister with a teacher on the village street when he arrives from Beirut. He kills her and claims the protection of a partial excuse on the grounds of a questionable attitude on the part of his sister. In another example, a brother sees his sister and a group of friends arrive at his house. He kills her. Subsequently, he claims that one of the young men of the group was her lover, citing a questionable attitude and obtaining a partial excuse.

This questionable attitude should be interpreted in a restricted sense. Only an attitude that creates doubt about the occurrence of adultery or sexual relations, or more precisely, an attitude that indicates a sexual act has occurred or is about to occur, should be called a questionable attitude. The witnessing of such a situation is supposed to have obscured the rational behavior of the perpetrator and to have limited his liberty. It should be the guideline for establishing the existence of a questionable attitude, when determining the possibility of mitigating the sentence of the accused.

A Comparative Analysis of Crimes of Honor

The Spanish penal code provides for a partial excuse for a husband, who by surprise has caught his wife in an adulterous situation, kills her and/or her lover immediately, or causes a serious injury to one or both parties. The partial excuse reduces the penalty of the husband's action, prohibiting him from free passage in the region where the case has taken place. In the case of less significant injury, he is totally exempted from punishment. These rules are also applicable in the same circumstances to parents of women less than 23 years of age who live in the family household. However, they do not apply to those who may have encouraged or facilitated the prostitution of the wife or daughters, nor to those who may have given their consent for such behavior.

The Portugese penal code reduces the punishment of the husband in certain circumstances if he kills his wife and/or her lover, or if he attempts to inflict a degree of bodily harm covered by Portugese statutes. The likely penalty is the forfeiture of the right of free passage in the region for a period of six months. He is, however, absolved of all punishment if these physical attacks are not serious in nature. These same rules are applicable to the wife who in the same circumstances kills her husband and/or his lover. They also apply to the parents of women less than 21 years of age in cases where the women are under parental supervision unless the parents have encouraged, facilitated, or favored corruption.

Special legal provisions also exist in Turkey, Italy, and France. The Turkish penal law lessens the punishment of the husband, wife, son, daughter, grandmother, or grandfather for violations of the law under certain circumstances. The Italian penal code provided for a partial excuse for the male member of the family in cases of homicide or personal injury for motives of honor. These measures, however, were struck down in 1979. The French penal code provided an excuse for a husband, who murdered his wife or her lover at the moment he surprised them *flagrante delicto* in the family household. This measure was struck down in 1975 by the divorce reform laws.

The Excuse Discriminates Against Women

Who profits from the granting of an excuse? It is a man: a spouse, brother, father, grandfather, great-grandfather, son, grandson, or great-grandson. In reality, any direct male relation fulfills the legal requirements. The victim is always female: a spouse, sister, mother, grandmother, great-grandmother, daughter, granddaughter, or great-grandaughter. In regard to a spouse, only a husband benefits from the possibility of an excuse. The term *husband* is used expressly in all legislation except the Lebanese and Syrian penal codes, which use the term *spouse*. But the intent of Syrian and Lebanese law is that only the husband can benefit from the excuse.

The Excuse Violates International Law

There are many motives and reasons to abrogate the measures which excuse crimes of honor. We will discuss the most important. Firstly, these texts are in blatant contradiction of the individual liberties guaranteed by the Universal Declaration of the Rights of Man (articles 3, 12 & 28) and the arguments relative to it, in particular, the agreement concerning civil and political rights. These measures establish male tutelage over women. They permit a man to kill a female relative even if she has reached the age of majority and is deprived of none of her faculties. Moreover, the male may be a husband, father, brother, or son. In fact, this power of life and death over a woman is extended even to a son who is a minor living under the responsibility of his mother. According to the Lebanese penal code, a son who kills his mother is punished less severely than a person who poisons his dog.

Secondly, these measures contradict the equality of human beings as guaranteed by the Universal Declaration of the Rights of Men (articles 1, 2, 3, 7 & 16), the aforementioned international agreements, and the Arab constitutions themselves. A number of these constitutions do not end by assuring the equality of all citizens (as is the case of Lebanon), but instead they expressly guarantee the equality of women and men and non-discrimination based on gender (*e.g.*, Egypt, Iraq, Jordan, Kuwait).

Thirdly, these measures are incompatible with the Declaration of the Elimination of Discrimination, which was unanimously approved by the United Nations General Assembly in 1967. Article 7 of that declaration advocates the abrogation of all legal measures which constitute discrimination against women. By virtue of the International Convention of the Elimination of All Forms of Discrimination Against Women (proposed in 1980 and ratified by a number of Arab states including Egypt, Jordan, and Tunisia), individual nations are moving to rescind such measures.

Our fourth to seventh points deal with contextual matters. Fourthly, these texts reestablish a limited notion of private justice. They grant individuals the right to pursue their own so-called justice and exempt the bearers of justice from part or all of the punishment prescribed for the committed act. Fifthly, the invoked excuses legally (both in spirit and in literal interpretation) remove the deterrent effect of the punishment. In expanding the possible applications to cases in which it is an issue of *questionable attitude*, these measures permit abusive interpretations. Sixthly, these texts perpetuate a tribal mentality, which does not conform to the evolution of customs. The penal code should be a living code, reflecting the customs and mores of a country during a given period of time. Seventhly, even when a judge does not apply a particular text to excuse a defendant, he may mitigate the sentence if circumstantial evidence warrants.

For these and other reasons, we must remove these texts from law. It is clear, however, that the abrogation of these measures will not be sufficient to deter crimes of honor, whose causes are numerous. Furthermore, multi-country studies have shown that the majority of criminals (82%) were illiterate, that they came from rural and poorer regions, and that most of them were young (15-25 years of age).

Strategy and Legal Measures
to Abrogate the Excuse of Crimes of Honor

In Lebanon, a committee of male and female jurists has been appointed to work towards abrogating the measures on crimes of honor. This committee made the necessary studies, conducted a large information program, proposed new laws, and presented their recommendations to the parliament and the government. The newly proposed legislation was adopted by a member of

Parliament, who passed it on to the Commission for Administration and Justice. This commission held two hearings to which the committee was invited. However, our efforts have been paralyzed by many events, most notably the political and security situation in Lebanon. The abrogation of the legal text regarding crimes of honor is part of a larger undertaking, started some time ago, to align national legislation with international standards.

This strategy began with a study, comparing Lebanese law with international, Arab and western legal policies. On the basis of this study, we have divided the established strategy into several phases. The first stage led us to obtain political equality (1953); the second, to obtain equality in inheritance rights (1959); and the third deals with various provisions of the penal code including those about crimes of honor. It would be time-consuming and superfluous to expound on the various points of our strategy, so we will mention only the principal points which include:

❑ a general study of the legislation as shown above

❑ a division of the activities into successive stages

❑ a narrowing of the goals and a precise formulation of the newly proposed law

❑ a consolidation of efforts and an establishment of an ad hoc representative committee

❑ a public awareness program

❑ a solicitation of support from political parties, labor unions, and other groups

❑ a presentation to responsible authorities of recommendations including the proposed new law

Such is the strategy we have followed in the past. Our present task is to translate this strategy into a national policy to bring about, both legally and practically, the equality of women and men and the full recognition and application of the fundamental rights of all human beings.

Laure Moghaizel is an attorney who works with the Institute for Women's Studies in the Arab World.

The Philippines:
Violence and Exploitation
of Women Workers in Southeast Asia
Jing Porte

Today, Southeast Asian women have become industrial workers who provide cheap and docile labor to multinational corporations. Throughout the Philippines, Thailand, Indonesia, and Malaysia, a growing number of women are working in the assembly lines of garment, textile, and electronics factories owned by the multinationals.

Export-oriented industrialization, a strategy for Third World development favored by the United Nations' International Development Organization (UNIDO), the World Bank, and the International Monetary Fund, has encouraged the exploitation of Third World workers. This policy has retarded the growth of local industries and thereby, employment. Multinationals, which establish plants that make use of cheap labor in activities such as assembly, repacking, or semi-processing, often compete with smaller local firms. Moreover, they do not transfer technology or skills to the local economy.

Cheap labor costs and regulated unionism are the two principal incentives to attract foreign capital investment in Southeast Asia. These countries establish free trade zones (FTZs) or export processing zones (EPZs) to lure the multinational corporations to invest in their economies.

In countries plagued by high unemployment and the presence of a vast reserve of workers, especially women, these multinationals can easily control labor with the help of puppet governments and repressive regimes. As a result, we find a depressed labor situation in Southeast Asia. Here, this situation means low wages, substandard working conditions, insufficient social security, job insecurity, and weak unionism.

Labor Conditions

In the Philippines and other parts of Southeast Asia, wages have not risen sufficiently to cope with rising prices and currency devaluation. The situation has been worsened by governmental restrictions on the right to strike. In fact, the government has threatened to ban strikes not only in the EPZs, but in all other industries. Workers have protested President Marcos' Presidential Decree 1033 of May 1, 1985, which created the Presidential Council for National Economic Recovery. The government has proposed that a non-renewable three-year ban on strikes and lockouts would solve industrial unrest and encourage economic recovery. Hence, it is blaming the workers for the country's economic recession. Anti-union policies, including the harrassment of union leaders, the suppression of organizing activities, and the restrictions on collective bargaining, have been a mainstay of the Marcos government.

These repressive conditions are reflected by worker unrest. In 1984, thirty establishments were the scenes of picketline violence, including the notorious Foamtex incident where two strikers were killed by police. In strike-related upheaval in 1984, more than 364 strikers were injured and at least 263 workers were arrested. Violence increased in 1985. Strikers have been gunned down by military agents and company security forces. In July, security guards at Stanford, Inc., in Pasig, Metro Manila shot and wounded three workers critically. In the same protest, twenty-one other workers were injured in picketline violence. Stanford's workers (90% of its 7,000 workers are women) were protesting the redundancy of approximately 1,500 workers, allegedly due to automation.

An upsurge in labor unrest is but one symptom of the explosive situation. It is also an indication that the system of labor relations as established by the Philippines' Labor Code has become obsolete and unresponsive to new conditions. Repressive governmental intervention in labor-management disputes has curtailed workers' rights and favored capital's interests. Nevertheless, workers continue to call strikes for better pay and working conditions and to struggle for political and labor rights.

Wages

In the garment and electronics industries, women workers are forced to increase their productivity periodically, as management raises production quotas without corresponding compensation.

Even though the legislated minimum wage in the Philippines and in Thailand cannot support a worker, companies often pay less. Women workers in EPZs in the Philippines receive about $78 per month while the basic cost of living is about $156 a month. These wages provide a bare subsistence: a diet of rice, fish, and water; lodging in small rooms with four or more people; and transportation to and from the factories. Most Thai women laborers work in small companies or sweatshops which generally pay only half of the legislated wage. To justify the lower wages, management permits them to live in a dormitory or boarding house and provides them a cup of rice for every meal.

Most women workers are important wage earners for their families. Meager as their wages are, they must scrimp on the necessities of life in order to send money to their families in the provinces. Despite their economic role, women generally receive lower wages than men. Moreover, because women workers have to attend to family problems and child-rearing functions, their absences reduce their take-home pay and their performance ratings which determine wage increases. With their dual responsibilities, women workers often have no more than four or five hours of rest.

An analysis of labor laws in the Philippines shows that they are hostile to collective bargaining. To preserve "industrial peace," the government may call for the cessation of collective bargaining to be replaced by compulsory arbitration. The potent weapon of the right to strike is restricted or banned to protect the interests of big businesses owned mostly by foreign nationals.

Substantial economic benefits are won by workers who militantly assert their right to unionize and strike. Through strikes workers are able to obtain wage increases. Of about 1,825 collective bargaining actions in the Philippines, the militant unions and federations under PKMK (a coalition of federations and unions against poverty) comprise the majority.

Job Security

With low-wage scales and high unemployment, business has been able to deny job security to workers. Even workers in labor-intensive and export-oriented industries have not been spared by massive lay-offs, redundancy, rotation, and suspensions.

The companies regularly circumvent laws on dismissals and lay-offs. They often use apprenticeship regulations to avoid regularizing some workers. Frequently, management responds violently to workers' protests about illegal termination of employment. In fact, it often targets union activists for dismissal.

Conditions in the Workplace

Due to the companies' desire to maximize profits, they maintain substandard conditions in the workplace. For example, garment factories are often sweatshops. Crowded rows of women bend over machines amidst piles of materials all day long. They endure poor lighting, ventilation, and toilet facilities, crowded mess halls if any, and intolerable heat. In electronics plants, exposure to chemicals and extremely cold air-conditioning (designed to protect the machines and materials) and other bad conditions often cause occupational illnesses such as stomach ulcers, mental stress, and strains. Unfortunately, some women die from these conditions and from accidents.

Health considerations are sacrificed to productivity. Furthermore, management does not acknowledge the existence of occupational hazards in the factories. The case of Elfreda Castellano illustrates this situation. For three years, this Filipino electronics worker at the Tin-Dip Station of Dynetics, Inc., worked during the night shift, soaking integrated circuits into acids and other chemicals. She died at the age of 22 from cancer of the lymph nodes. Management, who claimed that her death was not work-related, refused to make a settlement with her family.

Sexual Abuse and Harassment

Women on the assembly lines are usually subjected to sexual abuse and harassment. Often they must provide sexual favors for employment or promotion. "Lay-off or lay-down" has become a common occurrence. Hence, women workers are at the mercy of their supervisors or managers.

Virginity tests are given to applicants in the electronics industry to ensure that the women are single and without children. Management assumes that women workers with children are less productive than single women because of absenteeism.

Verbal and physical abuse have become common occurrences. For instance, male security guards can strip-search the women. And management dehumanizes the women by engaging in humiliating treatment and using foul language.

Maternity Benefits

Women workers are also beset by maternity and child care problems. In the Philippines, legislation has diminished the maternity benefits of women workers. Under the present law, women workers receive 100% of their basic wage for a period of six weeks for the first four pregnancies. If maternity benefits have been used up, sick leave benefits cannot be availed of as additional paid leave. The law provides for no paternity benefits at all.

The backbreaking factory work; the exposure to chemicals and dust; the unhealthy conditions; the absence of adequate nutrition and rest; and the domestic responsibilities; all have had a deleterious effect on the working women's ability to raise their children. The situation is worsened by the lack of social services such as nurseries and daycare facilities. Moreover, domestic tasks in the Philippines (and other Third World countries) are far more time-consuming than in the developed nations.

Living Conditions

Because of low wages, we find women workers being forced to find accommodation near the factory sites. Housing is scarce and expensive for their meager income. Their relatively high rent for a small room, which is shared with four to six roommates, consumes a large amount of their monthly income.

The housing accommodation near the factories are not clean and comfortable, and they do not have a good water supply or decent toilets. In the cases where the management provides dormitories for the workers (e.g., Thailand and Bataan Export Processing Zone), the rooms are small and crowded with beds for as many as three shifts of workers. Where housing is not available near the factory sites, the women workers must bear the costs of transportation. Very few companies provide shuttle buses to tranport their workers from the factory to town.

In Thailand, especially in smaller factories, workers live on a diet of rice and papaya salad. In the Philippines, a rice and fish diet must suffice for the 8-12 hour work day.

Workers do not receive free medical benefits. Therefore, women workers will obtain medical attention only after their illness is in an advanced stage. As a result, women do not receive adequate care for common diseases such as tuberculosis and pneumonia which are caused by the poor working and living conditions.

Unionism

The existence of yellow unions, the government's compulsary arbitration system, and repressive labor laws have weakened unionism in many countries in Southeast Asia. In spite of restrictions (or bans) on the right to strike, workers continue to defy these laws. Such actions often result in violence, injuries, and the imprisonment of workers. Hence, the workers have become radicalized and have turned to militant trade unionism to fight repression and exploitation.

Today, more and more women are actively participating in trade union activities. Women are union leaders; and on the picketlines, they face attacks from military and company agents. However, their full participation in union activities is complicated by their domestic roles. Often, women leaders must hurry home to attend to the marketing, cooking, washing, and baby sitting. As a consequence, they find it difficult to achieve their full potential of leadership and mobilization. Nevertheless, many women workers are devoted to organizing their fellow workers into progressive trade unions. They are confronting these pressing issues as both workers and women.

Jing Porte is the Southeast Asian Coordinator for the Committee for Asian Women.

Editor's note: This paper was drafted in 1985, and the author's critique of Philippine social and economic policy under the Marcos government may not apply to the current situation.

PART III

USING OR CHALLENGING THE LAW: THE STRATEGIES

5/STRATEGIES

Educating
and
Organizing

The papers in this and the following two chapters   look   at   actions   taken   by   women   and organizations   throughout   the   Third   World   to confront the variety of legal obstacles facing them. Strategies focusing on the *cultural component* of the law are included here under the general title of **Educating and Organizing,** which is in turn broken down   into   three   sub-sections   suggested   by   the nature of the strategies presented. The first deals with consciousness-raising efforts in a variety of formats   for   a   variety   of   purposes.   The   second examines those strategies which have chosen to develop paralegals or community *legal advisors* to educate or organize women about their rights or to offer them basic assistance in gaining access to the system. Since there are several instances of this approach   across   geographical   and   cultural boundaries, they are grouped here for comparative purposes. Third, those strategies which are multi-faceted   and   have   attempted   to   combine consciousness-raising   with   organizing   and mobilization are grouped together.

Finally, to clarify our editorial choices, it should be reiterated that many of these papers could be used as examples in several categories. If they appear under consciousness-raising, for example, it does not mean that the groups are necessarily doing no organizing or mobilizing. Rather, it was felt that the description of their consciousness-raising activities served as a good case in point. Likewise, the group of papers discussing paralegals does not include every strategy that has a paralegal component. Moreover, many strategies with educational activities carry them out out as part of legal reform, lobbying, or legal assistance activities.

Clearly, all the papers in the strategy section derive their respective strategies from an analysis of the underlying issues. Therefore, the reader should note the type of problem, the kind of analysis, and the structure of the strategy. This kind of contextual reading will enhance an understanding of the strategy. Since a complete analysis of each paper cannot be included here, we have chosen to mention only those aspects of the strategies which seem to be best exemplified or described by the paper.

❦❦❦❦

Raising Consciousness About the Problem

Beginning, then, with consciousness-raising efforts, we see represented a variety of approaches. In India, for example, *Krishnan* describes an awareness campaign that is multi-faceted. It is organized, in part, around slide shows and discussion groups in schools and colleges, and it also includes the publication of articles and letters in newspapers and journals. These activities are viewed as supportive to law reform and litigation activities designed to create popular demand for changes in the substance and practice of the law related to pornography and the unjust portrayal of women in the media. Similarly, *Rioja* and *Henault* recount the experience of an organization in Argentina which used consciousness-raising activities as part of a mass publicity drive to gain support for proposed legislative changes in family law. Included were a signature campaign, surveys, distribution of pamphlets and other publications, and workshops for teachers and students.

Other programs focus less on publicity than on direct educational work with targeted constituencies. For example, *Kaur* discusses a short-term legal literacy and education effort in Malaysia implemented by the University Women's Association of Malaya. Aimed at raising women's awareness about the law and their rights, a three-day seminar on family law for both Muslims and non-Muslims was conducted by experts in the field. It drew women leaders from community and political organizations. Mass distribution of pamphlets on the substantive themes discussed in the seminar supplemented the workshop pre-sentations. *Yamin* and *Sadli* in nearby Indonesia describe a longer-term, more structured strategy geared toward the legal education of Muslim women on a one-to-one basis in the context of a multi-service program of consultation for women. The program integrates legal, social, psychological, and religious components but does not include publicity or media elements. While both focus on awareness-raising and legal literacy, the methodology of the two programs is quite different.

Another example comes from *Campos* and *Beltré* from the Dominican Republic, who link consciousness-raising about rights and about the structural and cultural sources of discrimination to a program of legal assistance. However, a structured legal education program is the strategy's center-piece. It consists of a course which has biweekly sessions and is attended by women elected from urban and rural community groups. In addition to the course, program staff also produced a series of pamphlets summarizing the substantive information provided by the structured legal education program. Written in simple language, these pamphlets are for public dissemination. This case study from the Dominican Republic not only puts forward the goal of informing people about their rights but of developing the skills needed to assert rights, including an understanding of the sources of powerlessness. The paper contains a good discussion of empowering methodologies.

Vásquez also describes a program strategy which uses seminars and courses as primary vehicles for consciousness-raising. Within the strategy, educational activities are seen as a component of research aimed at assessing the consequences of the gap between theory and practice.

Methodologically, the program described by Vásquez begins as a dialogue with women participants from poor urban neighborhoods of Lima, Peru. Together the women explore their perceptions of the reality they live with regard to family violence and other problem areas. They articulate, for example, how they experience violence, how they see the options provided by the law, what their attitudes are toward the use of law and toward extra-legal solutions. These perceptions are then compared with the assumptions and provisions of the law in theory in order to assess where gaps exist. From there, it can be determined which perceptions of the women must be changed, which aspect of the law can be used, or which laws must be challenged or altered.

Yañez, also of Lima, Peru, describes a program utilizing a similar methodology. The program includes a phased educational component. After women attend a three-hour seminar, those most interested are invited to participate in a longer course which was cooperatively designed by the legal team. Out of this experience, a methodology was designed to be both participatory and adapted to the exigencies of the course's legal content.

❦❦❦❦

India: Women in the Media
Prabha Krishnan

Overview
Under Indian law, pornography does not exist; it is subsumed under the term *obscenity*. Some Delhi women's organizations are attempting to clarify this distinction and to make women understand that the expression of their sexuality is not obscene or indecent. The strategy of this case study has been developed by an *ad hoc* women-in-media group in New Dehli. Initially, we are working within the existing law to expose its inadequacies. Later, we plan to challenge the entire law in order to change it.

Our goal is the enactment of legislation that will effectively deter the exploitation of women's sexuality for commercial gain in the media. We aim to mobilize a mass base of enlightened women who will organize around the issue of the obscenity law to fight exploitation and who will support and help implement new laws. A long-term awareness campaign has been organized around slide shows and discussions groups, in schools, colleges, and elsewhere.

We also reach out to the general public through publishing articles and letters in major newspapers and journals. Simultaneously, we look for cases where we can effectively challenge the law. Our support comes from those individuals and groups with whom we have direct or indirect contact. Coincidentally, the Law Commission of India sought to amend sections of the Indian Penal Code dealing with obscene advertising and indecent displays. It circulated a working paper on the subject, seeking the views of citizens. We prepared a written statement of our views to enter into a discussion with the commission about pornographic images of women in the media.

Strategy Development
This strategy has evolved sporadically over a period of several years. In 1982, a group of Delhi women met to examine the portrayal of women in the media. The group decided to analyze existing images of women and to try to provide alternatives. However, after we attempted to share our

findings with larger groups, we discovered how limited discussions and posters (among other things) were. So, we developed a slide show, containing modules that show women in various media. Subsequently, the women working with the slide shows discovered that they had grave differences of perspective and ideology with women in the larger group.

One of the thorny issues was the use of demonstrations and protests against editors of journals which exploit the images of women. One such demonstration was followed up by a complaint against the targeted journal to the Press Council of India. Through this complaint, we sought to show how the existing laws, by concentrating on concepts of *obscenity* and *indecency*, did not express women's concerns. Moreover, they provided loopholes through which offenders escaped time and again, thus frustrating many concerned individuals.

We intend to continue our consciousness-raising program by reaching out to a greater number of groups of concerned people and various commercial associations, such as the manufacturers of photographic goods, tourism-promotion groups, film exhibitors, agencies, *etc*. Working within the constraints of time and money, we intend to look for possibilities to use the law creatively.

As time passed, we discovered a tendency among some women in the large group to use their access to influential individuals to press their viewpoint. While this certainly smoothed our way and won us a few initial victories, it soon became evident that we were not making a concerted effort to build a mass base. Many of us believed we must organize ordinary people who would seek change in the media's portrayal of women because they were concerned with justice, rather than rely on a small number of individuals who could use their influence and friendship with legislators. Therefore, we now seek access to various organizations on the strength of our previous work, but we maintain the initiative to institute and work for various reforms.

Focus
Our strategy focuses on the following groups of people: school children, college students, women's groups, other activist groups, and the media (such as writers and illustrators of children's books, ad agencies, TV and radio administrators,

etc.). We employ slide shows with different commentaries to fit the audience to examine the portrayal of women in commercials, children's entertainment, films, and the press. If convinced of the need to change the image of women, group participants then organize themselves. They provide the necessary support to change the laws and to pressure the government to enforce the new laws.

Major Legal Issues

We are concentrating on the major legal issues that revolve around the laws that govern the visual or verbal images of women in the media. These laws regulate commercials, advertisements, public displays, children's publications, and the use of postal facilities in the distribution of such materials. All of these laws stipulate that the use of nude and semi-nude images of women is *obscene* or *indecent*. The legal concept of pornography does not exist, but it is mentioned in case law as a synonym for *obscenity*. To distinguish between pornography and obscenity requires a different perspective. Therefore, we have refused support offered by many groups for reasons we consider wrong.

Organization and Participation

As indicated earlier, the strategy to change the law and make it more expressive of women's needs depends on the participation of large groups of women who will insist on the effective implementation of the changed laws. Hence, the creation of awareness of many groups of people is crucial.

At present, there are two main groups of women involved in the strategy. The first is a core group of women, who present the slide shows and who organize direct-action campaigns or activities. This group is not static in composition. The second group is composed of a larger number of women and men who either as individuals or as groups initiate and/or support the various activities.

A Class Action Suit

In December 1983, the issue of the monthly magazine, *India 2000*, which claims to articulate the aspirations of all Indians, accurately and forcefully presented a cover story entitled, "In the Scales of Justice: Rape." It purported to be a sober debate on the provisions of the Criminal Law Amendment Bill, 1980, which sought to remove existing inequities in the law governing rape trials. The amendment bill had followed on the heels of a nationwide uproar about the Mathura case. In 1972, a 15 year-old tribal girl Mathura complained that she was raped by two policemen at the police station where she had been summoned about a complaint of alleged abduction by her lover. The prosecution stated that Mathura had been forced to stay behind after her relations had left the police station. She was then raped.

Because Mathura was illiterate and unsophisticated, she contradicted herself in court. This contradiction and the fact that she had a lover, her fiancé, was enough for the court to rule that she had invited the attentions of the policemen. The lower court ruling was reversed by the high court, and again restored by the Supreme Court of India. This last judgement prompted four eminent law professors to ask the Supreme Court to reopen the case. In their written requests, they pointed out the grave inconsistencies and prejudices on the part of the court. Although the court refused to reopen the case, the women's movement was born anew as a result of the awareness and mobilization generated by the case.

In a related activity, the Law Commission of India spent nearly two years soliciting comments and suggestions about the rape laws from a wide spectrum of groups and individuals. Even though the resulting Criminal Law Amendment Bill, 1980 did not meet with uniform approval from all women's groups, it provided for a transfer of the burden of proof and for a wider recognition of custodial (police detainment) rape. These mild changes appear to have struck terror in the hearts of men, most of whom—whether educated or illiterate—tremble at the thought of false accusations of rape. But men's fear of false accusation, when considered in the context of a country where most rape victims are powerless and illiterate rural women and where a woman's fair name is the honor of her family, appears ludicrous.

Nevertheless, it is the basis for a four-page article in *India 2000* replete with pornographic illustrations and wild accusations of intoxicated women and female rape.

As noted before, the existing law, by defining such images as obscene and indecent, does not reflect our own perspective. We view the degrading portrayal of women as a tool of exploitative, powerful men for personal gain and as an incitement to gender hatred. As a result of our differences with the obscenity laws, our strategy has ruled out recourse to criminal courts. Instead, we turned to the Press Council of India. It has the duty to formulate guidelines on controversial cases and on the use of language and visuals; the council also has the power to censure violators of the press code. To further our continuing educational campaign, we sought the intervention of the Press Council by preparing a formal complaint about the offensive article.

Filing affidavits and counter-affidavits took almost a year to complete. On November 21, 1984, the Press Council held an *in camera* hearing. Our witnesses included lawyers, artists, psychologists, and civil libertarians. We argued that pornographic material incited gender hatred, and thus, seriously breached the provisions on public order and public morality contained in the Constitution of India. Therefore, pornography's effect of inciting gender hatred interfered with every woman's right of free movement and employment, due to the constraint of potential male violence. The respondents replied that they, as journalists, were exercising their right to inform the public and to create a debate on issues of public concern. Our action, they alleged, interfered with their freedom of speech and expression. Moreover, by present-day standards on nudity in the media, their pictures were not offensive.

The Press Council ruled in our favor, but it was quite clear that they viewed our arguments about pornography as flawed. However, members of the Enquiry Commission were also offended by the obscenity and indecency of the pictures and language. As provided by the Press Council Act, the offending journal was required to carry a retraction of the impugned article and a rebuttal by the complainants. We also asked the chairman of the council to intervene, so that a statement fair to both parties could be published. He agreed to examine our material and draft guidelines on the portrayal of women in the Indian press. Simultaneously, we approached the Law Commission of India to seek legislation that better expressed the position of women on their images in the media.

Results

Our campaign has not been an unqualified success as the confusion between pornography and obscenity continues to persist. Nevertheless, we believe that we have made great strides in opening up the topic to wider debate. Our interaction with people in various walks of life, such as artists, teachers, civil libertarians and many others, has convinced us that it is an important concern. Furthermore, our contact and work with the Law Commission of India hold great promises for the future of our struggle.

Prabha Krishnan is a freelance journalist in India.

Argentina: Changes in Family Law
Sara Rioja
Mirta Henault

Introduction

In Argentina, family law discriminates against women. Argentinean legislation, traditionally characterized as liberal, has permitted sex discrimination, although article 16 of the constitution expressly states that all inhabitants are equal before the law.

Since the beginning of this century, women's organizations and political parties have repeatedly called for changes in article 264 of the civil code which would increase the rights of both men and women. In 1919, Law 10.903 incorporated the current concept of paternal responsibilities and fathers' rights and authority over their children. This legal concept was ratified by Law 14.367 which extends the obligations of paternal authority to his illegitimate children. Although both spouses possessed these functions, they were attributed only to the father in practice. Only in extreme cases were mothers given these legal rights. Hence, women's social status and self-

199

esteem have suffered from these inegalitarian laws.

Process

Equal Rights for Argentinean Women (DIMA),which obtained legal status in 1980, was founded in 1976 by a group of women struggling for women's rights in the face of military repression. In 1979, a group of women renewed a campaign to change the paternal authority laws. DIMA immediately joined this struggle. The campaign coincided with a period in which the government allowed numerous Argentinean groups to travel abroad. Because husbands had to sign travel authorizations for children under 21 years of age, young married women felt they were the objects of discrimination. These events encouraged the growth of a collective conscience which was, perhaps, the most positive event of the decade for us.

Focus

The campaign to change the laws on paternal authority received popular support. It consisted of an important lobbying effort and a mass publicity drive. Fifty thousand signatures supporting this cause were submitted to the Ministry of Justice and to the Undersecretary of Youth and the Family. Although the military government did not acknowledge the demands, the campaign incited the two major parties to agree to include these reforms in their political platforms.

After the return of democracy, the Senate, which had studied the proposals of the political parties, addressed the issue of the existing laws on parental authority. The law was amended and approved by the Senate and was passed on to the House of Delegates for a final vote. In December 1984, we learned that the executive power had sent the reform bill to the Special House Sessions. We now know how the final text will read; it does not coincide fully with the one we requested.

Our movement developed in three phases. From 1976 to 1980, we organized panel and discussion groups, slide shows and films followed by debates. These activities were carried out privately and helped us to understand and unify ourselves. In 1980, Argentina signed the Convention on the Elimination of All Forms of Discrimination Against Women. In 1980, we reached a second phase as we lobbied for the ratification of the

1980 convention and began a campaign to suppress the paternal authority laws. Three congresses were organized: the Women in the World Today (with Argentinean participants) 1981; the Women in the World Today (with Latin American participants), 1982; and the Meeting of Feminine Creativity, 1983. A third stage of our activities began in 1983 when we organized an educational campaign—Intensification of the Paternal Authority Campaign—to eliminate sexism in textbooks, as well as to establish teaching programs and correspondence schools.

DIMA works through the educational system to create an awareness about women's rights, existing stereotypes, the social inequality of women, and the need to change existing textbooks. To date, we have gone to several schools and visited with a total of 3,000 students, staff, parents, and guests. We encourage comments and discussion among adult groups and we would like to extend these activities to the whole country.

We have printed twenty-four brochures and curricular aids for distribution. They contain lessons on women's rights, women's history, and women in the labor force and society. These publications will provide unpublished references which are not mentioned in official teaching. We plan to organize workshops for teachers and students to attract new people to our program and to disseminate our ideas.

Issues

In addition to the campaign about parental authority, we want to develop awareness about the following issues and themes that have been addressed by the congresses we have organized.

The issue of women with respect family, politics, morality, power structures, laws, *inter alia* must be addressed. Secondly, labor laws and prerogatives that protect or discriminate against women should be examined for their effects on women in the labor market and in the home. Thirdly, the unequal education of women, women's image in the media, and customs that devalue or distort the feminine image merit attention. The search for women's identity and an examination of the social devaluation of women are critical topics as are considerations of the historical development of the feminine image and the history of the struggle for women's liberation. Fourthly, we focus on issues of sexual development, sexuality, maternity, body language, *etc.* Finally, the future of women in society must be considered by those striving for an informed consciousness.

Results

We carried out an informal public opinion poll and found that the public believed that:

women are capable of obtaining a high level of training, and intelligent and motivated enough to achieve positions of responsibility, but they will not be able to integrate into these higher positions because of their special characteristics.

When questioned about these characteristics, the people responded that:

women could have problems with meetings and schedules because they always give priority to the family, vacations, illnesses and their own problems, showing that they have less freedom to devote to work outside the home.

The respondents did not consider single female workers, widows, separated or divorced women, or childless women. When pollsters questioned them on this point, they were evasive, stating that "the kindred/extended family would always come between a woman and her position of responsibility."

Our research shows that male opinion of women has only changed superficially. Analysis has revealed that men do not want women to compete with them in employment and prefer that women attend to domestic tasks and the children. These attitudes are reinforced by religion, society, media, and public opinion. They are also intensified by sexual harassment of women which is common in the workplace.

We have protested against the negative image of Argentinean women through many activities, known as the Campaign to Improve Women's Image in Communication Media. To accomplish this objective, we have designed an educational technique with which we are currently experimenting. It has been developed to counteract the harmful effects of the negative social image of women on their identity and self-respect.

Lessons

Since the establishment of the women's decade in 1975, the situation of women in Argentina has not improved in spite of the efforts of DIMA and other women's organizations. On the contrary, it has deteriorated in certain aspects.

While democracy has been restored, it has not improved significantly the conditions of, or attitudes toward, women. Conditions that would enable women to participate effectively in the country's development process have not yet materialized.

The initiation of the democratic process has not altered the nature of feminist activity, but it has brought a greater participation of women in the political parties. However, fewer women are represented in the legislature and in high governmental positions than in past democratic periods. Apart from the scarcity of women in high political or financial positions, there are also few female executives or union leaders—even in those sectors dominated by female workers, such as garment factories. In the labor force, traditional patterns of discrimination have not changed: higher positions are generally offered to men, while women continue to occupy the lower ranks and earn less than men.

In education, the traditional stereotypes have not been modified. The school textbooks are patently sexist. A few schools have established sex education courses, and some universities are organizing women's studies programs. Although women dominate teaching in the primary grades, they do not hold high positions within the Department of Education.

The media has intensified its portrayal of women as sex objects, capable only of serving and giving pleasure. This image is one-dimensional and precludes any mention of a woman's initiative or imagination. It is a caricature of women, distorting women's self-image.

In conclusion, although a greater number of women occupy positions in public life and the professions, their situation remains inferior to that of men. We have not been encouraged by a high level of activism and dedication among Argentinean women. In fact, they tend to uphold traditional stereotypes. Nevertheless, DIMA and the feminist movement will continue to struggle to eliminate discrimination against women and to promote their active and effective participation in the political, economic, and social life of this country. Our work will only be accomplished when women are able to benefit fully from the development and achievements of Argentinean society.

Sara Rioja and Mirta Henault are members of DIMA (Equal Rights for Argentinean Women) in Buenos Aires.

Malaysia: Educating about Rights
Amarjit Kaur

Overview

The strategy adopted by the University Women's Association, University of Malaya (UWA) has aimed at confronting the constraints on women in the area of family relations in Malaysia. The objectives have been to raise the status of Malaysian women by using the law—Islamic law for Muslim women and the Law Reform (Marriage and Divorce Act) of 1976 for non-Muslims—and to empower them through the increased awareness of their rights. The major activities of this strategy include legal literacy, education, and consciousness-raising. A three-day seminar was organized at the national level by legal experts to initiate the strategy. The seminar held five plenary sessions on topics including marriage and divorce; property, maintenance, and succession; children, guardianship, custody, and maintenance; battered wives and abused children; and legal aid facilities.

At each session, papers were presented from the point of view of academics, practitioners, and legal authorities (the Syariah Court officials in the case of Muslim law and a welfare officer for non-Muslim law). Each session was followed by workshops, which were chaired by law faculty students enrolled in the Professional Practice Course at the Law Faculty, University of Malaya. The UWA, in conjunction with the Federation of Women Lawyers, Malaysia, distributed pamphlets published in Malay, English, Mandarin, and Tamil about women's legal rights. These brochures are written in a simple and straightforward manner and discuss subjects such as women's rights under the new divorce law. Finally, the experts who gave papers at the seminar have agreed to give talks and to counsel women when requested by women's organizations.

Process

Through various UWA programs the organization came to recognize that both Muslim and non-Muslim women were basically ignorant of their legal status in Malaysia. As a result, the UWA decided that it would organize a national seminar to disseminate information on Malaysian family law to a wide cross-section of women.

The major share of the funds for this project came from an American agency, the Asia Foundation. Other contributions came from the vice-chancellor, University of Malaya, and commercial organizations. An important stimulus to this project was the impending implementation of the Law Reform (Marriage and Divorce Act) of 1976. This significant piece of legislation outlawed polygamy among non-Muslims and relaxed the conditions for non-Muslim women to obtain a divorce. There was also discussion about legislation in the individual states which would require a Muslim male to obtain the permission of his first wife before he could contract a second marriage.

Focus

The focus of the strategy was to organize a national seminar that would reach a representative group of women from women's political and community organizations. UWA invited both rural and urban women leaders to make them aware of Malaysian family law. These leaders were expected to disseminate information locally upon their return to their respective centers. These activities were to be followed by UWA visits to local centers to provide counseling, updated information, and personal contact. The women's political groups included the women's wings of the major political parties in Malaysia. These organizations have very wide grassroots support in their communities.

Major Legal Issues

The strategy has concentrated on family law, battered wives and abused children, and legal aid facilities. There is a real need to safeguard women's legal rights and to sensitize them to their legal status in the country so that they can both understand and challenge their position in Malaysian society.

Women constitute 49.6 per cent of the Malaysian population, 70 per cent of whom live in rural areas. Traditionally, the rural woman has been isolated from the major forces of modernization. However, urban women have fared little better. Increasingly, they have become alienated from urban society because of rapidly changing lifestyles. One indication is that divorce among Malaysian women is on the increase. Legal and social discrimination affects women in numerous ways. For example, the government's industrialization policy has resulted in the creation of a floating reserve of inexpensive female labor. The strategy, therefore, attempts to address the myriad needs of Malaysian women.

Organization and Participation

The strategy was conceived by the UWA, which was responsible for its overall organization. A total of 200 people participated in the seminar. Speakers included academics from the Law Faculty, University of Malaya, who discussed legal principles and consequences; private sector lawyers and legal practitioners, who presented case studies; religious officers from the Syariah Court who discussed Islamic law; and welfare officers who discussed non-Muslim law. Workshops were chaired by male and female law students who were enrolled in the Professional Practice Course conducted by the Law Faculty of the University of Malaya. Among the other participants were UWA members, and urban and rural women representatives of women's community and political groups. On a state basis, it was decided to invite ten women leaders each from the largely rural states, six women from the other West Malaysian states and four women from the East Malaysian states. A number of other interested individuals also attended the seminar.

Results

The strategy proved to be highly successful. It was evident that the participants were fired with enthusiasm after the talks and discussions. An awareness of their rights instilled within them the need to ensure that further action was taken, so that the experiences gained at the seminar did not just fizzle. No memoranda were drawn up, nor resolutions passed. It was clear, however, that the leaders of the various communities and members of numerous political organizations had gained an appreciation of the issues to carry out their tasks, to promote legal literacy, and to fight injustice. The papers on non-Muslim law were translated into Mandarin and Tamil, so that they could be distributed to the non-English speaking public. The strategy, therefore, has succeeded in increasing women's access to essential resources.

In March 1982, the Malaysian government finally implemented the Law Reform (Marriage and Divorce Act) of 1976. Later on in the same year, marriage tribunals were set up to handle marital separations. We, in UWA, feel that our strategy, and the publicity it generated, was partly responsible for the initiation of this move by the government. The paper, "Battered Wives and Abused Children," recommended the establishment of a center for battered wives in Malaysia. In 1983, one of the leaders from the women's wing of the Chinese political party (who had assisted UWA by printing and distributing the Mandarin version of the papers on non-Muslim law) took the initiative to set up a center for battered wives. This center is run by the Women's Aid Organization and currently has two full-time and several volunteer workers.

Seminar participants were also keen that the UWA organize seminars on other issues of relevance to women. UWA selected two topics: consumerism and women's employment. A panel discussion was organized on consumerism where information on applicable laws was disseminated. In the case of women and employment, the UWA, in conjunction with the United Nations agency A.P.D.C organized a two-day seminar in April 1984. This seminar highlighted the position of women workers in Malaysia. The participants consisted of representatives from workers' and women's organizations, academics, and activists. At this seminar, resolutions were passed for the improvement of the status and working conditions of women in agriculture and industry, and other sectors. These resolutions were delivered to the appropriate authorities.

Major Lessons

This strategy has been very effective in reaching a wide audience. It also helped the UWA to identify women activists in the country and to promote closer contacts among us. Participants have since approached us for advice and information on other issues relevant to women. Hence, the UWA has become a recognized resource on women's issues in Malaysia, mainly because its membership consists of educated women concerned with the betterment of women in general.

Amarjit Kaur is a professor of history at the University of Malaya in Kuala Lumpur.

Indonesia: Women and Legal Aid

Nani Yamin
Saparinah Sadli

Overview

With the many changes occurring in Indonesian society, the existing institutions and legal infrastructure have proved inadequate to deal with the problems of women and families. One such change was the reformed marriage law ratified on January 2, 1974 and the Implementing Government Regulation No. 9, 1975, which aimed at protecting the institution of marriage. Prominent women felt that further action was necessary to implement the ideals embodied in the government regulation and to promote further reform.

In response, the Indonesian Council of Ulamas and the Indonesian People for Humanity Foundation agreed to establish the Institute for Consultation and Legal Aid for Women and Families (LKBHuWK). The LKBHuWK, which is supported by the Al-Azhar Islamic Peasant Foundation, was established on December 21, 1979. Its activities are based in Jakarta, but it plans to establish branches in other regions.

The general aim of the institute is to fulfill women's and families' needs that have been created by the process of Indonesian national development. These needs often require legal, social, psychological, and religious assistance. With the help of supporting organizations (*e.g.*, the Indonesian Council of Ulamas and the Indonesian Lawyers Association) and knowledgeable individuals, the institute has organized experts in various disciplines to assist women and families with their problems.

The Muslim women staff consists of volunteers and mostly part-time professionals. The professionals are composed of social workers, lawyers, psychologists, and religious workers, all of whom work as a team. Because our ultimate goal is to enable the client to feel content, and not only to solve her legal problems, the institute uses an holistic approach. This approach involves viewing a client's problem as personal and psychological with legal implications. The emphasis on understanding the client's needs and anxieties is stressed. It requires that every client is first interviewed by a psychologist to determine the nature of the problem. If necessary, the case is then discussed with a lawyer, a social worker, and a religious worker. This approach helps the client to choose the most suitable solution to her particular problem. It also shortens the court procedures when they are required.

Legal experts play an essential role by advising clients in the preparation of their cases if litigation is required. They make the client aware of the costs and benefits of a legal resolution of the problem. They also represent the client in the court. Social workers deal with a wide variety of problems. For example, they provide technical support for the lawyers and psychologists in the preparation and resolution of a case. A social worker assists the client in preparing a legal case. The term *social worker* is very broadly defined here, and it includes medical doctors, architects, notary publics, *etc.* Finally, religious professionals are available to advise clients. As the role of religion is important in Indonesian society, religious faith is emphasized in a client's search for answers to her problems. Because the foremost concern of the institute is the individual, it thoroughly prepares and follows up each case. Hence, it may involve psychological counseling, helping the person to find suitable housing, or even finding the client a job.

Focus

The institute's activities include providing consultation, advice, and legal aid to women and families, legal education and information, informational activities to improve family welfare, and premarital consultation and advice. The institute also initiates research on women in the context of Indonesian society and it advises the government on the social welfare of women and families. It also publishes and sponsors discussion fora, symposia, and seminars to expand ideas on relevant subjects. Through the assistance of government and private organizations, it provides better educational and employment opportunities for women. Finally, the institute participates in international organizations concerned with women's problems.

The institute seeks to avoid total financial dependency on outside sources. As a private organization, we are prohibited from receiving regular governmental funds. To help finance the institute, we decided to enlist the support of 100 women sympathizers who would be made *Distinguished Women Members* of the institute. Each would contribute a one-time donation of Rp. 500,000 (equivalent to $500). Over the course of three years, seventy-five women have joined the ranks of *Distinguished Women Members*. Their contributions have not been used for routine activities, but are placed in an endowment fund. Routine activities are financed out of our daily revenues and interest income. The institute also receives funding from private sponsors (NGO's) for special activities. Another source of income is special projects, such as the Family Education Program at the LNG plant in Lhok Seumawe, North Sumatra. Other sources of income are lecture fees and donations from clients or their relatives.

Results

Although the institute is only five years old, it has already made a number of substantial achievements by empowering women in general, and by making the law more relevant to women's lives. The institute has established two other branches in Bandung and Yogyakarta, which employ similar strategies and policies to the one in Jakarta. As a result, the branch offices have operated efficiently from their inception.

The institute also assisted in the establishment of a similar institute at the Arun-LNG plant in Sumatra by preparing and training the staff in counseling principles. The institute continues to encourage the organization of new branches by attracting government officials to this endeavor and by recruiting trained professionals and volunteers to serve in the potential branches. Aid is currently being solicited from NGO's for this program.

Programs providing information and basic legal education have been established for women and families. The aim of the programs is to educate women about their rights in marriage and family life and about their civic and religious duties as responsible citizens. The programs have attempted to make the legal system relevant to women's lives. Where necessary, the institute has taken an active role in improving existing laws concerning women. However, the institute has continued to nurture a cordial relationship with the government by the activities it chooses to undertake.

No organization is without its problems. Ours are derived from two main factors: budgetary constraints and the need for more full-time professionals. Although the number of clients increases each year, programs cannot expand sufficiently within the existing budget. Since the institute serves its clients on a voluntary basis, its income from fees is very limited. While soliciting private funds is a tedious process, we are convinced that this source is the only solution to finance the further expansion of the institute's activities.

Given the present level of activities, the institute needs more professional staff. The present director and staff are doing a creditable job despite the prevailing conditions. But they are clearly overburdened by routine activities, leaving them little time to plan long-range strategies. To expand the organization, a critical, systematic, and professional evaluation of the institution and its activities is required. Hence, we need to staff a professional secretariat to plan and evaluate the future direction of the institute. Currently, we do not have the funds to employ these professionals. Related to this problem is recruiting women professionals who often require job security and good salaries. These demands cannot yet be fulfilled by the institute.

211

Up until this year, women professionals have volunteered their expertise by working part-time for the institute. However, to expand the activities of the institute, more than idealism is required. We hope to learn how to deal with these problems from the experiences of those here. Clearly, all of you have faced constraints on your activities to improve the well-being of women and their families. We have learned from others' past experiences in an attempt to further our goals. We therefore welcome all insights to help us prevail in our efforts to assist women.

Nani Yamin is the founder and director of the Institute for Consultation and Legal Aid for Women and Families. Saparinah Sadli is the founder and member of the Institute's Advisory Board.

Dominican Republic: Legal Aid and the Urban and Rural Poor

Luisa Campos
Mildred Beltré

Overview
The Dominican Center for Legal Counseling and Research (CEDAIL) focuses on the plight of women workers, women peasants, and unemployed women in the Dominican Republic. The strategy of the project confronts the diverse sources of the inequities which women suffer whether they are economic, social, historical, cultural, psychological, or legal. We have chosen here to address the common forms of abuse and exploitation of women that occur within the home and everyday life. The historical and cultural conditioning of impoverished and uneducated Dominican women leads to their poor perception and uncritical acceptance of abuse and exploitation. Hence, many of these women have no concept of the forces underlying their subordinate position.

The multiple forms of the abuse of Dominican women do not generally include cruel torture—illustrated historically by the Mirabal sisters (three women who rejected the attentions of dictator Rafael Trujillo) or political activitist Florinda Soriano (Mamá Tingó)—who refused to accept complacently the violation of their rights by those in power. On the contrary, the great majority of our women are subtly exploited in every-day life. However, in many ways, exploitation is no less incapacitating than the more brutal means of torture; it destroys hope, dignity, and even lives.

The basic legal education project aims to assist impoverished urban and rural women who are greatly abused and marginalized. The goals of our strategy focus on three main tasks. Firstly, we educate these women about their rights and how to exercise them. Secondly, we promote legislative reform so that the laws better reflect women's social reality; we are also working to increase women's access to the legal system. Thirdly, we are attempting to show women that their problems are not individual but social in origin, and they can best be confronted through collective action.

The main activities undertaken to achieve the objectives of the strategy include the following.

❑ the organization of classes, discussions and workshops, and the distribution of basic legal education publications (all of which take place within the framework of organized groups to increase the impact on the communities)

❑ the provision of legal counseling and representation (and using casework as an educational process)

❑ the encouragement of unity and solidarity to strengthen women's struggles

❑ the use of social communication channels to complement the struggles in the poor sectors

❑ the training and sensitizing of law students about the legal and social needs of the underprivileged.

Process

The development of a basic legal education strategy for poor women in rural and urban areas of the Dominican Republic was initiated jointly by the staff of CEDAIL and the base groups with whom they work. In the process of legal counseling, the CEDAIL team became disturbed by the ignorance of women about their most elementary rights and the means to exercise them. However, their clients were beginning to recognize the necessity of knowing their rights and the means to obtain them. The CEDAIL initiative was born out of this concern to respond to the problems witnessed in the legal assistance and defense work. As a result, the CEDAIL staff decided to prepare an education project study on human rights.

In 1982, the preparation of pamphlets on human rights was begun. Because it was difficult to obtain adequate financing and staff to carry out the project, we are only now in the printing stage of production. However, a trial edition of the pamphlets has been issued to elicit criticism, recommendations, and corrections from the women's groups using them. Because the printing of this material was delayed, our educational work has centered around talks, workshops, and the utilization of legal cases as they arose. No substantial changes have been made in the strategy. From the very beginning, the legal assistance and support services were envisioned as educational vehicles that would lead to women's awareness, organization, and action.

Focus

In our view, the legal difficulties of Dominican women stem from the content of the law itself, the institutions charged with applying the law, and the attitudes and behavior of the people. We decided to focus on the legal structure and legal culture of the society. Specifically, our project addresses the cultural aspect of women's legal status through legal assistance services and legal education programs. These activities have shown that the social conditioning of impoverished women has resulted not only in a lack of fundamental legal knowledge but also in their acceptance of unjust and discriminatory policies and practices. Emphasizing the structural and cultural aspects of the law is the first step in educating women about gaining and defending their rights. Nevertheless, we recognized that we could not ignore the content of the law because much of the Dominican legislation is imported and does not correspond to everyday life. However, addressing the problem of the law's content was secondary. It will be emphasized only when the impoverished women themselves can critically analyze laws that are unjust and discriminatory and can unite to demand changes in the legal system. We hope that this movement will become sufficiently strong to bring about legislative changes in response to worsening living conditions and the demand of popular struggles. Until now the Dominican government has not proposed any legal reforms.

Legal Issues

The project addresses six principal areas of the law: human rights; constitutional rights; women's rights; agrarian rights and land laws; labor law; and penal law. The selection of these legal issues emerged primarily from the concerns of the participants, who voiced their essential concerns to the CEDAIL team.

Organization and Participation

Participants in the educational program are chosen by their own local organizations, and they consist of poor women from both rural and urban areas. The women and CEDAIL jointly develop their courses; they meet with the CEDAIL team every two weeks in a two-hour working session. Both rural and urban women participate together so that they can familiarize them-selves with the many sources of discrimination and social inequities.

Due to the structural nature of the problems, the strategy requires the initiation of a process of dialogue, consciousness-raising, and organization that enables the women to act upon their demands. In this way, the strategy does not only respond to extreme cases, but also helps women to use the law in their everyday lives.

Results

Although the basic legal education project has been planned since 1980, the work consisted only of that involving our legal cases until recently. A systematic legal educational program began in March, 1985. Although it is too early to evaluate the systematic approach, we can assess the impact of our educational efforts geared toward legal counseling and representation.

Our basic premise of this form of education is that a victim of injustice is the principal actor in the struggle to obtain her rights. Therefore, we must train ordinary women to know their rights and to organize to defend them. We must not act as substitutes for these women in their struggles. The function of our team is to offer legal education and assistance to women to claim their rights. The women determine the nature of the research, education, and action to reach their goals. The participants then teach women in their communities basic legal knowledge. They also learn to confront appropriately those who violate their rights.

The diligence of the women, whether urban slum-dwellers or rural peasants, has been most pronounced in their active participation in many diverse struggles. In April, 1985, women peasants, members of community peasant associations from Los Coquitos in Monte Plata province, were arrested on three occasions while demonstrating for their land. One group remained in prison for five days; CEDAIL obtained their release through a *habeas corpus* provision. During the time they were imprisoned, a predominantly women's delegation of poor urban dwellers and rural peasants occupied a neighborhood church in solidarity with the prisoners' land struggle and in protest of their imprisonment. During the occupation of the church, the presence of the heavily armed National Police never deterred the people from supporting the peasants' struggle.

The solidarity of the rural and urban masses that emerged from this experience proved to be a source of strength and a stimulus to the popular struggles. As a result of this strategy, there has been an increased awareness by women about their rights and the need to defend them. One such indication is the growing caseload at CEDAIL. The women increasingly recognize human rights violations and have begun to fight against them. In addition, there is growing participation of women in the legal training programs. Currently, CEDAIL's legal education is being planned with the help of women from the neighborhoods and peasant communities. Furthermore, the implementation of the strategy has led to further contact with the peasants' groups and women's organizations.

Contact with women in the urban neighborhoods and

peasant communities has been established in order to provide necessary legal assistance and support services. The favorable results have been enhanced by the highlighting of everyday problems and ongoing legal cases as an educational component of the process. It has strengthened the unity and the struggle of CEDAIL and the communities with which it works.

Lessons Learned

An essential part of the strategy is the principal role played by women in demanding their own rights. The work of the CEDAIL staff is to provide legal and other relevant information to the participants. We are convinced of the important function of education in any legal services project, as it can empower people to demand that the law be an effective instrument for social equality.

Another important aspect is our recognition of the need for a continuous evaluation of the educational and participatory activities to rectify errors and to reinforce their merits. A great drawback in the strategy was our original assumption that those who were responsible for the legal assistance services could simultaneously undertake systematic educational work. We now recognize that we must employ a staff to carry out the educational program in close coordination with the legal team. With additional personnel, we can provide better assistance and support for the poor. Another significant limitation is the precarious nature of any project involving the poorest and most disadvantaged social groups. Much of these people's time is consumed just in the struggle for survival.

An important experience has been the coordination of our activities with those of other groups whose aims are not directly linked to the legal system. For example, some organizations have initiated a nutritional and health information project involving both urban dwellers and peasants. This project reinforces the process of consciousness-raising, organization, and popular struggle.

If we desire just and humane societies, it is necessary to oppose both the international capitalist system and the national structures of oppression. We must prepare united strategies to struggle against some of the common manifestations of these systems: the unequal wages received by women; the widespread exploitation of women by multinational corporations in the free zones; the rural exodus of peasants as a result of the international agro-industry; the international female prostitution networks; and the bad working conditions of domestic workers who have little or no access to a social support system.

The eradication of these dehumanizing conditions and the transformation of our societies demand international solidarity to confront these arduous tasks. We have no alternative other than to respond in solidarity to the historical challenges that have befallen us. We must create a humane world that negates the masculine attributes that characterize the current international order: competition and aggrandizement of the strongest; militarization; excessive consumption by the few; and indifference towards the suffering of the great majority. Female solidarity is essential to place cooperation before competition, democracy before authoritarianism and bureaucratism, the love of people before the love of things, egalitarian economic conditions before superfluous luxury, and peace before war.

Sister Luisa Campos, a Dominican nun, and Mildred Beltré are lawyers working   at the Dominican Center for Legal Counseling and Research.

Peru: The Exercise of Women's Rights
Roxana Vásquez Sotelo

Introduction

The civil and political rights guaranteed by Peru's constitution are not practical realities. The law, which only a minority of the population supports, is discriminatory and unfair. Women are unable to exercise their rights because they are not informed about them; nor do they have the means of acquiring legal knowledge. Because women's views are excluded in many areas of life, they are not incorporated within the legal structure. Moreover, the legislative bodies enact and maintain laws that discriminate against women.

Working in legal programs that focus on women has shown us how the law is used for social control. One of the best means of sustaining negative social attitudes toward women is the law which institutionalizes the oppression of women. Furthermore, in the patriarchal family, informed mechanisms are established to control women's work, sexuality, and reproduction.

Overview

Members of the Flora Tristán Center are dedicated to analyzing the causes of women's subordination and placing this oppression in a historical and contemporary perspective. We must broaden our understanding of women's socioeconomic conditions, including the interpersonal relations within the family structure. Most importantly, we are trying to translate this analysis into an activist program that promotes the organization, consciousness-raising, and social participation of Peruvian women. We believe that the women's movement must take a public stand against violence directed towards women. Such a position will facilitate public discussion and debate about this issue.

As a result of our exploration of women's socioeconomic conditions and legal status, we have systematized and exchanged our ideas and experiences with other women's organizations. Given the scarce theoretical and methodological resources, it is essential to produce publications and research on specific aspects of women's conditions. The center views the task of women's liberation as part of the fight for a true democracy. Therefore, it participates in all activities and initiatives that aim to defend democratic liberties, especially those of women.

Focus

From the legal perspective, our fundamental objective is to analyze and compare the theory with the reality of the law and to assess the social consequences of the contradictions of this relationship. To implement our goals, we evaluate current legal practices and examine, for example, the everyday lives of couples, specifically men's abuse of women, women's perceptions of violence, and ways to confront violence in the home. We examine how women's legal conflicts endanger the stability of the family. Moreover, we are analyzing the impact on women of marginal socioeconomic conditions and the various weaknesses of the law. We also assess the common people's understanding of legality and extra-legality.

The center organizes its programs around four substantive areas: women and employment; information and culture; urban development; and the law itself. The legal program focuses on training, counseling, and researching. In the areas of training, we organize legal seminars for women's groups from the *Pueblos Jóvenes* (marginal urban populations of Lima) to teach them about their rights. Our counseling activities focus on issues of separation, divorce, alimony, and violence. As researchers, we are proposing to study the various legal problems of women. We are particularly interested in analyzing the sexual division of labor and sexual discrimination. Our research will examine the functioning of the legal system and the social structure so that we have a better understanding of women's practical legal and social needs.

Participation

Our team members select, design, and execute the strategy. Groups of organized women participate from the Pueblos Jovenes of Lima and other similar locales. In ten days of legal workshops, approximately 300 women have participated to date. Women's groups have asked the center to organize various other activities as part of the legal workshop. Routinely, the center provides legal counseling in an environment that is open and secure. More informally, students, journalists, and other women who wish to discuss their experiences also participate.

Results

At this stage, the most important results have been the change of the program's focus and the redesigning of specific strategies to help women understand and use the law. Practical work has shown us that Peruvian law does not adequately provide for the socioeconomic realities of women today. Our goal to change the focus of the law and to redefine the law's role is inter-related to our work for a consistent legal system and viable alternatives for poor women.

We have had the opportunity to learn about the dynamics of some women's organizations. We have also observed how women tend to organize themselves during periods of crisis and how such an organization becomes the main vehicle for their action and participation in social change.

Roxana Vásquez Sotelo is one of the directors of Flora Tristán's legal program for women.

Peru: Legal Education for Poor Women
Gina Yañez de la Borda

Overview

The Manuela Ramos Movement of Peru has been operating for six years to change the oppressive conditions of women in all areas of society and life. Our strategy concentrates on work with women's organizations with whom we help develop training courses about the concepts of sexuality and the image and organization of women. At the end of 1983, we began to work on three main areas of legal assistance for women: training, services, and legal research. We initiated the project by demonstrating that women have very limited access to legal information. In our country, women do not use the legal system, which in any case is only marginally interested in the common people.

Development and Focus

Our general objectives include making women aware of and able to understand Peruvian law; publicizing the nature of the legal situation of women, minors, and the family; and assessing the need for legal reform. Our specific objectives are training paralegals living in poor areas and linking the women to the legal services that Manuela provides.

From March 12 to April 18, 1985, we taught one workshop in eleven work sessions. The subject matter of the course was published in a booklet containing the major points of the program; these were given to the women at the beginning of the course. Our legal team conducted a workshop in conjunction with women members of Manuela Ramos as part of the course preparation for paralegals. Comments and suggestions of the participants provided the workshop team the necessary feedback to revise the contents of the course. As a result, the subject matter of the training course for paralegals, which included civil, criminal, and administrative law, and the constitution (as they relate to women), was modified.

Legal Issues

Our project focuses on the legal issues that most affect women. Our legal education programs concentrate on the subjects of Peru's constitution, the civil and penal codes, personal law, and legislation about abuse, abortion, rape, and abandonment.

In the penal field, we addressed four delicate issues: abortion, abuse, rape, and abandonment. In the civil field, routine matters such as the registration of marriage and marital rights and responsibilities were discussed. These discussions permitted us to discuss the impact of the law on conjugal relationships. These talks were of particular interest because many participants were common law wives.

Organization and Participation

When we selected women to participate in the Meeting of Manuelas 83, we considered their educational level, their participation and position in community organizations, their relations with neighbors and friends, and their employment status.

We personally chose twenty-two women to participate. Some were community leaders; some had taken our three-hour *Women and the Law* seminar; and twenty of these women were regular participants in the course.

The legal team, supported by the Manuelas, collectively planned and conducted the course. Each session was headed by a person with three assistants. In the course, we provided texts of the constitution and other legal material. The *Women and the Law* course used drama, group discussions and question and answer sessions.

Results

Each stage in the development of the courses strengthened us as a team amd underscored the unsolved problems we faced. It became clear, for example, that we were working with a methodology that could be applied to other fields but not to the law.

We also found that among the people we assisted in divorce proceedings few of the couples actually divorced legally. Instead, they simply separated.

We sought to help participants overcome their anxieties about all legal processes emphasized using the judicial system.

Lessons

The participants and the organizations were challenged by the strategy, and we undertook the course as a shared task. In the development of each issue, we applied the law to concrete situations. In the course, we used an integrated approach through case examples rather than a simple application of the legal codes. After reviewing the course, we believe that beginnning with the constitution was a sound decision. Many participants were surprised that few people (not even their own legislators) or institutions complied with the provisions of the constitution.

One very important lesson we learned was that every year thousands of abortions are performed in terrible conditions and result in the death of these women. This situation, resulting from Peru's laws on abortion, must be changed by legal reform. Similarly, the Peruvian rape laws must be overhauled. Rape, which people commonly believe is committed by crazy or evil men, is—in fact—committed by uncles, brothers, stepfathers, and even fathers. We have learned that the issue of rape cannot be addressed outside the total social context in which it occurs because of the multifaceted social, economic, and ideological factors that enter into play.

Gina Yañez de la Borda is the coordinator of the Legal Program of the Manuela Ramos Movement in Lima, Peru.

Building in the Multiplier Effect

This set of five papers is of particular interest, for it provides concrete examples of programmatic efforts to use women paralegals or legal promoters. While many strategies acknowledge the importance of the "multiplier effect," few have actually designed a method to prepare and subsequently employ community members as multipliers, *i.e.*, educators, organizers, and legal assistants or advisors. These papers offer only a glimpse of such programs. Given their brief history to date, data required for a comprehensive evaluation is not yet available. Nevertheless, these case studies do serve for comparative purposes.

Dasso and *Lora* describe the use of paralegals as community organizers and mobilizers in Lima, Peru. *Awino Kaduru* describes paralegals as *legal extension workers* in rural Kenya, while *Singh* and *Huda* describe them as integral to legal literacy programs in rural Nepal and Bangladesh, respectively. Two levels of paralegals, can be distinguished in these projects. One is the community or village-level *legal counselor* or *promoter*, and the other is the *paraprofessional*. The functions of the paralegal as counselor include advising women on their rights, assisting them in making an initial diagnosis of their problem, and referring them to the appropriate resource for further assistance. This level of paralegal also assists in the delivery of more structured educational programs. The paraprofessional not only advises women about rights, but keeps records, fills out forms, and has the capacity to assist in resolving simple conflicts.

While these papers have been singled out as exemplifying strategies using paralegals, some of the programs mentioned in the previous section on consciousness-raising, and in the following section on combining organizing and education, also include paralegals. It is interesting to note that a distinction between the levels of paralegals is often not made. Nor is there always a clear distinction between the education or training of legal promoters on the one hand and general community-level education on the other. In a sense, both prepare people to be capable of advising their peers about the broad intent and procedures of the law in specific areas. The functional difference is often found in whether those having received some measure of training are formally integrated into a program or strategy or are expected to fulfill the multiplier effect on their own. What is clear, however, is that wherever structured legal training of community women is implemented, there is a recognition of the importance of grassroots education about the law and about rights.

᪣᪣᪣᪣

Peru: Strategies for Family Law
Elizabeth Dasso

Since November 14, 1984, women (half the population of Peru) have had a new civil code, improving the previous Code of 1936, so that both women and men seem to be sharing in marital life. The further need to introduce new concepts, modifications, and clarifications is also evident.

The 1984 modifications contain terms with ambiguous meanings, giving complete liberty to the judges and leaving the application of the law to their opinions. In a male-oriented, racist society with injustice toward the poor, such as that of Peru, it is women who suffer the most harm. Judges' interpretation of the law is based principally on custom. This guiding principle impedes an administration of justice in the interests of the marginated of society, and in particular, of women.

In our understanding, the real change is in article 326 referring to the legality of the de facto union (cohabitation) after a minimum of two continuous years; cohabitation had been considered an immoral, indecent, and punishable way of life in Peru.

Nevertheless, we will see that the fulfillment of the positive aspects of the current code depends on women's knowledge of it. The new code's family law provisions allow more room for work in education and legal services for women, and make it necessary to reflect on new strategies which women can use to exercise their rights.

I would like to share our experiences in this area, and describe some of the main elements of Peru-Mujer's successful legal work with women.

The first component of our program is a multidisciplinary support team working on legal consultations. Women often look for a person in whom they can confide problems. The support of a person versed in psychology is necessary, or persons trained in sociology and anthropology, to facilitate women's success in confronting power situations with the police and/or the judicial administration. Working in teams also permits devising strategies that take into account aspects of local social life.

Secondly, we join forces with other women's groups working in the legal field to propose changes in the laws as well as to demand compliance with the laws. For example, Peru-Mujer worked with the Flora Tristan Center and the Manuela Ramos Movement to create a project on alimony lawsuits. In alimony cases, a monthly cash payment is demanded; in situations of unemployment or incidental employment, however, it is difficult to keep financial records and obtain financial settlements. The current law also provides for in-kind compensation, an option generally not used. The alimony project is using and attempting to expand this compensation category to include the possibility of payment through community tasks which take up so much of women's time and energy. The project has drafted a modification of the current law and presented it to some members of the Law Association for their comments and their support in Congress.

The third, key component is a legal education program for women. Knowing their rights—how the laws were written, what the law says, and what they, as women, want—permits them to exercise their rights in everyday life. Law is not to be a dead letter, but understood as a permanent contrast between what should be and what is. Our educational materials permit easy learning and group dynamics. We have created sets of pictures referring to areas of law that concern women and their families (family, labor, penal law), drawn on large poster boards with messages on the back of each poster to help women remember the law. Recently we created a coloring book based on this experience.

Another vital component is training motivated community-based women in legal orientation and defense for other. Experience has demonstrated that previous self-affirmation, based on self-esteem and valuation of the self-image of women, is needed for these legal trainers. Through role-playing and working together, the women strengthen themselves and discover their power to act in defense of women's rights, to speak in public without fear of criticism, and to deal with police and judicial authorities.

The most frequent family law cases—registration of children, alimony lawsuits, the rectification of birth certificates, and family abondonment—require accurate information and the support of witnesses. The work of the trainers in the community is successful because of the information and advice they offer, and their ability to talk with all parties in the neighborhood. They reduce legal costs by providing a community-based service to which all women have access. In addition, the trainers motivate other women to learn their rights, using elements unknown to those who do not live in the neighborhood or in the community, such as local networks and radios in the markets. They create a multiplier effect in the community that ultimately check authorities' conduct and guarantees enforcement of the law.

A fifth component is preventive legal education. For example, in many cases, women have not been prepared to meet the requirements for carrying out an alimony lawsuit or to exercise other rights of the marital relationship, such as child support, which can delay or complicate negotiations. Women need to know how to register a baby, for to do so when marital relations are still good can help avoid future difficulties.

The sixth component is the exchange of experiences between legal trainers in different communities. At present, we are developing a legal services center in the Independence district (the northern zone of metropolitan Lima) with one of the trainers from a program established in another neighborhood, Pueblo Joven Márquez, participating as facilitator. Her presence helps make the idea of a legal center seem real and feasible. Potential trainers can say, "If Eloisa is a townsperson like me, and she is now a legal trainer, I could also be a legal trainer." Inter-community exchanges also permit the sharing of strategies for securing maintenance, for example, when the husband denies having fathered the children, or for conducting alimony lawsuits when it is not known where the husband lives or works.

How has the judicial apparatus responded to our efforts? For the most part, positively. When a woman appears knowledgable and confident about her rights and demands, the authorities find themselves in unusual circumstances and tend to act favorably. The women generally argue on their own behalf, accompanied by the trainer in the beginning; the authorities thus feel social pressure, a further reason to give credence to the women's argument.

Sonia's case is typical of the Peru-Mujer experience. A migrant from the mountains to Independence, Sonia meets a man, they fall in love. Their relationship is good until one day she tells him she is pregnant. He says he doesn't love her, that the pregnancy is her problem, that he has a girlfriend, and he disappears. Sonia decides to have her baby. Time passes. He changes his mind and wants to get married, but Sonia does not accept his offer of marriage. With great effort, she supports her daughter and decides to send her to school, but runs into an obstacle because the child is not registered. It is now that she learns about the legal program, and she goes there for help.

The trainers give her advice; she participates in the training, and she receives legal orientation. The trainers use various sources to find the father of her daughter, talk to him, and convince Sonia and the father to resolve the problem so the girl can have a birth certificate. Now that she knows her rights, Sonia is herself arguing a child support case for her daughter. And, like other trainers who were motivated by exercising their own rights, Sonia has decided to become a trainer to help other women.

Sonia found in the group of trainers not only legal but practical and emotional support, central elements in the successful continuation of any legal case.

Elizabeth Dasso is the director of the Peru-Mujer Community Legal Program.

Peru:
Paralegal Assistance
in Community Development
Victor Carlos Lora

Overview
Our strategy attempts to improve the socioeconomic situation of women through changing their legal status. The strategy has emphasized the culture of the law because it arouses and enables people to assert their rights.

The training encompasses three areas, namely, assertiveness, organization, and appropriate legal education.

Through training, we hope to alter the attitudes and behavior of the participants so that they may become paralegals, serving their own communities. The training of marginal women as paralegals and the creation of a legal office in which they can work with their clients (under the supervision of two lawyers) have begun to demystify the legal system. These activities are also endowing women with the confidence to confront and resolve their problems. In this participatory framework, the traditional relationship between lawyer and client is broken. The clients greatly contribute to the resolution of their conflicts with little or no dependence on a lawyer. The women are also educated through this process which is usually absent in traditional law practice.

In Peru, popular struggles have resulted in the creation of legal norms and standards that respond to the needs and rights of the people. In general, the laws are not discriminatory; theoretically they are egalitarian. Nevertheless, the November 1984 civil code contains legal ambiguities, which—because of cultural factors—condemn married women to dependency on their husbands. Furthermore, protective labor legislation (*e.g.*, prohibiting women from working at night except prostitutes and dancers) reduces the employment opportunities of women because of the risks and expense (of complying with social legislation) to companies.

Since the time of the Virreynato of Peru, the powerful have lived by the aphorism, "the law is to be respected, but not to be obeyed." Peru's legal system serves the political and socioeconomic power structure. Even Peruvian literature clearly reflects this attitude. For example, in Manuel Scorza's novel *History of Garabombo* the central character is told "in Peru, Indians never win trials." Without a doubt, the Indians, the poor and other marginal people of Peru lose trials because powerful interests control the judiciary and because the powerless have limited resources to fight the establishment.

Until today, the labor laws promulgated in 1918 have not been modified. This legislation covers a decreasing proportion of the population because it only applies to labor in the traditional labor market. The serious Peruvian economic crisis has brought about a dramatic increase in non-traditional forms of work which is performed primarily by female workers. This sector of the economy is not regulated by any labor legislation,

231

and hence, the women are totally unprotected.

Unions have diminished in importance in Peru. In the past few years, increasing numbers of marginal urban and rural population have entered the struggle for employment opportunities, housing, and public services. As a class, they are still forming and are not well organized. This group is in need of legal services.

Legal activists are able to challenge various aspects of the law which are contrary to the public interest. While our strategy uses the legal system to help the poor and powerless, it takes into consideration the limits of the law in the administration of justice. Finally, the Peruvian legal structure heeds the notions of equality before the law and respect for human rights, but even when these theories are applied, the problem of access to the legal system by the marginal populations remains.

Focus

Directed specifically at women, our legal services were initiated in Peru in 1981 in the settlement of Fundo Márquez, a marginal urban area located 45 kilometers from Lima. Later, in 1984 another project was initiated in El Ermitaño. This project came about at the request of its leaders who demonstrated the abuses and neglect of the law suffered by their community. The project tries to provide legal education to women and to forge a legal service that can be sustained under the women's control in their new settlement.

To implement the strategy, we undertook seven essential organizational activities. Firstly, we began to make the community aware of its social and legal status using cultural events and entertainment in which women participated. We also organized informal meetings with women's groups to address this and other issues. Secondly, we assessed the situation of the community and its socioeconomic and political conditions. We considered the Peruvian legal system, the people's concepts of justice, and their previous experiences with the authorities when attempting to assert their rights. In addition, we looked at the daily realities of women and their informal networks to manage their everyday problems. Thirdly, in conjunction with the community leaders, women participants, and the project team, we initiated a working plan.

We developed educational materials as our fourth step. These included a methodological guide, workbooks, self-instruction pamphlets and law texts suitable for the population and its culture. Fifthly, we trained sixty paralegals to work in the following areas: women's: identity; leadership and organization; women's rights; and the management of the legal services center. Sixthly, we equipped a community-based legal office to provide services such as information and education, legal aid, and guidance. Finally, the sixty paralegals elected five directors to coordinate the activities and services of the center.

The center has engaged in numerous support activities. It has publicly presented discussions on the assessment of various problems and the results of the project. It has also presented seminars on women's rights and provided an ongoing legal education program through the use of the mass media. Paralegals have distributed educational materials to the community and promoted socio-legal literacy. The project is evaluated by the participants, clients and community leaders. Furthermore, the paralegals and training team assess the training of the participants and effectiveness of the strategy.

The project responds not only to women's legal needs but also to the necessity to strengthen and unify them as a social force. A legal service run by the women themselves will provide them access to information which they have been systematically denied. Once the women know their rights and are capable of proposing substantial legal changes, legal reform becomes relevant to them and to the project. Then, they can unite and coordinate with other progressive groups to pressure the government for legal and social reforms. This education will also help women achieve greater sexual equality within the community.

Through the availability of paralegals and the control of Legal Services Center by the community, the women are accorded greater access to urban services. The activities of the center are affordable; and they are participatory alternatives to legal services which reinforce a traditional relationship between lawyer and client.

Legal Issues

The strategy concentrates on legal areas that the community viewed as most important. The community was questioned by community workers, and five priorities emerged from the survey results and from the opinions of community leaders. In order of importance, they are human, civil, and political rights; family rights; property rights; violence; and health.

Organization and Participation

We chose to work with the District of Independence, the only district in Lima with a woman mayor. We believed that our strategy could reach the entire population of 240,000 inhabitants in this district if we integrated and coordinated our activities with those of the municipality. To serve the needs of this community, we selected sixty women to train as paralegals. We visited all district organizations and women's groups to explain the strategy and to request that each organization appoint a delegate. The majority of the organizations accepted the concept of the strategy and our proposals; and they named representatives.

After we coordinated with the municipality and the neighborhood organizations, a committee was formed, composed of the training team, two district representatives, and four delegates from the neighborhood organizations. This committee makes local decisions, and it consults with the central committee of the district organization and with participating women. The community and our project emphasize the necessity to strengthen the democratic decision-making process and to restrict traditional power relationships.

Results

Since the strategy was implemented in 1981, we have had numerous successes. We will mention our most important accomplishments. In the marginal settlement of the Pueblo Jóven Márquez, legal services have been provided and the community organization has improved. These changes have facilitated community demands for electricity in the area. The project has also succeeded in discouraging illegal property sales, which were transacted in some cases by corrupt officials. It has resulted in organizing the entire group of women, incorporating them into the neighborhood organizations. Before the implementation of the strategy, only half were organized.

To date, twenty-two legal cases have been filed and resolved. Fifteen of the cases were handled by paralegals who required no assistance from lawyers. Others have been briefed about their legal cases. Some have chosen to represent themselves in the legal proceedings, while the remainder have opted for legal representation. In addition, the project offered seven courses on women's rights, which sensitized the women about their condition. Two women participants have proposed a legal services project to help their own rural community, located 90 kilometers from Lima. In the District of Independence, the consciousness of the community has been raised. As a result, organized groups have improved the communication networks and organizational solidarity and unity.

Lessons

The difficulty of extending the project from El Ermitaño to a district level was not adequately. The District of Independence is comprised of sixteen mountain areas; and as a result of its topography, it is without communications system. Moreover, we spent additional time in implementing the project due to complex political formalities.

We made one serious error in Fundo Márquez when we did not conduct a graduation ceremony. Such a ceremony would have demonstrated publicly that the paralegals had acquired the required expertise to advise about community legal affairs. Informing the community that the participants had completed a four and one-half month training course was insufficient. Another error was our neglect to obtain a clearly identifiable space for the legal office. Furthermore, many of the district's people objected to services from a paralegal who did not live in the neighborhood. Hence, it was necessary to establish in Independence a community-based legal services center where control of the center by the participants is assured.

Victor Lora lives in Lima, Peru. He has worked for several years in legal programs for women.

235

Kenya: Legal Services for Rural Women
Rosemary Awino Kaduru

Introduction

In this paper, I will discuss the legal status of women in Kenya by analyzing some of the laws that govern women's rights. I will also provide a case study on women, the law, and development which Partnership for Productivity (PfP) carried out.

Partnership for Productivity is an indigenous private voluntary organization which was started in western Kenya in 1969. PfP's primary goal is to assist in Kenya's economic development by permitting people to use their economic creativity. It aims to improve the ability of small business persons to manage their commercial enterprises. PfP's programs include business start-ups, agricultural activities, women in development, appropriate technology, and legal assistance. The law in development program complements PfP's other services.

The bulk of PfP activities are centered in western and central Kenya. Western Kenya, which is one of the poorest regions in Kenya, has an extremely high population growth rate. The inhabitants live primarily in rural areas in which the land holdings have been fragmented. Fifty percent of the small farm households in this area are under the poverty line. Women in this region are engaged largely in subsistence production supplemented by other small income-generating activities.

The majority of the households in Kenya are headed by women. As a result of polygamy and male migration, many Kenyan women bear the primary economic responsibilities for their families. However, most women do not have the legal and other knowledge to conduct their responsibilities adequately; they do not understand clearly their legal rights or obligations. But rural women in particular require a greater knowledge of the law and ability to use it. They must acquire legal education to understand their entitlements to essential resources and services, to defend their interests, and to press their claims against public and private centers of power.

The majority of the rural women lack access to legal services due to the costs and to the lack of interest of most lawyers about the needs of the rural poor. In Kenya, there are only about 1,000 lawyers serving a population of over 17,000,000 people. Hence, they cannot meet the needs of all Kenyans. The lawyers are mainly based in urban centers far from impoverished rural areas. Even if lawyers are physically accessible, the cost of legal services imposes a significant constraint. In addition, lawyers usually offer a limited range of skills to their clients; their talents are usually expended on litigation or on counseling individual clients about problems encountered by the urban upper-middle class. Moreover, lawyers who embrace the causes of poor rural clients risk alienating wealthier clients and jeopardizing their connections and status within the community.

State, Law, and Women

The law plays an important role in regulating the levels of participation by women in the development process. Law and social practice are dialectically related; hence, a discriminatory legal status based on sex plays a significant part in shaping the socioeconomic behavior brought about by a sexual division of labor in society.

The legal status of women helps shape the socioeconomic position of women in Kenyan society. Some hypothesize that the subservient role of women in society is due to their lack of decision-making power. However, in certain areas of the decision-making process, women appear to be more privileged than men. Legislation has given basic rights to women, but they remain basically ignorant about these rights.

The demographic distribution of women, who constitute more than 50% of the Kenyan population, also affects the role of women in society. Most Kenyan women reside in rural areas, lack educational advantages enjoyed by their male counterparts, and generally remain under the authority of their fathers and husbands. Although urbanization has brought radical changes in the status of a relatively small number of women, it has had little impact on the vast majority of Kenyan women. Much must be done to help both the elite and the majority of Kenyan women if social justice and economic development are to be attained.

Kenya has several different legal systems regulating various aspects of life. Customary law regulates the lives of the various ethnic groups in areas that have not been touched by state legislation. Religious laws (*e.g.*, Hindu and Islamic laws) apply to specific sectarian communities. Kenya also has an imported legal system, inherited from the colonial powers. The multiplicity and overlap of these systems complicate the task of ascertaining the precise status of women in Kenya. Out of necessity, emphasis is placed on the positive, legislatively-enacted law as the ultimate agent for change in Kenya's legal system.

Women's Political, Civil, and Property Rights

Section 82 of the Kenyan Constitution of 1969 prohibits discriminatory legislation. The term *discriminatory* is broadly defined; but significantly, this prohibition of discrimination does not apply to laws about matters of personal law (*e.g.*, marriage, divorce, devolution of property, or death). Under the constitution, therefore, many existing or newly established tribal, religious, and common laws and practices that discriminate against women are legal in Kenya.

Since the constitution serves as the superstructure upon which the government's legislation and policies rest, there is a inference that government policy condones gender-based discrimination. It is a compelling argument because the government failed to prohibit sex discrimination in the constitution. Moreover, many women over the age of 18 do not know they have the right to vote or equal rights in marriage.

In Kenya today, there are no laws that prevent a woman from owning property if she has the means. However, the majority of the women cannot acquire property because of their limited economic opportunities. Currently, the *Married Women's Property Act* protects married women who own property. The majority of Kenyan women are the wives of peasants whose property generally consists of small plots of land, a few head of cattle and small amounts of savings. Therefore, the issue of women's property rights is restricted to the few educated women who earn monthly salaries.

Women's Access to the Legal System

Failures in the legal system may contribute in a variety of ways to the unsatisfactory *access relations* between the economically and politically disadvantaged groups, consisting of the rural and urban poor, and the structure of resource administration. Firstly, legislative and administrative norms fail to emphasize development that satisfies basic human needs. Secondly, the law fails to encourage the participation of the disadvantaged in the administration of development programs. Thirdly, the legal and administrative systems fail to provide mechanisms for the masses to contest bureaucratic decisions and resource allocation.

In general, individual women do not have the power and resources to ensure the accessibility and accountability of the system. Only through collective action can they pressure the government to fulfill the basic human needs of Kenyan society. Consequently, Partnership for Productivity has initiated a women in development program to assist in providing some of the economic and legal needs of the majority of the disadvantaged women in the rural areas of Kenya.

Overview

The Women in Development (WID) program and various legal programs were initiated in 1981. The WID program was established to assist in the development of Kenya's economy by providing low-income women in rural and suburban areas with the means to manage their small economic units more efficiently, which would improve their socioeconomic status.

The program is devoted to making low-income and poor women aware of their capabilities and contributions to development. We endeavor to create self-reliance rather than dependency; women's participation and control rather than outside imposition; and holistic rather than segmented developmental attitudes. We are striving to center the process around people, not bureaucratic plans. We believe the abilities of low-income women should be developed so that they can educate, organize, and undertake projects themselves.

The Women, Law in Development (WLID) program was designed to complement all the other services offered to women by PfP. It provides legal education and legal assistance to rural women in the context of other programs. One basic goal of the program is to develop a cost effective and replicable model for addres-sing the lack of access by the rural women to legal and paralegal services. While working with women in the rural areas of Kenya, PfP realized that one of the greatest obstacles to rural development was a general lack of knowledge by the majority of the women of their legal rights and a limited access to legal services. PfP then began implementing a legal program to raise the socioeconomic conditions of the people by providing legal education and services.

The legal needs of rural women cannot be adequately identified and met through traditional legal aid programs. A nationalized legal system would run into serious political problems in providing assistance to the rural poor; and the high costs and restricted availability of private lawyers present severe limitations on the provision of extensive legal assistance to the disadvantaged social groups. Furthermore, traditional lawyer-client relationships often create dependency which is antithetical to the development of self-reliance and collective action in rural communities.

Focus

PfP's legal program does not represent clients in court. However, we have initiated a legal development fund which permits us to engage attorneys to represent our clients. The PfP Women, Law in Development program is implemented by two lawyers and twenty-one paralegals. Paralegals who have had some basic legal training live with the people in areas where PfP has projects. These paralegals are known as field extension officers. They have been trained in the basic principles of law so that they can educate our rural clients about the need to obtain legal assistance. They collect basic information from clients before PfP lawyers take action on the cases. In conjunction with local leaders, they also organize legal education meetings.

We will now illustrate how the program works. Although a small businesswoman believes she has a valid lease, some vital element of the agreement may be missing. A PfP paralegal can help the businesswoman by reviewing the contents of the lease. The PfP staff member can also inform the business woman about her rights and about the availability of legal assistance from PfP, if it is necessary.

After the paralegal establishes contact with local women, PfP legal officers arrange to visit the area to provide relevant legal and civic education sessions. For instance, land law is extremely important to the rural poor. The PfP educates them about the registration of titles; land transactions and procedures; business law; legal requirements about organizing and registering groups; the statute of limitations; the laws on compensation, insurance, *etc.*

Only a system of paralegal assistance can effectively empower the rural poor to use the law beneficially. The paralegal is not primarily a solicitor delivering traditional types of legal services. On the contrary, the paralegal becomes an integral part of the groups served—helping people understand their collective needs and how to use the law to assert their rights and claims. Furthermore, paralegals must facilitate the people's participation in decisions and collective action. Assisting the community in identifying legal needs and arranging for PfP lawyers to provide educational and discussion sessions are also important. While we recognize that clients may need competent professional intermediaries to perform traditional legal tasks (*e.g.*, courtroom representation and the drafting of complicated documents like mortgages), it is essential to provide broader assistance. We must develop new methods and means to educate the rural poor about their rights and to enable them to participate more effectively in business, politics, administration and law.

PfP has found public legal education to be a very useful tool in teaching the rural poor about their rights, their obligations under the law, and the legal resources available to them. We aim our education efforts at the target community groups—these include farmer's groups, market committees, church committees, women's groups and organizations, institutions, and the local chiefs' public meetings, popularly known in Kenya as the chiefs' *barazas*. Our public education sessions cover a range of legal subjects: the constitution; family law and inheritance; the structure and jurisdiction of courts; insurance laws; statute of limitations laws; the Chiefs' Authority Act; and acts concerning agriculture, water, police, local government, andland control and transactions, *etc.*

241

The PfP does not view legal education as a total solution to the problem of law in development. It is only the beginning of the process: the program provides people with legal knowledge to protect or advance their interests. Legal assistance and education must also assure the full participation of, and control by, the clients. In this manner, people can weigh the cost and benefits of particular actions and assert their rights. Since the education sessions began, we have found that many people express specific legal needs. It is clear that informed and educated rural people can assert their rights if given a chance.

When clients need legal representation in court, which the Kenyan Law Society does not permit us to do, we provide them alternatives. In simple cases, we do not hire attorneys; instead, we will usually prepare court papers (*e.g.*, plaints, defenses, petitions, affidavits, *etc.*). We also help clients to undertake searches in the land or business registries before they enter into land transactions or business deals. In addition, we fully explain to the client the nature and significance of her case should it end up in court. In more difficult cases, we engage lawyers to represent our clients.

We operate legal clinics in various rural areas. The PfP lawyers visit the areas to advise clients about their legal problems. We encourage our clients to settle their problems at the lowest level possible. Hence they only go to court as a last resort. For example, in separation or divorce cases in which the wife seeks a maintenance order for herself and her children, we ascertain whether or not she has tried to resolve the issue through her family, village elders, or the local leaders. If she has not, we urge her to do so. If she has, we insist that she provide us a letter from her chief or village administrator, stating that the discussions have been fruitless.

Conclusions

The PfP program has concentrated on providing legal education and legal advisory services to rural women engaged largely in subsistence production. PfP has found a cost-effective way of reaching larger numbers of clients, namely, working through women's groups. Its work with women has made a great impact on rural society. The PfP programs have provided rural women a social support system. The programs also provide institutional mechanisms to mobilize and channel local resources. Through participation in PfP programs, many members develop organizational, leadership and decision-making skills.

In recent years, PfP programs have focused more on social needs than on technical advice. Just as social factors are very important in developing small enterprises, technical inputs remain necessary. From its experience, PfP has learned that there is a great demand for legal services among its clients and others who have received legal education. It has also found that the existing legal system is expensive, complex, slow, remote, and insensitive to the needs of low-income rural women. Furthermore, the cost of litigation requires subsidies.

PfP paralegal field workers can raise awareness about legal issues, but they cannot effectively resolve all legal problems. The PfP legal staff has neither the resources nor the organization to pursue the clients' legal problems. Hence, we have initiated the legal development fund to cover the costs of broader legal services. Nevertheless, as no other organization has established a legal program for women and as PfP has developed the beginnings of a programmatic model, we believe we must continue our program, eliciting support from other women's organizations.

Rosemary Awino Kaduru is a lawyer in Nairobi, Kenya and director of legal programs for Partnership for Productivity.

Nepal: Women and Legal Aid
Silu Singh

Introduction

The Women's Legal Services Project (WLSP) was formed in 1982 as a result of the expansion of its predecessor, the Legal Aid Committee of the Nepal Women's Organization. This project, which provides legal services and legal education, has two main objectives: the provision of free legal counsel and services to poor and needy women to seek legal redress for the wrongs they have suffered; and the education of women about their rights through legal literacy campaigns in rural areas. The WLSP also conducts research and analysis to find new and better ways to emancipate women.

The reality of Nepalese society has shown that unless legal aid is available, the newly won legal rights of women could remain paper rights. Legal aid services and related activities can help women assert their rights, increase their legal awareness, and create favorable public opinion to press for greater legal rights for women.

Overview

Nepal is faced with the main challenge of development, specifically, mobilizing the entire population in the development process. The chief obstacle in realizing the participation of Nepalese women in development is their unequal legal status. Therefore, the law is a major problem. The Nepalese feminist movement is working to mobilize public opinion against the existing laws that discriminate against women or damage their interests.

Since the revolution of 1950-1951, the government has been more receptive to the idea of gradual change in the law to remove women's inferior legal status. The constitutional system established after the revolution gave equal political rights to women. Women were permitted to vote, stand for political office, and work in public administration. Although new legislation has significantly improved the status of women, the implementation and enforcement of the law is equally or more important. Every effort must be made to enable women to

244

exercise their rights effectively.

To guarantee women's active participation in Nepalese society, four basic conditions are necessary: the promulgation of legislation guaranteeing women's equal rights in all fields; the modification of social attitudes to ensure women's property and family rights; the encouragement of women to participate in politics; and the establishment of programs to integrate women fully in the development process. Members of the Women's Legal Services Project perceive the legal and social inequality of women as being rooted in the culture of the law, as well as in the structure of the legal system. Its strategy is designed to respond to the former; the latter does not fall within the activities of the project.

The project works to safeguard women's rights recognized by the constitution and the laws of the land. To achieve this goal, the project aims to provide free legal aid to women whose rights have been violated and to arouse women's consciousness about their legal rights. The perpetuation of the inferior legal status of Nepalese women is primarily due to their lack of knowledge about new progressive legislation and to their inability to assert their rights because of the inaccessibility of the legal system.

The project directly confronts these two obstacles by conducting an ongoing and widespread legal literacy campaign for poor women and by establishing a network of legal aid offices which can serve the needs of these women. Because illiterate women are more vulnerable to exploitation, they need legal knowledge far more than educated people. Thus, legal literacy is more imperative for a society in which general literacy is quite low.

The project has found that village women who have been educated about their basic rights have been able to assert their rights and to seek prompt assistance if any of their rights have been violated. They also effectively educate other village women about their legal rights. The legal literacy programs reach village women throughout the country. They are conducted by the project's network of offices on a continuously rotating basis. The executive director of the project travels regularly to areas surrounding each office to speak to village women. Under her initiative, local, short-term legal literacy classes are held. In these classes, well-known legal experts teach selected village women about the legal system. In addition, women are trained in a series of one-week intensive legal workshops at the central office and branch offices of the project.

Process

The Women's Legal Services Project and, indeed, even the system of free legal aid for needy women in Nepal, owe their existence to the initiative of the late Princess Pricep Shah. In 1964, after the establishment of a new legal code guaranteeing equality for all citizens, she urged public-spirited lawyers and other concerned people to work for the establishment of a free legal aid system for poor women. The Legal Aid Committee (predecessor of the WLSP) was established to meet this need. About a year after its establishment, the committee hired a staff of lawyers and paralegal workers. They worked under the direction of a senior woman lawyer who was responsible to the Nepal Women's Organization (NWO), a funder of the committee's activities. The committee adopted the twin objectives of providing legal assistance and conducting legal awareness campaigns.

Because the majority of Nepalese live in rural, mountainous areas, the WLSP has concentrated its efforts on expanding its network of offices outside the Katmandu Valley where regional courts are situated. Besides the routine legal aid work, the project is vigorously conducting legal literacy campaigns in the rural areas around the central cities of Katmandu, Patan, and Bhaktapur and in the areas that can be reached by the branch office.

Focus

The project's legal services provide help to a large number of individuals. However, the legal literacy campaign affects society as a whole. Hence, the WLSP's strategy has focused on legal literacy. It has enlisted the support of local NWO representatives and Panchayat (local councils of the state system) officials to promote and conduct its legal literacy classes. In the early years, the WLSP concentrated on organizing local short-term literacy classes to reach as many village women as possible; now it has placed more emphasis on intensified training of selected village women through legal workshops at project offices.

The WLSP is now planning to undertake a new project, the study of women in prison. It will conduct research on women convicts imprisoned on charges of infanticide. In mountainous areas of Nepal, most young men leave their native villages for long periods of time, and young wives often form extra-marital relationships. The social taboo against pregnancy under these circumstances is so severe that terrified expectant mothers often resort to illegal abortion or abandoning their newborn babies. For these acts, they can be prosecuted on charges of abortion or murder. The project plans to make a thorough study of these imprisoned women in an attempt to solve the problem of excessive punishment of women who are the victims of their circumstances. The results of this research are expected to make an important contribution to the Women's Legal Services Project.

Legal Issues

The WLSP is handling all types of legal problems including marriage, divorce, child custody, division of ancestral property, inheritance, personal property, and earned income. However, it does not neglect cases of eligible clients involving other areas of the law. The staff will provide legal representation to female victims to ensure that crimes against women are reported and prosecuted. The WLSP will also represent female defendants to guarantee their right to a fair trial. In addition, it also handles women's rights cases and cases of discrimination against women in employment, education, elections, or in other fields.

Organization and Participation

The Women's Legal Services Project operates under the aegis of the Nepal Women's Organization, an organization created under the provisions of the Nepalese Constitution to represent the interests of women. The chairwoman of the NWO is the ex-officio chairwoman of the WLSP Advisory Board; the executive director, a senior advocate, oversees and directs all aspects of the project. Prominent jurists and private attorneys are members of the WLSP Advisory Board, and other lawyers, paralegal workers, and agents serve as members of the project's staff. Furthermore, social workers are appointed by the WLSP to encourage women to use the project's legal services. Finally, the WLSP's administrators also are directly involved in the project's myriad strategy activities.

As the NWO local representatives and the people's representatives of the Panchayat actively assist the project's legal literacy program, the entire machinery of the NWO and the local Panchayats is involved in the project strategy as patrons.

Results

At present, the project is five years old. While its evaluation will be undertaken only at the end of this year, a rough assessment of the strategy can be made.

A total of 686 women have received legal assistance by the end of the first two years of the project. On their behalf, the project filed 340 cases in the law courts and 273 applications in the administrative and semi-judicial offices.

The WLSP has conducted a legal literacy campaign, holding classes in six locations with 785 women participating. It has identified the need to provide more intensive legal training. As a result, the WLSP has organized a seven-day legal workshop at its central office, training 105 women paralegals from 24 villages. Also, the project has produced some simple legal education publications, and it hopes to publish more very shortly.

The increasing number of women seeking legal redress through the Women's Legal Services Project is evidence of the growing consciousness among women of their rights and of the project's success. The program also reaches more rural women through social workers and paralegals, who are trained by the WLSP.

Lessons

Concrete conditions and specific realities differ from one country to another, and hence, the experiences of other societies cannot be applied mechanically. Yet, the common experiences of Third World countries show that their development efforts—essential for independence—cannot be successful without mobilizing the entire population, particularly women. To this end, women's independent legal status must be become a reality. A sad irony is that the legal status of women is inferior in the very countries where their participation in society is most needed. Laws must be enacted to improve the status of women.

However, the legislative process is complex. On the one hand, it is a tool for social change; on the other, it must respect popular tradition so as not to flout the sensibilities of the people. Legal education is, therefore, essential to galvanize popular support for progressive changes in the law. The promulgation of new legislation to improve the status of women can be buttressed only if women successfully assert their already-won rights.

Experience in Nepal has shown that religious beliefs are not fanatical and that social prejudice against women is not deeply rooted; consequently, there is no strong resistance to enacting egalitarian laws. Hence, if the law can serve as an instrument of change, a system of legal aid can accelerate the process of legal reform. It can also strengthen the force of the law by safeguarding the existing rights of women. Thus, legal projects can make a significant contribution to women's struggle for an independent legal status by using the law to protect women's existing rights and by changing the law to acquire new ones.

Silu Singh is the Executive Director of the Nepal Women's Legal Services Project.

Bangladesh:
Religion, Law, and Women's Rights
Sigma Huda

Focus

In Bangladesh, the existing laws that relate to women are comprehensive and adequate. Unfortunately, they remain merely legal theory. For the majority of people, over 80% of whom are illiterate and poor, the legal system is totally meaningless. These people continue to be exploited and oppressed by the more powerful.

As a result of this situation, the Bangladesh Jatiyo Mahila Ainjibi Samity (The Bangladesh National Women Lawyers Association) embarked on a program to bring the heart of the laws to the public. The association organized a full-time project which traveled to the 68,000 villages of Bangladesh and which aimed to teach some 50 million women (and in some places, men) their basic rights. The association felt that this program would help women to fight oppression.

It encouraged female law students to join the association and to visit rural areas whenever it conducted workshops and meetings. Unfortunately, while the association attracted a growing membership, it also collided with traditional restrictions placed on women. The social norms of the male-dominated society of Bangladesh determine how and where a woman, especially an unmarried one, can travel.

As a result, the association began to work on an experimental basis with a family planning group (The Bangladesh Women's Health Coalition). Members of the association visited the clinics on a fixed day of each week to educate the staff about basic laws affecting the status of women. The staff of the clinics was our target group because it had direct access to many women. Doctors, nurses, and counselors then could teach women about their rights. This successful experiment gave birth to the idea of working with paralegals.

After a year of experimenting with the Bangladesh Women's Health Coalition, we decided to open our own center. We located our center at the office of the Association of the Development Agencies of Bangladesh, as we recognized that coordinating with other development agencies would make a wider impact than working on our own. Field workers, project coordinators, and even group leaders affiliated with other agencies could effectively use our paralegal training.

We organized a three-month training course using a syllabus based on law concerning the every-day life of women. However, it did not work out as smoothly as we had expected. The principal reason for the center's difficulties was that most organizations with which we worked operated through a central office in Dacca. However, their staff was scattered throughout the rural areas. Because of finances and logistics, the development workers could attend neither our three-month training course nor our weekly lectures series. Moreover, we did not have sufficient funds to organize a fulltime fifteen-day workshop, and we could not expect our few volunteer lawyers to suspend their professional activities and devote themselves fulltime to the center. Nevertheless, the classes were not total failures. We attracted a large number of participants from the so-called social welfare organizations, which are run by society ladies. Even though we had not been able to work with the target group of rural organizations, we continued the center's activities. Last year, we began to operate two more centers in the downtown and suburban areas of Dacca; this year, a third center on the northern outskirts of Dacca has opened. The target group of these centers is the slum-dwellers—particularly the women, who tend to be more aggressive than their rural counterparts.

We felt that by providing legal education in colloquial, easy-to-understand Bengali, we could teach women about their religious misconceptions. Their understanding of religious law is often confused with the traditional customs, practices, and interpretations of uneducated priests. Through discussions with these women about their common problems of marriage, personal affairs or employment we are able to build a rapport. As we explain the law and guide the participants on legal principals, we try to convince them to make their owned informed decisions. We teach them to view themselves as persons and to cooperate with each other as a group. We also teach them to avoid confronting the legal power structure by themselves; instead, we advise them to petition to arbitrate the dispute with the help of representation by a group of women. This inclusive strategy helps counter an individual's susceptibility to the pressures of the Imams and local elders.

We also believed that the association must identify itself with other women's organizations that have similar objectives to be more effective. We cooperatively organized live-in workshops at the village level in all four jurisdictions of the country. We tried to gather many women who had leader-ship qualities to live with us as sisters with common interests, problems and struggles. The theme of these workshops was *Women, Development, and the Law.* To make legal concepts more comprehensible, we composed songs on the various aspects of personal law; we also composed short dramas on the violations of law, the legal remedies available, and the use of the law to fight social taboos and opposition.

Results

It is still too early to assess our impact on the public. However, the media are publicizing crimes against women such as rape, assaults, and abuse. Clearly, people are leaking these incidents to reporters to evoke a public protest. Moreover, village women are now taking public stands on important issues.

We face a lot of obstacles as we try to convince women that they are their own worst enemies. Women must realize that God created men and women as equals and that our constitution supports the tenets and teachings of the Holy Books. Society teaches that we must revere the man; yet, the *Koran* says: "And revere the womb that bore you." The practice of venerating males has grown out of the fundamental belief in worshipping the man after God. It has been made worse by cultural portrayals of women. For example, commercial films portray the heroine as trampled upon and show patience and sacrifice as virtues in women. We continue to attempt to develop the means by which these barriers can be overturned. We are teaching women that they must demand respect from their family and society. A woman is not doing herself or her children a favor by sacrificing her well-being to that of her husband in the name of respect.

In conclusion, I would like my sisters to assist me, my association, and other women in Bangladesh to overcome the awe and fear of their husbands, but at the same time to retain a true *respect* for them; and equally, to instill in their spouses the same *respect* for themselves. Furthermore, we urge that women's centers be established throughout Bangladesh so that women can exchange views with each other and learn from each other's experiences. Concerted efforts must also be made to encourage these organizations to publish simple books, which can be used to teach the basis of the legal system and its importance to women. Furthermore, unity must be created among women so that they can fight legal and other social battles together. Women who are well-versed in their religion should attempt to interpret correctly the meaning of the scriptures relating to women and their status. Then, they can spread this knowledge to assist their less fortunate sisters. Finally, women must organize to research religious dogma, customs, traditions, and superstitions in order to change discriminatory practices.

Sigma Huda is an advocate in the Supreme Court in Bangladesh and secretary of the Bangladesh National Women Lawyer's Association.

Mobilizing Around Issues

The papers in this section discuss strategies that include organizing and mobilizing women for the achievement of various specific objectives. In the examples given here, most frequently the objective is to change some aspect of legislation which negatively affects women. *Kumari* begins by describing a multi-faceted strategy to deal with the issues of harassment, torture, and murder of women related to the custom of dowry. The strategy includes a campaign to educate the public on the evils of dowry; assistance to victims or potential victims through a counseling program; litigation to bring the issue to the attention of the courts; mobilization of women through marches and demonstrations in order to pressure the police and other authorities; and lobbying for legislative changes in the dowry law.

Fernandez in the Philippines discusses an approach to mobilizing women at the grassroots to gain control of land for housing. This process includes gaining an understanding of the issues as well as the skills to deal effectively within the framework of the law and government policies. Stating that "a right is not a right until it is guaranteed," Fernandez describes a process through which people gain knowledge of their rights and mechanisms of the law (in relation to land issues), acquire skills to access the system, and develop methods to attain their rights that engage women directly and concretely. *Carrión* in Ecuador describes a similar approach with urban women in Quito. In the context of educating women about their basic social, political and legal rights, the strategy focuses on organization and planning in order to engage the women in a process they control. The emphasis is on *education in action*, which includes the development of both intellectual and organizing skills. It takes an integrated approach to the law, addressing not only the legal but also the social and political processes which ultimately determine the exercise of rights.

In discussing the experience of women in Nicaragua over the last few years, *Vargas* describes the kind of organization necessary for effective collective advocacy in the women's struggle and the role of law as an instrument in their struggle. She asserts that equality and the effective assertion of rights can never be achieved by decree and, therefore, women must be engaged directly in making them a reality.

Rocha describes a program in Brazil aimed at raising awareness of rural women, wage workers, and peasants of their actual or potential rights, and equipping them with the capability to obtain, defend, or apply those rights. The strategy includes consciousness-raising and organization, participation in rural trade unions, building solidarity with other groups, and finally, using the legislative process by lobbying and pressuring legislators to produce changes in labor and social security laws.

The paper by *Aumeeruddy-Cziffra* recounts developments of the feminist movement in Mauritius during the last decade, in which the law figured prominently in the movement's strategy. The strategy included mass education and organizing around issues affecting women. It also included lobbying for the creation of a ministry to address women's and family rights, and for legislative changes, particularly the addition of an equal rights clause in the constitution, changes in the labor laws, and improvements in the personal and inheritance rights of married women. The paper shows how critical the political climate of a country is in influencing the degree of flexibility, extent, and success of a strategy in educating and organizing women around legal issues.

The examples given here are all multi-faceted strategies that aim to create direct channels from the grassroots to legislators, the courts, and policy-makers and implementers, and to develop the political and organizing skills women need to assert a greater measure of direction over these processes of articulating and implementing the law.

❧❧❧❧

India: the Tradition of Dowry
Ranjana Kumari

Introduction

The social custom of dowry, so ingrained in a male-dominated society like ours, has had an alarming impact on India. In the last few years, it has had numerous consequences that increased the suffering of women. The custom involves the giving of a gift to a son-in-law or his parents, either in cash or in kind. From the point of view of women's status, the custom of dowry has to be looked at as consisting of three elements. Firstly, there is a prenuptial settlement on the bride which is disclosed to the groom's family. The gift, which is formally bestowed on the bride, is not her exclusive property. Secondly, there are gifts from the bride's family to the groom; and thirdly, there are additional gifts from the bride's family to the family of the groom. The settlement often includes the enormous expenses incurred as a result of travel and entertainment of the bridegroom's party.

In actual practice, the gift-giving continues throughout the first few years of marriage. In the beginning, the practice of dowry was meant to assist a newlywed couple to set up their new home and life. However, now it has taken the shape of commercial transactions in which monetary considerations receive priority over the merits of the bride. Never before have the demands for dowry been so insistent and so widespread, nor the amount so large as today. The bride's parents are further taxed by demands on other occasions such as festivals and social ceremonies even after marriage. Failure to meet these demands is frequently followed by abuse of the young wife, which can lead to either suicide or cold-blooded murder of the bride. These incidents are generally reported as accidents in which the husband claims that the wife caught on fire due to an explosion of kerosene.

The giving of the dowry is justified as a way of providing a woman with a share of the family property. The Hindu laws on property and ownership do not give women their proper and due ownership rights as independent entities as far as family income, assets, and property are concerned. The Hindu Succession Act does give women the right to inherit an equal share of the family property. But, the tradition against this right is so strong that in most cases the family's property is given to the sons or other male members; the women usually do not contest.

Focus

With the increased desire for quick money and luxuries the demands for a large dowry are not confined to the middle class; they have spiraled down to the lower classes. As a result, the harassment of women, including bride burning, has recently attained new proportions. The incidents which occurred in Delhi from 1980 onwards amply reflect the magnitude of the problem. In 1980–1981 there were 421 reported cases of death due to dowry ("accidental deaths due to burns"). A year later there were 568, rising to 610 in 1982–83. The following year, there were 690 deaths. In the first three months of 1984, 585 dowry-related deaths were reported.

Although there were 610 such deaths in Delhi in 1982-1983, only forty cases were recorded specifically as dowry offenses. Clearly, more must be done about the dowry and its horrors. Victims of this evil practice belong to all groups and classes of society. The law, which is weak and vague, and the police, who are ill-equipped and indifferent, often do not protect potential victims. The weakness of the legal system in dealing with dowry crimes leads to difficulties in convicting the culprit. In fourteen years, only one prosecution was initiated under the provision of the Dowry Prohibition Act of 1961.

The vulnerable position of women due to the dowry has activated women's organizations in India. Realizing the gravity of this problem, women's organizations have launched a campaign to mobilize public opinion to support the eradication of this practice.

I will discuss the role of one of the national women's organizations, Mahila Daxata Samiti in this campaign. I am actively involved in this struggle which attempts to make the law more relevant to women. Mahila Daxata Samiti, a non-partisan, non-sectarian body of women from all sections of society, strives to fight exploitation, injustice and oppression that affects women in Indian society.

Samiti works on a whole range of women's problems. The "anti-dowry cell" of the Samiti, a committed group of women led by Ms. Suman Krishnakant, have intervened directly in dowry death cases. A high priority was the adoption of a multi-faceted strategy to deal with issues promoted by the dowry, such as ruthless harrassment, torture and murder of women.

While becoming active in these cases, the members recognized that Samiti possessed no other power than moral persuasion. Also, they realized that the existing laws are of little help in restoring human dignity to women. Recognizing these constraints, Samiti organized a campaign with the help of other women's organizations to change the existing Dowry Prohibition Act of 1961, which has been frequently violated and evaded through legal loopholes. The members of Samiti, however, were aware that even if the law were to be amended, it would remain ineffective unless its spirit became an accepted part of social behavior. Therefore, an educational program to mobilize public opinion against the evils of dowry became the focus of this strategy.

There are other aspects to the strategy. Under the legal aid and assistance program, Samiti acts as a liaison between the Legal Aid Cell of the Government of India and the victims. Samiti has undertaken several legal programs to help women. It has established a paralegal training program which attempts to bring the law closer to lay-women. Such a training course of eight weeks was held for social workers in 1984. Samiti also has its own group of women lawyers which extends free legal aid services to dowry victims and other women.

Samiti also conducts an awareness week every October, beginning with the *Gandhi Jayanti* celebrations on the university campuses where debates, talks, and discussions as well as *Kavya Goshtis* are organized. Young students are particularly encouraged to participate. A mobile exhibition on dowry issues has been organized since 1982. Educating women about the law is intended to acquaint them with their legal rights and to equip them with the means to resolve their legal problems. Secondly, an awareness of the law can promote public opinion to press for the necessary changes in the legal system.

Cooperating with other women's organizations, the Samiti initiated the development of a broad front known as the Dahed Virodhi Chetna Manch to work for collective action.

These organizations have jointly organized demonstrations, public meetings, and media campaigns to create an awareness of, and to promote change in, the existing dowry legislation.

Legal Issues

The strategy combines the process of education and socialization of the public, the use of the legal system to protect women, and the provision of services to victims of crimes against women. As part of the public awareness campaign, numerous seminars have been conducted from 1978 onwards.

The Hindu Marriage Act provides a good example of a law that needs to be amended to reflect the changing social conditions. This act does not give to housewives the right to claim property which has been acquired by the husband after marriage. It places no monetary worth on housework; the Hindu wife is not protected from desertion by her husband. In most respects, a woman married under the Hindu Marriage Act faces handicaps which are not applicable to a man. Clearly, the law is vulnerable to manipulation by an unscrupulous party, either male or female, involved in a marriage dispute.

Samiti has worked for changes in the following laws: the Dowry Prohibition Act; the Criminal Law (Amendment) Bill, which deals with rape; the Criminal Law, Section 498A, which focuses on the issue of cruelty to women; and a bill proposing the establishment of family courts. All of these laws have been enacted or amended.

Results

The achievements of Samiti with respect to the Anti-Dowry Campaign are several. Firstly, the counseling program receives an average of 30-35 cases a month; it has become very popular among the women who face dowry threats in Delhi. Secondly, its initiative to join other women's organizations in the front Dahed Virodhi Chetna Manch lead to the largest demonstration ever organized against dowry on August 3, 1982. The front also pressured government to amend the existing dowry legislation. A private member bill was initiated by the president of the Mahila Daxata Samiti and as a result, the government appointed a joint committee to examine the Dowry

Prohibition Act of 1961. Thirdly, Samiti, along with other organizations, mobilized the public to pressure the joint committee to enact the Criminal Law (Amendment) Bill. Samiti's request to circulate the Hindu Marriage Amendment Bill was honored by the government. Fourthly, Samiti's efforts to establish family courts were well received by the Minister of Law; the Parliament later passed family court legislation. Fifthly, Samiti's efforts may create a conducive atmosphere to fight against the dowry because of its numerous actions in and around Delhi.

The struggle for obtaining justice for women through the activities of its Anti-Dowry Campaign is an important chapter in the history of Mahila Daxata Samiti. This campaign acquires particular importance because it seeks to use the law to protect women against many of the traditionally justified injustices.

Ranjana Kumari is a member of the Mahila Daxata Samiti and Director of the Center for Social Research in New Delhi, India.

The Philippines: Strategies for the Homeless
Teresa Fernandez

Introduction

I am a community organizer. I work with a group that specializes in the training of organizers by actually organizing the disadvantaged, using the action-reflection and conflict-confrontational approaches. I am also a member of a foundation that establishes low-cost housing cooperatives, and of PILIPINA, a group dedicated to equal rights and economic justice for women. Progressive individuals and organizations envision a Filipino society that is people-centered. To build such a society, we face many problems, particularly the vested interests of a small elite.

The problems confronting ordinary Filipinos include poverty, high prices, unemployment, malnutrition, corruption, homelessness, *etc.* They are both the causes and effects of intrinsic social conflict. Furthermore, these problems highlight the unbalanced Filipino socioeconomic structure which has been institutionalized. Hence, the rich are becoming richer. The landowners, big businessmen, government officials, and the multi-nationals own the land, capital and goods; and they control the state and enjoy its priviledges. In contrast, the poor are, indeed, becoming poorer. The slum-dwellers, tenants, and cultural minorities are not powerful or wealthy. Moreover, they are fearful, apathetic and weak. The source of their plight is rooted in the system whereby the structures are established, maintained, and perpetuated by the ruling class to safeguard its vested interests.

If the poor stand together in facing the authorities, the strength of their number will offset the weight of the powerful; in many cases, it will force the interaction of the two on a more equal footing. The participation of the weak in seeking social justice is a sham if it always confronts an exceedingly powerful opponent. In general, the *more-equal* dictates and the *less-equal* obeys.

However, the experience of group participation endows an individual with a sense of self-confidence, dignity and power. Empowering the poor signifies the establishment of participatory and powerful organizations to represent the poor and powerless, so that they can eventually play a role in decision-making.

A Brief Analysis of the Issues

In the Philippines, there is extensive poverty and a very unequal distribution of land. Vast tracks of land are owned by multinational corporations, farmed for export production of goods such as pineapples, coffee, and bananas. Apart from the large plantations, other industries like Kawasaki Steel also take advantage of Filipino conditions to produce mainly for export. Rural and cultural communities are frequently forced off their lands and compelled to squat in forest lands. Because of this situation and the growing upheaval in rural areas, many migrate to the cities, compounding the problems of urbanization. Moreover, squatters and other poor tenants in the cities are often threatened by eviction. The government has declared squatting a crime, punishable by eviction and imprisonment. In the cities where I work, twenty-five percent of the population are squatters—all of whom are categorized as criminals by the sheer circumstances of their being poor.

Another issue is the foreign origin of the law. The enactment and elaboration of legislation over past centuries primarily served colonial economic and political requirements. As an expression of rights, freedoms, and responsibilities, the law reflects foreign concepts and is written in a foreign language, thus excluding most people from access to the law. The legal system is highly complex and requires the services of a lawyer. The cost of legal services is far beyond the reach of the vast majority of people.

An additional problem exists for women. Property laws in the Philippines favor men. A husband has the sole right to manage family property. The wife cannot dispose of family property nor receive money (except from relatives up to the fourth degree) without the consent of the husband.

Responses to the Issues

Some squatters sought redress through legal channels. For example, a group of eighty residents living near the port of Cagayan de Oro were ordered to vacate property near the dockyard to expand the port. Now, although one law prohibits squatting, another law states that squatters cannot be evicted without being relocated. These people clung to the law. Thus, to delay eviction, a number of them avoided the service of subpoenas, and a greater number demanded their relocation before eviction. They were eventually evicted, but only after they were promised relocation and were compensated for relocation costs.

Squatters have also physically resisted eviction. In Cebu, the area inhabited by the squatters was previously part of the sea; the people eventually reclaimed the land by dumping all their waste materials under their houses. To their chagrin, they were served with a notice to vacate the land which now belonged to a foreigner named Wullbright. They could not imagine how a foreigner could have a title to a land which was formerly under water. They checked and reasoned with government officials, but to no avail. Finally they decided to stay no matter what. When the bulldozers arrived, all of the men were in their houses. The women and children were in the street, adjacent to the houses. The bulldozing crew did not know what to do. They threatened the women, who dared them in return. Eventually, some of the women convinced the crew to leave. Afterwards, the residents created a network to warn about any new demolition attempts. Over the next few years, several threats of demolition occurred.

When a leader of the movement was detained, women and men brought their children, animals, and kettles to the jail. They claimed they were also leaders of the squatter movement; if they were to be detained, they would bring their families and animals to jail, so that they would be fed. The jail warden became so worried—because he could not feed all these people—that he closed the jail gates to prevent them from entering. They went home with their freed leader.

Squatters have also sought financial assistance from outside groups. In Cagayan de Oro, a slum area was renovated through a loan from the World Bank. The people are obligated to pay for the costs of land acquisition and land development (the standards of which were prescribed by the World Bank), and the expenses of the agency's staff. The people will never be able to repay their debt in their lifetimes. Learning from this experience, another community of 841 families, whose property was to be redeveloped, decided to take a stand. As they would eventually assume the costs of the project, they believed they should have a say about the form of development, the various negotiations, the myriad aspects of construction, and the evaluation of the project. Otherwise, they asserted, they would not agree to the project. With the help of a researcher from Xavier University, they carried out their own feasibility survey to verify the government's survey. They also tried to elicit the support of the local government, which is sympathetic to their position. However, these tasks were easier said than done.

People's participation takes time, and it can sometimes test the patience of even those who are sensitive to their needs. The length of time that they can persevere remains to be seen. However, this community has it own project working-plan; it has set up committees to document, check, and solve problems. This process can be exhausting. Moreover, the government often responds by ignoring it.

Other landless people in Cebu have been helped to obtain land through group purchase. By searching for cheap property on the outskirts of the city and negotiating with neighboring landlords, one group has been able to buy land. It also has been assisted by a local foundation, which will accept installment payments for five years. The development process is the responsibility of the group, and it taps local resources to help implement the project. After the group provides common space, roads, and infrastructure, it divides the land among the inhabitants.

The group has encountered some problems. For example, the Human Settlement Regulatory Commission's (HSRC) requirement that subdivision roads be ten meters would incur additional costs for people, who do not require such large roads as they do not have cars. Lawyers explained to the people that this regulation exists to safeguard the interest of the buyers of subdivision lots. In this case, however, the owners and buyers were the same people, and therefore, the standard regulations should not apply to them. As a result, they are able to construct a 2-3 meter wide path walk without violating regulations.

Seven hundred and fifty families who obtained the tacit approval of the local government are benefiting from this scheme. This strategy is also being used by some 231 women in Davao City with the help of the PILIPINA Legal Resource Center, run by women lawyers and the Kahayag Foundation. They are negotiating to buy a piece of land on an installment basis, rather than accepting an eviction notice.

Another response to the problem of homelessness is the expropriation strategy adopted by some 140 families in the barrio of Cagayan de Oro. Most of them are tenants, who have lived in the area for 20-30 years. The amount of rent they paid over the years could have purchased land. The 140 families are using a new law which states that land can be expropriated for socialized housing. Writ of possession can be issued upon payment of 10% of the declared or assessed market value (whichever is the lowest) to the court. To implement this strategy, the people have organized to lobby the city legislators and to execute a public relations campaign. This case continues.

Other groups have responded in myriad ways. It would take hours to enumerate them. In general, the strategies are easier to describe than to implement. In theory, none is better than the other; the various situations and circumstances determine the best strategy. Common to all these experiences are two key points: the main actors are those affected; the organizers and lawyers are merely supporters; also, more important than the legal battle is the moral struggle, which implies that every person has the right to a home on his own land.

The process of organizing the poor homeless people involves three major steps. Firstly, the organizer must begin from the people's point of view. She must understand the objective reality of their situations and empathize with their subjective perception of the circumstances. In many cases, it is most effective to live among the people. Secondly, an organizer must not merely follow the people; she must not mythologize their situation, but rather encourage and motivate them into action. Thirdly, however much effort and time an organizer expends on these cases, it is ultimately the people who must make the final decisions about development projects. Therefore, the organizer's tasks include data collection, planning and preparation, motivation, and mobilization; this assistance eventually enables the people to act alone. In short, she must actually prepare the people for her departure.

The problem of land and property requires time, effort and know-how to solve. People are usually encouraged to tackle simpler and more easily achievable issues like water and health services. Experience in these issues can help them avoid mistakes when confronting the more complex issue of land.

The Role of Women

While property remains a man's prerogative, it is interesting that the majority, and the most active, of those involved in the land cases have been women. This experience is understandable as most women are bound to the home. Even working women must contend with the responsibilities of the household, and hence, are doubly burdened. It is they who bear the burden of eviction or demolition. Women squatters suffer more greatly from their deprivation of water, light, and a healthful environment. As they are more directly affected, women respond favorably to organizing efforts. The men are forced to accede to these tactics.

In fact, there have been instances in which meetings or activities have been postponed or unsuccessful because the husband of a female leader would not permit her to attend; sometimes, a child gets sick and the husband simply will not take charge. These considerations must be taken into account when the strategy is developed and implemented. These difficulties stem from the economic dependence of women, no matter how active they are. In response to this situation, we attempt to provide loans to initiate income-generating activities. Some women are faring well; others are still learning to assume new responsibilities.

The Role of the Law

Access to the legal system does not necessarily signify access to justice. Organizational lawyers recognize that it is not sufficient to inform the people about their rights and the mechanics of the law. They must also make legal concepts real and tangible to the people. Once they are aware of the justness of their demands, they develop methods to attain them. In addition, the lawyers should attempt to communicate a healthy irreverence towards the law so that the poor and powerless are not afraid to challenge governmental policies.

Finally, whatever strategy the people adopt, they must persevere in its implementation. A right is not a right until it is guaranteed. The disadvantaged, particularly women, must struggle and assert their rights, if they are ever to attain justice and equality.

Theresa Fernandez is a community-organizing trainer in the Philippines.

[Editor's note: This paper was drafted in 1985, and the author's critique of Philippine social and economic policy under the Marcos government may not apply to the current situation in the Philippines.]

Ecuador: Organization of Women in the Working Class Districts of Quito

Lucía Carrión

Overview

Women, particularly housewives in the working-class districts of Quito, are the greatest victims of these slums. As the center of the family unit, poor women confront daily the dearth of economic and public resources with which they must shape their families lives. Hence, they must develop mutual aid systems with their neighbors and relatives. Women are thus key players in the informal dynamics of the community. Yet, their economic power is limited. Furthermore, they have little or no decision-making power in the local, regional, or national arenas.

One of the central problems of people living in these poor districts is their low level of organization. Such a situation restricts their ability to pressure authorities to channel greater resources to the poor, women, and the underpriveleged. In many cases, state funding for working-class neighborhoods is not forthcoming because of inadequate communication between the state and these districts. Other factors such as administrative problems, organizational inefficiency, the passivity of the people, and the political patron-client system, *inter alia*, compound the problems.

Women's participation in the existing local organizations is low. These organizations lack the strength needed to improve public infrastructure and community life to benefit women. They do not address women's identity problems nor do they acknowledge women's participation in those community activities which are not seen by the public. The community, the organization, and the family generate mechanisms that obviate people's appreciation of women's participation in daily affairs. At the same time, organizations do not understand or value the domestic role of women. It is important then that new means are created to organize, to break the public/private dichotomy, and to highlight the plight and potential of women.

Women began a gradual process of reexamining their identities as a result of socioeconomic changes undergone by the country in the 1960's (*e.g.*, industrialization through import substitution, the restructuring of the agrarian system with the dissolution of the traditional hacienda system, the consolidation of the peasant unit of production, urbanization, and the transformation of the state's role and the changing structure of the family). These processes encouraged individualization and women's search for identity through the attainment of rights and responsibilities within the social system.

Process

The process of re-democratizing Ecuador which was begun in 1979 resulted in state involvement in women's issues. It attempted to integrate women into the process of democratization through mass organizations and state programs for development, self-management, and economic redistribution.

The National Women's Office (OFNAMU) under the Ministry of Social Welfare requested that the Center for Planning and Social Studies (CEPLAES) develop a strategy and implement a social program directed at the poor working-class districts, focusing especially on women. CEPLAES secured funds from the International Development Research Center of the government of Canada to implement its proposal.

The process of social change, the history of women and the state's initiative to benefit women helped the CEPLAES program to be accepted in these districts. In addition such factors as the House of Representatives' debate on criminal legislation, country-wide elections, and new economic legislation all affected the domestic economy, the survival of the districts, and favored the implementation of CEPLAES strategy.

Focus

The strategy focuses on educating women about their basic social, political, and legal rights. It also emphasizes the social and political processes that permit discrimination and oppression of women. Moreover, the strategy highlights the structural roots of powerlessness and socioeconomic inequality to combat inequality, it emphasizes the many aspects of organization and planning.

The program proposed to organize women's groups in two working-class districts. It aims to publicize women's issues, to integrate women's public and private lives, and to improve the quality of life for poor women. It also seeks to clarify the problems of ordinary women so that women's organizations can provide basic education and information. Finally, the program is attempting to develop a methodology to organize and assist these women, which can be easily reproduced and implemented by other institutions.

We developed five specific activities to implement our strategy. Within the concept of *education in action*, relevant educational activities are offered. Education is conceived as a process that begins in concrete practices, needs, and interests. The educational program encompasses the following: an analysis of social, economic, and political reality; discussions about democratic planning and evaluation; the teaching of leadership, cooperative skills, and social welfare rights; and interpersonal and domestic relations. Training activities are oriented towards teaching women particular skills in various fields, such as the domestic and health fields. They also seek to improve the conditions of community life by teaching skills which are expected to be re-invested into the community.

Our other actions for change include activities which respond to the immediate needs of the group and those that promote participation in long-term organized programs. Basically, they incorporate activities that help develop alternative ways for poor women to deal with the structural problems of poverty, unemployment, *etc*. They encompass ongoing programs which seek to address community problems (*e.g.*, improving health standards).

Research includes activities that encourage the processes of reflection and consciousness-raising of women and their organizations. Ongoing research helps the center to evaluate the program's goals and the impact of its activities at each stage of implementation.

The strategy does not concentrate exclusively on legal aspects. It aspires to have an integrated focus that addresses the many social and political processes that affect women. This perspective is necessary because the Ecuadorian legal system is

271

more advanced than actual social processes. This is not to say that the legal system is equal for both men and women. Legal discrimination still exists. For example, one article of the civil code states that "the husband has the right to decide the domicile of the couple; he is the head of the household; the wife must obey her husband ..."

Our project seeks to identify the cultural elements that impede the enactment of progressive legislation as well as the political limits of the legislation. For instance, a high priority of women in the La Primavera district is health. In that district, we found few formal health resources (*e.g.*, medical care and health infrastructure). In addition, we discovered that there was a need to train and organize women to demand sanitary facilities for the family and the district. We published a health manual, and formulated a system of health assistance that could be used in an organized way by the women of the district. We also provided health training courses. One course contained four main proposals : training women as health promoters; reinstituting folk medicine; teaching the treatment of prevalent illnesses; and providing medical alternatives in the district which would be implemented through women's groups.

Organization

The participants, principally housewives, were not organized. The strategy planned by CEPLAES was modified after the staff became acquainted with the reality of the districts. The project was composed of the CEPLAES promotion/research team, women participants from the two districts of Quito, and state institutions. The women participated in three different aspects: program participants, program promoters, and program and activity coordinators.

Results

As a result of this strategy, two organizations in each of the districts have been formed. They have established planning, development, and evaluation guidelines to implement the various programs. The programs have brought about a modification of the women's self-perception. The women have gradually overcome their fear of speaking in public; they have sought alternative forms of communication; they have developed their critical and analytical faculties; and they have a greater ability to voice demands. In addition, the strategy has helped the women to participate in decision-making and to organize community activities.

For example, people from diverse socioeconomic backgrounds were brought together to encourage greater social integration. These experiences opened up a new world for these marginal women. The program provided a place for the women to gain new friends and to work together for social change.

Lessons

A strength—but also sometimes a weakness—has been the wide range of problems that the strategy has addressed. This breadth facilitates a creative inter-relationship between the outside agent and beneficiaries. This dynamic promotes democratic and collective organization; and at the same time, it discourages some forms of authoritarianism. However, the wide range of themes weakens the strategy because of the tendency to diffuse broadly the program's resources. Another drawback has been the difficulty in establishing criteria for a systematic evaluation.

The programs should evolve from the concrete demands of the people and be integrated within the structure of the poular movements. CEPLAES has been requested to work with and support popular organizations. Such coordination will modify and enrich CEPLAES work in the future.

Lucía Carrión is an economist and the Executive Director of the Center for Planning and Social Studies in Quito, Ecuador.

Nicaragua:
The Law and Women's Emancipation
Milú Vargas

Women cannot adapt themselves to their history unless they begin to collectivize their experiences, which will help them to overcome the structural isolation they suffer and to understand the social causes of their individual suffering.

Maria Mies

Introduction

Under the Somozan dictatorship, Nicaraguan women along with all common people were condemned to illiteracy, hunger, unemployment, poverty, and exploitation. Men and women were denied the most basic human rights, and as a result, many suffered imprisonment, exile, and death. Mere physical survival was threatened.

Women participated collectively in the struggle for liberation and the triumph of the Popular Sandinista Revolution. They were organized as the Association of Women to Confront the National Issue (AMPRONAC); its struggle represents a long chapter of women's participation in national liberation.

The association was established to demand the freedoms of expression, association, and organization (particularly for unions) and to free political prisoners. In addition, it sought to punish those who killed defenseless demonstrators; those who tortured prisoners; and civil and military officials who engaged in plunder and fraudulent operations.

Among AMPRONAC's specific demands were the banning of prostitution, ending of the commercialization of women, and introducing equal civil rights for women. The national and international chapters of the women's association demonstrated its extensive organizational capacity and its ability to fight the dictatorship. AMPRONAC played an important role in organizing peasant and poor urban women. It also denounced the crimes of the dictatorship and prepared logistical support for insurrection. Our activities contributed to the Sandinista victory.

The Women's Movement
and the Sandinista Revolution

The broad participation of women in Nicaragua today is in part due to the existence and work of AMPRONAC. Its legitimate demands are a product of the long struggle of the Nicaraguan people. The participation of Nicaraguan women in society and politics is integrated in the continuing revolutionary process, which ensures the achievement, of total emancipation.[1]

Women were integrated into the national liberation movement; to have isolated them from the historical conditions in Nicaragua would have only demonstrated chauvinism. Hence, AMPRONAC directly contributed to the struggle for social change, freedom, and the transformation of the economic, political, and social structures.

The attitude of the Sandinista National Liberation Front (FSLN) towards women is reflected by the integration of the priniciples enunciated in the *Emancipation of Women* into its general program.

The victory of the popular Sandinistan Revolution has brought about a new period and perspective in politics. The just aspirations of our women to integrate into all facets of the political and social process can only result from their participation in the new society, from the gradual development of new socioeconomic structures, and from the ideological development of the revolutionary society.

With the victory of the revolution, with our collective integration into the revolutionary process, and with the recognition and support of the government, women are taking the first steps towards emancipation.

The FSLN women's program encompasses three objectives:

❑ the transformation of the social relations of production to ensure the complete incorporation of women into the productive process and into the society as a whole.

❑ the ideological transformation of society (which will eliminate a basis of inequality) in order to develop relations of mutual respect between men and women, to establish social equality, and to end the vertical cleavages

275

of the male-female relationship

❏ legal reforms in the law which reflect those made at the economic, political, and social levels.

Organizational Issues of the Women's Movement

First of all, we must differentiate between private and social issues. An issue is private if it involves only an individual and his or her narrow circle. It is of social interest, however, if it deals with questions that transcend the individual's circle and affects the whole social structure.

For example, if a pregnant domestic worker is fired because the employer wishes to avoid paying maternity benefits, it is her problem. But, when 5,000 workers are fired for similar reasons, this issue ceases to be the problem of one domestic worker. If a woman has an abortion, it is her problem. But, when 10,000 abortions are performed a year (in a population of 500,000), abortion is no longer an individual problem, but signifies a larger social problem.

We could mention many more similar examples: the widespread unemployment of women; the low wages of female workers; and the financial abandonment by fathers of their children. When thousands of women are found in these situations, the problems cease to be those of Juanita or Lupita, and they become public issues that must be solved.

Secondly, we must consider the nature of the organization needed to carry out a collective women's struggle Many believe that it should include both males and females. I believe, however, that it should be composed of women only. Although women's particular problems affect the whole society, they suffer from doubly savage discrimination and terrible alienation.

By organizing women in their own association, we run the risk of being labeled contemptuously as feminists. Previously, feminism has not been viewed as a force to fight traditional roles and characteristics which have been used to justify discrimination against women. Revolutionary feminism has often been misrepresented as being opposed to men. On the contrary, revolutionary feminism seeks to destroy the aggressive machismo in men and the passivity of women.[3]

276

The structure of the organization must be flexible and democratic in order to permit free communication among its members. The women's organization should be built from the level of local committees, on to the regional level, and up to the national level. This structure will insure greater accountability and effectiveness.[4]

A third issue consists of determining which women we should organize. We believe we must build a women's organization that fights for the real liberation of our sex and at the same time, works to build a new society. Therefore, we must organize women who are exploited, unemployed, illiterate and impoverished. They include housewives, domestics, peasants, other workers, and nurses, *inter alia*. All they have in common is their precarious material conditions. We must organize them so that the battle for the economic well-being of them and their children is won.

Another segment of women that should be organized is the middle-class, including professionals, intellectuals, state and private sector employees. These women resist the imposition on them of traditional values, ideas, and morals. They do not submit easily to social control or neutralization, and they are anxious to change the social rules for women.

Although the two groups are different in terms of socioeconomic standards, life-styles, and attitudes, both are committed to social change, especially on women's issues.[5]

Legal Reform and Women's Emancipation

The law can be used as an effective instrument in the fight for women's emancipation. Laws regulate our everyday lives (*e.g.* marriage, motherhood, work, *etc.*) After women study and analyze the use of the law in everyday situations, they will be better able to determine their destinies. The following issues are of great importance to women in determining their lives.

Firstly, paternal authority consists of the corpus of legislative rights, powers, and responsibilities conferred upon the father to care for and govern his children from conception until their majority. In most Third World societies, the law establishes the right of the father to impose his will on his children and on their mother. A woman may question the justice of this legal norm (which is reinforced by social conditions):

"Why does the law neglect my real situation? I care for my children. Why am I not permitted to make decisions? This law does not reflect my reality! For whom was it created?"

Secondly, according to the marriage law, the husband has legal power over his wife and the right to her domestic services. As the principal provider, the man occupies a central position in the family; he determines the family'stheir living conditions. In this context, the woman may ask: "When did the difference between the duties of mother and father come into existence? Why is there a difference?"

Thirdly, pregnant women have the right to a paid-leave of six weeks before and six weeks after delivery—a minimum right of women. However, it has not been effectively applied. Here, the woman may ask: "Who will ensure that my employer will not fire me upon learning that I am pregnant?" Of course, the employer cannot state that he is dismissing a woman for being pregnant because that is prohibited. Nevertheless, common practice has demonstrated that the employer will use a variety of other reasons to justify the woman's dismissal.

Fourthly, domestic work is not subject to normal working hours. Regulations only require that a minimum of ten hours of rest per day be given to the worker. Furthermore, the worker does not have sick leave or social security, illness, disability, or death benefits. We must ask ourselves, "Why is the working day fourteen hours long? Who will pay the domestic worker when she is sick? If she cannot work, how will she live? If she dies, what will become of her children?"

The answers to all these questions are harsh and cruel. The magnitude of the women's problem must guide us along the long and painful road to the liberation of women.

Conclusion

The laws are instruments to fight for women's emancipation, but they never comprise the sole solution to their problems. The emancipation of women will not be achieved by decree. If that were possible, the establishment of legal equality of women is a relatively easy matter. The real problem we face, however, is the actual realization of women's rights and equality.

Milú Vargas is Legal Advisor for the Council of State in Nicaragua.

Brazil: Women in the Rural Sector
Ayala de Almeida Rocha

Overview

The strategy addresses the legal issues of labor and social security provisions which, either by restriction or by omission, deny women's rights. Women's lack of awareness about their rights in general—and those rights which affect their working conditions in particular—helps to perpetuate the abuse and exploitation of women.

The cases in this report refer specifically to women in the rural sector. Rural legislation which this strategy addresses is characteristically discriminatory in terms of labor or social security regulations; it does not provide the protection of urban legislation. Furthermore, laws on women in the rural sector are doubly discriminatory and they do not reflect the reality of their situations.

Therefore, the legal norm shapes a rural world where there is little awareness of the law's content and   its weaknesses. Frequently, unjust and discriminatory laws encourage a passive acceptance of injustice and discrimination. Faced with these problems, our primary goal is to bring about the inclusion of the legal norms of recognition and protection of women peasants and rural workers in ordinary, supplementary, or transitory laws such as collective dissent rulings.

Our goal is much broader than simply changing legislation: it is consciousness-raising, training, and implementation. In working towards this goal, we hope that legislation will also be changed. The ultimate result for which we strive is equipping women with an awareness of their actual or potential rights and the capability to obtain, defend, or apply their rights.

Many diverse activities are required to attain the goals. Four broad categories of activities or elements of the strategy are described below.

In the first place, we conduct consciousness-raising and organizational meetings to mobilize and educate women.

Secondly, we participate in the rural labor unions. In this context, we also organize a women's group which discusses and develops their demands so that both working-class men and

279

women can cooperate to achieve their objectives. The strategy promotes the participation of women in the working class movement in order that their grievances will be recognized as a general demand of the entire class.

Thirdly, we seek to maximize the impact of our work by extending our activities beyond rural women and the working class. We seek to unify various groups and individuals around common concerns.

Fourthly, we use the legislative process in the strategy. Although various groups and individuals pressure the legislators, the influence of women peasants as a social force is a constant in our strategy and activities. In addition, we have established training courses, an evaluation process, specific group activities at the center, and joint activities with the labor unions, *inter alia.*

The organizing of the rural sector must be considered in the context of its history of patriarchy, male domination, obscurantism, and backwardness, all of which obstruct simple goals. Therefore, it is necessary to modify our activities due to the entrenched attitudes of the dominator who happens to be the husband of the peasant woman. Moreover, it is essential to integrate him into our program and activities.

Process

First, the structure and dynamic of CDDH/AEP (Centro de Defesa Dos Direitos Humanos/Assessoria e Educacão Popular) must be considered. The popular council is composed of people from the rank and file of the rural sector. The dynamic of this center is generated by its ability to examine problems appropriately. The many agrarian issues in this northeast region of Brazil as well as the present learning process of CDDH/AEP require constant interaction with rural grassroots groups in the rural environment. Specific issues have been highlighted by the demonstration of peasant women.

Preparations for the first sugar cane cutters' strike in the northeast marked a significant awakening of the workers and brought about the formulation of their grievances. The workers discussed and developed the general framework of demands to be presented for negotiation. During this process, matters relating to women's working conditions took on a different tone and were evaluated according to the actual situation in which the women were working. Later in the process, significant possibilities for action opened up while building the strike.

Focus

The strategy is comprised of a collection of tactical components ranging from the small motivational meetings at the grassroots level to participation in labor union activities to the determination of a precept as a legal norm.

These elements of the strategy's focus are integrally linked to the realities of a peasant woman's life The components of the strategy focus on the improvement of her conditions by increasing her awareness, clarifying the need for and the method of change; and motivating her participation. One of the first steps is to provide the peasant woman with access to basic resources in terms of knowledge and skills. Also, it is important to provide training that will have a multiplier effect in order to make a larger impact on society.

In summary, the main focus of the strategy is to formulate guidelines for collective dissent cases which have been used to draft and enact legislation; in addition, it aims to develop people's critical awareness and to create a power base to press for change and reform.

Legal Issues

Our legislative focus concentrates on labor legislation. We seek security for pregnant women including remuneration and guarantees during pregnancy; recognition of women's needs for rest; equal rights in the choice of work and residence; and other rights related to equal work for equal pay. In the area of social security legislation, we seek the elimination of dependence on the man and the reversal of legislation which confers upon the man the head of household status. We also argue for equal retirement rights and for the the right of women to join unions.

Organization and Participation

The participants are rural women, both wage workers and peasants who attended meetings which initially were infrequent. For the most part, they emerged from general worker meetings to discuss various aspects of land disputes. As with the discussions to formulate collective dissent and strike issues, the meetings took on their own dynamic among the grassroots groups and within the unions. CDDH/AEP aimed to increase the frequency of the meetings and to help with their organization. Eventually, the meetings occurred more regularly and included elements of organization and evaluation.

Results

Evaluations about motivation, participation, tactics, achievements, *inter alia*, are conducted regularly. In October 1984, and more recently, the Fourth National Congress of Rural Workers has witnessed several successes. In the first case, an important success consisted of the inclusion of issues related to women workers' rights in the collective dissent demands. With the participation of women peasants in the strikes, these demands were granted by the final ruling of the court. Moreover, the worker's congress included women's social security and worker's rights on its agenda and recommended corresponding legislative proposals.

Lessons

It is essential to place the situation of rural women in the appropriate context. The quasi-feudal system presents many obstacles to the rural woman: paternalism; the domination of the landowner over the rural worker and his family; and other socioeconomic and cultural problems. Also the logistics of transportation make work with rural woman difficult.

Nevertheless, the barriers have been overcome through parallel community activities (*e.g.* community health projects and planting projects, *etc.*), which permit more participation and which raise self-esteem within the family and the community. When difficulties in implementing some aspects of the strategy were overcome, the gains from collective dissent rulings and their inclusion in the worker's congress agenda advanced the strategy.

Ayala de Almeida Rocha is the legal and educational counsel for the Centro de Defesa Dos Direitos Humanos, Assessoria e Educacão Popular.

Mauritius:
Women, Legal Education and Legal Reform
Shirin Aumeeruddy-Cziffra

Introduction

The Feminist League was born out of the Mauritian Militant Movement (MMM), a growing mass movement. The MMM's 1973 manifesto made clear its intention to encourage feminist movements. wo In 1974, just prior to the International Women's Year, a group of Mauritian women created the Feminist League to press for women's rights and to raise the consciousness of women. Until this time, women had been largely absent from the social, economic, and political arenas. Married women were considered minors without their own legal identity. No group had ever organized to change the discriminatory laws and to improve the situation of women.

The Feminist League took advantage of the popular MMM to spearhead a campaign to educate people about women's rights. Soon after its creation, the Feminist League began publicizing the social, economic, and political problems of women. The International Women's Year in 1975 and the United Nations' Decade for Women spurred a wide debate on all these questions and raised a new consciousness among women as well as the public.

Since its creation, the women's movement has opted for a strategy which envisioned using the law and the judiciary to the utmost to safeguard women's rights. This strategy has led to a fight for legal reform. The results since 1980 have been the reorganization and modernization of family and civil laws which affect married women. As a result of these changes, women can now take advantage of reforms which protect women and children. Legal reform has made a considerable impact on women's attitudes. As a consequence, women have acquired a new legal status and a new self-confidence.

The Feminist League together with the MMM obtained the creation of a Ministry of Women's and Family Rights in 1982. Its minister, who is a woman, also assumes the function of attorney general. Governments since that time have continued to follow the strategy initiated by two organizations.

Focus

In order to improve the legal and social conditions of women, the Feminist League sought to raise the consciousness of women and men, to popularize and utilize the laws which protect women, and to demand legal reforms which would eliminate sex-based discrimination and safeguard women's rights.

After 1981, when new organizations succeeded the Feminist League, the goals of organizing women to take collective action for change and of giving women the effective tool of the law were added. We have used all available means to sensitize the masses about these issues. These methods have included demonstrations, media promotion, national fora, debates, and graphics. We have also produced and distributed leaflets and feminist journals.

In order to make people aware of the laws, we are translating and explaining publicly the laws. We have provided legal advice at various locations including events such as large demonstrations. To promote legal reform, we have used the press to communicate the major themes of our movement. After 1976, women deputies who were members of our movement pressed their claims by shifting the focus of the debates in the legislative assembly. A continuous dialogue took place with experts who are drafting legal texts at the Ministry of Justice.

For previously-stated historical reasons, our movement was launched from a political party. Originally, it was a mixed group. Very quickly, however, it became necessary to organize women outside of the party, while at the same time remaining close to the party and its underlying objectives. We chose to pursue our strategy as an autonomous feminist movement, attempting to avoid the constraints of male paternalism and women's lack of self-confidence. Increasingly, our political label divided us from some parts of the society, permitting us only to reach women who were close to the MMM. This was a handicap in the 1970's. On the other hand, the wave of change which unfurled in Mauritius beginning in 1981 overturned all previous political facts and reduced the importance of everything outside the political domain. These changes included the end of the Feminist League, the creation of a Ministry of Women's and Family Rights in 1982, and the beginning of a women's commission in the MMM. This commission took over the coordination of feminist efforts in the party.

During the period of 1975-1981 when the Feminist League undertook most of its work, it sought to create a common women's platform and to encourage solidarity among newly-formed groups. The campaign to educate Mauritians began in 1974; the campaign concluded by reaching those groups which were dedicated to feminist ideals. In 1977, a common platform reunited several groups of women for collective action against newly enacted repressive and discriminatory laws. This permitted the feminist front to bring a suit before the Commission on Civil and Political Rights at the United Nations in Geneva. In 1978, the activities of this front widened the issues of concern to women. Subsequently, a non-political, radical movement, Women's Solidarity, was born. This movement continues to fight feminist battles.

Legal Issues

In the area of civil and political rights, we sought a constitutional amendment to guarantee equal rights for women; an amendment to the 1974 Jury Act to permit women to sit on juries; and finally an amendment to the Immigration and Deportation Acts of 1977. Another area of concern was women's rights in marriage, in other words, their personal and inheritance rights. To that end, we argued for an amendment to the Napoleonic Code of 1804. This amendment would permit women to work freely and to earn and spend their wages as they see fit after contributing to household expenses. It would permit women to hold a bank account and freely engage in real estate and financial transactions. In addition, if women choose to be married, they would have the right to manage the family finances jointly or to exercise separate finances, if that is in the interest of the household. Women would also have the right to exercise joint parental authority over children and to obtain custody of children under five years of age if there is a marital separation or legal divorce.

The rights of women as workers also drew our interest. We wanted an amendment to the Labor Act of 1975 providing for

285

equal pay for equal work, and better protection for pregnant and nursing women. We have chosen to work on these legal areas because of three major considerations.

Firstly, the exercise of civil rights is fundamental to gain other rights and to give women confidence. Secondly, as long as married women remain legal minors and under the fule of men, they cannot develop individually and participate fully in social, political and economic life. Thirdly, as long as women are not respected, protected, and paid equally, they will not be free, nor able to contribute fully to the development of their country.

Participation

Between 1974 and 1982, members of the Feminist League in collaboration with other women's organizations brought the struggle for women's legal and social rights to the forefront. Deputies of the opposition MMM party in the legislative assembly worked from 1976 to 1982 to reform discriminatory laws and fought against the promulgation of unfair legislation. In 1982–1983, the government adopted and assumed the leadership of the feminist programs. Since 1983, the Women's Commission of the MMM continues to lead the fight for women's rights and various necessary changes.

Results

The strategy has been implemented for the past ten years and inspired real changes which affected the law and Mauritians' attitudes. It has a snowball effect: other groups have organized and strive for similar objectives. The strategy has had a direct impact on the lives of women, especially married women. Now, they have acquired their own legal identity and the rights to work, manage their property, and take part in all aspects of civil life without obtaining permission from their husbands. These new rights signal the beginning of freer and more equal relations between men and women. Also, the strategy opened new professions for women and brought improved working conditions. Women are now more informed about their rights and they are better able to defend existing rights and gain new ones. Finally, the strategy contributed directly to wider political participation by women.

Lessons

Our strategy has been limited; the means we used were inadequate for a rapid and effective consciousness-raising of the people. Our political label impeded our work during the first years of existence (1974-1981).

One area in which we have underestimated the weight of tradition is marriage, particularly, the raising of the legal age of marriage to eighteen years for young women. The pressure of political and social forces has forced the government to retreat. Therefore, we have concluded that an autonomous feminist group is indispensable to pressure the political parties. It is equally necessary that feminist women work inside these parties so that they can raise the consciousness of the party-members and form interest groups to defend women's rights.

We believe that our link with a political party was positive because we were assured of its support in most of our battles. Problems only arose over sensitive issues, such as the age of marriage and abortion. Our strategy has been validated by the policies of the MMM after it took power.

Conclusion

In Mauritius, the evolution of politics has greatly influenced our initial strategy. The Feminist League, born out of the MMM in 1974, left the party in 1975. In 1977, the Feminist League initiated the creation of a unified platform which became Women's Solidarity in 1978. From 1982 to 1983, the MMM monopolized the political terrain. In 1983, a strained political situation divided the country, forcing groups to side with the different politcal parties. In the MMM, a commission of women took over the coordination of women's issues in the party. The MMM, as the strongest political party confronting a coalition government, remains the alternative of tomorrow. For women, the picture is cloudy. The organizations which have survived are all politically marked. At this time, we clearly recognize the need for an autonomous women's movement, but the socio-political atmosphere does not favor its development.

Shirin Aumeeruddy-Cziffra is Deputy Senior Minister of Justice, Women's and Family Rights, Mauritius.

287

Changing
the Law

All the papers contained in this chapter describe efforts to change specific legislation. In most cases, the strategies adopted are multi-faceted and include constituency-building and public education together with other approaches to mobilize women to effect changes in the law.

Mason's paper on the effort to enact legislation requiring equal pay for equal work in Jamaica describes this approach to law reform. The Jamaican strategy included, in addition to lobbying, a public education campaign accompanied by efforts to improve the education and training of women in all occupations. The targets of the lobbying efforts were carefully defined, as were the collaborators in the strategy—trade unions, vocational institutions, educators, and employer organizations, among others. Recognizing that changing the law would not be enough to assure real and lasting change, the strategy also focused on changing attitudes.

Kazembe and *Mol* describe an effort in Zimbabwe to make known to women throughout the country the content of the 1982 Legal Age of

Majority Act. Because women were not involved in formulating the new law—even though it marked an improvement in their situation—there was an urgent need to make the law known to women and to develop positive attitudes toward it. This task was achieved though a project that combined an information campaign to publicize the law with research to assess its degree of implementation and its effect on women. These efforts have pointed out the need for adequate educational methodologies to communicate the content of the laws in ways that begin to affect attitudes and behaviors. They also indicate the importance of involving the intended beneficiaries in the law reform process.

Tai-Young Lee from Korea also addresses the need for changes in attitudes as a prerequisite for effective law reform. Over the past twenty-five years, Korean women's efforts to reform family laws have been relatively successful. Their strategy included a wide range of activities, from signature campaigns to media blitzes, from the formation of coalitions to the creation of legal service centers. Nevertheless, the struggle to change traditional attitudes that consider women inferior continues. Creating the popular support to make further changes remains a challenge for women in Korea.

Pulea describes the participation of women in the Pacific island Vanuatu in the formulation of a new family law through a comprehensive process of research and education. This strategy was geared toward increasing awareness about legal rights and specifically toward involving women in formulating provisions of a family law that would favor their interests. Women were helped to understand the political process, the functioning of the legal system and the content of the law. This understanding, in turn, pushed them to clarify their own interests and concerns in the framework of formulating new and more adequate legislation.

Jamaica: Equal Pay for Equal Work
Myrtle Mason

Overview

Jamaican women, who constitute about 51% of the island's 2.1 million people, have actively participated in the workforce since the introduction of the slave-labor plantation system. They have been forced to work in order to survive.

Until the early 1970's, women's participation in the workforce was largely confined to traditional employment and to low-paying jobs. They were most highly represented in the service sector, particularly domestic service, about 76% of which were women. While women workers formed 56.3% of the professional and technical sector, most of these were teachers and nurses. A more accurate picture of the status of women in the labor force in 1974 can be drawn from their representation in the administrative and management sector, merely 11.8%.

More often than not, women workers have received lower pay than men for the same work. They have been denied equality of job opportunities because a substantial proportion of jobs were designed exclusively for men. Women have had little or no voice at all in the decision-making process, and sex discrimination has been common.

At the same time, many Jamaican women have had sole economic responsibility for themselves and their families. Of all households, approximately one-third were headed by women in 1974. Furthermore, in the majority of all households, women have sought employment to supplement the family income. Government employment statistics for 1974 indicated that the level of female participation in the labor force was relatively high: 34.8% of the female population was either employed or seeking employment.

The Soroptimist Club of Jamaica, a women's service organization committed to the advancement of the status of women, has long been aware of the important role played by Jamaican women in the economic and social life of the country. It was equally concerned about sex discrimination in the workplace because it resulted in unfair treatment and limited opportunities for women. The club's Civic Committee saw the need for change in attitudes and policies regarding women. It responded to that need by articulating a strategy geared to the creation of new laws and policies which would encourage the elimination of discriminatory practices against women at the workplace.

It was quite clear from the outset that while it was possible to legislate against discrimination, it was also necessary for women to obtain training opportunities which would equip them to benefit fully from the new legislation. Consequently, the strategy had two major objectives. The first aimed at the elimination of the inferior status of women in the job market. Because women have been treated as inferior and subordinate to men, they were not entitled to equal pay for equal work.

The second objective has been the provision of adequate training opportunities for women in all occupations, including those which have been traditionally accessible only to men.

The Soroptimist Club embarked on a program of consciousness-raising; it organized seminars, at which other women's organizations participated, and discussed at public fora the goals and objectives of the strategy. One such seminar, entitled *Perspectives on the Social and Economic Status of Women in Jamaica*, sponsored by the Soroptimist Club in April 1975, enlisted the cooperation of some twenty-five women's organizations representing many aspects of Jamaican religious, political, social, and educational life. At this seminar, participants made some important and clearly defined decisions.

As a result of the decisions, representations were made to government and quasi-government agencies concerned with employment and training. They urged these agencies to make all training centers co-educational and to make available to women a wider range of courses so that they could become qualified for better paying jobs.

The other groups the club aimed to influence were employers' organizations, trade unions, educators, guidance counselors, and parents. Educators were requested to examine the education system's role in the perpetuation of sexual inequality, especially curriculua based on sexual stereo-types. The club also requested that vocational counseling be introduced in all schools to facilitate a change in attitudes towards the traditional sexual division of labor. Special attention was also directed at parents to seek their cooperation in discouraging the promotion of sex roles for children and in enlightening their children about the vast new areas of employment available in non-traditional occupations.

Employers' organizations were asked to give equal opportunity to women workers and to provide daycare facilities for working mothers. Our organization strongly requested that trade unions: create more opportunities for women in leadership and representational positions; be more vigilant about ensuring equal pay for male and female workers engaged in the same category of work; encourage employers to make special efforts in providing middle and upper level management training for women; and develop new attitudes towards the concept of equal opportunity and participation for women.

The Soroptimist Club lobbied the government to appoint women to all decision-making and policy-making bodies which affect vocational and technical training, employment, and education. It also pressed the Ministry of Labor to enact legislation requiring that men and women receive equal pay for equal work. Eventually, this concept was accepted by the government, and legislation was enacted in the Parliament. The club monitored the various steps required in the legislative process.

Process

During the early 1970's, a socialist government assumed the reins of power in the country and set out to correct many of the social ills which plagued society. The role of women in the social and economic life of the country was highlighted, and sex inequality was actively discussed. Women's organizations became very vocal about sex discrimination, and the government listened. The government publicly stated its commitment to the improvement of the status of women. It created a Women's Desk which later became the Bureau of Women's Affairs in the Office of the Prime Minister. This addition to the bureaucracy lent support to the fight for women's rights. The Soroptimist Club translated the growing concerns of many working women into a plan of action and took steps to initiate change. The club collaborated with other women's organizations and the Women's Desk to press for change. The receptiveness of the government to change facilitated the initiation of the strategy.

In addition, the club supported those women's organizations which spearheaded the call for the provision of daycare facilities for the children of working mothers and for the payment of maternity leave benefits to all pregnant working women. A national program of daycare centers has been implemented; also, legislation guaranteeing maternity leave with pay to all working women was enacted in 1979.

Focus

The strategy focused on the enactment of legislation to require equal pay for equal work; the education and technical training of women in all occupations; and public enlightenment.

Although the urgent problem of discrimination needed to be addressed, emphasis had to be placed on education and training. If women are to benefit fully from the legislation, they must be equipped to assume their new responsibilities. Nevertheless, the strategy addressed the issues of both men's and women's attitudes and behavior at the workplace.

The myth that some jobs, positions, and responsibilities are best handled by men had to be dispelled. The club considered other approaches to achieve these objectives, but rejected a more aggressive approach because of the deeply rooted bias that has favored male domination at the workplace. Any measure which seriously challenged that domination would have been viewed suspiciously and would not have been supported by some women workers. In addition, the high level of unemployment in the country, especially among women, made it prudent to adopt a cautious approach.

Legal Issues

The strategy concentrated on one major legal issue, namely, the inequality of remuneration of male and female workers for the same work. By and large, the attitude of the society has been heavily biased towards male dominance. In general, it has accepted the myth that a man is the head of the household and is, therefore, entitled to better pay than a woman. This bias found expression in various facets of social life and was particularly visible at the workplace. The strategy focused on the attitude of all people, but it had to deal expressly with making women aware of this bias and the resulting discrimination.

This aspect of discrimination against women was selected as it affected the economic survival of many working women. In a matrifocal society, such as Jamaica, where many women were, and are today, the sole economic support of themselves and their families, social justice demands that women be given an equal share of the cake.

The Soroptimist Club recognized these injustices, sensed the mood of the society, and felt this was an area of greatest need requiring corrective action at that time. In 1974, the level of unemployment among female workers was more than twice as high as that of men—30% female to 12.5% male. Not only was unemployment greater among female workers, but their participation at the workplace was largely confined to the less prestigious and low-paying jobs. Income distribution statistics in 1974 support the argument that more women were employed in the lowest paid occupations. It was, therefore, necessary for women to obtain employment in the non-traditional fields if they were to participate equally with men at the workplace. However, before this could be achieved, new vocational skills and a change in attitudes were essential.

Organization and Participation

The strategy focused on legislation, training, and public enlightenment. The groups targeted for action included government agencies involved with labor relations and training. Constant contact was maintained with the Ministry of Labor to press for legislation that would eliminate sex pay discrimination and provide equal training opportunities for women and men. To make legislation effective, attitudes had to be changed and training provided. This required the participation of other groups. They included the trade unions, employer organizations, vocational training institutions, educators, guidance counselors, Parent-Teacher Associations, and women workers.

Each group participated at varying levels. The trade unions monitored the workplace to ensure that the principle of equality between the sexes was observed as far as possible.

Some employers and vocational training institutions opened their doors to women and provided employment and training opportunities for them. Educators, guidance counselors, and some parents participated in effecting changes in attitudes towards stereotyped sex roles. Women's organizations educated women workers so that they would be capable of managing non-traditional jobs.

Results

The Employment (Equal Pay for Men and Women) Act was passed by Parliament and came into effect on January 1, 1976. This act provides for the payment of equal remuneration to male and female employees for work performed for the same employer when the duties, responsibilities, or services are similar or substantially similar in kind, quality, and amount.

Training opportunities for women have increased. For example, the official enrollment figures of the University of the West Indies show that the number of women admitted to that institution increased from 38% in 1970 to 47% per cent in 1979. Women have received training in many non-traditional fields; more women are employed in those fields today than when the strategy was first initiated. We find women employed as carpenters, masons, auto-mechanics, drivers of heavy equipment, navigators, engineers, *etc.* Visible benefits have been achieved by women workers in non-traditional occupations.

However, without precise information about the demand for trained manpower, an assessment of the adequacy of integration is difficult. Government employment statistics for 1982 indicate that the level of female participation in the labor force was 45.2% of the female population; an increase of 10.4% over the 1974 figures of 34.8%. Women employed in professional, technical, administrative, executive, managerial, and related occupations composed 59.6% of that occupational sector in 1982, a dramatic increase over the 1974 figures.

A proper evaluation of the impact of the Employment (Equal Pay for Men and Women) Act presents some difficulty as statistics are not readily available. From recent informal discussions with officials of the Ministry of Labor, it appears that some employers have endeavored to perpetuate the notion of unequal pay by such clever devices as manipulating the duties, responsibilities, or services of male and female employees. Vigilance by women workers at the workplace is likely to counteract abuses of the legal process. Possibly this vigilance accounts for the fact that only one complaint under the act has been received from a trade union on behalf of a woman worker; this case was settled. No complaints have been received from non-unionized workers. Not all women benefit from the legislation, but it is a start in the right direction. As more women grasp the opportunities of education and training, the law will serve them better.

In a recent newspaper article "Male Dominance in Jamaica," Professor Carl Stone, a distinguished political scientist and pollster, wrote:

The major factor blocking the progress of women from middle and upper middle occupations, where they outnumber the men, into top positions appears to be male chauvinism and protectionism of their virtual monopoly control over top jobs in the society.

The myth that certain jobs and levels of responsibility are best handled by men has been used in both the public and private sector organizations to prevent women from moving into more positions of power and dominance at the workplace. Women have to be super-qualified or super-efficient to get jobs that would be given to unqualified and mediocre men without a second thought.

Professor Stone's frank and forthright views are commendable. He has pinpointed some of the obstacles to be overcome by women if they are to reach the supreme goal of leadership at the workplace.

Lessons

One important lesson learned is that consciousness-raising is a significant component of the formula for the success of the strategy. Programs designed to create awareness must constantly be pursued. Since the latter part of the 1970's, Jamaica—as other Third World countries—has been deeply affected by world recession. Hence, the resources available for programs aimed at correcting many of the social and economic ills affecting women have been greatly restricted. However, in our view, consciousness-raising must be an ongoing exercise if necessary improvements are to be achieved. The lack of adequate financial resources to facilitate greater training opportunities and public enlightenment has been a weakness of the strategy.

One very significant factor which has emerged from the strategy is the ability of this underdeveloped country to mobilize women's groups of differing social and economic status and of differing political views into a cohesive force to fight for a common cause. However, the struggle for rights and reforms is not attained simply by legislation. Whether it becomes a reality or remains an illusion depends on the attitude of the society in general and of the persons most affected in particular. We believe legislation is a tool for action which can and should be developed in order to serve better those for whom it was created. Therefore, it should constantly be reviewed; disparities must be pointed out; and where necessary, we must press for its just application.

Myrtle Mason is a judge of the Family Court in Jamaica.

Zimbabwe: State, Law, and Women
Joyce Kazembe
Marjon Mol

Overview

The Fundamental Rights and Personal Law Project was initiated in 1981 following a private discussion with the Minister of Justice Simbi Mubako. The minister's primary aim was to remove all forms of discrimination in customary and general law and to create a body of law consonant with the doctrine of human rights as set out in the United Nations' Declaration of Human Rights.

Legal reform is too important to be left in the hands of lawyers only. The proper and effective planning of law reform goes far beyond the drafting of official policy into the form of legislation. Amendments must be consistent with the spirit of the legislation, and sanctions against non-compliance must be provided. Hence, the thrust of legal reform focuses on various factors. Firstly, there is the technical imperative, whereby legislation is formulated or amended to put into effect in a consistent manner a stated policy. Secondly, there is the administrative imperative, whereby the law can be made effective, including the providing of adequate sanctions, the informing of the executive judiciary, and the training of administrative personnel. Consulting with private experts, individuals, and organizations is also very important. Therefore, the draft bill, preferably in the form of a white paper, will be scrutinized by parties outside the government. Implementing effective reform requires the cooperation of various governmental ministries and the education of the public about the intent and content of the legal reform.[1]

The justice minister established an advisory research group composed of experts from different disciplines to determine the weakness of family and personal law under both customary and general law. The preliminary aim of the research was to formulate, analyze, and test alternatives to the present discriminatory system of personal law, especially as that law pertains to black Zimbabwean women. The research group would test public reaction to the reforms by using various methods including surveys. It would also recommend the most efficient method of implementing the reforms. The government and the research group would then discuss the potential social effects of the proposed legal reforms. The whole exercise would enable the minister to decide which options, if any, were legally and politically acceptable to him. This original plan has been somewhat successful but required modifications.

A Women's Advisory Legal Council, consisting of experts from the law department and from the Center for Applied Social Sciences (CASS) at the University of Zimbabwe, was established. Members of the council were to work with various governmental offices, ministries and community organizations. The council met frequently, discussing the numerous considerations of the introduction of the Legal Age of Majority Act (LAMA). Later, the council made recommendations about this bill, which were passed to the cabinet by the Minister of Community Development and Women's Affairs. Indeed, many were consulted before the LAMA became law in December 1982. Since that time, the Women's Advisory Legal Council has fallen into abeyance due to the government's inattentive attitude toward the council. The government chose to ignore the council. Nonetheless, informal consultation continues between the Fundamental Rights and Personal Law (FRPL) project team at the Center for Applied Social Sciences and the Ministry of Justice, Legal, and Parliamentary Affairs, and the Ministry of Community Development and Women's Affairs. Rather than remaining silent, CASS members decided to carry on with the FRPL project.[2]

Focus

Legislation defines the objectives, structures, and functions of an organization. The extent to which the objectives are realized can only be determined by empirical research. For example, the aim of the Customary Law and Primary Courts Act (No. 6, 1981, amended by Act 21/1982) was:

To provide for the application of customary law in the determination of civil cases; to provide for the constitution and jurisdiction of primary courts; to provide for appeals from the decisions of such courts;...to repeal the African Law and Tribal Court Act (Chapter 237, 1969);...and to amend the Maintenance Act (Chapter 35)....

Now, it is up to the sociologists to determine how well the legislation is functioning. The structures of the primary courts have an important impact on the organization of the family because they compose the principal judicial forum (in the adjudicative sense) to resolve family disputes. Therefore, sociologists were enlisted to examine what the courts were doing and how well they were doing. Hence, the rationale behind the project was to understand the actual working of the legislation in order to determine its potential impact.

To conduct this research, we sampled nineteen out of sixty-two community courts, with at least two courts from each of the eight provinces. The sample reflected the different socio-economic conditions of the people in Zimbabwe. We transcribed all the cases that had been tried at the community courts in February, June, and November 1983 with the exception of Harare, where we looked at the cases tried during this period by three out of the eight presiding officers. To ascertain the general attitudes of people who dealt with community courts, we interviewed the concerned presiding officers at the beginning of the project in February and March, 1984 and then in April, 1985. We also conducted an extensive survey of 519 litigants who had used six of the sampled community courts during this period.

We have found that while males involved in court litigation number more than three times the female litigants, women are far more likely to be complainants than respondents. The preponderance of women's complaints related to maintenance claims—financial support of families. Between June, 1981 and February, 1982, maintenance claims accounted for 5.5% of all cases heard at thirty-three community courts around the country. After the amendment to the Customary Law and Primary Court Act in October, 1982, the percentage of claims lodged at nineteen community courts in February, June, and November, 1983, increased. This rise may reflect that, in custody cases, a greater consideration is now given to the interests of the children. Therefore, more women are being awarded the custody of their children and concomitant financial support from the fathers.

301

Women appear to be increasing their contacts with the community courts, which have become refuge centers for divorced and deserted wives and unmarried mothers. Community courts have a growing role in assisting women with family problems and in enforcing women's legal rights. As a matter of fact, 18% of the 206 males interviewed for the survey of six community courts thought they were actually women's courts, as the men perceived that women were favored in the judgements. Where the courts had to enforce their judgements, the enforcement of maintenance claims (14.1%) followed those of debts and contracts (15.9%). Furthermore, women are now faring better in matrimonial property disputes. These findings, which we are still in the process of analyzing, indicate that the legal status of women, at least before the courts if not in society as a whole, is improving. It is hoped that the number of female presiding officers will increase, or at least that those presiding over these courts will become more sympathetic to women. At present, seventeen of the 160 presiding officers are women.

In addition to the sociological research project, we have also embarked on an information campaign, using all available media, including the press, radio, and television. This campaign, which targeted primarily lower and middle class women, aimed to make women aware of their rights (*e.g.*, Legal Age of Majority Act) and the procedures to claim them (*e.g.*, Customary Law and Primary Courts Act). This campaign was essential because the people of Zimbabwe were never consulted about these legal changes.

Professionals who were not lawyers interpreted both laws and produced seven pamphlets in a series called *Paths are Made by Walking,* a phrase coined by the South American revolutionary, Antonio Machado. The booklets were written in simple language, and they were translated into Shona and Ndebele. The information was related through everyday examples and illustrated by cartoons. They focus on the legal age of majority and on marriage, maintenance, and property. Discussion issues were provided to elicit response and a prize was offered for the best group response. The pamphlets were distributed free of charge. Alice Chikodzero, a composite figure representing the Fundamental Rights and Personal Law team, was created by the authors of the phamphlet.

Cooperation from the press and the government was sought to advertise and distribute the pamphlets. The Ministry of Community Development and Women's Affairs distributed over 1500 copies in English, Shona, and Ndebele to their community development workers. It also organized follow-up meetings that publicized the pamphlets. The community courts are also disseminating information on legal changes. In addition, the help of private organizations has been sought and obtained in the distribution of information. They include the Adult Literacy Organization of Zimbabwe, the Citizens' Advice Bureaus, the Centers for Social Services, all national women's organizations and church, health and youth organizations. They began to distribute our publications in September, 1984 and will continue until June 1985. In the period from September, 1984 to May, 1985, we have distributed approximately 75,000 pamphlets (13,570 series).

In one of the publications, our Alice authors a legal advice column based on issues raised by readers. Another Alice project was *Citizens' Law*, a five-minute television program that informed people about the consequences of the Legal Age of Majority Act. At the moment, we are preparing a radio program aimed at high school students to be aired in the last school term of 1985. We are also encouraging drama groups to act out the stories in the pamphlets before adult literacy organizations.

Mixed reactions to the publications have surfaced. Some people, both men and women, are opposed to the whole concept of equality. Others entirely support the new legal reforms. Possibly, the most unreasonable response has come out of the Ministry of Justice, Legal, and Parliamentary Affairs. Some of its officials have accused us of undertaking work for which we were not trained. They have asserted that we sociologists with no legal background should stick to our areas of expertise. On the other hand, many private organizations and even many officials in other ministries have commended our efforts.

We continue to receive written inquiries for information on specific problems. All of these letters are answered individually. We have also received a total of 350 responses to the questions on the back of the pamphlets, and we have just finished selecting the winners. The Adult Literacy Organization of Zimbabwe, ALOZ, has planned a follow-up on the use of the pamphlets in their groups. If sufficient demand exists, they will reprint these publications.

Lessons

We have learned that our methods of dissemination of information were not adequate to explain and to affect issues such as the Legal Age of Majority Act. LAMA, for example, carries major consequences and implications, which deeply affect the lives of ordinary, traditional people. The leaders of women's rural women's groups have asked us to organize workshops and to distribute detailed information about their new rights. They feel that such assistance is necessary before they can begin to explain LAMA (and other issues) to their own constituents. Increased coordination with other organizations is needed to disseminate information on legal issues.

Since legal reform is often a politically hot issue, it is wise not to depend on governmental cooperation only. The role of private organizations cannot be overemphasized. A well organized communication, information, and distribution network located throughout this country is essential. The establishment of a network will require close cooperation among private organizations and between government and other groups. Financial, material, and human resources must be solicited for this undertaking.

Legal aid offices must be established throughout the country with the help of the University of Zimbabwe and the government. New training and educational facilities to help women obtain their legal and economic rights are also greatly needed. In addition, programs that focus on legal and family issues must be directed at high school children. This program, which would prepare students to enter society, should be included in the curriculum.

While women have made some gains in the workplace, they need more and better training facilities to take advantage of employment opportunities. At present, most female workers are unskilled, and they are rarely able to move up the ranks to better jobs. Many women advocate a quota system to correct the sexual imbalance in managerial positions. They also would like the government to establish a review system to deal with cases of job discrimination against women. Furthermore, many women's rights advocates want the government to implement paid maternity leave in the public sector (which already exists in the private sector) and to facilitate a system of child daycare centers.

The powers of the Ministry of Community Development and Women's Affairs, which has no administrative authority, must be strengthened. Even though women commend the government for establishing a ministry of women's affairs, many note that it is somewhat ineffective because it depends on the goodwill of the Ministry of Justice, Legal, and Parliamentary Affairs to introduce or implement legislation.

Other governmental reforms to improve women's status in society include a commendation by the Ministry of Community Development and Women's Affairs; a recommendation to the Tax Commission for separate taxation; a proposal by the Colloquium on Women's Rights in Zimbabwe (held in November, 1984) that the government legislate one marriage act and one succession act which would govern all citizens of Zimbabwe, irrespective of race or sex; and a suggestion that the government extend equal loan and credit facilities, trading and licensing opportunities, and property rights to women, as men have had. These proposals and others are the legal reforms that must be considered in Zimbabwe to further egalitarian ideals and to improve the status of women in society.

Joyce Kazembe is a resident fellow and Marjon Mol a research associate at the Center for Applied Social Sciences at the University of Zimbabwe.

Korea: Customs and Family Law Reform
Tai-Young Lee

Customary Law, Patriarchy,
and the Status of Women

Customary law, which reifies traditional social attitudes, is a formidable force that must be considered in any attempt to improve women's status in society. An acceptance of the inferior nature of women weakens the demand for the restoration of their human rights. Those urging change are considered to be against traditional customs and values which have been accepted as a component of a unique culture. These attitudes are the greatest obstacle to the achievement of the basic rights of women and the expression of the values of human rights for all people.

Patriarchy has long dominated Asian culture. Korean culture is no exception. It boasts of a 5000-year history, the last 550 years of which have been influenced by the foreign Confucian value system. Confucian thought, which has exerted a pervasive influence on Korean society, does not stress the innate rights of individuals. On the contrary, it perceives social relationships in terms of domination and subordination.

These inegalitarian views have had a major impact on the roles of Korean women in the family and society. The relationship between a male and female has always been that of domination and subservience. Throughout her life a woman is an appendage to another person: a father, husband, or son. As a consequence, a daughter is less desirable than a son; a wife is inferior to her husband; and a mother is less important than a father. While a woman has many duties and responsibilities, she possesses few rights.

According to the patrilinealism of our culture, the male blood line determines descent and inheritance. It is perpetuated by the discriminatory family laws, known as the *head of household system*. It emerges from the customary law requiring that a family be headed by the eldest son of an eldest son. This tradition continues to oppress women living in a modern democratic country.

The Development of the Law Reform Movement

After the defeat of Japanese colonial rule and the abolition of the Korean monarchy in 1948, the Republic of Korea was established, and a constitution which proclaimed the principles of human equality was promulgated. Many institutional changes occurred throughout the society, particularly in the educational system. However attitudes, customs, and customary laws essentially remained intact.

No matter how articulate the lawyer or how wise the judge, a woman was a victim of the customary law which governed most areas of human relations at that time. Therefore, in 1953 legislative reform became a priority in my struggle to improve the status of women. The focus of the legislative reform was family law because of its historical legitimization of entrenched discrimination against women.

The Korean Constitution affirms the equality of the sexes. After I submitted a reform bill on family law in 1957 with the help of my legislator husband, the legislature approved it to avoid conflict with constitutional principles. This reform, in effect in 1960, became Korea's first family code.

Thereafter, I began to organize women friends to initiate a new campaign to fight discrimination against women. This campaign would take twenty years to bring about necessary revisions in the family law. In 1973, sixty-three women's organizations formed the Pan Women's Committee for Promoting the Revision of the Family Law. For four years, we used all of our combined imagination and power to design and implement diverse strategies to achieve our goals. We held public lectures to inform and educate. We organized rallies and collected signatures to submit to the National Assembly. We worked with family law scholars to draft our recommendations on specific desired changes of the law. We used posters and brochures to explain and depict the contents of our proposals. The mass media, especially women journalists, helped highlight our demands for law reform. We spoke on the radio and argued on TV panel shows. Furthermore, we lobbied politicians and government officials, as well as participated in committee hearings on this issue. All of these activities were essential to nudge our society to make important changes.

307

Finally, in December, 1977 a number of our ten major proposals were approved and these went into effect on January 1, 1979. So far, we had progressed about two-thirds of the way towards eliminating legal discrimination in the areas that most affect women. Reform had come about primarily because of the support of the women legislators who knew that their situation was comparable to that of Korean women. However, this partial revision had not been accomplished smoothly. Along the way, opposition had formed, indicating the continuation of strong resistance by some traditional and conservative individuals and groups.

Nevertheless, one-third of the law—containing the most difficult but essential provisions to reform—remained unchanged. In July, 1984, a new organization, the Women's Union for Family Law Revision (of which I was elected president) was established. It was initially composed of seventy-five women's organizations; since then, nine men's groups have affiliated with us. We refined and improved our various strategies as we determined to complete our task of family law reform.

The timing of our movement to implement reform was crucial. The elections for a new assembly were not far off, and we urged women to use their voting power to elect legislators who would cooperate in revising the law. Moreover, in preparation for the end of the UN Decade for Women, we strongly urged our legislators to ensure that Korean women would have something to boast about in Nairobi! And finally, the government had recently become a signatory to the UN Convention on the Elimination of All Forms of Discrimination Against Women; we pointed out that it would be a contradiction for the government not to move quickly to abolish the existing discrimination in its own civil code.

Eighty-four organizations and numerous family scholars gave their best efforts to increase awareness about the need for family law reform and to work for its implementation. I am sad to confess we were not successful. The fact is that Koreans are still steeped in the traditional ways of thinking. Although the laws may be unconstitutional, the reverence for old customs and the conflict between unwritten and written regulations causes such confusion and division that we still have not been able to establish equality for women under the family law. As long as legislators and public figures do not have the courage to speak and act for change, thereby disturbing their society, the urgency and justification of change are extinguished. More importantly, the roots of discrimination remain.

Current Situation

The acceptance of male superiority and female inferiority (even in the minds of women themselves) has immobilized our movement. At the same time, Korean women are not the same victims of Confucian values and traditional thought that they were 40 years ago.

We still have a long way to go until working women and housewives claim the due worth of their work. It is still very difficult for a married woman to work outside the home. The entry of women into many realms of society is still barred by custom, if not by law. This lack of acceptance amply demonstrates the strength of the unyielding traditions and customs. We must bring about a revolution in the consciousness of all our people so that they espouse that, in the words of our poster, "All Human Beings are the Same."

Conclusion

Women must raise their voices for change. Women must raise their voices to awaken the other half of humanity and show it how to distinguish between justice and injustice. They must demonstrate that the condition of women is not ordained by nature, but is caused by the perpetuation of custom. People can and must change this situation to develop all spheres of their societies.

Therefore, I challenge all of you to see this meeting as more than a finale of the women's decade. I challenge you to encourage other and exchange information. As for me, I pledge today to dedicate the rest of my life to continue to work for the betterment of women and the human family. Will you join your voices with mine in this pledge so that the echoes from Nairobi will be heard around the world, and so that men will join us in this movement for peace?

Tai-Young Lee is Director of the Korea Legal Aid Center for Family Relations.

Vanuatu:
Development of a New Family Law
Mere Pulea

Introduction to the Legal System of Vanuatu

Vanuatu, formerly known as New Hebrides, was governed under an Anglo-French condominium status until its independence on July 30, 1980. Prior to independence, Vanuatu had three separate legal systems: British subjects were governed under British law; French nationals under French law; and the indigenous New Hebrideans (who by virtue of the 1914 Protocol were stateless persons) were governed under joint condominium laws.

The Constitution of the Republic of Vanuatu provides for the continued enforcement of the Joint Regulations and subsidiary legislation made before independence. The British and French laws are applied to the extent that they respect the independent status of New Hebrides, wherever possible taking account of custom. Customary law continues in effect as part of the law of the republic.

Vanuatu as yet has no national divorce laws. While the indigenous Ni-Vanuatu follow customary law for divorce, provided they are married under customary law, there are no legal provisions for dissolving a Ni-Vanuatu civil marriage.

Overview

A number of new national laws have been promulgated since independence. A new family law is envisaged to come before Parliament in 1985. Although there is no shortage of models for family law in the Pacific, a small group of concerned Ni-Vanuatu women feel that there are philosophies, ideals, and traditions of Vanuatu society that need to be fully addressed before any family law is promoted and developed.

The Vanuatu National Council of Women has decided that any issue affecting family life, and in particular, the proposed family law should be thoroughly discussed at all levels of society so that informed submissions can be made to the government. This is buttressed by the council's resolution that women must be involved in political decision-making and the development process; the government has also recognized the value of women's participation in national development.

Funds were sought from the Commonwealth Secretariat to enable the National Council of Women to obtain legal assistance from outside the country. In November, 1984, a three-day forum was held in the capital, Port Vila, which brought together a small group of women to serve as a women's task force. Exploratory discussions at the forum focused on four issues: the inter-relationship between law and society; the law-making process; the basic legal principles on equality, rights, and status of women, children and parents; and the meaning of legal terminology.

The women then agreed that one priority was to develop the group's knowledge and understanding of the existing legal system. It argued that without a basic understanding of the legal system, it would be difficult to develop a systematic plan, timeframe, and strategies to achieve their objectives. To implement this priority, the group reviewed existing legal provisions relating to women. It also compared Vanuatu social law with that of other Pacific countries. A written review of eight Pacific countries' legislation *Aspects of the Legal Status of Women* served as background information.

The design and thrust of the strategies developed by the National Council of Women were dependent first on the availability and ability of women to be involved in facilitating small-scale research, surveys, and discussions. The ability to create awareness in, communicate with, and educate as wide a group as possible was a second crucial factor. Finally, our strategy depended on the ability to collect, collate, and evaluate information on matters relevant to the proposed family law to facilitate the drafting of the submissions.

The agreed-upon methodology was a combination of informal interviews and discussions with women's groups. Also, written questionnaires were submitted to police, court officers, and other officials, and two national workshops were held for women's representatives. The first workshop was designed to involve women representatives from all over Vanuatu to discuss the proposed program and elicit their views. The second two-day workshop, conducted a few weeks later was designed to evaluate the collected information and draft submissions to be presented to the government.

311

Goals

The process of formulating the project goals was influenced by many factors. These include the consideration of development of policies that affect both men and women; policies to make benefits, rights, and the legal system more accessible; policies towards the multi-legal systems alternatives available in both the law and society; and policies aiming to develop an indigenous body of law to incorporate into the legal system, thereby reflecting the spirit of the constitution.

The overall project goal—women's participation in the development of the proposed family law—was broken down into three categories. The development of women's awareness and knowledge of their legal rights was the first sub-goal. The second was effective participation by women at all levels in the development of a legal culture and a more accessible legal system. A third sub-goal was addressing the concerns of women within the proposed family law.

The first sub-goal is designed to empower women through an increased general knowledge and awareness of the legal system in order to develop an understanding of their legal rights.

The second sub-goal follows from the first. It involves educating women to develop their options to improve their status and welfare; they also must be encouraged to participate in the establishment of a legal culture which will favor their interests. The third sub-goal is the desired result from the first two in order that informed submissions could be made to the government on legal issues affecting women, children, and the family.

Major Activities

Because of the need to be informed of the range of laws and legal provisions that affect women, a system of survey and research was designed to collect and collate such information. In November, 1984, a three-day forum was held in which a small number of women discussed the process of lawmaking. It demonstrated how law is the end result of a series of steps taken to define the problems, evaluate the information, and identify the issues that need to be addressed through legislation. In addition, a series of meetings were held with legal officials and administrators to elicit their cooperation, to clarify the role of the National Council of Women, and to express its hope to contribute to the development of the proposed family law.

With the assistance of court officials, the council developed a questionnaire that was later used to gather statistical information to evaluate women's problems. A survey of police statistics was also conducted to see if women were seeking police assistance in family crises, and whether there was a large disparity between court and police statistics.

Two country workshops were planned for April and May, 1985. The first aimed to elicit the views of women on the design of the survey and then to equip them for the task of presenting the survey to their communities. The second workshop was designed as a feedback process and an evaluation of the information gathered: it would help determine the strategy to be used for drafting submissions for governmental consideration.

In an attempt to attain a realistic profile of existing laws, a legislative inventory was prepared to inform women of the laws affecting family life. Women were also asked about their experiences regarding family problems.

This method answered as well as raised questions. A number of issues came to light: the appropriateness and adequacy of existing legal provisions to protect the rights of women and children; conflicting or overlapping legal jurisdictions; the actual implementation of the laws; and the weakness and deficiencies in the law. In light of identified deficiencies, what kinds of strategies should be developed to initiate new laws? Which sectors need a new or revised legal base? Should legislative provisions have a particular focus?

These issues require further consideration. It is envisaged that both the strategies and the working principles will be constantly assessed in the light of changing circumstances throughout the period of the project.

Process

The initiative to participate in the development of a new family law came from the Ni-Vanuatu Council of Women. It reflects the growing awareness of women of their vital role in the process of constitutional development. Political awareness combined with a cadre of professional women will catalyze the changes needed to improve the legal status of women. This plan to develop national policies and laws will involve both urban and rural women.

There is an ongoing search for a new and more meaningful family legal code; it will recognize the role of customary law laid down by the constitution. In order to decide whether precolonial concepts are culturally acceptable or inappropriate in Ni-Vanuatu society, a period of revision is now taking place. The object of this revision is to prevent the unnecessary criminalization of people due to the adoption of western legal and/or moral norms. After a period of discussion and research, informed decisions can then be made about which aspects of traditional culture need to be incorporated within the proposed family law and legal culture.

Focus

Because lawmaking in the Pacific has become the exclusive preserve of political leaders, lawyers, and other legal experts, it is rare that women's and citizen's groups are asked to participate in the legislative process. State power has placed the development of the law in the hands of the few.

Given this situation, the strategies of the National Council of Women are focused upon three major considerations. Firstly, the council is attempting to develop a dialogue with the state authorities so that in the long term they will seek women's opinions on pertinent matters.

Secondly, because women have limited knowledge and access to the legal system, the previously mentioned workshops and social surveys have been designed to educate women about their rights and the ways to achieve them. They also identified legal and administrative provisions that discriminate against women and recommended improvements in policies, laws, and the delivery of legal and social services.

Thirdly, the National Council of Women is exploring various alternatives to legal remedies by using informal mechanisms that already exist in the community. For example, it is looking at the customary forms of dispute settlement to provide additional choices for the resolution of problems.

Legal Issues

Although the law alone cannot save the family as an institution, many women feel that certain measures can contribute to the stability of the family. Several areas involving family issues have been identified and are discussed below.

Social resources available for family conciliation such as churches, courts, and other groups must be evaluated. Specifically, some legal machinery may be necessary to provide remedial action at an early stage for issues regarding marriage, separation, or divorce. However, the boundaries between customary and civil marriages need to be distinguished as they directly affect the status of women and their children. Not enough is known in the Pacific of the difficulties which women and children suffer from the application of the dual systems. The issues of parental misconduct and/or abuse of children and of child custody claims in a polygamous marriage are greatly affected by the dual system of customary and civil marriages. It is an extremely complex area, particularly where both systems of polygamy and monogamy interact. Furthermore, the question of customary law rights and the status of an unmarried mother and the father of the children requires investigation and clarification. Presently, the law permits a range of conditions by which a putative father could abandon his responsibilities towards his children. The formulation of measures to strengthen the rights and status of women so that they are not penalized in either system requires detailed research, analysis, and collaboration.

Although there is a trend in some countries to adopt the no-fault ground for divorce, it has far-reaching implications in Pacific communities and may be culturally inappropriate. Surveying individuals (who are guaranteed anonymity) through church, women's, and youth groups could provide useful information.

Financial assistance for abandoned wives and children is another serious problem. In general, women are not aware of their rights to seek legal action, and enforcement procedures are cumbersome. Moreover, where a spouse is poor, unemployed, or dependent on meager wages or on an extended family system, a financial package is needed to provide adequate welfare and assistance to the entire family.

Participation

The organization and participation in these strategies will be a collective decision made by the National Council. Research techniques, methodologies, surveys, and informational programs will be defined at the first workshop, scheduled for April, 1985.

The methodology will differ from area to area, according to the various levels of education and culture. Whether the information is obtained by individuals or in teams will be dependent on the availability of personnel and the nature of the task.

In January, 1985, a small group of women who hold senior national positions surveyed government officials in Port Vila about important women's issues. At the same time, leaders of women's groups used informal methods of discussion to help women articulate their concerns and desires about the family. Information gathered from the survey and fora will be added to the general body of information for evaluation at the workshops.

Results

Since the inception of the project, there have been a number of achievements. The National Council of Women has taken numerous steps to assure that women's concerns are addressed in the proposed family law, and it has arranged for an outside legal consultant to assist them. It organized a three-day discussion in November, 1984, bringing together a small task force of women to facilitate the various requirements of the project. The council also organized and secured funds for two country workshops of women's representatives in April and May, 1985. Through discussions and surveys to obtain statistical data, the council has encouraged smaller local groups to discuss and inform themselves about the proposed family law.

The National Council of Women has also encouraged direct contact between a small group of educated women with officials in Port Vila. These contacts have opened the way for collaboration (*e.g.*, the assistance by a senior court official in the design of a survey to gain legal statistical information).

The conduct of research and survey by the women themselves is an achievement in itself. Generally, in Pacific societies, men are the main sources of information. Hence, those who are directly involved with designing questionnaires, research methodologies, data collection, evaluation, and work-shop organization are benefiting from these opportunities and training. The council plans to expand the research and education programs to the rural and outlying island areas in order to provide their women with these powerful tools and to build up a wide body of comparative data.

These efforts are only the beginning. Indications suggest that the Vanuatu Council of Women can provide a unique forum for collaboration on myriad women's issues. It can make an important contribution to Vanuatu social development by educating and training women, by collecting information and data, and by sponsoring strategies to bring about changes in legislation, policies, and attitudes that discriminate against women.

Mere Pulea works as a legal consultant for various organizations and governments in the Pacific region.

Advocating
for
Justice

Most of the papers in this section describe advocacy strategies directed toward specific problem areas. They all include some form of legal literacy or training, but their primary focus is on providing access to the system through legal advocacy. Five of the papers focus on assisting and organizing women workers in the informal or formal sectors; two focus on women as victims of violence; and one describes an advocacy strategy in an urban land dispute. The other five papers describe legal assistance centers providing a variety of services on a range of issues.

Many of the programs described in this chapter, as well as those in previous chapters, are only beginning or had very little experience at the time their case studies were prepared. Because they initially lacked the necessary resources, some of the program organizers began slowly—albeit with determination. Since that time, many have gained considerable skill and insight and would be in a better position today to describe their learnings.

The setting for advocacy in most, but not all, cases is the *legal services center*. In this context, some of the papers assert the superiority of the collective over the individual approach to advocacy and legal services. Most of the authors discuss the notion of *structural legal assistance* (in those or other words) and understand that advocacy, if it is to be effective, entails more than *acting on another's behalf*. Rather it must integrate the participants into problem-solving processes traditionally left to the lawyer and into the struggles to secure their own rights. This approach will ultimately lead to the development of greater self-advocacy skills. Because of women's limited awareness and traditionally passive attitudes, however, the required methodology is neither simple nor automatic and emphasizes the consciousness-raising, organizing, and mobilizing activities that lead to empowerment.

❧❧❧❧

Family-Oriented Centers

In almost all cases of strategies rooted in service centers, the primary legal area of concern is that pertaining to family matters, such as inheritance, maintenance, child support, and domestic violence.

Rodríguez discusses the role of the legal services center in strengthening women's organizations in Ecuador to influence political decision-making. Similar to other programs mentioned under the section on legal education, the center, located in Quito, works to enhance women's understanding of their situation and to promote initiatives to change legislation detrimental to women. In addition, the center offers legal assistance in specific cases. *Montaño* from Bolivia articulates a similar goal of strengthening women's organizations by providing them with legal assistance, encouragement and information. Hence, these two programs are alike in that they include both an education component (consciousness-raising and organizing) and a services component (pro bono legal assistance) in their strategies. *Salih* describes a Sudanese program working on both public education and the provision of free legal services to low-income women. Similarly, the goal is to increase the awareness of women about their rights and to assure their participation in developing the means to defend those rights. The major legal concerns that surfaced relate to family, labor relations, and personal and societal violence against women—not unlike the problems facing women in Ecuador and Bolivia.

Akande from Nigeria describes a family law center which gives *pro bono* assistance (on family problems) to low-income women exclusively. The focus on family is highly relevant in the Nigerian context, given the strong cultural and religious influence in family matters. The center also serves as a training ground for young lawyers and encourages them to practice family law as a specialty. In addition, the center designs and implements public education programs, including a weekly television program and various publi-cations. *Zurutuza* describes a program in Argentina which also aims to sensitize legal professionals to the plight of women. Like the other multi-faceted legal services centers, it offers free legal assistance and an educational program to train group leaders and paralegals as well as the general public.

❦❦❦❦

Ecuador: Women and Legal Services
Lilia Rodríguez

Introduction

While Ecuadorian legislation is viewed as relatively advanced, the social reality is quite a different matter. Even though male marital authority has been legally abolished the law continues to reinforce male authority in the marital relationship. Ecuadorian law provides that the husband has the right to decide where he and his wife will reside and that the husband is the head of the household. Furthermore, the wife must obey her husband.

Crimes of honor are excused by the law. Thus, the penal code allows a man to attack or kill his daughter, niece, or sister if he discovers her in premarital or extramarital relations.

Property and financial issues are also structured in ways that are disadvantageous to women. Single women on their own are not entitled to social benefits. A wife is obligated to use her own resources to pay her husband's debts. While a married woman can administer her own property, she is not permitted to make decisions about communal household property.

Even though these laws and regulations are in effect, they are unconstitutional because they violate the principle of equality, which the constitution provides to all individuals. Ecuadorian law reflects the patriarchal concept incorporated in the French Napoleonic Code, which states, "Nature has made our women slaves. The husband has the right to forbid his wife not to leave...she belongs to him, body and soul."

In this context, the U.N. Convention on the Elimination of All Forms of Discrimination Against Women is an important mechanism to pressure the government to repeal anachronistic and discriminatory laws. Ecuador signed this agreement on July 17, 1980, in Copenhagen at the Decennial World Conference. It was ratified unanimously by the National House of Representatives on October 7, 1981. However, despite the existence of this agreement and the efforts of women's organizations, the congress has not yet approved any legal reforms concerning women's rights.

The reality of the law continues to reflect the *machismo* of the culture and social prejudice against women. Therefore, we believe that the legal structure alone cannot change the situation of women. It is little more than a standard by which to measure political and socioeconomic conditions (which, in the last analysis, will ensure change). Moreover, in many cases, legislation has been influenced and manipulated by interest groups. Legal change on women's issues has been the result of organized actions of Ecuadorian women.

Focus

Our organization, the Center for the Promotion and Action of Women (CEPAM), began by recognizing that the law reflects the organization of society and the interests of the dominant classes, strata, and groups. We also considered the influence of patriarchy on legislation which discriminates against women and legitimizes the oppression and subordination of women. While the law discriminates against all women, ordinary Latin American women suffer more because of their limited access to political and economic resources.

Our strategy has been influenced by an awareness that the law benefits the powerful and oppresses the masses. But the masses, particularly women, are not organized to pressure the power structure. We also recognize that customs, culture, and tradition have a stronger impact on society than the law. Furthermore, we believe the people as a whole do not understand their rights.

Given the reality of our situation, we have formulated three major goals. Firstly, we are striving to strengthen the participation of women and their organizations in developing and reforming laws on women's rights and status. Secondly, we are promoting education, information, and the development of awareness about the law. Thirdly, we offer legal assistance on specific cases.

Participation

CEPAM has established a primary project, Women and the Household, in which various programs—including training, information, and services—are brought together. It initiated the project in response to the needs of the women's, labor, and peasant organizations with which we work. This project emphasizes the development of women's awareness about their rights, thereby changing women's outlook on life in general. Thus, legal education not only provides information on the law, but also promotes a critical attitude about the social and legal systems. It also encourages the organization of women to work for the implementation of progressive legislation.

The field of training is organized around the substantive areas of health, nutrition, law, child care, and organizational assessment. The project examines the training of paralegals, who are selected by local organizations. It is also trying to develop a pilot program to train paralegals. In addition, the project provides legal advisory services for poor women. In addition to these legal services, the project offers courses, seminars, and workshops, and it disseminates legal pamphlets and publications.

The participants in the programs represent various classes, strata, and groups: workers, peasants, professionals, and marginal urban dwellers. They participate in the whole educational process, including the design of courses and evaluation of programs in consultation with CEPAM and women's organizations. The process of legal training generates an important dynamic in the organization that broadens its circle of interests.

Lessons

Women's legal education programs are important for the achievement of the goals of the women's decade: equality, development and peace. However, they constitute only a part of our overall strategy to improve education, health, employment and the standard of living of women in Ecuador. These objectives, which will bring about a more just and humane world, can be ensured only by profound changes in today's social system.

We have also learned that it is important at this time to strengthen women's organizations to influence political decision-making. These organizations must develop political and legal initiatives to benefit the interests of women. In this context, legal aid centers can play an important role in educating women about political participation.

We must encourage local groups to undertake research, analysis, and surveys about the legal situation of women. Such an exercise is needed to evaluate women's legal status and rights. In addition, we must develop or integrate mechanisms to compare and coordinate local and regional requirements, programs and experiences. Finally, we must strengthen our resolve and determination to establish an overall alternative—beyond mere legalism—that will ensure the establishment and fulfillment of women's rights.

Lilia Rodríguez is Executive Director of the Ecuadorian Center for the Promotion and Action of Women (CEPAM) in Quito, Ecuador.

Bolivia: Legal Assistance to Poor Women
Julieta Montaño

Overview

The program consists of establishing the Women's Legal Office to provide legal advice on social, domestic, political, civil, penal, and human rights issues to organized women through unions, cooperatives, mother's groups, and other organizations.[1] The project also trains organizational leaders in the legal system and other social issues that affect women. The strategy focuses on providing legal and social education and other services to poor women in rural, urban, and suburban areas of Bolivia.

As the legal office becomes better known, it is increasing its legal and social services for women. The staff is particularly interested in the psychological states of the clients because they reveal underlying family problems. These problems often create emotional instability in the women and their entire families. In these situations, the program provides psychological counseling for the client.

To introduce the program to women, legal workers visit various associations, women's centers, and women's cooperatives. They meet with the leaders and ask for suggestions about how to improve the project's services. They also explain any aspects of the program or the legal system which the women do not understand. Moreover, they emphasize that the law can benefit ordinary people and not only the elite. Finally, the women consult with and question the professional staff about their personal problems.

Focus

The Women's Legal Office organizes short courses that introduce women to the law. They stress the nature of injustice—particularly towards women—that pervades this country. The group leaders examine existing laws which do not serve women's interests even though they are supposed to protect them. Through these brief and elementary courses, our office is striving to educate leaders to help resolve the legal problems of their groups.

The Women's Legal Office encourages women to organize themselves and to remain united. Our purpose is to strengthen their organizations by providing them legal assistance, encouragement, and information about their rights. The legal office fills a void in urban and rural Cochabamba for women and their organizations. These women can turn to our office where they are able to discuss their problems in complete confidence and obtain reliable assistance.

The basic goals of the Women's Legal Office are making women aware of their role in social change; educating poor women about the law and providing them legal assistance; and strengthening various women's organizations.

Legal Issues

The office provides legal assistance and services to women with social, family, police, civil, criminal, and human rights problems. The majority of the cases have centered around domestic issues. The five most important legal issues faced by our clients are requests for alimony or maintenance because of abandonment; separation and divorce (often as a result of abuse); recognition of illegitimate children; legal assistance for organizations and criminal cases. To date, the office has worked on 391 legal cases, 256 of which were brought by organized groups. The remaining 135 cases involved individual women. These cases concerned women between the ages of 20 and 40 years old. The center also trains organizational leaders to deal with the legal and social problems facing their members. It presses for favorable legislation and social change that affects women. Moreover, it develops legal and educational materials to benefit women specifically.

Participation

Legal aid services of the office were initiated on January 2, 1984. Legal assistance is organized by individual visits and dialogues with women's groups which request our assistance. Our staff is prepared to communicate in Spanish as well as in Quechua, whose speakers have been systematically isolated from Bolivian law. (While the official language is Spanish, a significant proportion of the population—especially rural women—speak the Andean languages Quechua and Aymara.) In the course of six months, we have filed 164 cases in a jurisdiction of approximately 200,000 people.

To help women better understand the legal problems facing them, we organized a short course for leaders of mothers' associations. The theme of Rights and Constitutional Guarantees was chosen. We published pamphlets, explaining the basic norms of the constitution; we also translated this information into language that was easily understandable by ordinary people. The theory of the law was examined and compared with its daily practice. Many of the women were aware of the fact that the majority of legal abuses and weaknesses are due to their lack of knowledge about their legal rights, and hence, their inability to defend these rights.

As part of the course, the Women's Union of Bolivia (UMBO) also discussed Bolivian history. For the first time, many peasant women were presented a critical interpretation of the history of the formation of the country. The methodology used in the course consisted of the use of participatory discussion, workbooks, and slide shows. At the end of the course, the participants asked that we organize another forum to explain the norms of the family code.

Results

While visiting women's organizations in urban, suburban, and rural areas, we saw that they wanted to learn about their fundamental legal rights and ways to claim and defend them. For many rural women, the concepts discussed in legal education programs were totally new. Furthermore, the participation of poor rural women has increased. At the end of the workshops, the participants displayed an understanding of what had been explained. With the help of visual and curricular aids, they returned to their districts, organizations, or communities and informed the members about their legal rights.

Lessons

We learned that the team's experience was not adequate for the tasks of teaching and evaluating. We also discovered that participants in the workshops found it difficult to disseminate information to their peers because of their lack of experience. Some of the women were not confident enough to convey information learned in the workshops. Moreover, some of the delegates were not committed enough to share their educational experiences.

Two unanticipated issues taught us other lessons. The lack of good transportation highlighted the need to improve logistics. (During the course, the transport workers had struck; therefore, we had to depend on various organizations to take the women to the workshops.) The second is more complicated. We learned that some religious conservatives are wary about examining family legislation because it discusses subjects such as divorce, concubinage, and sexual relations. One segment of the Catholic Church does not want to discuss these subjects at all.

Ultimately, we learned that a measure of efficiency and success can be achieved in qualitative terms, even if team members are challenged by quantitative limitations.

Julieta Montaño, a lawyer, is Director of the Women's Legal Office in Cochabamba, Bolivia.

Sudan: Legal Aid
Mahjouba Salih

Overview

Sudan is a predominantly rural country with a majority of farmers and nomads. It is among the twenty-five least developed countries, having an estimated per capita GNP of US $320. Over 98% of Sudanese women are illiterate. Legal illiteracy is even higher. Most of the people, whether rural or urban, rich or poor, male or female, are almost totally ignorant of their legal rights. As written, the laws and policies of Sudan are not discriminatory towards women. Article 38 of the Permanent Constitution of Sudan provides that "All persons in the Democratic Republic of the Sudan are equal before courts of law. The Sudanese have equal rights and duties, irrespective of origin, race, locality, sex, language, or religion."

It becomes clear, therefore, that the legal problems that women face do not lie with the actual laws or legal structure, but with the application of those laws and the discriminatory attitudes and actions towards women. Women's ignorance of their legal rights increases the scope of the problem. Furthermore, practices and attitudes affect the legal status of Sudanese women, either because they promote or condone discrimination against women, or because they demonstrate a lack of understanding and awareness of the intent and procedures of the law. Whatever the impulse, the result is that women are excluded from full participation in production and benefits of development.

Therefore, the problem really lies with those who administer the law and with the ignorance of the populace. The strategy we are proposing deals not with the actual letter of the law, but rather with its implementation and with the general consciousness of the people. We emphasize the necessity to increase the awareness of women about their legal rights and their involvement in the development of the means to defend those rights.

Objectives

The major objective of the Sudan Legal Aid Association is to conduct a legal education campaign to change people's attitudes towards women. To implement this campaign, individuals will have to be convinced that legal education will contribute to the overall well-being, productivity, and prosperity of the nation.

The association also aims to provide free legal aid and representation of and for women on specific cases. It hopes to increase women's access to the legal system in order to secure their basic legal rights and to redress injustices. Finally, the association aims to increase women's awareness of the constitutional, legal, and Sha'ria rights (especially in relation to the family and labor law) through the mass media.

During the last decade, various attempts have been made to use the mass media to introduce legal education and increase the awareness of women about their legal rights. The association has effectively participated in these attempts. We believe other activities could be effective. By using volunteers and law students to provide basic legal services, we could increase the access of the poor and women to the legal system and thereby bring about social justice and progress.

The association has organized many activities designed to confront the legal constraints placed on women. An advisory committee composed of volunteer members of the association has been established. The mandate of this committee is to reform family law and submit comments and recommendations to improve legislation.

The association has organized seminars and workshops. In addition, the association has published and distributed pamphlets and conducted informal classes, both of which educate women about wages, working conditions, maternity benefits, legal rights, and other relevant issues. As the association emphasizes education, it has helped establish informal discussion groups at the workplace of women to promote an awareness of the legal system. It has also established mobile legal aid centers to travel to rural areas to provide women with legal counseling, advice and other services. Finally, the association has provided legal representation for women in cases of marriage, divorce, child-custody, financial support, and related topics.

331

Process

The idea of the association was initially conceived after I graduated from the Faculty of Law at Khartoum University and joined the attorney general's office in 1976 as a legal assistant. Recognizing that women who are the victims in legal disputes are usually ignorant of their basic rights, I decided to offer legal advice to women who needed it. I began informally providing this service to any woman who came to my office or home to discuss her legal problems. I also tried to follow the progress of cases which women had already initiated.

In 1979, I was appointed by a presidential decree as a member of the Executive Committee of the Sudan Women's Union, affiliated to the sole political organization in the Sudan, the Sudan Socialist Union. I was responsible for the Office of Women's Legal Affairs for five years. During this time I provided free legal aid and advice to women with legal problems.

In 1982, the Ford Foundation awarded me a grant to study legal aid institutions in India and Indonesia, followed by a grant to undertake similar research in the United States. As I was very impressed by the activities and functions of the centers in these countries, I decided that an independent legal aid center offering services for women and the poor could benefit Sudan.

At that time, the Sudan Legal Aid Association came into being. The association has been established as an independent, non-profit, non-governmental organization, which is open to all those from the legal profession who support its aims and ideals and to anyone who wishes to offer financial help. A twenty-member advisory committee was established. It consists of the attorney general, chief justice, chairman of the bar association, the dean of the Faculty of Law at Khartoum University, and various other members of the legal profession. Its constitution was promulgated, and the association was officially registered in April, 1984. Since then, it has provided legal assistance; however, the lack of financial resources has restricted the services that the non-profit association can offer.

Focus

The main focus of the association is in the area of law and behavior which oppresses women. Women in Sudan are particularly disadvantaged in the areas of law that deal with family, labor relations, and personal, and social violence.

Family law in Sudan, based on Islamic law, is complex. Given the high rate of illiteracy, women are rarely able to obtain information about their rights. There is, therefore, a considerable need to provide simple and easily accessible information about family law. There is also a pressing need to develop the commitment of present and future Sudanese lawyers towards providing family law services to women and the poor.

Although the intent of labor relations law does not discriminate against women, in practice it tends to have an adverse effect on women, their employment, and development. Because working women face many legal problems, the association aims to provide a service to help them in this area. At present, the only legal aid service available to disadvantaged and low-income groups in Sudan is restricted to criminal cases. Even here, the service is limited to the appointment of defense attorneys by the court. Civil cases which involve women or the poor rarely reach the courts since no low-cost or free advice and counsel is available to plaintiffs. The association, therefore, seeks to rectify this situation. Apart from providing free legal advice, the association wants to organize a widespread campaign to raise the awareness of people about the discrimination against women.

Legal Areas

An educational campaign to inform women of their economic and legal rights is vital. The primary aim of such a program is to provide information about such topics as economic autonomy, inheritance laws, child-custody, financial support, and domestic violence. Seminars, conferences, workshops, the mass media, and community education projects are all useful. Furthermore, the association wishes to provide a free and readily available legal aid advice and counseling service addressing the concerns of women and low-income people.

Participation

It is envisaged that all members of the association will participate in providing legal and educational services. It is organized so that all interested persons are able to participate, whether in a legal or support capacity. Those involved in the legal profession will be responsible for the planning and execution of the association's programs, while others will provide economic and public support and essential back-up facilities.

Results and Lessons

Because the association is so new, there are few results to report. In light of the personal experiences of those working with the association and the work that the association has undertaken in its brief existence, we know there is a grave need for this service. Free legal aid coupled with an informational campaign will substantially benefit women. Not only will it increase awareness of their basic economic and legal rights, it will also allow women access to services that will reduce the magnitude of their abuse. It will also permit women the right to redress various discriminatory practices and legal offenses.

We are committed to continuing to provide legal and support services to the disadvantaged. We aim to create social awareness of these needs and to gain support of influential persons to pressure the power structure. To further these objectives, we have elected prominent persons to the association committee. Finally, we have been made aware of the critical need for secure funding to implement the goals of the association, namely, legal assistance and social services that will facilitate the full and equal participation of women in the development process.

Mahjouba Salih, a lawyer, is Director of the Sudan Legal Aid Association in Khartoum.

Nigeria: Family Law Project

Jade O. Akande
Priscilla O. Kuye

Overview

Nigeria is a patriarchal society, perhaps more male-oriented than is normally appreciated by Western observers. This is evident in many ways, but a few examples will suffice. Firstly, a large section of women in the vast northern region of the country were denied political rights—including the right to vote—until the new constitution (now suspended by the military regime) was enacted in 1979. Secondly, education was denied to a large portion of females, not because it was the policy of the government, but because of ignorance. As parents could not afford to educate all their children, the boys were given preference for very valid reasons (e.g., the boy will eventually be the bread-winner of a family, the girl will marry into another family). Also, girls are better hawkers and are of immediate help to their petty-trading mothers. This led society to believe that most women were less intelligent than men and, therefore, should be under the guidance and protection of men. The extensive patronage of women has resulted in the denial of their right of access to the courts for resolution of family problems.

As a corollary, education can also lead to removing the fear of the courts and litigation which has been ingrained in many women. The general attitude is that the litigation of a family problem will break up the family. Women have been conditioned to believe that it is their duty to preserve the family at all costs. No amount of suffering should warrant the need for court intervention. The law to some extent may have encouraged this feeling and attitude, particularly by provisions such as those that make a woman's adultery, but not a man's, grounds for divorce.

It is precisely because the primary institution of socialization is the family that any assault on discrimination against women must attack all inhibitive factors of both the culture and structure inherent in the family.

The objectives of this project are two-pronged. It is believed that many injustices are perpetrated because the majority of women are unaware of their rights; and the few who are aware, do not know how to protect such rights. Therefore, one objective is to make women aware of the existence of their rights, and through this, to understand their legal and social status. In Nigeria, many legal rights are not enforced due to customary and traditional practices. Hence in this regard it is necessary to make women appreciate the structural sources of their powerlessness.

The second objective, following from the first one, is to open up avenues to secure the enjoyment of these rights and to redress injustices. Where there are limitations in the law, demands will be made to correct such limitations. Where there are practices inhibiting the implementation of the law, conscious efforts will be made to initiate changes in traditional patterns that should have become obsolete. The thrust, then, is to make the women themselves feel the need for change so they will want to be active participants, both individually and collectively, in bringing about these changes.

The goals of this strategy are to make women aware of their rights so they can use their capabilities to enhance their own status. We want to break down barriers that inhibit their own development and that hinder their effective participation in the developmental process of the nation. Equally, it will be important to break down both legal and practical constraints by eliminating discriminatory practices embedded in certain institutions such as marriage, which are of no visible benefit either to the institution itself or to the contributions of women to the society.

Specific activities organized to implement these goals are two-fold. The first one was the establishment of a family law center—a legal services advisory center which gives free legal advice on all family legal problems to low-income people. Initially, the service was not restricted to women because of the fear that it would have been regarded as another women's liberation project. This label might have jeopardized its existence because the government might have been reluctant to commit itself to a project which seemingly encourages women to attack established practices. In addition, the class of women to which it is directed might be frightened away if it were seen as an exclusively female preserve. Hence, an appearance of secrecy could result in the attempt by some men to prevent women from using the service.

This center, which is staffed by a committee of four legal experts (two women and two men), publishes booklets on legal rights in the four main languages of Nigeria. The publications are given free of charge to all clients of the center and also circulated to women's voluntary organizations in all the states of the federation. Although many low-income women are unable to read, their school-age children can be persuaded to read and explain the contents to them. This situation has another advantage: children will begin to learn about their rights at an early age.

The center also serves as a training ground for lawyers interested in family law practice. At the beginning of the academic year at the law school (all graduates of law spend a year in professional training), the center calls for volunteers. Volunteers are given an orientation course on how the center operates and what is expected of them. They are given the necessary and relevant materials on family law; next they are divided up into two groups. Each group has a day of meeting clients and working with them under the guidance and supervision of the legal experts. By the end of their law school course, the center would have trained a group of young lawyers actively interested in the practice of family law.

The second part of the action program is public education. A steering committee composed of lawyers and journalists is responsible for projecting the work of the center to the mass media. Family law experts are invited to appear on radio and television to answer legal questions and to emphasize particular issues. Each of the audio-visual media is committed to at least fifteen minutes of air-time twice a month. The press publishes articles on the center's work as often as possible. Emphasis is placed on radio broadcasting because of the audience it reaches.

Process

The initiative for the program came primarily from one individual, Professor Jade Akande. Various groups of women (and sometimes men) over the years have discussed the need to enhance the status of women in Nigeria. Among them are the International Federation of Women Lawyers (Nigeria), the Nigerian Association of University Women, and the National Council of Women's Societies (particularly, the Status of Women Committee).

Professor Akande was commissioned by the federal ministry to undertake a tour of the whole country to assess and identify the various practices and customs inhibiting the enhancement of the status of women. She undertook the study tour in 1979–1980 and submitted her report in late 1980. By this time, the Constitution of the Federal Republic of Nigeria of 1979 had been enacted, and the country had returned to a civilian regime. That constitution legislated against discrimination on the grounds of sex. It was, therefore, felt that the circumstances were auspicious for a campaign to improve the conditions of women.

It was discovered during the study tour that perhaps the greatest obstacle to women's progress was the lack of knowledge of their rights, especially among the rural low-income groups, who were also largely illiterate. Among the middle and upper classes , literate and mainly urban women, the greatest barrier was their lack of understanding of how to claim their rights without offending society.

As a result, a pilot legal center project was initiated. It was a pilot in the sense that it would be established first in the federal capital where its influence would be felt quickly by the government. If it succeeded in the capital, then the project could be extended to other parts of the federation. After the initiation of the pilot project, the establishment of centers in outlying regions would be made considerably easier because more people would have become acquainted with it and its objectives.

With a favorable political atmosphere and a relatively secure source of funding, a group of women headed by Professor Akande constituted the initial planning committee. The Nigerian Institute of Advanced Legal Studies (NIALS) was selected as the implementing agency. Not only is Professor

Akande a research professor there, but this legal research institute (the only one of its kind in Africa) also has the resources, manpower and physical plant to facilitate the implementation of the proposed project. In addition, the Director-General of the NIALS became chairman of the planning committee and one of the legal experts working at the center. The Director of the Nigerian Law School was also invited to participate because of the need to use some of his students for training at the center.

The center had to be located away from the institute because of the difficulty which clients might have in getting onto the campus of the University of Lagos, the site of the institute. The Lagos Island was chosen as the site for the center because it is more easily accessible to the class of people for whom the project is meant. The premises of the Y.W.C.A. was selected for the center's offices because it is centrally located; it was offered free of charge; and a large number of young women are trained in various fields of home economics there. Through them, information from and about the center is passed to the public.

Focus

The strategy has focused on culture, education, and sometimes the reeducation of women about their rights and the impact of custom and traditions on women's social status. A focus on family relations was chosen because it embraces almost all aspects of life, and it is perhaps the only sphere of life in which women cannot be ignored.

The use of the Legal Advisory Center will break the barriers for women to seek legal help, thus opening up avenues to a greater understanding of legal processes and structures. Through counseling services, women can familiarize themselves with ways to exercise their rights without neglecting their responsibilities. It will help build their confidence by encouraging them to participate more fully in society.

We hope that the idea of a family law center will spread throughout the federation. It might eventually influence the policy-makers to expand the scope of the offical Legal Aid Council to embrace family law issues.

Legal Issues

Most women in Nigeria are affected by family law. It is the area in which legislation has been least successful in changing attitudes, customs and practices. To a very large extent, religion dictates peoples' attitudes on many vital issues of family law. Furthermore, religious issues are among the most volatile in Nigeria today.

Various legal workshops, seminars and conferences seeking to enhance the status of women in Third World countries have shown that the decision-making process in the family is not advantageous to women. This situation affects women's participation in society. Thus, family relations and family law must be reformed.

One problem faced by Nigerian family law is the elevated position in which customs and customary law are held, even by the educated elite. It is only in the area of family law that customary law predominates. Therefore, when one speaks about these changes, one is thinking more of customs and practices, which perhaps can best be changed by education.

Participation

The primary participants are lawyers and women from the mass media; secondary participants are low-income people, and the Women's Voluntary Association, and the National Council of Women's Societies, which distribute the center's publications.

The government also indirectly participates through the Nigerian Institute of Advanced Legal Studies and the Nigerian Law School. The funding agency, the Ford Foundation, will continue to participate for another year and thereafter, it is hoped that the government will assume full financial responsibility.

Results

The center has been in existence for about one year. The number of women seeking help from the center has been very encouraging. Media reports indicate that both men and women are benefiting from the project: also, the center has received many letters requesting the establishment of centers in other states to provide more women with legal counseling services.

Branches of the National Council of Women's Societies have reported that the center's *enlightenment program* has been received even in some remote rural areas. One cannot assess the impact of the programs in such a short time. There is no doubt, however, that increasing numbers of women are more aware of their rights and are more prepared to assert these rights. While it may be presumptuous to claim that it has been entirely due to this project, one cannot dismiss its contributions.

On the first anniversary of the project, a thorough and public evaluation of the center will be conducted. It will determine the future direction of the center and its work.

Lessons

The major strength of the strategy is its *public enlightenment program*, but the large demand for its publications has strained the center's limited financial resources. A major weakness is the relatively small number of cases that the center can handle expeditiously. Initially, no clients were turned away, but in keeping with our stated objective, the center caters only to low-income women who cannot afford legal services otherwise. We hesitate to refuse many clients as we do not want to create a wrong public impression. In a vastly illiterate society where information is communicated orally, the rejection of a client can do untold damage by her misrepresentation of the situation, and thereby discourage other needy persons from coming forward.

Because the center does not usually handle litigation directly, some prospective clients do not appreciate the value of its services. The center will review this matter in considering future policies.

Jade O. Akande is Regional Vice-President for Africa of the International Federation of Women Lawyers and is a research professor at the Nigerian Institute of Advanced Legal Studies. Priscilla O. Kuye is a member of the National Council of Women's Societies.

Argentina: Women's Legal Activism
Cristina Zurutuza

Introduction

For eight years, Argentineans have endured one of the harshest military dictatorships in Latin America. Professionals endured a repressive political system which controlled politics, ideas, and thought. Only since 1984 have the people tried to reclaim their rights. Because of state repression, the women's movement was relatively inactive during the years of the women's decade, 1975–1985. Our women's program is especially interesting because of the socio-political context in which it originated.

Sexist ideology affects women most during a period of crisis. The most serious forms of discrimination against women involve society's interpretation of the law and women's legal and social status. The legal establishment has always ignored women; and often it has subjected them to unequal and discriminatory conditions. For example, under the military dictatorship, law schools tended to disregard legislation that discriminated against women and the obvious inequality of women.

With the return to civilian government, all institutions have been receptive to new ideas. The possibility of changing the legal system also emerged. The new civilian authorities have removed judges whose decisions only served military interests. Council members, whose activities were very objectionable, have been replaced. The National Congress and other representative bodies, all of which were suspended for the eight years of the dictatorship, have begun to deliberate again. They are addressing numerous legal issues, including women's rights and development.

Overview

Initially, the principal problem in improving women's rights in Argentina was the discrepancy between the theory and practice of the law. Some legislation was potentially beneficial to women; however, in practice, the law tended to discriminate against women. Moreover, women from all socioeconomic strata lack the necessary legal knowledge to claim and defend their rights. As a result, they passively submit to the manipulation and suppression of their prerogatives.

The strategy was designed to respond to three important needs. The first need was to train and sensitize legal experts, paralegals, and group leaders through workshops, seminars, courses, conferences, research, and publications. Informing people about women's rights was a second necessity; it was accomplished by the free distribution of publications to institutions. The third need was the establishment of a center to provide legal assistance and education.

These three objectives are now being implemented. The center has developed a group of experts since August, 1982. It organized seminars, conferences, and workshops on women and the law. The organization is currently developing its capacity to publish and distribute materials to institutions that reach ordinary people. Finally, the legal services office has been operating for one year.

The work of the center is developed by women lawyers, psychologists, and social and medical assistants. For two and one-half years, it has been developing and implementing a systematic program. The project strives to reach various experts and leaders so that they can educate and inform a larger number of people. It seeks to improve the conditions of women by encouraging their participation in the legal system and the development of their awareness about their rights.

Legal Issues

Our program relies on the use of advanced labor legislation, the fulfillment of which is restricted and conditioned by economic and political factors. Our program is seeking to address this issue.

Another area of importance is family legislation, which is in a nascent stage compared to some other countries. For example, an executive decree prohibits the sale of contraceptives. In practice, this regulation is not widely enforced, and contraceptives are commercially available. Abortion is also prohibited. This law is enforced, and it provides for criminal sanctions against the person who performs an abortion and for the woman who requests it. Men and women are treated differently by the law on the issue of adultery. Women are legally prohibited from engaging in extramarital relations. In contrast, in order to accuse a man of adultery, it must be proven that he maintains a mistress at a separate residence.

Participation

The strategy of the Center for Women's Studies uses various group methods. Seminars are multi-disciplinary in nature. All programs are based on an ideological analysis of the subject, the code, legal cases, and specific laws. Workshops are directed by a lawyer, psychologist, and paralegal.

The strategy addresses laws that are not executed because of resistant social attitudes, customs, and ideology, as well as an inadequate enforcement system. The strategy underscores the rights and privileges that the law grants to women, but the law is not implemented because women are either unaware of their rights or are resigned to their subservience.

The strategy challenges the law in cases that flagrantly violate women's rights (*e.g.*, the discriminatory legislation on adultery). It focuses on this aspect because the written law is more beneficial to women than are the customs and ideologies prevalent in Argentinean society. The strategy focuses on changing the spirit and letter of the law in cases of manifest injustice (*e.g.*, legislation dealing with paternal authority, abortion, and adultery).

It also addresses the issue of inalienable human rights: the law sould protect rather than abuse. The themes of family, labor, and economics are considered appropriate issues for action. The diverse tactics and issues of the strategy must aim at the fundamental premise that women and men are equal. The strategy then can address the whole legal system and social attitudes towards women.

Results

When democratic rule returned to Argentina, new political and social conditions emerged which granted a measure of liberty to the people. Democracy opened up new legal avenues for women.

The altered structural conditions of the country have improved the possibility of strengthening women's rights. As women begin to participate again in political activities, they will reintegrate into the public arena in order to reclaim their rights and to demand protection or modification of the law.

Our methods are political in the broad sense of the word. They include ideological support, consciousness-raising, and the organization and mobilization of women. We have organized the specific activities of the center to improve the conditions and status of women by addressing the legal structure and institutions in Argentina.

Cristina Zurutuza is coordinator of the legal program of the Center for Women's Studies in Buenos Aires, Argentina.

Centers Addressing Violence and Abuse

The next two papers are unique in that they focus on a single family-related issue—one that is increasingly felt by women throughout the world—domestic violence. *Sánchez* and *Uribe* describe a program whose goals are very similar to those of the programs discussed in the previous section: to promote social change by increasing women's awareness about their rights and by making the legal system more accessible to women. While family and labor law are the major concerns, the majority of their cases deal with some form of abuse suffered by women. In addition to strict legal assistance, therefore, the program also offers psychological counseling and group therapy. In a different geographical and cultural context, *Mukherjee* from India describes another strategy to minister to the victims of *dowry violence.* Her case study documents the extreme vulnerability and plight of a woman who was subjected to physical abuse as a result of her family's inability to provide the dowry demanded by her husband and in-laws. She also describes efforts made to press for the expeditious and just handling of the case by the police and the courts.

ꕤꕤꕤꕤ

Colombia:
Legal Assistance Program
Olga Amparo Sánchez
Marta Uribe

Overview

Based on an analysis of the specific situation of women in our environment, we have identified three central legal problems. Firstly, women are basically ignorant of their legal rights, and they possess no means to exercise their prerogatives. Secondly, there are no alternative legal services that address women's problems. Finally, women are handicapped by their subordinate status and lack of identity and organizational role models.

The objectives of our legal assistance program are to provide legal services to individual women and to promote positive legal change. The program considers the situation of women and the family in terms of their actual experience. It analyzes Colombian legislation that affects women, focusing specifically on the family, the workforce, and the multiple forms of abuse to which women are subjected. It assists women in confronting their legal problems with greater assurance. The program also offers legal counseling from a comprehensive perspective. In addition, it prepares educational material to inform women about the law and its administration.

These objectives are met by organizing activities such as women and family workshops, legal counseling, and group therapy for women in crisis. We also prepare educational materials, share experiences, and conduct field research on the abuse experienced by Colombian women.

Process

Casa de la Mujer was formed by a group of people concerned with women's problems. Its services began on March 8, 1982; the legal service program began on August 1, 1983. All of the *Casa's* programs are closely linked. The legal services program meet the needs of women for appropriate legal assistance. The initial aims of the program are being attained; women are increasing their awareness, utilizing the law more effectively, and shedding their subservient outlook.

Focus

Studying the situation of Colombian women leads us to examine the diverse facets of women's dual condition of subordination and discrimination. These facets include the legal view of women, women's awareness of their rights, and the actual availability of legal services.

The strategy focuses on the content of the law, the structure of the legal system, and the legal culture. Therefore, in addition to providing women with legal services, it targets the level at which the law treats women. Furthermore, the strategy concentrates on raising women's consciousness of their rights, legislation, and concrete actions that affect women's exercise of their rights.

The focus is fundamental. It encourages the women to reflect on their daily lives to identify their problems, and to recognize their vital role in the family and society. Hence, women decide to determine their own destinies.

Legal Issues

The strategy addresses the concerns of family, labor, and penal law (mainly the issues of violence and exploitation). It concentrates on areas of most concern to women. The counseling services largely involve family matters and abuse. The majority of our clients have experienced some form of abuse in the family, at work, or in society at large.

Participation

Participants in the development of the legal services program are the legal aid staff of *Casa de la Mujer*, which has progressively evaluated and consolidated its work. Women who participate in the women and family workshops, group therapy, and other *Casa* programs (such as those on health, sexuality, and creativity) do not necessarily use the legal sevices.

The workshops, which began operation in 1983, meet weekly or biweekly for two hours. The initial motivation of women participating in the workshops usually stems from the need to resolve a specific problem, to overcome a crisis, or to understand the legal aspects of a particular problem.

The organization of the strategy is based on *Casa's* experience, the concrete needs of women who request services, and the analysis of the situation of women in our environment. Our method of work can be summarized by two concepts: research and action, and learning by doing.

Results

The *Casa* has consolidated the legal aid program and evaluated the staff and the work. It has developed a methodology and course materials for the women and family workshops. It has also incorporated legal aid clients into the workshops and other activities of *Casa*, which broadens the analysis of women's problems. The integration of the legal services program with all the other work of *Casa de la Mujer* is essential. Our strong, alternative legal services focus on the roots of woman's specific problems.

These services are designed especially for women who are most vulnerable—the poorly educated, the deprived and disadvantaged, and those without means to obtain private legal services. From partial evaluation of all our services and workshops, we have concluded that we can provide better legal services.

Furthermore, we have witnessed a strengthening of the women on a personal level, as they search for new forms of affirmation for changes in everyday relationships, and for strengthened bonds of solidarity to face their problems. These processes are essential to the formation of organizational structures which will advance the women's struggle for their rights.

The evaluation of the programs was based on two types of data. Firstly, *Casa* collected information from women involved in different phases of the process (initial contact, interviews, case follow-up). Secondly, we obtained personal assessments from the clients and workshop participants. Every year, two meetings are used to evaluate the programs.

Casa members believe that the methodology is directly related to the attainment of the proposed objectives. Moreover, it is a concrete response to the various legal problems of women.

Lessons

The relatively isolated life of women, along with their limited access to education and training, perpetuates women's ignorance of their legal rights. Our situation immobilizes women and creates serious problems that cannot be removed without legal assistance. Our legal aid services represent an important alternative for women. In cooperation with other groups, we are attempting to tackle the serious legal and social problems of women in Colombian society. We have been particularly challenged by the problems of violence toward women and the necessity to reach broader segments of women.

It is important to place women's legal problems in a larger perspective than the strictly legal plane. The legal services program attempts to integrate women's legal situation within a wider social framework. Hence, legal services in combination with the search for non-traditional responses to women's problems can become an instrument of change for the personal and social conditions of women. A new force for change is the collective search, a search that is initiated by women who share their experiences, seeking recourse for common problems, and encounter new forms of support and solidarity.

Olga Amparo Sánchez, a sociologist, is the Director of Casa de la Mujer and Marta Uribe, a psychologist, is coordinator of its Women and Family program.

India: Dowry Violence
Sheila Mukherjee

Overview

This case study addresses a problem that came to the attention of the Community Welfare and Research Society in Varanasi, India: a young bride was set on fire by her husband and in-laws. The immediate goals were to save her life and to gather sufficient evidence to prosecute the perpetrators. We took the woman to the university hospital immediately after the incident. Despite many threats, we registered a complaint of attempted murder against her husband and his family. In addition, we publicized this case to elicit public opinion against this act and collected donations to enable her family to meet the necessary legal expenses.

Focus

Because we were known here, the woman's family asked us to assist them as they were essentially helpless. The primary goal was, of course, to help the woman to survive. After her survival was assured, we focused on providing her with legal representation to ensure that the perpetrators were brought to court. Moreover, we worked for the conviction and appropriate sentencing of the husband and his family.

Legal Issues

We worked through the Indian Penal Code as this was the only legislation by which the perpetrators could be arrested. India is only now in the process of introducing family law and family courts. Because of the passivity and prevailing social attitudes, many culprits escape prosecution or conviction. We were, however, successful in obtaining an indictment of the husband and his family.

Results

The case is progressing in favor of our client. The culprits are threatened with the possibility of a fourteen-year prison sentence. The defendants have proposed to the client's family a reconciliation of the couple, promising humane treatment for the woman. Throughout the ordeal, we have collected donations from the community to help the victim with the expenses of this case.

Lessons

Our strategy has been very effective and successful in that it has made both the criminals and society aware that they cannot commit such acts with impunity. Hence, the major lesson of this case is that women's organizations must be absolutely firm and determined in dealing with the oppressors of women. They must bring the oppressors of women to justice despite all threats and intimidation. Determination and energetic action have stimulated the support of the public to help the victims of these terrible crimes.

The Case of Mrs. S

Mrs. S, formerly Miss B until her marriage about one year ago, is a young woman of about 20 years of age. She comes from a lower middle class Brahmin family in the Bengali community of Varanasi, India. She has little education. Miss B has no father, and before her marriage she lived with her mother, grandmother, and an unmarried brother (Mr. B). They lived in the Sonarpura area of Varanasi, which is inhabited mostly by middle or lower middle-class families.

Her brother was graduated from high school. Mr. B has a women's apparel business that deals in Banarasi saris for which Varanasi is famous. The family does not own its home and lives in a rented house in Sonarpura in south Varanasi. The area is close to the Ganges, a center of religious activities. The area is also the home of some hippies and a few anti-social elements (who engage in stealing, smuggling, and dealing in drugs).

Miss B was married about a year ago into the S family. Her husband, Mr. S, is about 24 years of age and has a business in Banarasi saries like the B family. The S family, who owns its home, lives about one-half a kilometer from the B family. Economically, the S family is better-off than the woman's family. Mr. S, the eldest son, was responsible for his parents, two brothers, and three sisters at the time of his marriage.

The bride, Mrs. S, was treated decently for three to four months after her marriage. After that period, her husband and in-laws began to quarrel with her about the dowry goods which they claimed were of low quality. Relations between Mrs. S and her in-laws continued to deteriorate. Mrs. S reported the bad treatment she was receiving to her own family.

About four months ago as she was sleeping, her clothes and bed were set on fire by her mother-in-law and her husband. They tried to restrain her when she began to scream. The neighbors who came to investigate were prevented by the S family from entering the house. However, the news spread immediately. Our organization and the B family arrived quickly. Her brother, some neighbors, and our representative rushed Mrs. S to the university hospital, which is about two kilometers away. We arranged for her to receive prompt medical attention. We paid regular visits to the hospital to ensure that she received good medical treatment. Mrs. S gradually recovered and returned to her mother's home to live.

At the hospital, Mrs. S had stated that her mother-in-law set fire to her clothes. After she returned home, she added that her husband had also participated in the attempted murder. She said that at the hospital she had been in such a state of shock, she was unable to make a full statement. In contrast, the in-laws claimed that she caught fire while she was cooking and that the rest of her story was a fabrication.

This incident aroused the concern of the community, but no one had the courage, motivation, or the initiative to report the matter to the police. We urged her brother, Mr. B, to lodge a complaint against the perpetrators at the Bhelupura Police Station.

Meanwhile, the S family continually threatened Mr. B about going to the police. With our support and assistance, Mr. B lodged a formal complaint against the perpetrators. The husband and his mother were immediately arrested and sent to jail; she was released on bail after fifteen days in jail, and the husband after three months. The S family continued to mount pressure on the B family not to pursue the case. In fact, we were forced to send two of our male employees to protect the B family. We mobilized public support for the B family, and thereby, obtained police protection for this family.

Because the B family was unable to meet the legal expenses of the court, we appealed for public donations. Initially, we raised Rs. 1500 for the B family. On the other hand, the richer S family was able to engage a top lawyer to plead its case. The case is currently being heard. If it is proved, the husband faces a fourteen-year prison sentence. While the S family has stepped up its campaign to induce the B family to withdraw the case, our organization continues to support their prosecution by helping the B family in any way possible. We have worked to ensure that no political pressure is placed on the police to weaken this case. On the contrary, we have continually pressed to expedite the investigation and judicial procedures.

The S family now realizes that we are determined to see this case through to the very end. Our firm support and active interest in the case has made them discuss reconciliation. In return for the dropping of the charges, the S family is promising good treatment for Mrs. S if she will return to her husband. In spite of the many promises of the S family, Mrs. S is unwilling to drop the matter and return to live with her husband and in-laws. The case is continuing.

Sheila Mukherjee is President of the Community Welfare and Research Society in Varanasi, India.

Advocating for Labor Rights

Labor issues provide another category and focus for advocacy strategies. The papers included here document three programs involving workers in the informal sector and two in the formal sector. The major difficulty is, of course, that most labor legislation is not applicable to informal sector workers—especially if they are not unionized. Legislation that does exist is vague and not easily enforced. *Bhatt* and *Patel* describe the comprehensive advocacy strategies developed and implemented to confront the special problems of self-employed women in India. One of the major accomplishments of their organization, the Self-Employed Women's Association, was to gain status as a registered trade union. This permits the association to advocate on behalf of women workers even where there is no recognized employer-employee relationship. The paper documents the legal struggles undertaken with and on behalf of vendors and home-based workers to gain basic benefits such as minimum wage and access to markets previously closed to them.

León describes and analyzes the situation of the domestic worker in Colombia and the strategy undertaken to confront the contradictions between "domestic service" and "domestic labor." The strategy is geared toward transforming the labor relation between the domestic worker and her employer and organizing domestic workers to defend their legal rights. This strategy includes legal advocacy and education components. The advocacy component includes assistance to individual domestic workers, as well as efforts to press for improved legislation and correct interpretation of the law by the courts, government agencies, and lawyers. The educational component integrates legal education and consciousness-raising activities by offering workshops to domestic workers on the substance and procedures of the law, on gender identity, and on their social situation and options for political participation. Moreover, the educational component of the program provides employers with information about their contractual obligations to domestic employees.

The situation of contract workers migrating from Indonesia to the Middle East is the theme of *Saleh's* paper. She points out that most women contract workers are domestic workers. Private agencies recruit women workers with the promise of higher salaries than they are making in Indonesia, and offer a trip to Mecca as a further incentive. While these benefits appear to be an improvement in their situations, once the women arrive in the host country, they find intolerable working conditions, cultural isolation, and no legal protection. Given the complexity of the problem, due to its international dimensions, an effective strategy to protect migrant women workers is still being formulated. Saleh discusses the assistance her legal services center offers a migrant worker before her departure and upon her return. The main objectives are to assure a fair and protective labor agreement including number of work hours per day, holidays, sick leave, and other related issues, and to provide the migrant worker with sufficient information about her rights so that she will not find herself exploited and without recourse.

In the formal sector, *Quesada, Martínez*, and *Zaldaña* describe a strategy implemented by a women's organization to recover wages and fight against the suspension of tobacco workers in Honduras. Although the workers belonged to a labor union, they were unfamiliar with their rights. To address the problem, the strategy included education and organization of the workers while simultaneously pursuing all available legal avenues. This case study suggests that legal illiteracy and lack of consciousness among women can hinder the development and success of an advocacy strategy. In this case, some of the workers decided they could not hold out until the end and they settled for less. Those who did see it through to the end, however, were rewarded for their persistence with increased knowledge and skills and managed to recover their wages and their jobs.

Jara describes a program geared specifically toward women workers in the formal sector and the improvement of women's labor organizations in Peru. Echoing the Honduran experience, Jara outlines the difficulties encountered in legal advocacy work related to women workers. The passive role many women accept, due to cultural and economic conditions, hinders the effectiveness of work with female factory workers. The strategy adopted, therefore, includes the following features: an interdisciplinary approach integrating law, the social sciences, and psychology; legal counseling linked with group training; and the use of both traditional and non-traditional dispute-settlement methods.

❧❧❧❧

India: Self-Employed Women Workers
Ela Bhatt
Veena Patel

Introduction

SEWA, which means *service* in several Indian languages, is the acronym of the Self-Employed Women's Association. SEWA, a registered trade union, struggles for the rights of poor, self-employed women. Although these women work very hard and make a significant contribution to the national economy, their activity is not recognized as work. As a result, either they are not paid or they are paid at very low rates.

This sector of self-employed workers does not have the benefits prescribed in labor regulations. As no recognized employer–employee relationship exists, few of the labor laws or protective regulations apply to them. This situation leads to rampant exploitation of the self-employed, particularly by the middleman.

Overview

SEWA seeks to help the self-employed to increase their income, their living standards, and their control over the family income. It is attempting to publicize its work by conducting demographic and sociological studies and surveys on particular trades. The studies investigate the working conditions, the sources of work, and the nature of exploitation. This information then becomes the basis of SEWA's efforts in organizing the members of a specific trade.

There are 22,700 members registered with SEWA. Its membership is composed of three categories. The first group is home-based petty producers who make such products as *bidis* (indigenous cigarettes), incense sticks, garments, small furniture, fabric, and handicrafts. Secondly are small vendors who sell goods such as vegetables, fruits, fish, eggs, garments, and similar types of products in the market. Lastly the service workers provide various services, including head-loading, handcart-pulling, scrap collection, wastepaper collection, and farm labor.

In this paper, I will use case examples of particular trades to illustrate SEWA's legal intervention on behalf of the self-employed women workers.

The Manekchow Vegetable Vendors

Three hundred vegetable vendors belong to SEWA in the Manekchok region, the main fruit and vegetable market. They are productive and contribute significantly to the economy of the city of Ahmedabad. They have been in business for the past fifty or sixty years; and by now, they should be recognized as lawful traders. However, the municipality does not recognize their rights or their functions in the marketplace. It has consistently refused to give them vending licenses, making them illegal vendors. They were prosecuted and fined at least four or five times a month with fines ranging from Rs. 50–500 per month. The police constables and other officers regularly visited the Manekchowk vegetable vendors demanding a bribe of Rs. 1–2 a day. If the bribe was paid, the officer would go away and allow the vendor to carry on her business. If, however, the vegetable vendor refused to pay the bribe, her name was recorded and she was promptly sent a summons for a traffic offense resulting in exorbitant fines. From time to time, the municipal authorities confiscated their goods. While ordinary people were allowed to park their cars, scooters, and rickshaws throughout the day without any charge, the poor vegetable vendors were prohibited from sitting on the side of the street to sell their vegetables.

These vendors have been members of SEWA for many years. SEWA has tried to ameliorate their harassment problem through direct action, including demonstrations, *satyagrahs* (sit-ins), and marches. Although these actions temporarily stopped the harassment, they did not tackle the basic problem: the refusal of the municipality to issue licenses to the vendors.

As a last resort, SEWA took this issue to the Supreme Court. SEWA argued in court that the hawkers have fundamental rights (*i.e.* rights given in the Indian Constitution) to carry on any profession, trade, or business into the city of Ahmedabad. The hawkers are engaged in lawful trade of fruits and vegetables and other marketable commodities in exercise of their fundamental rights under article 19(i) of the Constitution of India.

The Supreme Court responded favorably, ordering the Municipal Corporation to cooperate with SEWA in working out a mutually acceptable proposal by which these vendors would be issued licenses. Although at first the Municipal Corporation was reluctant, it could not openly disobey the orders of the highest court. Finally, a common solution was worked out and presented to the court. The court then passed the following order:

> We hope and trust at some point of time in the future the Municipal Corporation might be able to provide a lift so that the vendors do not have to carry the burden of vegetable baskets on their heads up to the terrace and the customers also may have more convenient access to vegetable vendors on the terrace.
>
> The authorities of the Municipal Corporation will issue licenses in favor of 313 vendors which shall be on usual terms.
>
> The male vegetable vendors shall be provided accomodation in separate rows from female vegetable vendors, and each vegetable vendor who has been provided accomodation on the terrace shall carry an identity card with his or her photograph thereon. The terrace should be reserved only for vegetable vendors who are selling vegetables from toplas, i.e., baskets....

The order of the Supreme Court has transformed illegal vendors into respectable citizens, who control their marketplace through their own committees.

Home-Based Workers

Our second focus is on the home-based workers, who can be classified into two groups. The first are those who are provided raw materials by an employer and are paid by the piece-rate. The second group consists of those who buy all their raw materials and sell their finished goods. These women are invisible to society, literally, because they work in their homes, and officially, because they are not counted in the official statistics.

These workers are generally women who combine their household tasks with production work. They process the raw materials at home and return the finished goods to the employer. *Bidis,* (cigarettes), *aggarbattis,* garments, block printing, hand embroidery, and spices are some of the goods produced by piece-rate. The worker's home serves as a workplace, which can adversely affect the health of family members. For example, in the case of bidi rolling, tobacco leaves are released into the air. In addition, the work often infringes on the family members' living space.

The hours of work vary from part-time work of four to five hours a day to a heavy workload of a fifteen hour day. Workers are paid according to the number (or weight or size) of items they have produced. For an 8-hour work day, they generally earn about Rs 5. Piece-rate workers do not receive minimum wages. There is a high rate of rejection of goods; for example, about 100–300 bidis out of 2000. Often, employers use contractors to employ piece-rate workers, or employers use the sale purchase system to avoid any existing legal obligations.

Home based piece-rate workers are not workers as defined by the Factories Act and, thus, are not covered by most labor laws. However, the broad definition of worker in the Minimum Wages Act of 1948 does cover home workers. Therefore, one would expect that even though home workers may not get other benefits that factory laborers enjoy, they would at least receive minimum wages.

Unfortunately, it is not so. The Minimum Wages Act does not automatically cover all trades. A trade has to be included in the Minimum Wages Schedule before it is covered by the act. Most trades in which home workers are active are not included in this schedule.

Even when the trade is in the schedule, the act is often not implemented because of the time-consuming legal processes. The implementing agency is a special government department, the Labor Department. If an employer is found to be violating a labor law, an inspector of the Labor Department lodges a complaint against him. Initially, the inspector attempts to resolve the matter by negotiation and conciliation. If he is unsuccessful, a case is filed in the labor courts, which have the power to decide all cases involving violations of labor laws.

Among the piece-rate workers, the garment makers have had some success in organizing. Many of SEWA's members are ready-to-wear garment makers, who work for garment merchants by the piece-rate at very low wages. No minimum wage for garment workers has yet been established by the government. Because they must pay for their own thread, needles, and for the oiling and repairing of the sewing machine, they receive no more than Rs. 2.50–3 for their labor per day. The garment workers have organized a SEWA union. As a consequence, they are demanding that their employers increase their wages.

As part of the agitation, SEWA filed a complaint with the Labor Department, which initially did not want to process the complaint. The workers' demonstrations and agitations forced the Labor Department to file a complaint and pressured the employers to negotiate with SEWA. Under the influence of the government and the workers, the employers finally capitulated. In negotiations, they agreed to a 50% increase in wages.

The only home-based industry extensively covered by the labor laws is bidi. There are two acts covering bidi workers: the Bidi and Cigar Act of 1966, regulating conditions of employment; and the Bidi Workers Welfare Fund Act of 1976. The first act provides for minimum wages, maternity leave, identity cards, and unemployment compensation for bidi workers. The second act stipulates that a fund, established from a tax on bidis, be used to benefit bidi workers.

When SEWA first began organizing bidi workers, we found that neither of the acts was being implemented. In the case of the 1976 welfare act, a fund had been established, but was not being disbursed. This act required that the bidi worker beneficiary must have an identity card signed by the employer. However, no employer would sign an identity card, as it would prove his employer status, and thus make him liable for providing benefits to the workers under the Bidi and Cigar Workers Act. To solve this legal problem, SEWA pressured and negotiated with the government. After years of discussions, the government finally agreed to accept identity cards signed by a labor officer and countersigned by SEWA.

Bidi workers are entitled to minimum wages under the Minimum Wages Act, but this act is hard to enforce. The basic problem is the difficulty of locating individual employers to take responsibility for their workers. After the act was passed, most employers began to work through contractors. These contractors work only on a commission basis and are unable to provide the workers their benefits under the provisions of the act. Hence, the principal employer avoids location and his responsibilities by operating through contractors.

Another system adopted by the owner to circumvent the laws is the sale-purchase system. In this system, an employer forces workers to buy raw materials from him, process the good, and sell the finished product back to him. In this way, the employers claim that the worker is now a small trader and is no longer covered by labor laws. However, in reality, the worker is not allowed by the owner to operate freely in the marketplace as a small trader. In any case, the workers does not have the capital and know-how to do so. SEWA is attempting to prove an employer-worker relationship in six filings.

SEWA has been lobbying for a comprehensive labor law which would cover home-based workers. This law would be in the form of a home workers protection bill. The government and some organizations have proposed to improve the conditions of piece-rate workers by equalizing their rights, benefits, and wage-scale with those of factory workers. Such an action would impose uniform working hours, minimum wages, paid holidays, leaves, pensions, healthcare, bonuses and gratuities, workers' and termination compensation, and other benefits. Policymakers and grassroots organizations are now discussing these issues and tackling the problem of the piece-rate workers. Nevertheless, it is a constant battle and struggle to obtain the enforcement of the laws, even after the workers are organized. Legal recourse is very difficult, time-consuming, and expensive for poor workers.

Why must all workers who are in need of protection and better facilities conform to the legal definition of recognized employees? While traditionally all forms of labor have been recognized as work, our legal system and policymakers perceive only recognized employees (the notion of workers in the capitalist system) as true workers. Adequate protection has been provided historically for the self-employed worker in the forms of customary rights over land use, raw materials, and the marketplace. Unfortunately, none of these customary rights have been integrated into our laws.

Ela Bhatt is the General Secretary and Veena Patel is a member of the Self-Employed Women's Association (SEWA).

Colombia:
Domestic Labor and Domestic Service
Magdalena León

This paper describes and analyzes the series of activities comprising the project *Actions to Transform Socio-Labor Conditions of Domestic Service in Colombia,* in the context of the relation between domestic labor and domestic service. It also considers the social context of the empleada* (literally *employee,*) used colloquially for maid or domestic worker, and the problems faced and the lessons learned. Work on the project began in Bogota in March 1981 and some of the activities were extended to the cities of Medellín, Cali, Barranquilla and Bucaramanga in 1984.

The Social Context of the
Domestic Empleada's Labor Relation
The labor relation of domestic service which the project seeks to understand and transform extends beyond a strictly labor-legal context. A domestic empleada's work is not only an external relation—a market activity wherein labor is bought and sold—but a way of life. It is the relation between domestic labor and domestic service that allows us to transcend casting the problem strictly in terms of employment.

Domestic labor has been culturally assigned to the woman as her fundamental role and defines her socially as *ama de casa** (mistress of the house), mother or wife. Domestic labor becomes wage labor when the ama de casa delegates part of her responsibilities to another woman who, within the very same ideology of service to others, seeks payment for performing personal services within another woman's house. Wage labor performed by paid domestic workers is subject to the same social stigma as domestic labor carried out by the ama de casa. Their devalued social role, derived from an ideology considering

*These terms are used throughout the article in the original Spanish. They are not italicized.

364

their service to others as natural, involves the *patrona** (employer) and her empleada in a relation of identity. Because domestic service is supplied by women from the popular sectors, and set up as a vertical-asymmetric power relation with the patrona, the social devaluation is augmented, and contradictions are generated between women of different social classes. The labor relation between patronas and empleadas is clouded, therefore, with effects both of the class contradictions and the gender identification established between the women. On the one hand, it is possible to speak of women's social subordination, and on the other, of class exploitation.

The labor relation becomes a way of life for the empleada in several ways. Setting the salary does not follow strictly economic considerations; factors such as those the empleada calls "good treatment" interact in the development of the relation. The relation established on the job is a combination of the work, and emotional, and personal aspects; the empleada's workplace is also her living place, but she is confined to a physical space different from that of the family, rendering explicitly the class difference. Because the live-in empleada's social and sexual relationships are restricted, her entire life is a function of the labor relation, which in itself carries a sense of around-the-clock availability, a phenomenon arising from the lack of legal regulation of work hours.

Furthermore, when the workplace is also home and place of consumption, it is impossible for the relation to be an impersonal one. The empleada who has just left her family of origin is in a situation of cultural and emotional dislocation and she transfers her attachments to those who live in her new, substitute home. As long as the relationship does not cross the class lines this attachment is permitted. As a result, the empleada internalizes a sense of inferiority and is unable to develop the class consciousness that would otherwise allow her to perceive the contradictions in the relation.

Under these circumstances, what strategies could be implemented that would allow us to change these relations? Two points must first be clarified. We reject the ideological position that considers domestic service essential. Those who hold to this position assert that paid personal services are needed to reproduce the labor force in the home, and they propose providing training courses to improve the social position of the *gremio* (occupational group). This approach continues to relegate domestic labor to women through paid services. It also fails to take into account the government's obligations with regard to the cost of reproducing the labor force. In an inegalitarian society, the private responses of domestic service only perpetuate social inequality.

Another thesis suggests that domestic service will be phased out as the society develops and modernizes. This would mean that sufficient female employment must eventually be generated to absorb the large numbers of women who currently use domestic service as a work strategy. As these large numbers of women domestic workers are, in themselves, evidence of how important domestic service is for reproduction of the labor force, this hypothesis is not the most accurate for developing societies. In addition, this thesis ignores the fact that there are no collective services to replace the empleada's personal services.

Domestic service is not declining in Colombia or in Latin American society. Conventional data are misleading because live-in domestic service is statistically underestimated, and secondly, because live-out domestic service, a recent and increasingly common phenomenon, is excluded. This sector is undergoing internal structural transformation, changing from the live-in to the live-out mode. It is not being phased out. At the end of the last decade, 37% of the female labor force worked as domestic servants (live-in and live-out) in the five largest Colombian cities.

The second clarification is the composition of the domestic workers. Migrants from rural areas with peasant and/or agricultural-proletariat family origins concentrated in young age groups predominate in this sector. Some withdraw from the labor market at the beginning of their reproductive cycle to set up their own households and to raise their children. Others re-enter the work force upon completing these life cycles, and the majority of these swell the ranks of the live-out empleadas.

A high proportion are single, and among these, the group of unmarried mothers is very important. Many women who work as live-in empleadas have been abandoned by their husbands or partners. The majority of women who work as empleadas have very little education; many (especially the older women) are illiterate or have not completed primary school.

To address these multifaceted issues, we have searched for strategies that are governed by the following considerations. Because the majority of the empleadas live and work under discriminatory conditions, the strategy must develop programs directed toward transforming the labor relations of domestic service and organizing the occupational group to defend its legal rights. Secondly, as the the gender ideology binding both empleada and patronas to domestic labor is deeply rooted, the strategy must develop programs that would promote a process of conscientization leading to personal autonomy-identity (empowerment). Thus, we saw the need to undertake two complementary actions: one to stimulate gender awareness among empleadas and patronas, and the other, class consciousness among the empleadas. Gender awareness endeavors to demystify women who are assigned domestic labor, and class consciousness will allow empleadas to identify with each other, to perceive the contradictions inherent in the class relation, and to create an organized movement.

The strategy's activities are classified into two main categories: *apoyo laboral* (labor support)—services and support by which empleadas learn of their labor rights, as well as the various aspects of class and gender identification, and about organizing. We also offered support for the empleadas' identity-autonomy (empowerment) process; and finally, socio-labor reflection with patronas. The second category involves organizing the empleadas and strengthening union activities, and exposing and modifying the subordination-exploitation structure of the patrona-empleada relation at an ideological level. The third category involves fostering the legal profession's correct interpretation and application of the law; and promoting governmental reform to benefit the domestic workers.

Direct Actions

Direct actions are those in which the participants are empleadas or patronas with whom we have personal contact. We explain the content and nature of the existing labor laws to the empleadas. Then the domestic workers discuss how to understand, enforce, and challenge the laws. The empleada's sense of autonomy-identity (empowerment) is explored and developed in the context of her situation both as a woman and as a citizen. Connections between these two levels, (*i.e.*, daily personal problems and general work problems) are stressed in order to penetrate into the hidden determiniation their personal and collective situations and encourage the empleada to organize themselves.

Having considered the individual labor relation, the project then moves to the collective nature of the empleada-patrona problem; it attempts to awaken class consciousness by collectivizing individual claims and exposing the contradictions in the labor relation, not as conflicts between individuals, but as functions of class positions. We hope that the mutual reinforcement of the empleada's identity as a person and as a social being combined with an awareness of class contradictions will encourage them as a group to mobilize and organize.

Patronas, on the other hand, are offered courses whose purpose is to demythologize the ideological values underlying their social assignment of domestic labor. In this context, they are also presented with the labor legislation that contains contractual obligations toward their domestic workers.

Labor Support for the Empleada

The principal goal of this action is to enable empleadas to use the law as a tool to improve working and living conditions. Legal assistance, legal education, and other service are provided to the empleada.

Legal Assistance

Given that they have never been aware of, or protected by, their legal rights, empleadas recognize the need for legal counsel. They have developed a fatalistic attitude wherein change is considered a matter of luck rather than a result of specific actions. So long as there was no legal support for their demands, the word of the patrona was the only one having any validity. Disclosing the existence of legislation and ensuring its compliance by means of legal assistance provided needed services to the empleadas.

Analysis of Colombian laws shows the following: the legislation considers that the empleada was part of the family and that the family is not a production unit (neither is true and both are discriminatory).

The legislation has gaps and weaknesses. Due to the nature of Colombian law, it does not address some essential issues relevant to the empleadas. Because the law's content is limited, it does not provide for comprehensive social justice.

Our project distributes information booklets summarizing the relevant existing laws to the patronas, and the empleadas. We advertise about the availability of our legal services for empleada through the mass media, personal contacts, trade unions, women's organizations and employment agencies. In addition, we offer a benefits settlement service to empleadas who have terminated their employment contracts or intend to do so.

This service encompasses a proper accounting of benefits due the empleada, namely severance pay, vacation, remuneration, and the accrued interest on severance pay.

If the settlement calculations are rejected either partially or totally by the patrona, we initiate proceedings. Initially, we seek to settle the issue through direct contact with the patrona, which has proven to be the most useful way to reach a positive solution. If the empleada and patrona are unable to negotiate a settlement, the only available recourse is to initiate a court case. Fortunately, most of our cases have been resolved at the negotiation stage. Moreover, the empleada actively participate throughout the benefits settlement process. This service aims to transcend a dependency mentality by emphasizing that the empleada be responsible for her individual problem and apply it to the wider group.

Education

As a first step in the process of education and conscientization, empleadas are offered courses in labor law. The objective is to interest them in learning the relevant law, so they can understand and conduct their individual cases.

The course's methodology is participatory and aims to develop topics from the viewpoint of participants. The facilitator-teacher encourages dialogue, and from the comments that are forthcoming, draws together the various experiences to highlight how the law applies to each topic. The methodology also seeks to convey the complex content of the law in simple form to people whose educational level is very low. To do this, teaching aids are employed based on the qualitative information developed from the legal consultations between empleadas and patronas. Conversion into teaching material of information gathered during the judicial activities is one way to return their experiences to the participants.

The course covers seven topics including work contract, probationary period, hours, salary, paid time-off (Sundays and national holidays, vacations and family crises), benefits (severance pay and compensation for on-the-job injury, sickness, pregnancy, abortion and uniforms), and terminations of contract.

Apart from providing the empleadas with information, the workshops are occasions when they can meet and build solidarity and when they can collectivize their problematic situation. Realizing that their situation—being a domestic workers who participate in unequal power relations—is not simply a personal one makes a strong impression on the empleadas.

Empowerment: Support for Development of the Empleada's Autonomy-Identity

The empowerment program complements the legal education and consciousness-raising activities. The autonomy-identity workshop aims to demythologize patriarchal ideology. It demonstrates how subordinate familial relations are transferred to the substitute home of the employer's family, and hence hinder the development of class consciousness. The methodology of the workshop is participatory and it permits the empleada to develop her identity both as a woman and as a social being.

It is important to stress that participants do not come from a single community, but because of the nature of their work, they live apart. Workshops attempt to break through the isolation and silence. They offer alternatives and the necessary security and motivation to unite and organize the empleadas as workers and as women, and ultimately to precipitate social change.

Workshop on Identity as a Woman

This workshop, by extracting the culturally-defined aspects of domestic roles and sexuality, and exploring strategies to challenge them, encourages individual and group reflection on the elements that comprise gender identity. This approach centers on the personal experiences of the empleadas, and other information presented by the facilitator. The workshop's objective is to present different aspects of women's sexuality. While the workshop agenda includes a technical session on family planning and contraception, it also touches on concepts such as the importance of bearing children who are wanted, and sexual relations for the woman's sexual pleasure, rather than simply as a reproductive function.

Civic Identity Workshop

To enable the empleada to better perceive her social roles as woman, worker and citizen, participants in this workshop describe, analyze and compare their individual situations. The general purpose is to show the empleadas that they have a place in social life and to help them to understand their problematic.

Other discussions center on employment, unemployment and rural–urban migration. In particular, it considers the causes of female migration to the cities (such as the lack of educational and training opportunities) and the problem of female domestic workers in the city (*e.g.*, limited public services). To elucidate the various types of violence that women are subject to in the city, participants talk about situations in which they feel insecure and afraid. In other sessions, they review health problems and their access to health care; finally, they discuss how they participate in city life.

Socio-labor Reflection for Patronas

The aim of these courses, which deal with the social and labor aspects of domestic service, is twofold: to stimulate an understanding of the concept of gender and to clarify their contractual obligations to the domestic service sector.

These courses encourage patronas to think about the relation between their own domestic labor and the paid service provided by the empleada. The social value of domestic activities and the social role of women to "serve others" is analyzed, and stimulated participants to consider women's social conditioning and subordination within the family and community.

The labor legislation governing contracts with empleadas is introduced in this context. The course demonstrates that the patrona–empleada relationship is drawn from the paternalist framework that considers empleadas as members of the family and, as such, without any rights or full enjoyment of the same.

Motivating patronas to participate has not been easy, Class consciousness prevents them from facing their labor obligations, and their own oppression as women prevents them from reflecting on their social role. Twenty-three courses having a total of 633 participants were given in the first part of 1985.

Outreach

These activities involve work with representatives of the domestic service sector, outreach to the community, discussions with legal professionals, and pressure for policy change.

Actions with Representatives of the Domestic Service Sector

These have a twofold objective. Firstly, they serve as a bridge between the rank and file and the leadership, and secondly, they *support and assist* the organized sector of the domestic service workers. Class and gender awareness instilled in the rank and file through earlier direct actions provide the foundation for the mobilizing and unionizing phases. The Association for Population Studies (ACEP) has not attempted to create an organization. It refers program participants showing interest in collective action to the SINTRASEDOM, *Sindicato de Trabajadores del Servicio Domestico,* (National Union of Household Workers). Union representatives and program participants collaborate.

The research team provides support for the organized sector of the occupational group by working directly with the union. It offers support for the union's different events, and trains leaders on the substance of labor law and methods used to settle claims. Preparation of teaching material and proposals to reform the law are also coordinated with the union.

In an effort to mobilize the rank and file, ACEP has also organized larger meetings. For example on May 1, 1985, it held an event held to celebrate May Day and to call for the enforcement of health provisions found in the labor legislation. Several other events that year emphasized social security programs.

Changing Social Ideology

This aspect of outreach focuses on making the labor legislation known to the general public, analyzing and clarifying the devaluation of domestic labor, and highlighting the veneer of servitude that persists in domestic service relations.

Articles, interviews and programs about this subject have appeared consistently in the mass media. A legal education radio program was broadcast for three months, and popular magazines have published articles about labor legislation. In additon, we have distributed pamphlets on labor regulations to patronas and others. By discussion of this project at national and international seminars and conferences, the research team has reached the professional community, social and community agencies, agencies working for change, and to other groups engaged in research–action projects.

Outreach to Legal Professionals

Serious legal problems of interpretation arise from the state of existing law and the from the limited rights of the domestic empleadas. This problem is further aggravated by the deeply rooted patriarchal ideology in professional communities which devalues the work performed by the domestic service sector. The specifics of the law as it relates to the domestic service sector are not taught in law faculties, or in individual labor law courses. The program's legal work has demonstrated that both practicing lawyers and students are unaware of the law's content and, worse still, of how to make the law operative on a mass level. Debate with legal professionals has been encouraged with a view to resolving these problems and enforcing the rights conferred by the law. Dispute about whether or not a body of law even exists has, to a large extent, been overcome and constitutes one of the most important victories of the program.

Actions at the Government Level

There is no government activity designated to respond to the empleadas' labor demands. Consequently, we have designed a series of actions to reform the legislation, to correct its interpretation, and to encourage further legislative activity.

Legislative Reform

One would think that the chances for changing legislation are next to impossible, given both the political structure of the government and the interests represented by those who manage the state apparatus. We, however, have tried to take advantage of all favorable circumstance to promote reform. The female deputy minister of labor from 1983-1984 shared and defended the interests of working women. During this period, we began to survey the most important aspects of the labor legislation in need of reform. Our basic goal was for domestic workers to achieve equal rights with other laborers. Unfortunately, this project languished due to the lack of governmental interest.

Corrective Interpretation and
Enforcement of Existing Legislation

Three basic actions have been developed. Firstly, because the Minister of Labor work inspector's interpretation of the law plays a fundamental role in the arbitration of conflicts between workers and employers, we have stressed both ideological and theoretical factors with this group of officials. We emphasize that legal interpretation does not hinge simply on points of law; patriarchal ideology, which devalues domestic service work, also comes into play.

Secondly, during 1985, the project campaigned to enroll empleadas in Social Security programs. Because there are no sanctions to enforce the existing law, and because enrollment procedures are very confusing, few empleadas are affiliated. Officials at the Social Security Institute say that their doors are always open for any patrona or empleada wishing to apply, but in practice one can say that it is a law that is obeyed but not enforced. Basic information about the procedures and potential benefits is contained in a leaflet prepared by our research team, and distributed to the participating patrona , and empleadas.

Thirdly, by taking an increasing number of our legal aid cases to the administrative tribunals and other structures, we sought to gain access to the government. Response to these initiatives has not been encouraging, and we believe that the government will continue to fail in its social responsibility to enforce the laws for the foreseeable future.

Problems of the Strategy

We will refer only to the problems we encountered about the empleada's personal situation, the patronal ideology and difficulties derived from the labor relation.

The Empleada's Personal Stituation

Some empleadas will not initiate labor claims at all, while others simply drop out of the process after making ther claims. Others do not see education in terms of specific rights as promising anything substantial. We have been resolving these problems gradually, especially in Bogota, where the activities are more developed. The high enrollment for the labor law workshop shows that empleadas who participated in the groups went on to become outreach workers.

Another problem is the frustration of the domestic workers in obtaining their rights after they are made aware of them. Equally, when the empleada begins to feel a sense of empowerment and to question her subordination, the clash between her newly found sense of power and her precarious socioeconomic situation may cause her to feel a loss of control over her life. The live-out empleada experiences this phenomenon more acutely because she must overcome considerable housing, health and recreational problems.

As long as there is a labor market for domestic service workers, an increase in class and gender awareness must be incorporated into a larger program for structural change. The alternative is to alleviate only individual situations and create slightly more pleasant living conditions for a few. It is crucial, therefore, to encourage empleadas to organize.

The Patronal Ideology

The ama de casa who is conscious of her own subordination is hostile to a project that defends empleadas. The amas de casas are very afraid of having claims initiated against them and argue that publicizing and working for the enforcement of legislation will raise unemployment rates because many well-off women would rather do things themselves than employ people with so many demands. These attitudes reflect the ideology of the patrona. Alternatively, once the patronal ideology is infused with reflection on their own subordination, complex attitudes and responses are released in the amas de casas. These range from political considerations implying new life-styles and concern for social justice concerns, to fear of being outside the law and to hiding behind classist ideology, refusing any type of concession or change, however insignificant.

Why the Labor Relation is Unclear

Because confusion surrounds the domestic service labor relation, difficulties arise when the attempt is made to enforce the law. Confusion arises because the relation is usually derived from a verbal contract, is affective and personal, and because fallacious arguments, such as considering the empleada to be a member of the family within moral law are adduced. This is why severance pay is usually calculated on an annual basis, and is neither retroactive nor cumulative; why interest is not paid regularly; why full vacation time is either denied or demanded by an empleada who may not yet have earned it; and finally, why she may be dismissed while pregnant. The problems are aggravated during the empleada's probationary period as contracts usually are verbal and the tribunal must weigh the patrona's word against the empleada's, thereby creating bitterness on both sides.

Lessons Learned

These fall into different categories, of which we will consider only four having broader application.

Legal Recognition

Progress has been made in the recognition of the empleadas' legal rights. This stage of development is to a great extent over, and the work is being consolidated among legal professionals. Patronas are less receptive, and rather than presenting legal arguments, revert to emotional or paternalistic tactics. We try to counter these tactics by defining inherent class and gender contradictions in terms of their patronal obligations.

The legal aid work has focused fundamentally on assuring empleada's their basic fringe benefits: severance pay, interest on severance pay, vacations, maternity leave and compensation for unjust dismissal. These elements do not exhaust the patronal obligations, however. Other aspects such as the obligation to provide medical attention during illness, vacation compensation, or double pay for work during holidays are more difficult to enforce. We use these claims in the negotiation process which promotes the recognition of patronal obligations and an altered mentality about these practices.

Legal Assistance as a Point of Departure

Legal assistance is provided to the empleadas as an integral part of the and not as an act of charity. It is a tool for personal and social change.

Mobilizing the Sector for Organization

Despite the empleadas' social conditions of isolation, alienation and work, they can be mobilized and organized if the proper methods are used. Appropriate activities can satisfy individual material demands; and by reshaping gender and class consciousness, they can motivate the sector to organize.

Actions in Search of Wider Change

Work on the issue of domestic service outside the context of its relation to domestic labor would be incomplete. The actions described in this paper are strategies to demystify the situation in which domestic empleadas are subordinated and exploited, and to stimulate collective activities that will lead to organization. At the same time, we are working with the ama de casa in her double role: as the patrona who represents the opposite pole in the labor relation, she is urged to comply with her contractual obligations; as a woman subject to the social subordination imposed on her by the assignment of domestic labor, she is stimulated to develop gender awareness.

It is extremely complex work to design actions that lead to a sense of the inherent class contradictions in the empleada's labor relation, while instilling gender awareness in both the empleadas and amas de casa. At the same time however, both are able to translate their newfound awareness into a search for wider change that will eventually dismantle classist and patriarchal social structures.

Dr. Magdalena León, a noted sociologist and researcher on women's issues in Latin America, is director of the program about which she writes in this article.

Indonesia:
Female Migrant Workers in Saudi Arabia
Amartiwi M. Saleh

Overview

The Legal Aid Institute in Indonesia has aimed to assist the poor who need legal assistance. Through experience, however, it has recognized that this assistance is inadequate. Too many of its clients have depended on the Legal Aid Institute to solve their problems. They have not actively participated in the process of addressing their situation. Therefore, this form of legal assistance is not sufficient in the long-term. The institute believes that it must improve its services by providing structural legal assistance: it must educate its clients to participate in their own problem-solving and to struggle for their rights.

Both individuals and groups have come to the institute for help in redressing unfair treatment. Most have viewed their problems as isolated cases; they have not linked their poverty and ill-treatment with the structure of the system. Without an awareness of the system and a strong desire to alter the structure, they will never be able to escape the debilitating conditions of poverty and discrimination.

A main objective in implementing structural legal aid is the development of awareness in order to build a more just and equitable society It also seeks to create power resources in the periphery to face oppression in the center. Structural legal aid connotes a struggle to implement legislation that will alter the balance of forces to bring about a more just structure. The structure must guarantee equality in law. Such egalitarianism must also be realized in the economic and political areas. Hence, development and legal reform, as seen from the structural legal aid aspect, must be carried out in the context of the realization of a just and prosperous society. Such work cannot be accomplished in a short period of time. It is a long-term program that requires diligence and patience.

In an effort to promote structural legal assistance for Indonesian women, I am providing a case study Indonesian women migrating to Saudi Arabia as contract workers.

Women Guestworkers in Saudi Arabia

As in the case of many countries, Indonesia has to cope with unemployment. Although Indonesia is industrialized, industry has not absorbed the available labor force. The establishment of large factories financed by foreign capital has contributed to this problem. Often these big factories destroy the economic viability of smaller ones, increasing the number of unemployed every year.

In the past few years, opportunities have opened up for women to work in Saudi Arabia. The majority of them are offered jobs as household assistants. These women sign a two-year contract and receive a salary of approximately US $150 per month. While housemaids in Indonesia do not earn as much, these women must leave their homes, husbands, and children to work abroad. Moreover, the standard salary of $150 is not commensurate with the extensive services, long hours, and sacrifices required of these women.

As a result of the large demand for female workers in Saudi Arabia, many companies have been established to supply these needs. At first, little attention was given to the arrangements of these developing enterprises. The problems became apparent after reports and rumors were spread about the terrible conditions under which many of these women lived. Women complained of excessive work loads, little rest, abuse, and even rape. A number of these women workers gradually returned before their contracts were completed because they could not endure the treatment they experienced from their employers.

Clearly, there exists a problem of the Indonesian female guestworkers in Saudi Arabia. The *Saudi Gazette* has entered the discussion. In its March 7, 1984 issue, the Gazette discussed this problem in an article entitled, "Maid or Slave?" The debate over this issue finds proponents on both sides. Those who support the supply of female workers to Saudi Arabia claim that it reduces the number of unemployed in Indonesia; it brings in foreign exchange; and a job in Saudi Arabia is preferable to unemployment in Indonesia.

Supporters often deny that these women are badly treated. They note that the number of those who return before the expiration of their contracts is small. Thousands remain in Saudi Arabia. Others have charged that it is impossible to assess what is actually happening to these women. Only when a large number of them return to Indonesia will some of the truth emerge.

Those who oppose the migration of Indonesian female workers to Saudi Arabia argue that it reduces the women's and the nation's dignity; they note that no protection is provided for these women; finally, opponents say it is not acceptable for women—from a religious viewpoint—to leave their homes and families.

Although this issue has created controversy, many women are still interested in working in Saudi Arabia. In fact, reports indicate that there are approximately 35,000 Indonesian women working in Saudi Arabia. They are attracted by the hope of being able to save a lot of money and of making the pilgrimage to Mecca at the expense of the employer (which is provided for in the contract).

Many of these workers are married women and have children. They leave their husbands and children to provide money for their families. Most are fairly emancipated since they dare to leave their families to go to a strange land with strange habits, language, culture, and customs. They are poor, often illiterate, and do not know Arabic or English (or even the Indonesian national language very well). Nor do they know what, if any, type of social support network exists in Saudi Arabia. The only thing they know for certain is they are going to have a Moslem boss. In spite of all these constraints, many women are even prepared to pay a large fee to brokers to recruit them due to the lure of money.

Those who oppose the supply of women to Saudi Arabia have filed a request to the Indonesian government to ban all such activities. Others claim that if a prohibition existed, many would still go there illegally. It would, therefore, create a worse situation as the women would have no protection at all.

A similar situation has been experienced by Sri Lankan women working in the Middle East. A Sri Lankan newspaper reported the following account:

I have seen and heard of several tragedies that had befallen the babysitter housemaids who left for the Middle East with great expectations, not of marrying the master of the house, but of earning and saving what to most in their poverty appeared to be a forturne

Several have had to return at their own expense, before expiry of the usual two year contract, because the lady of the house made their life miserable; the master thought he had not only hired a babysitter, but a concubine, and finally, the adult sons thought of the babysitter as a plaything for the adult babies.

The blame for this is not only on the Middle East employer, but should be shared by the employment agencies in Sri Lanka and their agents in the Middle East. Most agencies in the Middle East deal with these women as mere merchandise in a business that is nothing more than slavery.

The contracts between the agents and women (and not between workers and employers) provide no protection whatsoever for the women workers. Their contractual relationship is one between the powerful and the powerless: it always favors the agent at the expense of the woman. Because the agents receive a $300 recruiting fee from an employer, they generally favor the employer's point of view. However, the fees that some women pay these agents do not seem to ameliorate their working conditions in Saudi Arabia. The contracts do not specify the working conditions—e.g., the number of hours per day, holidays, sick leave, or other types of compensation. These workers must agree to carry out all duties efficiently and responsibly. In contrast, there are no sanctions against employers who change the conditions of employment. The employers have total rights and control over the women workers.

The contracts always contain one notable provision: the employer will bear all the expenses for the women workers to make a pilgrimage to Mecca during the period of her employment. This article attracts many of these workers, but it does not make legal provisions for its implementation. For example, to whom does the worker complain to, if the employer refuses to grant her a leave of absence to go to Mecca?

Because most of these women are totally ignorant about the law, they rarely question the terms of the contracts. They sign them with little or no hesitation.

Women come to the Legal Aid Institute for its assistance after they have returned from Saudi Arabia with complaints of exploitation. If they had consulted the institute before leaving, they would have received some warnings and helpful advice.

The institute would also provide assistance to these women in negotiating a fair and protective labor agreement with the recruiters. Moreover, it would attempt to take legal steps to protect the women by sanctioning employers who take advantage of them.

We hope that by bringing this issue to this forum, we can forge closer relationships with international women's organizations and learn from the experiences of others in solving their problems. If women's organizations exist in Saudi Arabia, we would like to work with them on this serious problem. In fact, women's organizations from all countries involved in supplying women guestworkers to Saudi Arabia should cooperate with Saudi women to reduce the exploitation and abuse of these workers.

Amartiwi M. Saleh is Director of the Bandung Legal Aid Institute in Bandung, Indonesia.

Honduras:
Legal Assistance to a Workers' Group
Alba de Quesada
Mirna de Zaldaña
Violeta Martínez

Overview

The Center for Legal Services (CLS) of the Federation of Honduran Women's Associations (FAFH) received in August, 1982, a request to help a group of women workers in the tobacco industry to resolve specific labor problems facing them at that time. The issues were non-payment of two month's salary and probable suspension.

Process

The following facts set the working situation of the women. Firstly, the company was unable to introduce into the country a specific process to cure the tobacco leaves. Secondly, the company did not have sufficient materials to permit the women to work regularly. Finally, there was growing anxiety about future economic resources to meet daily production requirements. The women initiated requests for legal and social assistance from the Center for Legal Services and from social workers at the Women's Division of Social Security Management in the Ministry of Labor, who suggested that they obtain help from the CLS.

Focus

To implement this particular strategy, the center used cultural, structural, and legal approaches. Some of the women's rights had been violated many times by the union under direction of officials in the capital. Because the women tobacco workers were unaware of (or had ignored) their labor rights despite their union membership, the CLS initiated an educational process, consisting of discussions and group study. Individual defense was used by leaders of the group in three loan cases. At the collective level, a council was established to inform the women of their rights and to formulate a series of steps to guarantee these rights.

Initially, the strategy concentrated on labor issues, specifically the payment of salaries and labor loans. Subsequently, it focused on the introduction of domestic legislation to raise the consciousness of women about personal identity and inter-family relations. It also taught them how to obtain credit to finance the initiation of productive jobs.

The first stage of the strategy involved the pressuring of the company to pay the delayed wages. To do this, the center worked with the labor inspector until it obtained the salaries. This process was occurring while the company continued its suspension of the workers. During this period, the center established an informational program for the women. It explained their rights and organized them into smaller groups to discuss their labor problems in detail. Interestingly, the company's male workers who held similar positions as the women asked to join the groups and to participate in the struggle. Some of the women agreed to compromise about the settlement with the company due to the influence of their families or to their urgent needs. These settlements were loans provided by the company; unfortunately, the amounts were smaller than originally demanded. Subsequently, the contracts of most of the women were terminated. In addition, the company discontinued its production activities in this area.

Motivated by the ruin of the company, the CLS organized a course on legal education and women's advancement. In this course, the women discussed and analyzed their socioeconomic problems at the individual and community levels to help them in their search for alternative forms of employment. Some of the unemployed established—with the help of volunteers from the U.S. Peace Corps—bird breeding, gardening, and beekeeping enterprises on their small landholdings—usually, a quarter to a half an acre.

After carrying out a feasibility study, the center also helped the women organize sewing and handicraft training, which was supported by the Ministry of Labor. Furthermore, those who owned ovens were provided start-up capital to establish a cottage industry of breadmaking, a product in great demand in Tegucigalpa.

Results

The major result was the company's action in canceling its wage-debts. Further, the company gave loans to eighty-nine women. When the problem was resolved, the majority returned to their jobs. While fifty-seven of them were rehired under similar conditions, the remainder obtained arrangements that were less beneficial. Women learned that they are as important as men and that they cannot fight in isolation. All of the women attended courses, and many of the women want their daughters to enroll in the center's educational courses.

The legal and functional illiteracy of the women hindered their participation in, and the implementation of, the strategy. Furthermore, the project ecountered the prejudicial attitudes of many men, whether they were husbands, family members, or friends. These men feared that their female companions would become more knowledgeable than they. As a result, we recognized that we must open our doors to men.

When the company—which had dissolved its productive activities—reopened two cigar and cigarette wrapping units, fifty-seven women chose to return to the factory rather than to struggle for new employment. They were influenced by their clergymen, husbands, and male companions to return to the company. The strategy, nevertheless, helped the women change their attitudes in confronting their socioeconomic problems.

Lessons

One manifest lesson was the hostile response of company management towards the women leaders of the movement. For example, CLS workers encountered difficulties in entering the site of the labor conflict. From these experiences we concluded that legal problems never can be tackled in isolation from the social situation. Thus, women workers must be encouraged to strengthen their resolve and solidarity to confront their problems. On our part, we must offer theoretical and practical courses in order that women can find productive employment and apply their theoretical knowledge. Also, we must coordinate activities with union officials to avoid duplicating efforts. Finally, we learned that the government can function as an ally; we obtained the cooperation of the Labor Inspector and

Social Security Management to pressure the company into paying the women's wages.

Alba de Quesada, Mirna de Zaldaña, and Violeta Martínez are lawyers working with the Federation of Honduran Women's Associations (FAFH).

Peru:
Women Workers and the Law
Luz Elena Jara

Introduction

In 1982, approximately 25% of Peru's 5,958,000 work force were women. Women earn roughly one-half of that of men. Labor laws heavily regulate working conditions for women. For example, women are prohibited from working past 10 P.M. and on Sundays and holidays. Nor are women permitted to stand on their feet all day. Businesses that employ over twenty-five women must provide day care for the women's children and allow breaks to feed their babies. However, these rights are rarely enforced because of women's lack of awareness about the labor regulations and because of the effects of modernization on production, which require cheap, submissive and unskilled women laborers.

Women's jobs and working conditions reflect the isolation, discrimination, and extra-exploitation they suffer. Their status as working women is often a source of discrimination. Society assumes that women should not work outside the home; and only those forced by economic circumstances do so. However, such work contributes to the greater independence and security of women.

Overview

The Center for Legal Assistance, Research and Training (CICAL) seeks to promote awareness and defend women's rights, to strengthen women's labor organizations, and to encourage women's participation in activities pertaining to the improvement of their conditions in the work force. It has designed and implemented a training program to meet these aims.

Numerous problems and issues are encountered in the legal counseling and the representation of women workers. A major problem faced by women workers is discriminatory treatment by employers and male workers.

Female labor issues are also perceived as having minor importance in comparison to collective workers' issues such as struggles for unionization or the composition of the *Pliego de Reclamos* (list of demands). Other difficulties are caused by the subjective view of many women about the nature of their labor problems. Frequently, women do not see them as structural problems, but rather as personal differences with the boss or fellow workers. Moreover, women often depend on male relations to resolve their various labor matters.

Female labor union members are frequently treated unequally or ignored. As a result, women are not active in the movement. In some cases, they are deterred from actively participating in the union because of pressures from the family or from their fellow workers. We have seen that the most aware and active women workers are attacked by accusations of being unfeminine or licentious in their personal conduct. There are few women leaders who are able to overcome this hostility and win respect and solidarity. Such personal attacks against women activists are very characteristic of the manufacturing sector, but much less so in government employment (perhaps because women government workers have more professional training, *etc.*).

Peru's economic crisis has resulted in many women workers

reverting to a more passive role. Fewer are actively struggling for better working and living conditions. Furthermore, the activist role assumed by some women workers has led them to imitate male behavior in organized labor (inefficiency, labor-boss domination, absence of democratic union practices, *etc*.).

Focus

We developed a systematic and clearly defined program to improve the conditions of women workers. Firstly, we decided to provide services only to women who work for a business, a work center, or independently (*e.g.*, street vendors or *Clubes de Madres* [Mother's Clubs]), and who have few resources to defend themselves adequately.

Secondly, we chose to take only labor cases (*e.g.*, cases involving reinstatement, harassment, failure to comply with laws or agreements), and civil cases (*e.g.*, separations, divorces, alimony, custody, wills, social security pensions, birth certification, *etc*.).

Thirdly, we recognized that it is not possible to change conditions or reduce discrimination by legal means alone. We must coordinate with sociologists, psychologists, economists, and others to analyze the particular situation of women workers and to promote and support their interests.

Fourthly, we adopted a legal counseling system closely linked with personal and group training. Each staff member is thoroughly familiar with legal methods. They teach the clients the legal procedures and alternatives of various cases and situations. This form of counseling allows us not only to inform, but also to train, which will have an important multiplier effect. Furthermore, the teaching and training, undertaken jointly with other institutions, provides opportunities to analyze the relative importance and content of legal norms. Hence, clients are able to determine the need to maintain, derogate, or improve the norms and laws.

We offer professional legal services, and include economists, accountants and other professionals in preparing cases, but we also defend women through less traditional approaches. For example, a 45-year old woman came to us for assistance in drafting a letter of resignation. We inquired about the circumstances and learned that her boss had harassed her about being less efficient than younger workers and had demanded her resignation. After describing all the events to us, she realized that the boss simply wanted to avoid paying mandatory social benefits for laid-off workers. Rather than resign, she initiated a summary grievance process which would allow her to leave her job but maintain benefits.

The woman worker subjected to labor abuse receives our commitment to defend her and also our support to help her face an employer's unlawful actions. Thus, the legal counselor and the client share responsibility for resolving the case which imparts a sense of self-esteem and security to the worker.

We have initiated a specific methodology in our approach to women's labor grievances. Initially, we notify an employer through a letter or other out-of-court channels, asking them to respect the rights of our client and to discontinue their legal violations. In some cases, this action resolves the situation, particularly when the problems are not very serious and do not involve major economic ramifications. When it is not resolved at this stage, this notification serves as evidence of the deliberate refusal of the employer to comply with the law and of our initial intention to resolve the matter through extra-legal means. In the worst cases, it has frequently caused employers to be wary about committing the same infraction, as they know that it will generate a protest from the workers and constitute a precedent for future conflicts.

We maintain that labor violations of legal labor agreements should be handled by the union organization (when it exists), whereby the woman worker actively participates in the process. When there is no union, CICAL aided by the client, demonstrates the collective relevance of the case to obtain consensus support from the women. This action helps to slow down, if not stop, the infractions.

We urge our clients to participate actively in all legal proceedings so that they will learn about the legal system. In the beginning we represent them, but at later stages they play a decisive role in solving the conflict. If the clients lose their case, they understand why. Hence, they acquire experience in defending and gaining their rights.

In the matters of collective bargaining, unionizing, or enforcing the right to strike, labor activists receive special training before calling a strike: This training seminar covers legal, labor, union, and economic issues. No collective bargaining negotiation is begun without an analysis of working conditions and a financial report on the company so that we can bargain with hard data. Moreover, no collective action is initiated without prior general consent and support of the workers. For example, the Clinica Italiana employees' union is all women. During this year's bargaining, they agreed to use numerous means—work stoppages, legal pressure, negotiations, etc.—to obtain their list of demands. This year, their demands were met in four months; while last year, it took the whole year.

When the individual or collective case is finalized, we urge the client to establish a permanent counseling agreement with CICAL. This service includes a monthly bulletin, written or oral responses to client inquiries, inclusion in the general training plan, and access to the services of an economist or accountant. This service provides essential and continuing support for all workers who belong to the system.

Results

No specific coordinated strategy of legal defense and counseling for women workers yet exists in Peru. Our own work is still at an incipient stage. There is, therefore, a great need to coordinate and cooperate with other organizations to improve substantially women's living and working conditions. Clearly, there is insufficient research, discussion, and debate about the problems of working women.

Nevertheless, during the last few years, we have systematized and differentiated our work as legal advisers to women workers. From the work summarized above, we can make several observations. Working women have specific labor problems which require separate legal treatment from general labor matters. They are different in nature due to the enduring discrimination and isolation of women, regardless of their contribution to and participation in the national economy.

Our work involving inspection reports and the presentation of complaints and petitions to civil or labor fora has been 70% effective in solving labor problems. The remaining portion reflects the significant political power of some public officials or the great economic power of many enterprises. This power is not effectively countered by a force of organized labor.

Despite the difficulties in defending their rights, women workers can resolve a labor dispute by obtaining support from co-workers and guidance from labor organizations.

The juridical aspect is important in empowering working women to defend their rights, but it is only one component of women's development. The roles of economics, sociology, and psychology are essential. In addition, labor training of women workers should contribute to social change, thereby overcoming the discrimination and isolation of women.

Labor law offers in and of itself an important field of action for women. Through labor law, women can express their interests and obtain the means to improve their living and working conditions. However, these objectives are difficult to achieve and they require much coordinated effort. Through collective bargaining, women find a channel to gain new and more extensive rights; it also provides them an opportunity to discuss management, administration, the division of labor, the nature and structure of production, and the uses of their own productive power.

The law regulates most aspects of everyday life, and it reflects specific interests. The political and social education of women workers will help them participate in the society at large. To date, Peruvian women have not won access to political power, precisely because of their embryonic stage of organization. Moreover, as a result of the struggle for basic working rights and higher wages, the issue of disenfranchisement has not been confronted openly by the women's labor sector. We must show society the importance of women in the labor force. We must also strive for political power so that women can adequately express themselves, obtain respect as women workers, and gain the right to determine the future of their lives, their families, and their country.

Luz Elena Jara works with the Center for Legal Assistance, Research, and Training (CICAL) in Lima, Peru.

Advocating for Land Rights

In the sole paper presented in this section, *Quintillan* documents an advocacy strategy to equip low-income women in the Philippines to secure land for housing. Specifically, the strategy focused on equipping women with the knowledge and skills needed to participate in community decision-making and negotiations to secure ownership and control of a disputed piece of land. While this is the only example of strategies focused on urban land acquisition, similar struggles are widespread throughout the Third World. The suggestions, therefore, contained in this particular study transcend its specific geographical context. Combining political and legal methods, community organizing, and legal literacy and services, the strategy included community legal education, collective action and mobilization, lobbying, pressuring government officials and agencies, training activists, and building grassroots organizations and networks. The paper shows the concrete ways in which the women's access to economic and political resources were increased.

The Philippines:
Legal Acquisition of Property
Emelina O. Quintillan

Overview

The strategy addresses the socioeconomic issue of unequal distribution of land in the Philippines and the problem faced by women of a poor fishing community in Toril, Davao City, in securing title to the property they occupy.

The strategy aims to empower low-income women by educating them about their rights and the available legal and socioeconomic resources to enable them to fully participate in community decision-making and in negotiations on securing ownership, title, and control of the land for housing.

Major activities that have been undertaken and continue are the following: establishing community legal education programs; undertaking collective action and mobilization; lobbying at policy-making levels; pressuring government officials and agencies; building effective grassroots organizations; training activists; and building networks.

Strategy

Since 1981, the Kahayag Foundation has been sponsoring consultations on "Alternative Law" to bring together various individuals and groups who have been using law to empower the poor. Some of the low-income women living on the shoreline of Lizada, Toril, Davao City, attended one of these consultations. In September, 1984, a typhoon destroyed the shanties of the fishing village where these women lived, forcing them to move to higher land. There they rebuilt their shanties. They were arrested and then released after a representative of the Ministry of Social Services and Development arrived and certified that they were, indeed, victims of the typhoon. These people later discovered that the land they moved to was owned by a banking corporation. Representatives from the Metropolitan District Command and the bank ordered the people to vacate the land immediately. The problem was that they had no other place to go. Soon after, they began meeting to search for solutions to their problem. A group of women from this community decided to confer with the branch manager of the bank to find out the possiblity of buying the land. However, the price and the terms of the payment were not feasible for the people in the poor fishing village.

The women sought the help of the Mindanao Development Center, a community development center run by priests and layworkers in the city slum area, and of the Kahayag Foundation. Both agencies referred them to the PILIPINA Legal Resources Center. PILIPINA wrote to the vice-president of the banking corporation in the head office in Manila about the people's problem. The women were told if they needed help in organizing and more legal information, the PILIPINA Legal Resources Center could provide them with assistance.

PILIPINA, then, got together with a trained grassroots organizer to study the case of the people of Lizada, Toril, and to determine the best approach. When the women from Lizada, Toril, returned to the Legal Resources Center with the news that the people of the community were eager to organize and to consult a lawyer, a meeting was scheduled.

The heads of the 231 families of this community and the community organizer discussed the land problem from morning until evening at the town hall near the area occupied by the people. At that time, attorney Quintillan explained in layperson's language the relevant laws that could be used for or against the people in their quest for land ownership. Various options and legal remedies were also presented to the people. This meeting was followed by an open forum. Because the discussion was led by women, the participants were more confident and were ensured equal opportunity to participate in the deliberations and to express their ideas.

The people finally opted to buy the land. They agreed to propose to the landowner to make installment payments through the formal representation of a lawyer from the PILIPINA Legal Resources Center. While formal discussions were underway with the top officials of the bank, the women continued mobilizing to pressure government officials and agencies to implement social welfare laws vis-à-vis the property rights of the owner.

The strategy and activities adopted to solve the

community's problem were formulated by the women of Lizada, Toril, as well as the community organizer, the lawyer, and the rest of the staff of the PILIPINA Legal Resources Center. The initiative came from the women of Lizada, Toril; the organizing and mobilizing skills were provided by a trained community organizer; the legal literacy and other necessary legal services were provided by the lawyers and the staff of the PILIPINA Legal Resources Center; and the linkage and network support was provided by the Kahayag Foundation.

Focus

The strategy used in this case is action-oriented and is focused on the cultural aspect of the legal system which restricts women's ability to provide for their personal and family needs. The activities were directed towards demystifying the law and establishing a more accessible legal system for women.

The socioeconomic and psycho-cultural condition of the women in the community dictated the appropriate approach. In a fishing community, women are left at home while men are at sea. The lack of security in their homes, the fear of being evicted, and the harassment of the landowners are more keenly felt by the women. Finding solutions to their land problem was, therefore, more imperative for the women. The strategy, however, had to be within their capabilities and resources. The women are on a minimum subsistence level and have had very little education.

In contrast, the laws are written in a foreign language (English), and traditional legal services are on a lawyer-client basis; they are also litigation-oriented and expensive. To enable the women in this particular community to use the legal system in their favor, they had to have knowledge of the relevant laws and an understanding of the legal system. Moreover, to be able to act on what they know, they had to have accessible alternative remedies. For more educational purposes, the women of Lizada, Toril were involved in almost all the procedures and activities undertaken by the PILIPINA Legal Resources Center concerning their problem. With their active participation, the community had the prerogative of deciding what course of action to take in every stage of the negotiations with the landowner. For a traditional lawyer, this process is tedious; but it is necessary if the aim is to minimize, if not completely eliminate, constraints that restrict women's development.

Legal Issues

The strategy in this case concentrates on basic human and civil rights, particularly property rights, social welfare and economic issues. The problem of the poor women of Lizada, Toril revolves around these issues.

On the one hand, the banking corporation was invoking its property rights over the land occupied by the subject community. On the other hand, the basic needs of the people of the community and the social welfare laws required fulfillment. The needs of the people and the failure of the government to implement the social welfare laws are basic socioeconomic issues that have to be resolved. The problem of the women began when the bank demanded that they vacate the land they were occupying and threatened to sue them for squatting (which has been made a criminal act) and to evict them. Because the threat of imprisonment and eviction was immediate, the strategy had to concentrate on legitimizing the occupation of the land by the women and their families. With the proposal from the community to buy the property and the intercession of government officials and agencies, the filing of a suit against the women and their families was precluded.

The problem of the women of Lizada, Toril was not just a simple case of acquiring land for the landless. It was also a problem of protecting the marginalized sector of society from the legal repercussions of acts against property which were necessary for their survival. The property rights of the bank, however, are unique. Banks in the Philippines are required by law to liquidate or dispose of their acquired real property assets within a period of five years. The land occupied by this particular community was an acquired asset of the bank which needed to be disposed. Hence, the people came up with the proposal to buy the land. Collective action and mobilization pressured government officials and implemented social welfare laws to facilitate the transfer of ownership from the bank that did not need the land to the people who were in dire need of a place to live.

Participation

The participants in the strategy activities included the women of Lizada, Toril, a community organizer, the complete staff of PILIPINA Legal Resources Center, and the Kahayag Foundation.

The activities of the strategy were planned collectively through constant consultations between the PILIPINA Legal Resources Center and the women of Lizada, Toril. The people of the community have formed an association, most of whose officers are women. Furthermore, the working committees of the association are headed mainly by women.

The women of Lizada, Toril mobilized the people in their community. The community organizer, who immersed herself in the community, linked the PILIPINA Legal Resources Center with the community. Hence, she disseminated information, received feedback, advised on non-legal matters, monitored the progress of the planned activities, and reported with the women to the PILIPINA Legal Resources Center. The PILIPINA Legal Resources Center provided a legal consultant for the people of Lizada, Toril and a lawyer to represent them at the bank's headquarters. The center helped organize women's consciousness-raising and community legal education seminars. The center also quiered people about their other problems. Finally, it documented all proceedings with the assistance of the community organizer and a representative from the women's group of Lizada, Toril. The community organizer and the PILIPINA Legal Resources Center staff translated relevant laws into a language understandable at the grassroots level.

The Kahayag Foundation played a supportive role in the purely legal aspect of the strategy. It, however, played a major role in providing linkage, networks, advocacy skills, and resources.

Results

The strategy, as planned, has been well implemented. It has deterred the bank from proceeding with its intended court action; it is now willing to negotiate with the people on the proposed purchase. The collective action of the people has drawn the attention of government officials to the plight of the people in Lizada, Toril, and they are being pressured to implement social welfare laws. An alternative plan was prepared: it requested the purchase of the land for the people. The agency's initial response was that it did not have funding for the project at that time. However, the city could be pressured to assume responsibility for this problem if the landowner refuses to sell the property to the people.

Therefore, the immediate aims of the strategy have been achieved. The legal literacy activity has had a tremendous impact on the confidence and motivation of the people. The understanding of the laws relevant to their problem has given them direction. The presence of the community organizer facilitated their activities. The initiative of the women of Lizada, Toril has led to the mobilization and collective action of the community.

The strategy has increased poor women's access to various resources. The PILIPINA Legal Resources Center has provided them with the needed legal services. They have benefited from the Kahayag Foundation's assistance in teaching employment skills and conducting consciousness-raising seminars. The theory-action approach of the PILIPINA Legal Literacy Program gave them the opportunity to negotiate with government officials who could help solve their problem. The fact that the community organizer, the lawyer, and the staff of the PILIPINA Legal Resources Center and most of the staff of the Kahayag Foundation are all women may have facilitated communication with the women of Lizada, Toril.

Through the constant discussion with the women of Lizada, Toril, and the monitoring by the community organizer, the strategy has been evaluated regularly in terms of its impact on the situation. The women have been taught to document their activities; they regularly submit progress reports to the PILIPINA Legal Resources Center.

While no discernible improvement in the general economic situation of the community is yet evident, the confidence, motivation, and resourcefulness of the people, particularly the women, have greatly improved. Negative attitudes, arising out of frustration and feelings of helplessness, have been overcome. Recently, however, reports have been received about the beginnings of intrigue among the community leaders which could lead to a split in the community organization if the situation remains unchecked. Having identified the problem, the community organizer is now working on strengthening and solidifying the grassroots organization before the intrigues could affect the whole strategy. The PILIPINA Legal Resources Center plans to involve women psychologists and social workers to assist the community organizer on this problem.

Lessons

The implementation of the strategy has been a concerted effort of deeply committed women who have donated their expertise. The strength of the strategy lies in the legal literacy program, which adopted the theory-action method, and in the effective organization of the grassroots. It is, however, limited by the lack of proper orientation and experience of the PILIPINA Legal Resources Center support staff, who are being exposed to this type of case for the first time. Since the traditional training of the law schools presents the law in isolation from the social and economic forces that affect its formulation and implementation, very few lawyers and law students have viewed it as an activist and developmental instrument. Hence, more lawyers and law students must be trained as activists. They must be educated about problems at the grassroots level and about women's issues.

Women may have access to the legal system because of the legal aid services offered by many lawyers' organizations. But access to the law does not necessarily mean access to justice. What is legal is not always just and equitable. Therefore, it is necessary that the legal system and the confronting problem be viewed in a holistic manner. Moreover, the aims must be clear. It is necessary to understand the attitudes, behavior, and needs of the beneficiaries of the legal system to plan effective activities. Monitoring activities is an important priority. The strategy, however, can only be effective if the people see it as necessary and relevant to the solution of their problems.

Emelina O. Quintillan, a lawyer, heads the PILIPINA Legal Resources Center.

PART IV

THE
NAIROBI MEETING
OF THE THIRD WORLD
FORUM ON
WOMEN, LAW, AND
DEVELOPMENT

Addresses
of
Dr. Nawal El Saadawi
and
Honorable Justice A.R. Jiagge

Dr. Nawal El Saadawi, Egypt

While I was on my way to this hall, I ran into friends going to a workshop on women and health. They said to me, "You are a medical doctor, you should be here, not there."

But that is just the point. I think that if women are to contribute to modern scientific thought, they must treat the gap between specialties. We were educated as doctors, as lawyers, as engineers, and with this split between different kinds of knowledge, we divided our head into different departments. We put law here, religion there, and separated technology, science, history, anthropology, and so on.

It is a tragedy because when I graduated from medical school, I felt that I hadn't learned much. Even my image of the human being was distorted because all of its components were set apart from each other. The body was divided into individual organs, the mind was divorced from the body, and the whole human being was totally isolated from society, history, religion, economics, and politics. Unless we study all these things, we are not going to understand why women are oppressed.

When I started to read history, I discovered that women had been oppressed not by a divine law, as my mother and my

403

grandmother had told me: "It's god that discriminated between you and your brother." I discovered it's not god, it's man-made. It's done by men, by people, by societies. We discovered that what we called natural law is not natural because nature did not make women inferior. That's why we should go beyond our specialities and study history, law, etc. That's why I'm here. I am not going to speak about law as a lawyer, but I would like to discuss how this law came into effect.

Who makes the law in our societies? Do women participate in making the laws? Do poor people participate in making the laws? No, it's the ruling system, a minority of men who own wealth and power who really make the law. This minority group who writes history also defines the value of scientific thought in medicine, in law.

I would like to discuss the concepts of equality, development, and peace because they are very much related to law. Law should be just, whether it is international law or national, or family, or personal. We cannot have peace without justice. Yet a powerful military machine is allowed to invade a country. Is this justice? Regarding development in the Third World, how can we develop our countries unless we control our resources, unless we have economic independence? But how can we have economic independence if we have an unjust international economic law? We have to make a link between international law and the other unjust laws that govern other domains of life. The international information law is also not just. We in the Third World, because of the media technology, are brainwashed by the culture of a few countries that have power and wealth. We cannot speak about justice without exposing these international economic, political, and military laws.

These unjust international laws are based on patriarchy and class. Patriarchy and class are reflected in every law that governs people, especially women, and particularly women in developing countries. We women in developing countries suffer from lack of democracy, we suffer from lack of freedom of thought. If you write a book, you can go to jail. When you make a speech, you can lose your job. This is not a common experience in the so-called "democratic" countries, which I would call "pseudo-democracies." Yet in most of the developing countries, we still don't even have a pseudo-democracy. For us, religion has a very big impact. Religion is not only in the political rooms, it is also in the bedrooms. We do not separate between religion and state, so whenever we have a resurgence of religious fundamentalism, it affects women. Women are the first victims.

One of the main characteristics of the patriarchal class system is injustice. They say law is just and they use the balance, the symbol of justice, to illustrate this, but I think the scale is not equal at all. There is injustice in every law because it's based on sex and class discrimination. You find this division and duality in economics and in personal life. In the family code, the man owns the woman, but the woman does not own the man. I'm not only speaking about the Arab countries; I'm speaking about almost every country: Christian, Muslim, Jewish, Buddhist—under all religions, women are inferior to their husbands. It is the husband's duty to provide for his wife, and it's her duty to obey him. It's more or less a master- slave relationship.

Changing the family code takes political power. Changing any law takes political power. In many countries, the labor laws are progressive because the working class fought for their rights. But women never had the political power to change the law, especially the family code. That's why you find that the most backward, the most unjust law in any country, is the family code. You find that the labor laws are much better for women. They say men and women are equal with regard to employment. This equality, this right that is given to women, is taken back in the family code which says that the husband can prevent his wife from working. Lately, due to a universal religious revival, societies are starting to make the family code more oppressive. You cannot separate politics and law. The powerful political groups in society change the laws. If women start to organize and have political power, then they can change the laws.

Women who do not have so-called "respectable" professions are also discriminated against. As a medical doctor or as a writer, I am respected. A lawyer, a judge is respected. But how about women who are forced through economic need to have professions, like prostitution, which are created by patriarchal societies? These women are discriminated against by the law. If you look at prostitution laws in many countries,

405

you find it is always the same. Man is innocent. Adam is innocent; Eve is responsible. They do the same act, but it's the woman who pays the price. In the laws, the man who practices sex with a prostitute is a "witness"; he is not punished. The profession was created by the patriarchal system through its laws, which forced monogamy on women but allowed men to be polygamous. Women are the victims; they are the ones punished. This is the philosophy of patriarchy—to punish the victim.

Honorable Justice Annie R. Jiagge, Ghana

A confidential report on human rights in the 1960s was, like all other confidential reports, considered in a closed session. The report stated that in the writer's country, when human heads were being counted, women and girls were excluded. Another report revealed that in the writer's country, it was lawful for a brother to kill a sister for defaming the family name and honor by committing adultery, but a brother did not forfeit his life for the same offense. Other confidential reports stressed the need for greater understanding of the human rights declaration to ensure that the declaration was accepted as applicable to men and women without distinction.

All over the world, women have at one time or the other been subjected to various forms of discrimination, sometimes under the guise of so-called "protection" and women on the whole have accepted such discrimination as privilege. Women have also accepted discrimination as justifiable on religious grounds. Women themselves are conditioned into thinking that there is only one way of life for them, only one means of fulfillment, and that is motherhood and homemaker. And so women have connived at the inferior status imposed on them and willingly submitted themselves to male domination.

When women started fighting for their rights, it was considered unnatural. In fact anything outside passive, modest, gentle, submissive, and demure behavior was condemned as not being feminine. Women fighting for the right to vote in the early years of this century were given stiff jail sentences, but the struggle continued.

At the time the United Nations was founded in San Francisco in 1945, only half the member states had extended the franchise or the power to vote to women. The UN Charter includes among its purposes, "the achievement of international cooperation in solving international problems of an economic, social, cultural, or humanitarian character and in promoting and encouraging respect for human rights and for fundamental freedom for all without distinction as to race, sex, language or religion." When the Commission on the Status of Women came into existence in June 1946, its mandate was to prepare recommendations and reports for the UN Economic and Social Council (ECOSOC) on promoting women's rights in political, economic, civil, social, and educational fields. The commission from its inception has worked steadily for the achievement of political rights for women in all countries. The commission considered as essential the possession of political rights as the means of securing other rights—political rights ensured participation in government, in legislature and the judiciary. The UN General Assembly in 1946 adopted Resolution 56: (1) calling on "All member states which have not already done so, to adopt measures necessary to fulfill the purposes and aims of the Charter in this respect by granting to women the same political rights as men."

In 1952, the UN General Assembly adopted the Convention on the Political Rights of Women providing that:

❑ Women shall be entitled to vote in all elections on equal terms with men without distinction.

❑ Women shall be eligible to all publicly elected bodies established by national law on equal terms with men without any discrimination.

❑ Women shall be entitled to hold public office and to exercise all public functions established by national law on equal terms with men without any discrimination.

The Commission on the Status of Women through ECOSOC requested the Secretary General of the United Nations to prepare annual reports on constitutions, electoral laws, and other instruments affecting political rights of women in all countries and to submit these reports to the General Assembly. Every year the Secretary General sent questionnaires to member states on these matters and presented the yearly reports compiled from the answers to the questionnaires. These soon began to indicate progressive reforms in national legislation to give effect to the political rights of women as spelled out in the Convention on Political Rights of Women.

The strategy of sending a yearly questionnaire to enquire about laws affecting the political rights of women, focused the attention of member states on the condition of women and influenced public opinion. This strategy had notable success because today, women in almost all member states of the UN have the right to vote. The new independent states in the 1960s incorporated into their national constitutions, substantial human rights provisions.

The strategy of a constant reminder of actions to be taken to conform with the provisions of the UN Charter and the Convention on Political Rights of Women worked, and discriminatory laws were amended, and more and more women took their seats in Parliament, served as cabinet ministers, judges of the superior courts, and several other posts that were not before accessible to women.

The constant focus on laws discriminatory against women is, in a way, education of public opinion. This strategy requires vigilance, perseverance, and dedication of women's groups to the removal of such laws. Women, as well as men of understanding, must endeavor to draw public attention to all discriminatory laws and seek their abolition. The mass media and other appropriate means of communication can play a vital part in educating public opinion. Hardly any government can effectively resist the pressure for change from well-informed sources which have the support of the majority. Organization is a necessary tool for this strategy.

In the early 1960s in independent Ghana, a bill was laid on the table in Parliament seeking in effect to abolish polygamy. There are two forms of marriage in Ghana—the monogamous marriage which is in accordance with statutory law, and the polygamous marriage conducted under customary law. The parties are free to choose one or the other form of marriage but not both. A person married under customary law loses the capacity to marry under the statutory provisions while the marriage under customary law exists. Any purported marriage under statutory law by a person already married under customary law while this marriage subsists, is void ab initio.

The bill before Parliament was to make all marriages monogamous. The intention was good and would have enhanced the status of women. The bill, however, made no provisions for the second, third, and fourth wives already married under customary law. The bill, if passed, would have deprived the second, third, and fourth wives of their marital status and turned all their children illegitimate.

When women of Ghana learned of the bill, they sought explanation about all the implications and realized that women married under customary law would suffer great injustice if the bill were passed as law. The women, making use of the political parties' organizational set-up, communicated with women all over the country. Women leaders met and planned a strategy to oppose the bill. On the day the bill was to be debated, women from all over the country descended on Accra and grouped themselves at the market, from where they marched on Parliament House beating on pots and pans and demanding the withdrawal of the bill. The bill was withdrawn and has since not seen the light of day. This strategy may seem unorthodox but it worked and provides some useful lessons: the importance of good communication links; the effectiveness of good organization, and; the determination to pursue a cause to a successful end.

Various factors go into the structure of a good strategy—a strategy that succeeds in one country may not necessarily succeed in another. Each case must be dealt with on its own merits, but women all over the world can learn from the experience of women in other countries, and can adopt and adapt, if necessary, a strategy that is appropriate to their situation.

Legislation is an important first step, but only a first step. Laws may be amended by simple words, but tradition can be modified only by radical changes in attitude, outlook, and behavior. Unless women know and understand the law, there cannot be meaningful awareness of the rights and liabilities created under the law. Therefore, good legislation must be accompanied by a strategy for educating women about their rights. When women realize what needs doing to improve their condition of life, when they appreciate that they themselves must act, then political maturity has begun. It is up to women to liberate themselves. There is hardly any example of oppressed people being freed by others, although outside help is useful. The real struggle is in the camp of the oppressed to free themselves and there are quite a few male allies anxious to help.

Take for instance the case of women in Southern Africa. Under customary law, women remain minors all their lives. Before marriage they are wards of their fathers, and after marriage the masculine authority over the woman is transferred to the husband. Women are not free to sue and be sued. They cannot transact any business in their own right. They cannot own nor inherit landed property and so on. During the battle for independence in Zimbabwe, the women played such a vital part to win the battle for freedom that it was inconceivable for them to remain minors all through life and so, in 1982, legislation abolished their status as minors and all women of age are free to transact business of any kind in their own capacity. But customary practices die hard, and the women of Zimbabwe are still struggling for equal rights with men in such areas as ownership and inheritance of landed property.

Legislation alone cannot abolish deep-rooted prejudice and structural obstacles. Years of domination by men have resulted in women underrating their own potential and thereby failing to undertake the necessary struggle to sharpen their own capabilities. In addition, women, especially those in the rural areas, are the custodians of tradition and custom and often hold onto these traditions and customs even though they are detrimental to their welfare. No strategy can succeed if women themselves are not motivated to remove the obstacles that impede their advancement.

In Ghana, a married woman is entitled to work, earn an income and use it for what she needs. Work is not only for economic necessity, but a fulfillment of a personal need. A personal income can boost a woman's self-made image and self-confidence. In the informal sector, women combine happily their role as mother and wife with some economic activity in self-employment. In the modern sector, a woman who works outside her home is forced to do a double day's work. In addition to her task at work, she must take opportunities available for training on the job to qualify for promotion. Her activities outside the home do not in any way minimize her workload at home. She is still responsible for housekeeping and looking after the husband and the children. These make very heavy demands on the woman.

The 1975 International Women's Year has brought solidarity among women in the struggle for their rights. However, we must sound a note of caution where customary practices and traditional attitudes are concerned. Some of these issues are linked with the culture of the people and better dealt with by the women living within a particular society. Women have to help women at the national level to overcome the many obstacles and be given the chance to prove themselves. However, the international solidarity of women is very important to help and inspire women who give up the struggle in the face of opposition, to exchange ideas and experiences, and build mutual confidence and respect and also learn from one another.

Report
and
Recommendations

State, Law, and Development

1. The nature of law in a given society is inextricably linked to the character of the state. Especially in developing countries where autonomous legal institutions have yet to take root, law cannot be separated from politics. Any understanding of law must be supplemented by political and economic analysis.

2. One cannot understand the issues of *state, law, and development* in Third World societies without reference to the international exploitative system. Problems such as foreign debt, unequal exchange, and multinational investment have made women's struggles increasingly difficult in the Third World. In fighting for their rights, women must join other forces in society struggling against exploitation at all levels.

Constitutional Issues

1. There was general agreement that throughout the UN Decade for Women, the principle of *equality between men and women* was formally enacted as a constitutional provision in many Third World countries. This was done either as part of a nationalist movement, as in India, as an aspect of social liberation, as in Nicaragua, or with the ratification of the Convention on the Elimination of All

413

Forms of Discrimination Against Women, as in Argentina and Bangladesh. A comparative analysis of constitutions of Arab states shows that, despite Islamic revivalist movements, the principle of equality between the sexes has been accepted as a constitutional norm in that region of the world as well.

2. Though formally acknowledged in the constitutions of the Third World, equality has not been achieved in fact and is not a part of the daily lives of most Third World women. Women's organizations throughout Latin America, Asia, and Africa have begun to devise various strategies to make equality real and relevant to the majority of women in these societies.

3. For many women, the search for equality during the past decade was part of the struggle for greater democratic rights within their society. For example, in Brazil, after pressure from women's organizations which played an active part in the struggle for democracy, the House of Representatives approved the project of a new civil code.

4. In other parts of the world, women's search for equality was part of social liberation struggles. In Nicaragua, after the revolution, women began to draft and lobby for just laws through large public meetings. As a result, they have managed to bring about constitutional and legislative changes in the civil code and in the mass media laws.

5. In some countries, women activists put pressure directly on the existing legal system, especially the courts, to bring about far-reaching changes. In India, for example, *open letter jurisdiction* allowed courts to entertain cases of oppression against women, such as dowry violence, rape, and women's remand home. Moreover, women activists have brought cases before the court in an attempt to challenge oppressive aspects of the family law.

6. In most countries, however, the equality clause of the constitution and ratification of the convention on discrimination have not been truly implemented. Women's rights have remained on paper, formal and meaningless. It is hoped that the next decade will ensure that these formal provisions become the living law, and as such, instruments for social change and social transformation which will result in true equality for women.

7. Many participants felt that during the next decade women should strive for the establishment of tribunals at the regional and international levels which would take an active interest in protecting the rights of women.

Development

1. Economic development programs generally have been discriminatory toward women because they assume men are heads of households and the primary producers in society. As a result, women are excluded from economic modernization, often being denied access to technical skills and credit facilities. Women's organizations have spent much of the decade attempting to remedy this imbalance in development planning.

2. Throughout the decade, it was assumed that development would be a benevolent process. However, economic structures of patriarchy, class, and race at national and international levels have ensured that women of the poorest classes reap the least benefit from the so-called development process. It is essential that these women be organized to acquire economic power and to use that power to assure that development leads to social transformation.

3. Though some participants felt that economic development is the key to the empowerment of women, the majority felt that women's strategies should be multi-pronged, *i.e.*, that consciousness-raising and organizing are vital components of any empowering processes and should, therefore, accompany economic development.

Land

1. Traditional patterns of landholding in many Third World

societies were often biased against women. Inheritance laws and systems of community property often ensured that women did not receive their due share. Thus, many campaigns in the Third World have centered around making the family law more equitable with regard to inheritance.

2. Modernization, especially in rural areas where land has been nationalized or sold to large companies, has resulted in hardships for women who have been primary producers in the agricultural sector. Women's organizations in Asia and Latin America have been organizing women to secure their legal property rights, thereby defending their right to livelihood. In the Philippines, women who have begun to organize themselves are squatting on their land to pressure the authorities to recognize their right to ownership. In India, women in the Chipko movement hugged trees which had provided them with firewood when bulldozers arrived to level the forest, forcing the authorities to reverse their decision to deforest the area. It is essential that women, in particular rural women, organize themselves and pressure patriarchial development organizations, which traditionally have been insensitive to the plight of poor rural women.

Family

1. Family law, especially when expressed as customary law, is generally weighted against women on the issues of divorce, property ownership, maintenance, and child custody.

2. Women's organizations during the last decade have pushed for amendments in family laws so as to remedy this imbalance. For example, in Kenya, new succession laws have been enacted; in Indonesia, new marriage laws have been passed; and in Zimbabwe, women's minor status has been elevated to that of major.

3. Though several countries have passed progressive laws and have made family law slightly more equitable, these actions are meaningless unless and until women are made aware of their newly acquired rights. Thus, women's organizations have become involved in fostering legal literacy. For example, Peru Mujer in Peru and the Women's Legal Services Project in Nepal have been actively engaged in legal liter-

acy schemes to educate women about their legal status and rights. The Family Law Centre in Nigeria, CESAP (Centro al Servicio de la Acción Popular) in Venezuela, and projects in Zimbabwe have been similarly engaged. In Vanuatu, in the Central Pacific, legal literacy has been connected to grassroots discussions on gaps in the law that could be amended. In the next decade, participants agreed, legal literacy will be a major goal of women in Third World countries. In addition, it was felt that law and legal clinics must not be the monopoly of lawyers, and that women must equip themselves to defend their own rights.

4. Though some participants felt that government cooperation is necessary for the success of these programs, the majority believe that autonomous women's organizations should take the initiative in organizing, designing, and planning such programs.

Labor

1. Occupations in which women are primarily engaged usually offer little protection in terms of labor rights. In addition, these occupations are devalued and are located at the lowest level of the wage structure. Women workers often are not organized and are, therefore, subject to greater exploitation, as is the case with women domestic laborers and others working in the informal sector.

2. The productive and reproductive value of the labor of unprotected women workers is either underestimated or ignored. The problem is compounded by the reluctance of women in some labor sectors, particularly domestic laborers, to organize themselves for fear of losing their jobs in conditions of high unemployment, as in Mauritius and Colombia. Nevertheless, some legal aid organizations and other concerned groups have been successful in encouraging women in such occupations to mobilize or unionize to confront issues which concern and affect them, and in sensitizing other women to these problems.

3. Women vendors in the informal sector are an important part of Third World social and economic reality. Once these women mobilize and unionize, they can gain greater dignity

for their occupations and ensure both a minimal level of monetary remuneration and reasonable working conditions. In India, women vendors have used their collective strength to articulate their demands to the state, which then responded by setting up facilities corresponding to their needs.

Custom, Law, and Ethnicity

1. Throughout the Third World, especially in Asia and Africa, there appears to be an ethnic revivalism, often connected to nationalism and national liberation movements. There has also been a resurgence of religious fundamentalism. These developments have become some of the most dynamic forces in Asia and North Africa.

2. Ethnic revivalism and religious fundamentalism have major implications for the status of women because it is in the area of family life and social relations that they are given maximum expression. They contribute to the duality in legal systems which reflects an artificial distinction between *public* and *personal* life, whereby laws with regard to public life grow and change with time, but laws and practices regarding personal life are stagnant, unchanging, and oppressive to women.

3. Ethnic minority women within a particular nation-state have special difficulties in demanding their rights because they do not wish to dilute and divide their group identity. Special strategies are necessary to help these women come to terms with both their ethnicity and their womanhood. It was noted that women members of minority communities remain tied to their traditions, while their sisters in countries where their community is a majority have begun to enjoy equal rights.

4. Ethnic revivalism and religious fundamentalism are phenomena yet to be understood by the disciplines of politics, economics, and law. Existing legal concepts, instititions, and strategies are not adequate to confront the many dilemmas of ethnicity and religiosity, especially with regard to the status of women. What is needed are strategies and concepts which will allow for diversity of cultural traditions without isolating fundamental human rights—such as the

rights of women. This is a major challenge for women in the next decade.

5. It was reiterated by many participants that religion, as a spiritual humanistic force, is not oppressive to women. Religious interpretation and practice, though, do discriminate against women. It is the latter aspect which must be challenged and transformed. However, some participants were of the belief that these practices are so closely linked to religion that only secular strategies will truly help women fight oppression.

6. Many participants felt that women in the next decade should strive for the formulation and enactment of uniform civil codes based on common values of justice and equality.

7. Some participants were of the belief that custom and customary law are reflections of men's desire to perpetuate their ownership of property and to control female sexuality. It was felt by these participants that even the modern family law and amendments suggested should be critically assessed as they are also generated by a capitalist, patriarchial order.

Custom and Customary Law

1. Several Third World countries, particularly those in Asia and Africa, have more than one body of law used in the implementation of justice. There is a body of *state law* or *general law*, and one or more bodies of *customary law*. The general law usually has its roots in those laws that were imposed on indigenous peoples by colonial powers, while customary law refers to that which was utilized in the pre-colonial era. Today, while the general law informs transactions in the so-called public sphere, customary law regulates interpersonal relationships and dynamics within the family. Since it is applied in matters of inheritance, divorce, and maintenance, for example, it affects women to a significant degree.

2. Initially, the colonizing powers usually permitted indigenous peoples to maintain their customary laws. Subsequently, they implanted their own sexist laws, particularly Roman-Dutch law, and labor markets which

419

took precedence over indigenous systems and undermined women's existing positions in society. Codes of indigenous law that were comparatively liberal toward women (for example, the Kandyan Sinhalese in Sri Lanka) were overridden by the strongly patriarchal legal systems of the imperialist powers.

3. In certain national contexts, customs and customary laws have affected women adversely. In many countries it is not usually acceptable for women to participate in activities of communal leadership, and social acceptance of male-dominated kinship hierarchies makes it difficult for women to attempt transformation of their position in society. In addition, customary laws of patrilineal inheritance, and marriage and divorce laws which favor men, deny women socioeconomic independence. Communities may tend to cling to customary practices by romanticizing them, or due to fear of change. While some customs, such as the communal ownership of land, may be beneficial to both women and men, it is necessary that communities find means of rejecting practices that are detrimental to women.

4. Women from indigenous minorities and tribal groups face special problems. They often must protect their livelihood, which is linked to the land in their traditional homelands. Kalinga women in the Philippines, for example, have been in the forefront of the struggle against attempts to divest them of their land rights, and have succeeded in making the authorities reverse their insensitive land policies.

Religion

1. It was generally accepted that religious traditions in their truly spiritual sense do not necessarily discriminate against women. However, religious interpretation and custom in certain localities have led to oppressive conditions for women living within particular religious traditions.

2. Ethnic revivalism and religious fundamentalism have often served to reinforce these practices which have relegated women to a subordinate position in society. For example, progressive laws, such as the family law in Pakistan, have

been threatened with repeal as a concession to fundamentalism.

3. Women's groups in some countries, however, have begun to
   organize effectively within religious traditions to forestall
   the repeal of just laws and to raise awareness of the true
   nature of rights to be enjoyed by women if the spirit of
   religion were accepted without distorted interpretation by
   men. They have done this by taking their battle to the
   courts, as in Pakistan, or by popularizing the issues of social
   justice, as in Bangladesh.

4. In other countries, where the state has made an explicit
   commitment to secularism, as in India, women are attempting
   to challenge religious practices that discriminate against
   them by invoking the equal protection clauses of their
   constitutions, which provide that all women, regardless of
   religion, should be treated alike. In addition, they have
   been pushing for a uniform civil code. The *secular* strategy is
   particularly effective in a multi-racial, multi-religious
   society.

Violence and Exploitation

1. Violence directed at women by men knows no boundaries—neither of age, caste, class, nor ethnicity. It takes
   the form of either physical mutilation and/or sexual
   aggression. Violence may be direct or indirect; it may be
   aimed at an individual or a group, or it may take the form of
   institu-tionalized violence, exploitative of the lower classes
   in particular.

2. While violence is universal, exploitation is particularly the
   lot of Third World women, due to a combination of
   oppressive forces—patriarchy, class, and race. The global
   economic system places a heavy burden on Third World
   nations in general, but it leaves women in these societies
   particularly vulnerable. Even in the family context, women's
   labor is exploited, as is their sexuality through pornography
   and prostitution. Hence, exploitation, a form of violence in
   itself, permeates nearly every aspect of life for Third World
   women.

Rape, Prostitution, and Domestic Violence

1. In discussing violence, the socioeconomic and political reality of the society under examination must be considered. Certain types of violence directed at women, such as battering, are not solely acts of aggression by an individual; they are a reflection of the power struggles in greater society.

2. Domestic violence, ranging from woman battering to conjugal rape, often tends to be underplayed because the patriarchal family is deemed sacrosanct and intervention by forces outside this unit is unacceptable. Society's condoning of such violent means of control has often left women with little support and few means of counteraction. Moreover, law itself tends to be dismissive of domestic violence. It was suggested that women work for the establishment of "battered homes" so that victims of this type of violence have a refuge and do not feel isolated.

3. Acts of violence range from genital mutilation and battering to rape and murder of women. They are basically attempts to control women's sexuality. While battering and rape are universal, genital mutilation and crimes of honor are relatively more culture-specific. Regarding rape and crimes of honor, legal systems, such as those in the Mediterranean countries, tend to further victimize the victim, while permitting the perpetrators of this violence, always men, either to go free or serve greatly mitigated sentences. Rape has been a weapon used in wars between nations, and in caste and class struggles. The rape of women of lower classes and castes by the powerful not only subjugates women, but attempts to humiliate the comparatively powerless men of these groups. It is also true that in certain contexts, women perpetrate violence against other women, such as in cases of dowry deaths in India.

4. Prostitution is a major problem in many of our countries where, due to economic deprivation, increasing numbers of women are resorting to exploiting their sexuality. Prostitution has been accentuated in recent years through certain forms of economic development, such as tourism. In some countries, such as the Philippines, organized sex tours,

a phenomenon emerging from the development process, have aided in exploiting women *en masse*, including children. Although society takes a condemnatory stand against prostitution, its condemnation is directed only toward the woman. This attitude is reflected in the laws, which weigh heavily against prostitutes, while permitting their clients to go free.

5. Several women's groups and legal organizations have mobilized against violence directed at women and the exploitation of their sexuality. However, to confront these issues effectively, groups must simultaneously address the political and economic conditions prevailing in their societies.

6. Pornography and the use of women as sexual commodities in the media must be combatted by women everywhere. The debasement of the female body is an affront to the dignity of women and constitutes the worst type of exploitation.

7. Many participants felt that penal codes are outdated and do not consider the new types of violence directed against women. For example, there is often no remedy against custodial rape, where the victim is supposedly under the protection of the law. Women throughout the world should push for changes in the laws so that they more adequately reflect contemporary social reality.

Workplace Exploitation

1. The past decade witnessed new economic developments in the Third World which are particularly exploitative of women's labor. One such development was the proliferation of Free Trade Zones, where multinationals invest capital, but rely on cheap labor to produce their goods for international markets. This new phase of the international capitalist system relies predominantly on female labor. Women are, in fact, the new industrial proletariat of the Third World. They are factory workers, laboring long hours for low wages. They are prevented by law or by coercion from organizing themselves into unions. During the next decade, women in Free Trade Zones should be mobilized and unionized to fight for and to defend their rights.

2. The women's decade also witnessed a large exodus of women domestic servants and unskilled laborers from their native countries, searching for opportunities in other parts of the world. Little attention has been paid to this situation, in which women are separated from their families and have to suffer difficulties due to ignorance of the customs of other societies. They are often the victims of international labor brokers who provide them with no protection and little security. During the next decade women should strive for international regulation which will prevent this type of exploitation.

3. Women's search for justice must be closely linked to labor's struggle for equality. The labor laws of any society are the most pertinent area of the laws for working women. It is essential that women lobby and struggle for changes in labor legislation which will protect their interests, as well as those of the larger working class.

Human Rights

1. Women in many Third World societies live in extremely repressive *national security states*, which resist even minimum expression of democratic rights. Even in societies deemed democratic, periods of emergency often result in large-scale violations of human rights. All participants felt that superpowers which support repressive regimes with military aid should be condemned. Women in such societies are politically oppressed and are, therefore, denied freedom to speak out against injustice. Those women who do, risk imprisonment and torture. Women's organizations throughout the world must show solidarity and support for women prisoners of conscience. The next decade should witness the establishment of an international commission so as to bring about international pressure in the eventuality of human rights violations directed against women.

2. Torture and cruel conditions of imprisonment are a reality for many women political activists in the Third World. Though the problem of torture is receiving worldwide attention, its effect on women, which is particularly devastating, is not fully addressed. The grave repercussions of torture go beyond

the individual, for the brutalization of a personality always results in the brutalization of society.

3. Women in many countries have realized that organizing around legal rights serves to raise awareness of human rights in general. It results in empowerment and political activism which makes women acutely sensitive to injustice. A *rights-conscious* women's movement will further the cause of justice in society as a whole.

4. Many participants pointed to the issue of large-scale deprivations of collective rights, such as the right to self-determination of ethnic groups and indigenous peoples. Women in these groups are especially vulnerable to human rights violations, and, as a result, suffer dual oppression—as women and as members of an ethnic group.

5. Most participants agreed that the question of political rights is integrally linked to the issues of poverty and exploitation. Individual political rights are only one part of the struggle for justice. They must be supplemented by an understanding of economic, social, and cultural rights. In societies where less than ten percent of the population owns eighty percent of the resources, where the unemployment rate is over twenty percent, and the minimum wage is below subsistence level, the struggle for women's rights must be part of the broader search for social justice.

Strategies for Collective Action

Successful strategies for the realization of women's rights during the past decade have fallen into three major categories:

- ◆ legal education and legal literacy
- ◆ legal aid
- ◆ law reform

1. Legal education strategies have involved setting up programs which:

- ◆ popularize the issue of women's rights by using booklets in the venacular language;
- ◆ train paralegals to work in communities and to educate

425

women about their rights;

◆ work with the mass media (television and radio) on education programs regarding the law;

◆ work with labor unions and community organizations to incorporate women's rights into their agendas.

2. **Legal aid strategies** usually have involved the establishment of legal aid and family law centers which give free legal advice to women, especially low-income women. In some parts of the world, the concept of *legal aid* is that of taking the law to the people. Lawyers and women activists, on a regular basis, visit remote villages and barrios, ascertain the problems of women living in those areas, and provide advice regarding possible courses of action.

3. National campaigns for **law reform** have been very successful in some countries, often focusing on traditional practices which are oppressive to women, such as dowry. In these cases, women have campaigned to pressure legislative bodies, staged sit-ins and demonstrations, and conducted plays and sing-ins in an effort to focus public attention on the need for effective legal remedies. In other cases, women have lobbied and used the media and other tactics to mobilize support and to influence lawmakers.

4. Each societal context poses particular problems to women, as well as its own set of parameters within which to work. Therefore, women have adapted the above strategies, emphasizing some more than others, to respond to their own situations. For example:

◆ In countries where trends have created a climate unfavorable for the exercise of women's rights, strategies of **vigilance** to safeguard legislated rights have been particularly important. In this context, women have had to organize to prevent existing rights from being taken away and/or to ensure proper application of laws protecting those rights.

◆ Many countries in the Third World are post-revolutionary societies living in the aftermath of armed struggle for national or social liberation. In these societies, the ideological force for equality which inspired the armed struggle created a favorable climate for women to secure their rights. However, women in these societies recognize that lasting changes in ideology require the transformation of societal attitudes and values. Their efforts, therefore, have focused on long-term strategies for **conscientization.**

5. With so many women's organizations working on women's rights, many groups were unaware of one another and therefore had not shared information and experiences. Increasing emphasis on **networking** has since ensured coordination and lack of duplication among these groups so that women's efforts toward justice can be maximized.

Future Direction

The last decade witnessed an upsurge of activity and the creation of a wide variety of women's organizations working toward the realization of women's rights. The vast majority of their strategies included one or more of the elements described above. The next decade requires women to build on and broaden these strategies of education, service, and reform, making them tools of empowerment for women. This is the goal for the upcoming decade: empowerment of women—so they can make law a truly effective instrument to further justice and equality for all women.

Recommendations

The Third World Forum on Women, Law, and Development, which concluded its week-long sesssions in Nairobi on July 18, 1985, decided by consensus to:

1. Establish an Emergency Committee of Third World Women for voicing concern about, and mobilizing world opinion against, any violations of the civil, legal, and human rights of women in Asia, Africa, and Latin America;

2. Work toward the establishment of an International Commission on Women's Rights which would:
   ◆ create a network of women's organizations throughout Asia, Africa, and Latin America to share information

and experiences about women's struggles for their rights in various parts of the Third World;

♦ formulate draft legislation on specific issues concerning women at regional and international levels. Specifically, the group expressed an urgent need to draft a uniform code on family relations which would articulate and protect fundamental rights for women *vis-à-vis* their position in the family;

♦ conduct research in areas of special concern to women in Asia, Africa, and Latin America;

3. Implement regional conferences which will bring together women's organizations in order to exchange information and share experiences with strategies addressing issues of women, law, and development, and to coordinate research and action at the regional level;

4. Launch a campaign entitled *Know Your Legal Rights* with the goal of empowering women throughout the Third World. Such a campaign would include:

♦ popularizing the language of the law by using mass media and other strategies to demystify the law and make it more accessible to the people;

♦ working toward an "alternative law," which maximizes women's rights and which is drawn from the language, reality, and experiences of the vast majority of Third World peoples, whose interests historically have been ignored.

NOTES

Introduction

1. For a more complete analysis of women in development approaches, see **Suggested Readings**. Of particular interest are: Jane Jaquette, Kathleen Staudt and Jane Jaquette, Carolyn Elliott.
2. For a discussion of public vs. private sphere ideology in law, see Diane Polan, "Toward a Theory of Law and Patriarchy," in *The Politics of Law: A Progressive Critique*, edited by David Kairys, (New York: Pantheon Books, 1982).
3. References for Alternative Law and Legal Resources approaches suggest publications of the International Center for Law and Development, New York.

1/ Approach: Conceptualizing and Exploring Issues and Strategies

1. The final report of the Third World Forum on Women, Law, and Development develops these themes in greater detail and links them with specific strategies being implemented.
2. *Webster's Dictionary.*
3. We acknowledge the existence of academic definitions of "strategy" that are different from our definition. However, since we are constrained by the need for a functional term capable of transcending particular usages, the term "strategy" will, therefore, be our preferred term and will be considered synonymous with the concepts of "program," "organizational response," *etc.*
4. Freidman, Lawrence M., "Legal Culture and Social Development," *Law and Society Review*, no. 4, 1973, pp. 29-44.
5. See Freire, Paulo, *Pedagogy of the Oppressed*, (New York: Seabury Press, 1978); *Education for Critical*

Consciousness, (New York: Seabury Press, 1973).
6. Upendra Baxi, quoted in "Report of the ESCAP/Marga Institute Expert Group Meeting on the Use of Experience in Participation/Law and Participation" (Bangkok: ESCAP, 1982).

2/Issues: The State, Law, and Development

India, Jethmalani
1. Robin Morgan, (ed.), *Sisterhood Is Global,* (New York: Anchor Press/Doubleday, 1984), pp.14-15.

Colombia, Velásquez
1. In Colombia, the last census was carried out in 1973. During that decade, urbanization (a product of the violence and poverty in the countryside), has transformed the character of the country. The rural population has declined from 61% to 30% of the total. (This data, collected in 1980 by the National Home Survey for seven cities at nineteen stations, represents only partial information.)
2. Abad Gómez Héctor, "It Happened in Amaga," *El Mundo,* July 9, 1983.
3. Calculated on the basis of tabulations from DANE. Taken from Norma Rubiano, "Elements for a Discussion on Discrimination of the Women's Labor Force in Economic Production," Bogotá, Buscando Caminos, 1982.

Sudan, Badri
1. M. Khidir, "Women's Participation in Agricultural Activities in Sudan" (unpublished Ph.D. thesis, 1981); Abdil Jalil, *Rural Women in Small-Scale Irrigated Agriculture* (1984).
2. *Khidir.*
3. This case study is based on an abstract of a 1983 study by A. Jalil and Umbada, "Rural Women in Small-Scale Irrigated Agriculture in the Case of Wadi Kutum." Kutum is located in western Sudan.
4. Jalil and Umbada. They and F. Barth (The Farm of Western Sudan, 1967) have clearly shown that high economic

participation of women is encouraged by a traditional
acceptance of women's work.

5. I. Fuad, *Ecological Imbalance in the Republic of the Sudan* (1984).

6. Figures below are taken from K. Afan, "On the Role of the Regions in the National Development of Sudan" (1984).

7. Sudan, Ministry of Finance, *The Economic Survey Yearbook*, 1982-1983.

8. *Ibid.*

9. Gassim Al-Said, *Off-Tenancy Activities of Tenants in the Rahad Scheme* (unpublished M.Sc. thesis, 1983).

10. *Ibid.*

11. Badri and Bashir, "Women, Education, and Development," *Proceedings of Population and Development in Sudan* (1982).

12. *Ibid.*

13. *Ibid.*

14. *Khidir.*

15. *Ibid.*

16. *Ibid.*

3/Custom, Religion, Ethnicity, and Law

Sri Lanka, Coomaraswamy

1. Susan Bourque and Kay B. Warren, *Women of the Andes, Patriarchy and Social Change in Two Peruvian Towns* (Ann Arbor: University of Michigan, 1984), p. 57.

2. Nawal El Saadawi, *The Hidden Face of Eve: Women in the Arab World* (London: Zed Press, 1980), p. 1.

3. Kumari Jayawardene, *Feminism and Nationalism in the Third World* (The Hague: ISS, 1982), pp. 15-17.

4. *Jayawardene*, pp. 77-103.

5. See Anthony Smith, *Theories of Nationalism* (London: Duckworth, 1983).

6. *Jayawardene*, pp. 137-151.

7. One of the demands of the Sikh separatist movement is the removal of legislation which gives married women individual property rights.

8. Madhu Kishwar and Ruth Vanita, eds., *In Search of Answers* (London: Zed Press), p. 14.

9. *Jayawardene*, p. 9.

10. *Bourque et al,* p. 132.
12. *El Saadawi,* p. 204.
13. Maria Rosa Cutrufelli, *Women of Africa, Roots Of Oppression* (London: Zed Press, 1983), p. 4.
14. *El Saadawi,* p. 93.
15. *El Saadawi,* pp. 93-100.
16. See Carmen Diana Deere, "Rural Women's Subsistence Production in the Capitalist Periphery," *Review of Radical Political Economics,* no. 8, 1976, pp. 9-18.
17. *Kishwar et al,* pp. 26, 28, 17.
18. *Kishwar et al,* p. 17.
19. For an interesting analysis, see Eleanor and Nash Leacock, "Ideology of Sex: Archetypes and Stereotypes," *Annals of the New York Academy of Sciences,* no. 288, 1977, p. 618.
20. See Ahmed Kharat, *The Status of Women in Islam* (Cairo: Dar El-Maarif, 1975).
21. See Shulamith Firestone, *The Dialectics of Sex* (London: Jonathan Cape, 1971).
22. See H.J. Hartmann, "The Unhappy Marriage of Marxism & Feminism: Towards a Progressive Union," *Capital and Class,* no. 8, pp. 1-33.
23. *Bourque et al,* p. 48.
24. See Asma El Dareer, *Woman,Why Do You Weep?: Circumcision and its Consequences* (London: Zed Press, 1982).
25. *El Saadawi,* p. 64.
26. *Kishwar et al,* p. 13.
27. *Cutrufelli,* p. 54.
28. G.P. Murdock and C. Provost, "Factors in the Division of Labor by Sex: Cross-Cultural Analysis," *Ethnology,* no. 12, 1973, pp. 203-225.
29. See E. Friedl, *Women and Men: An Anthropologist's View* (New York: Holt, Rinehart, & Winston, 1975).
30. See Flerida Romero, ed. *Women and the Law* (Manila: University of Philippines Law Center, 1983).
31. *Kishwar et al,* p. 13.
32. See C.S. Lakshmi, *The Face Behind The Mask: Women in Tamil Literature* (New Delhi: Vikas).
33. Maria Mies, *Indian Women and Patriarchy* (New Delhi:

Concept, 1980).
34. *Kishwar et al*, p. 47.

Pakistan, Patel
1. Pakistan Legal Decisions, 1983, Federal Shariat Court, p. 37.

Botswana, Molokomme
1. See Snyder: "Colonialism and Legal Form: the Creation of 'Customary Law' in Senegal," *Crime, Justice and Underdevelopment*, ed. Colin Sumner (London: Heinemann, 1982). This chapter contains a useful summary of various schools of thought on customary law.
2. "Toward a General Theory about African Law, Social Change and Development in the Individual Under African Law," Proceedings of the First All-Africa Law Conference, ed. P.N. Takirimbudde [no publishing data].
3. *ibid*.
4. *ibid*.
5. Isaac Schapera, *A Handbook of Tswana Land and Custom* (London: Frank Cass and Co., Ltd., 1938).
6. J. Kimble and A. Molokomme, "Gender and Politics in Botswana, Some Thoughts on the 1984 Elections," forthcoming workshop report.
7. *ibid*.

4/Violence and Exploitation

Sri Lanka, Tambiah
1. Asma El Dareer, *Woman, Why Do You Weep?: Circumcision and its Consequences* (London: Zed Press, 1982). See also: Nawal El Saadawi, *The Hidden Face of Eve: Women in the Arab World* (London: Zed Press, 1980; Boston: Beacon Press, 1982), pp. 33-43.
2. Kumari Jayawardene, "A Note on Violence Against Women," *Voice of Women*, Sri Lanka, no. 7, vol. 2, 1985, pp. 23-25.
3. Madhu Kishwar and Ruth Vanita, eds., *In Search of Answers: Indian Women's Voices from 'Manushi'*, (London: Zed Press, 1984), pp. 143-147, 158-161.
4. *Kishwar and Vanita*, pp. 154-155.

5. *Women Workers in the Free Trade Zone of Sri Lanka: A Survey,* (Colombo, Sri Lanka: Voice of Women Publication, no. 1, April 1983), pp. 63-70.

6. Yolla Polity Sharara, "Women and Politics in Lebanon," Miranda Davies, ed., *Third World, Second Sex: Women's Struggles and National Liberation,* (London: Zed Press, 1983), p. 27.

7. *El Saadawi,* p. 2.

8. Stree Shakti Sanghatana, "The War Against Rape: A Report from Karimnagar," in *Davies,* p. 199; *Kishwar and Vanita,* pp. 181-183.

9. *Kishwar and Vanita,* p. 135, 177-180.

10. Gita Sen, "Subordination and Sexual Control: A Comparative View of the Control of Women," *Review of Radical Political Economics,* New York, vol. 16, no. 1, Spring 1984, pp. 113-142.

11. *Kishwar and Vanita,* pp. 144-145, 162.

12. *Kishwar and Vanita,* pp. 186-195. "The Sad Plight of Iranian Women," *Bulletin,* (New Delhi, India: Center for Women's Development Studies), vol. 2, no. 2, November 1984.

13. Forum Against Rape, "The Anti-Rape Movement in India" in *Davies,* p. 182.

14. *Davies,* pp. 179-186.

15. "Holy War of Women in Lahore," *Voice of Women,* no. 7, pp. 3-5.

16. "Islamic Law in Pakistan Punishes Rape Victims," *Voice of Women,* no. 7, p. 38. See also: London Iranian Women's Liberation Group, "Iranian Women: The Struggle Since the Revolution" in *Davies,* pp. 151-155.

17. "Islamic Law" p. 38; and *Davies,* p. 151

18. *ibid.*

19. *Kishwar and Vanita,* pp. 203-207, 209-211, 213-216, 222-229.

20. "Dowry Deaths," Daily News (Sri Lanka), March 21, 1985.

21. "New Law to Check Dowry Deaths," *Daily News* (Sri Lanka), May 3, 1984, p. 7.

22. Manushi, "Indian Women Speak Out Against Dowry" in *Davies,* pp. 201-213.

23. A. Lin Neumann, "Hospitality Girls in the Philippines," Woman's Subordination: Asian Perspectives (Colombo,

Sri Lanka: Center for Society and Religion), *Logos*, vol. 20, no. 4, December 1981, pp. 70-76.

24. *Neumann*, pp. 78-79.

25. For example: *Women Workers of the Free Trade Zone of Sri Lanka: A Survey*, pp. 11-13; Committee for Asian Women, ed., *Tales of the Filipino Working Women* (Hong Kong, 1984).

26. A general assumption is that women are overly exploited, denied rights to organize, *etc.*, only in the FTZ's. In certain countries (*e.g.*, India and Sri Lanka), there is evidence that working conditions in factories outside the FTZ's are little better. While the work demand may be slightly less, the wage rates may also be less. Also a comparatively small number of women in industry are unionized outside the FTZ's and are, hence, likely to face similar disadvantages.

27. Bina Agarwal, "Women and Technological Change in Agriculture: The Asian and African Experience," paper presented at the Second National Conference on Women's Studies, Trivandrum, India, April 1984, forthcoming in *Technology & Rural Women: Conceptual and Empirical Issues*, ed., Iftikar Ahmed (Geneva: ILO).

28. *Agarwal*, p. 7.

29. *Agarwal*, pp. 8-10; *Kishwar and Vanita*, pp. 81-84.

30. *Agarwal*, pp. 41-42.

31. *Agarwal*, p. 40.

5/Educating and Organizing

Nicaragua, Vargas

1. Luisa Amanda Espinoza, *Women's Revolution Public Document*, (Managua: Association of Nicaraguan Women).

2. In developing a women's organization, we do not oppose the participation of women in a political party; on the contrary, we are in favor of it. The political militants will guarantee that the concerns of women are not overlooked by the party.

3. The feminist movement consists of women's organizations that work for emancipation in distinctive ways. We

distinguish among the following three movements: reformist feminist movements that fight within the existing structures of economic, political, and social exploitation (with a goal of legal equality for women); radical feminist movements that view women as a social class, hence, opposing men directly and denying the cooperative male-female relationship; and revolutionary feminism movements that combine the struggle for women's liberation with that of overcoming conditions of socioeconomic exploitation (which are found together in the majority of cases).

4. It should be noted that the group of women who will guide and lead the process of women's liberation will come from the marginal populations.

5. No organization begins with broad mass participation; usually, it is established by a relatively small group of people. Its structures must be transformed continually to allow new participants to integrate effectively and democratically.

6/Changing the Law

Zimbabwe, Kazembe

1. Joan May and Joyce Kazembe, paper presented at the Nairobi International Conference on Women and Development in Africa, September, 1984.

2. Funding for the project came from the USAID Human Rights Fund covering salaries and expenses of two research fellows, and from NOVIB, a Netherlands donor agency, compensating one research associate. All other expenses are borne by the Ford Foundation.

7/Advocating for Justice

Bolivia, Montaño

1. A proposal to establish a legal office for Bolivian women in poor areas of the country was approved by Bread for the World in December 1983. That organization provided almost U.S. $16,000 for the initial project.

SELECTED READINGS

I list here only resources that have been of use in making this book. This bibliography indicates a range of readings relevant to the study of women, law, and development.

Abu Nasr, Julinda. "Institute for Women's Studies in the Arab World." *International Supplement to the Women's Studies Quarterly 1* (January 1982): 15-18.

Barndt, Deborah. *Education and Social Change: A Photographic Study of Peru.* Kendall/Hunt Publishing Company, 1980.

Beneria, Lourdes, ed. *Women and Development, the Sexual Division of Labor in Rural Societies.* New York: Praeger, for the International Labour Office, 1982.

Bennett, Lynn. *Tradition and Change in the Legal Status of Women in Nepal.* Kathmandu, Nepal: Center for Economic Development and Administration, Tribhuvan University, 1979.

———. *Dangerous Wives and Sacred Sisters.* New York: Columbia University Press, 1983.

Black, Naomi and Ann Baker Cottrell, eds. *Women and World Change.* Beverly Hills and London: Sage Publications, 1981.

Blumberg, Rae L. *Stratification: Socioeconomic and Sexual Stratification.* Dubuque, Iowa: William C. Brown, 1978.

Boserup, Esther. *Woman's Role in Economic Development.* New York: St. Martin's Press, 1970.

Bourque, Susan and Kay B. Warren. "Female Participation, Perception and Power: An Examination of Two Andean Communities." In *Political Participation and the Poor,* edited by J. Booth & M. Seligson. New York: Holmes & Meier, 1979.

———. *Women of the Andes: Patriarchy and Change in Two Peruvian Towns.* Ann Arbor: University of Michigan, 1984.

Center for Women's Development Studies. "The Sad Plight of Iranian Women." *Bulletin 2*, no. 2 (November 1984).

Charlton, Sue Ellen M. *Women in Third World Development.* Boulder: Westview Press, 1984.

Chilcote, Ronald H. *Theories of Development and Underdevelopment.* Boulder: Westview Press, 1984.

Columbia Human Rights Law Review, ed. "Law and the Status of Women." *Columbia Human Rights Law Review* 8 (1977).

Comisión Interamericana de Mujeres. *Estudio Comparativo de la Legislación de los Países Americanos Respecto a la Mujer* (Serie Estudios No. 7, 1982). Washington, D.C.

Committee for Asian Women, ed. *Tales of the Filipino Working Women.* Hong Kong: Committee for Asian Women, 1984.

Cutrufelli, Maria Rosa. *Women of Africa, Roots of Oppression.* London: Zed Press, 1983.

Dalla Costa, Mariarosa, and Selma James. "The Power of Women and the Subversion of the Community." In *The Politics of Housework,* edited by Ellen Mallos. London: Allison and Bosby, 1980.

Davies, Miranda, ed. *Third World, Second Sex: Women's Struggles and National Liberation.* London: Zed Press, 1983.

Deere, Carmen Diana. "Rural Women's Subsistence Production in the Capitalist Periphery." *Review of Radical Political Economics 8* (1976): 9-18.

Dodd, David J., Paul Liebenson, and S. Rubin. "The Inter-American Legal Services Association: Promoting the Role of Law in Social Change in Latin America and the Caribbean." *Lawyer of the Americas: The University of Miami Journal of International Law 3* (Fall 1980): 533-572.

Economic and Social Commission for Asia and the Pacific. *Report of the ESCAP/Marga Institute Expert Group Meeting on the Use of Experience in Participation/Law and Participation.* Bangkok: ESCAP, 1982.

El Dareer, Asma. *Woman, Why Do You Weep?: Circumcision and its Consequences.* London: Zed Press, 1982.

El Saadawi, Nawal. *The Hidden Face of Eve: Women in the Arab World.* London: Zed Press, 1980; Boston: Beacon Press, 1982.

Elliott, Carolyn M. "Theories of Development: An Assessment." *Signs 3* (Fall 1977): 1-8.

Feldman, R. "Rural Women in Kenya." *Review of African Political Economy* 27/28 (1984).

Figueroa, Blanca G. *Incorporation of Women into Development Planning: Peru.* Lima: Asociación Peru-Mujer, 1983.

Forum Against Rape. "The Anti-Rape Movement in India." In *Third World, Second Sex: Women's Struggles and National Liberation,* edited by Miranda Davies. London: Zed Press, 1983.

Freidman, Lawrence M. "Legal Culture and Social Development." *Law and Society Review* 4 (1973): 29.

Freire, Paulo. "Cultural Action for Freedom." *Harvard Educational Review Monograph* 1 (1970).

———. *Education for Critical Consciousness.* New York: Seabury Press, 1973.

———. *Pedagogy of the Oppressed.* New York: Seabury Press, 1978.

Friedl, E. *Women and Men: An Anthropologist's View.* New York: Holt, Rinehart, & Winston, 1975.

Giele, Janet Zollinger and Audry Chapman Smock. *Women: Roles and Status in Eight Countries.* New York: John Wiley and Sons, 1977.

Huntington, Sue Ellen. "Issues in Women's Role in Economic Development: Critique and Alternatives." *Journal of Marriage and the Family* 37 (November 1975): 1008.

International Center for Law in Development. *Working Paper on a Three-Year Program.* New York: Author, 1983.

International Labor Organization. *Employment, Incomes and Equality.* Geneva: ILO, 1972.

Jahan, Rounaq and Hanna Papanek. *Women and Development:*

Perspectives from South and Southeast Asia. Dacca: Bangladesh Institute of Law and International Affairs, 1979.

Jaquette, Jane. "Women and Modernization Theory: A Decade of Criticism." *World Politics* 3 (Winter 1982): 267-284.

Jayawardene, Kumari. *Feminism and Nationalism in the Third World.* The Hague: ISS, 1982.

————. "A Note on Violence Against Women." *Voice of Women* 2, no. 7 (1985): 23-25.

Kairys, David, ed. *The Politics of Law: A Progressive Critique.* New York: Pantheon Books, 1982.

Kishwar, Madhu and Ruth Vanita, eds. *In Search of Answers: Indian Women's Voices from "Manushi."* London: Zed Press, 1984.

Lappe, Frances M., Joseph Collins, and D. Kinley. *Aid as Obstacle.* San Francisco: Institute for Food and Development Policy, 1980.

Leacock, Eleanor. "Introduction." In *The Origin of the Family, Private Property, and the State,* by Frederick Engels. New York: International Publishers, 1972.

Leacock, Eleanor and June Nash. "Ideology of Sex: Archetypes and Stereotypes." *Annals of the New York Academy of Sciences* 288 (1977): 618.

Lindsey, Beverly. *Comparative Perspectives of Third World Women: The Impact of Race, Sex, and Class.* New York: Praeger, 1980.

Lynch. "Lawyers in Colombia: Perspectives on the Organization and Allocation of Legal Services." *Texas International Law Journal* 13 (1978): 199.

Mies, Maria. *Indian Women and Patriarchy.* New Delhi: Concept, 1980.

Miller, Valerie. *Between Struggle and Hope: The Nicaraguan Literacy Campaign.* Boulder: Westview Press, 1985.

Morgan, Robin, ed. *Sisterhood is Global.* New York: Anchor Books/Doubleday, 1984.

Murdock, G. P. and C. Provost. "Factors in the Division of Labor by Sex: Cross-Cultural Analysis." *Ethnology* 12 (1973): 203-225.

Nader, Laura and H. F. Todd, Jr. *The Disputing Process—Law in Ten Societies.* New York: Columbia University Press, 1978.

Nash, June. "Critique of Social Science Roles." In *Sex and Class in Latin America,* edited by June Nash & Helen Safa. Massachusetts: Bergin & Garvey Publishers, 1980.

Neumann, A. Lin. "Hospitality Girls in the Philippines." *Woman's Subordination: Asian Perspectives.* Colombo, Sri Lanka: Center for Society and Religion; *Logos* 20, no. 4 (December 1981): 70-76.

Newland, Kathleen. *The Sisterhood of Man.* New York: W. W. Norton & Company, 1979.

————. *Men, Women, and the Division of Labor.* Worldwatch Paper 37 (May 1980).

Obbo, Christine. *African Women: Their Struggle for Economic Independence.* London: Zed Press, 1980.

Paul, James N. and Clarence J. Dias. *The Importance of Legal Resources in Strategies for the Rural Poor in Sub-Saharan Africa.* New York: International Center for Law in Development, 1983.

Polan, Diane. "Toward a Theory of Law and Patriarchy." In *The Politics of Law: A Progressive Critique,* edited by David Kairys. New York: Pantheon Books, 1982.

Reiter, Rayna R., ed. *Toward an Anthropology of Women.* New York and London: Monthly Review Press, 1975.

Romero, Flerida R. P., ed. *Women and the Law.* Manila: University of the Philippines Law Center and the Asia Foundation, 1983.

Rosaldo, Michelle Z. and L. Lamphere, eds. *Women, Culture, and Society.* Stanford: Stanford University Press, 1974.

Saffioti, Heleieth. *Women in Class Society.* Translated by Michael Vale. New York and London: Monthly Review Press, 1978.

Sanghat, Stree Shakti. "The War Against Rape: A Report from Karimnagar." In *Third World, Second Sex: Women's Struggles and National Liberation,* edited by Miranda Davies. London: Zed Press, 1983.

Schlegel, Alice, ed. *Sexual Stratification: A Cross-Cultural View.* New York: Columbia University Press, 1977.

Schuler, Margaret A. "Ownership of the Law." *New World Outlook,* no. 4 (January 1985), pp. 18-22.

————. *Women, Law, and Development: An Exploration of Legal, Educational, and Organizational Strategies to Raise the Status of Low-Income Third World Women.* Ann Arbor, Michigan: University Microfilms, 1985.

Sen, Gita. "Subordination and Sexual Control: A Comparative View of the Control of Women." *Review of Radical Political Economics 16,* no. 1 (Spring 1984): 113-142.

Sharara, Yolla Sharara. "Women and Politics in Lebanon." In *Third World, Second Sex: Women's Struggles and National Liberation,* edited by Miranda Davies. London: Zed Press, 1983.

Snyder. "Colonialism and Legal Form: The Creation of 'Customary Law' in Senegal." In *Crime, Justice, and Understanding,* edited by Colin Sumner. London: Heinemann, 1982.

Staudt, Kathleen A. and Jane Jaquette, eds. *Women in Developing Countries: A Policy Focus.* New York: The Hayworth Press, 1983.

Steiner. "Legal Education and Socio-Economic Change: Brazilian Perspectives." *American Journal of Comparative Law* 19 (1971): 39.

Taub, Nadine, and Elizabeth M. Schneider. "Perspectives on Women's Subordination and the Role of Law." In *The Politics of Law: A Progressive Critique,* edited by David Kairys. New York: Pantheon Books, 1982.

Tinker, Irene and M. B. Bramson, eds. *Women and World Development.* Washington, D.C.: Overseas Development Council, 1976.

"Toward a General Theory about African Law, Social Change and Development in the Individual under African Law." *Proceedings of the First All-Africa Law Conference*, edited by P. N. Takirimbudde (no publishing data).

Trubek, David M. "Unequal Protection: Thoughts on Legal Services and Income Distribution in Latin America." *Texas International Law Journal 13* (Spring, 1978).

Voice of Women. *Women Workers in the Free Trade Zone of Sri Lanka: A Survey.* Colombo, Sri Lanka: Voice of Women, 1983.

Were, Gideon S. *Leadership and Underdevelopment in Africa.* Nairobi: Gideon S. Were, 1983.

——ed. "Women and Development in Africa." *Journal of East African Research and Development 15* (1985).

Youssef, Nadia and Myra Bovinic. *The Productivity of Women in Developing Countries: Measurement Issues and Recommendations.* Washington, D.C.: International Center for Research on Women.

Special Journal Issues:

Development and the Sexual Division of Labor, *Signs,* 7 (Winter 1981).

Education as Transformation, Identity, Change, and Development, *Harvard Educational Review 51* (February 1981).

Forum '85 Nairobi, Kenya, *Connexions 17/18,* (Summer/Fall 1985).

Models of Development, *Signs* 3 (Spring 1977).

The Political Economy of Women, *Review of Radical Political Economy* 4 (Summer 1972).

Special Issue on the Political Economy of Women, *Review of Radical Political Economy* 12 (Summer 1980).

Women: Protagonists of Change, *Development* 4 1984.

Women and Class Struggle, *Latin American Perspectives* (Winter/Spring 1977).

Women Challenging the World, *New World Outlook* (January 1985).

Women, Class, and the Family, *Review of Radical Political Economy* 9 (Fall 1977).

Women and the Economy, *Review of Radical Political Economy* 8 (Spring 1976).

DIRECTORY OF CONTRIBUTORS

Jade O. Akande
University of Lagos
P.M.B. 12820
Lagos, Nigeria

Alba Alonzo de Quesada
Federación de Asociaciones Femeninas Hondureñas (FAFH)
Apartado Postal 935
Tegucigalpa, Honduras

Shirin Aumeeruddy-Cziffra
La Commission des Femmes
Mouvement Militant Mauricien
Rue de la Poudrière
Port Louis, Mauritius

Balghis Badri
Ahfad College
Omdurman 167, Sudan

Mildred Beltré
Centro Dominicano de Asesoría e Investigaciones Legales
(CEDAIL)
Apartado 2457
Santo Domingo, Dominican Republic

Ela Bhatt
Self-Employed Women's Association (SEWA)
c/o Gandhi Majoor Sewalaya
Bhadra
Ahmedabad 380001, India

Rabia Bhuiyan
The Institute of Democratic Rights
House No. 14, Road No. 7
Dhanmondi R/A
Dhaka 5, Bangladesh

Luisa Campos
Centro Dominicano de Asesoría e Investigaciones Legales
(CEDAIL)
Apartado 2457
Santo Domingo, Dominican Republic

Lucía Carrión
Centro de Planificación y Estudios Sociales (CEPLAES)
Casilla 6127 CCI
Quito, Ecuador

Chandermani Chopra
Chamber No 22
High Court Chambers
Sher Shah Road
New Delhi, India

Radhika Coomaraswamy
International Centre for Ethnic Studies
8 Kynsey Terrace
Colombo 8, Sri Lanka

Elizabeth Dasso
Peru Mujer
Apartado 949
Correo Central
Lima 100, Peru

Asma El Dareer
P.O. Box 3977
Khartoum, Sudan

Nawal El Saadawi
Arab Women's Solidarity Union
25 Murad Street
Giza, Egypt

Teresa Fernandez
PILIPINA - Cebu
102 P. del Rosario Ext.
Cebu City, Philippines

Savitri Goonesekere
Open University
P.O. Box 21
Nawala
Nugegoda, Sri Lanka

Mirta Henault
Derechos Iguales Para la Mujer Argentina (DIMA)
Av. Luis Maria Campos 1616
Planta Baja "B"
1426 Buenos Aires, Argentina

Sigma Huda
Bangladesh National Women Lawyers Association
c/o Chancery Chambers
7th Floor, Amin Court
62-63 Motijheel Commercial Area
Dhaka, Bangladesh

Lucy Jara
Centro de Investigación, Capacitación y Asesoría Legal
(CICAL)
Avenida 6 de Agosto 589
Oficina 202
Jesus María
Lima, Peru

Rani Jethmalani
Hotel Manor
77 Friends Colony West
New Delhi 110 065, India

Justice A. R. Jiagge
P.O. Box 119
Accra, Ghana

Rosemary Awino Kaduru
Partnership for Productivity/Kenya
P.O. Box 52800
Nairobi, Kenya

Amarjit Kaur
c/o Department of History
University of Malaya
Kuala Lumpur, Malaysia

Joyce Kazembe
Center for Applied Social Sciences (CASS)
University of Zimbabwe
P.O. Box MP 167
Mount Pleasant
Harare, Zimbabwe

Prabha Krishnan
C/6-34 SDA
New Delhi 110016, India

Ranjana Kumari
Center for Social Research
E 82
Saket
New Delhi 110017, India

Tai-Young Lee
Korea Legal Aid Center for Family Relations
1-866 Yoido-dong
Youngdeungpo-ku
Seoul 150, Korea

Magdalena León
Asociación Colombiana para el Estudio de la Población (ACEP)
Carrera 23, No. 39-82
Bogotá, Colombia

Fabiola Letelier
Catedral 1063
Oficina 40
Santiago, Chile

Victor Lora
El Alcazar 142
Urb. La Castellana
Lima 33 (Surco), Peru

Mothokoa Mamashela
National University of Lesotho
Faculty of Law
P.O. Roma 180
Lesotho

Myrtle Mason
6 Cherry Garden Avenue
Kingston 8, Jamaica

Laure Moghaizel
Institute for Women's Studies in the Arab World
Beirut University College
P.O. Box 130 5053
Beirut, Lebanon

Marjon Mol
Center for Applied Social Sciences (CASS)
University of Zimbabwe
P.O. Box MP 167
Mount Pleasant
Harare, Zimbabwe

Athaliah Molokomme
Law Department
University of Botswana
P/Bag 0022
Gaborone, Botswana

Julieta Montaño
Oficina Jurídica para la Mujer
Jordán 388
Casilla 2287
Cochabamba, Bolivia

Sheila Mukherjee
Community Welfare and Research Society
P8/3, Lane No. 16
Ravindrapuri
Varanasi 221005, India

Rosa Paredes
Centro al Servicio de la Acción Popular (CESAP)
Apartado Postal 4240
Caracas 1010-A, Venezuela

Rashida Patel
All Pakistan Women's Association
67 B Garden Road
Karachi, Pakistan

Veena Patel
Self-Employed Women's Association (SEWA)
c/o Gandhi Majoor Sewalaya
Bhadra
Ahmedabad 380001, India

Soledad Perpiñan
Third World Movement Against the Exploitation of Women
(TW-MAE-W)
P.O. Box SM-366
Manila, Philippines

Silvia Pimentel
Rua Barbosa Lopes 350
Granja Julieta, Santo Amaro
CEP 04720
São Paulo ESP, Brazil

Jing Porte
Women's Center
Room 406, R & G Tirol Bldg.
831 EDSA
corner Scout Albano Street
Quezon City, Philippines

Mere Pulea
P.O. Box 316
Nauru (Central Pacific)

Emelina Quintillan
Quintillan, Adao & Yenco
Leonor Bldg.
Magallanes Street
Davao City 9501, Philippines

Sara Rioja
Derechos Iguales para la Mujer Argentina (DIMA)
Av. Luis María Campos 1616
Planta Baja "B"
1426 Buenos Aires, Argentina

Ayala Rocha
Centro de Defensa Dos Direitos Humanos
58.000 João Pessoa
Caixa Postal 93
Paraíba, Brazil

Lilia Rodríguez
Centro Ecuatoriano para la Promoción y Acción de la Mujer
(CEPAM)
Apartado Postal 182 C
Sucursal 15
Quito, Ecuador

Saparinah Sadli
The Institute of Consultation and Legal Aid for Women and
Families
Mesjid Agung Al-Azhar
Jl. Sisingamangaraja No. 12
Jakarta Selatan, Indonesia

Amartiwi Saleh
LBH Bandung
Jl. Ir. H. Juanda 98
Bandung, Indonesia

Mahjouba Mohamed Salih
Sudan Legal Aid Association
Box 302
Khartoum, Sudan

Olga Amparo Sánchez
Casa de la Mujer
Servicio de Asesoria Legal
Carrera 18 No. 59-60
Bogota, Colombia

Silu Singh
Nepal Women's Legal Services Project
P. O. Box 3241
Kathmandu, Nepal

Yasmin Tambiah
International Centre for Ethnic Studies
8 Kynsey Terrace
Colombo 8, Sri Lanka

Marta Uribe
Casa de la Mujer
Servicio de Asesoriá Legal
Carrera 18 No. 59-60
Bogotá, Colombia

Milú Vargas
Asesora Legal
Consejo de Estado
Managua, Nicaragua

Roxana Vásquez
Centro Flora Tristán
Parque Hernán Velarde No 42
Lima, Peru

Nani Yamin
The Institute of Consultation and Legal Aid for Women and
Families
Mesjid Agung Al-Azhar
Jl. Sisingamangaraja No. 12
Jakarta Selatan, Indonesia

Gina Yañez
Movimiento Manuela Ramos
Apartado 11176
Lima 14, Peru

Cristina Zurutuza
Centro de Estudios de la Mujer
Nicaragua 4908
Buenos Aires 1414, Argentina

Dr. Margaret Schuler has been director of the Women, Law, and Development Program from its inception. With a background in sociology and non-formal education, she holds an Ed.D. from George Washington University and has researched legal strategies to raise the status of women in several parts of the world. She was instrumental in designing the forum that led to this book and in developing the WLD network of Third World women active in the field of women's rights.

OEF International is a private, non-profit organization, based in the United States, which focuses on creating economic opportunities for low-income women in the Third World and expanding their contribution to the development of their communities and countries.

OEF believes that the empowerment of women and the strengthening of their economic roles is of critical importance for achieving development goals. OEF's training and technical assistance programs provide the tools and skills which enable Third World organizations and women to increase food production, launch and expand small enterprises, and mobilize resources to improve women's legal status.

Throughout the United States, OEF works on many levels to increase public understanding and support for policies and programs which recognize the critical role Third World women play in food production and economic development.